BRADFORD'S HISTORY
"OF PLIMOTH PLANTATION."

FROM THE ORIGINAL MANUSCRIPT.

WITH A REPORT OF THE PROCEEDINGS INCIDENT
TO THE RETURN OF THE MANUSCRIPT
TO MASSACHUSETTS.

Bradford's History of 'Plimoth Plantation'

by William Bradford

This work is in the public domain.

Published by Frugal Reads.

William Bradford (1590–1657) was a leader of the Pilgrims and the long-serving Governor of Plymouth Colony. He authored 'History of Plimoth Plantation', documenting the Pilgrims' journey, hardships, and early American colonial life, making him a key figure in early American history.

Table of Contents

INTRODUCTION.

To many people the return of the Bradford Manuscript is a fresh discovery of colonial history. By very many it has been called, incorrectly, the log of the "Mayflower." Indeed, that is the title by which it is described in the decree of the Consistorial Court of London. The fact is, however, that Governor Bradford undertook its preparation long after the arrival of the Pilgrims, and it cannot be properly considered as in any sense a log or daily journal of the voyage of the "Mayflower." It is, in point of fact, a history of the Plymouth Colony, chiefly in the form of annals, extending from the inception of the colony down to the year 1647. The matter has been in print since 1856, put forth through the public spirit of the Massachusetts Historical Society, which secured a transcript of the document from London, and printed it in the society's proceedings of the above-named year. As thus presented, it had copious notes, prepared with great care by the late Charles Deane; but these are not given in the present volume, wherein only such comments as seem indispensable to a proper understanding of the story have been made, leaving whatever elaboration may seem desirable to some future private enterprise.

It is a matter of regret that no picture of Governor Bradford exists. Only Edward Winslow of the Mayflower Company left an authenticated portrait of himself, and that, painted in England, is reproduced in this volume. In those early days Plymouth would have been a poor field for portrait painters. The people were struggling for their daily bread rather than for to-morrow's fame through the transmission of their features to posterity.

The volume of the original manuscript, as it was presented to the Governor of the Commonwealth and is now deposited in the State Library, is a folio measuring eleven and one-half inches in length, seven and seven-eighths inches in width and one and one-half inches in thickness. It is bound in parchment, once white, but now grimy and much the worse for wear, being somewhat cracked and considerably scaled. Much scribbling, evidently by the Bradford family, is to be seen upon its surface, and out of the confusion may be read the name of Mercy Bradford, a daughter of the governor. On the inside of the front cover is pasted a sheet of manilla paper, on which is written the following:—

"Consistory Court of the Diocese of London

In the matter of the application of The Honorable Thomas Francis Bayard, Ambassador Extraordinary and Plenipotentiary in London of the United States of America, for the delivery to him, on behalf of the President and Citizens of the said States, of the original manuscript book entitled and known as The Log of the Mayflower.

Produced in Court this 25th day of March, 1897, and marked with the letter A.

HARRY W. LEE

Registrar.

1 Deans Court

Doctors Commons"

Then come two manilla leaves, on both sides of which is written the decree of the Consistorial Court. These leaves and the manilla sheet pasted on the inside of the front cover were evidently inserted after the decree was passed.

Next comes a leaf (apparently the original first leaf of the book), and on it are verses, signed "A. M.," on the death of Mrs. Bradford. The next is evidently one of the leaves of the original book. At the top of the page is written the following:—

This book was rit by govener William bradford and given to his son mager William Bradford and by him to his son mager John Bradford. rit by me Samuel bradford mach 20, 1705.

At the bottom of the same page the name John Bradford appears in different handwriting, evidently written with the book turned wrong side up.

The next is a leaf bearing the following, in the handwriting of Thomas Prince:—

TUESDAY, June 4—1728

Calling at *Major John Bradford's* at Kingston near Plimouth, son of Major Wm. Bradford formerly Dep Gov'r of Plimouth Colony, who was eldest son of Wm. Bradford Esq their 2nd Gov'r, & author of this History; ye sd Major John Bradford gave me *several manuscript octavoes* wh he assured me were written with his said Grandfather Gov'r Bradford's own hand. He also gave me a *little Pencil Book* wrote with a Blew lead Pencil by his sd Father ye Dep Gov'r. And He also told me yt He had lent & only lent his sd Grandfather Gov'r Bradford's History of Plimouth Colony wrote by his own Hand also, to judg Sewall; and desired me to get it of Him or find it out, & take out of it what I thought proper for my New-England Chronology: wh I accordingly obtained, and This is ye sd History: wh I found wrote in ye same Handwriting as ye Octavo manuscripts above sd.

THOMAS PRINCE.

N.B. I also mentioned to him my Desire of lodging this History in ye New England Library of Prints & manuscripts, wh I had been then collecting for 23 years, to wh He signified his willingness—only yt He might have the Perusal of it while He lived.

T. PRINCE.

Following this, on the same page, is Thomas Prince's printed book-mark, as follows:—

This Book belongs to
The New-England-Library,

Begun to be collected by Thomas Prince, upon
his entring Harvard-College, July 6
1703; and was given by

On the lower part of a blank space which follows the word "by" is written:—

It now belongs to the Bishop of London's Library at Fulham.

There are evidences that this leaf did not belong to the original book, but was inserted by Mr. Prince.

At the top of the first page of the next leaf, which was evidently one of the original leaves of the book, is written in Samuel Bradford's hand, "march 20 Samuel Bradford;" and just below there appears, in Thomas Prince's handwriting, the following:—

But major Bradford tells me & assures me that He only lent this Book of his Grandfather's to Mr. Sewall & that it being of his Grandfather's own hand writing He had so high a value of it that he would never Part with ye Property, but would lend it to me & desired me to get it, which I did, & write down this that sd Major Bradford and his Heirs may be known to be the right owners.

Below this, also in Thomas Prince's handwriting, appears this line:—

"Page 243 missing when ye Book came into my Hands at 1st."

Just above the inscription by Prince there is a line or two of writing, marked over in ink so carefully as to be wholly undecipherable. On the reverse page of this leaf and on the first page of the next are written Hebrew words, with definitions. These are all in Governor Bradford's handwriting. On the next page appears the following:—

Though I am growne aged, yet I have had a long-
ing desire, to see with my own eyes, something of

that most ancient language, and holy tongue,
in which the Law, and oracles of God were
write; and in which God, and angels, spake to
the holy patriarks, of old time; and what
names were given to things, from the
creation. And though I cañot attaine
to much herein, yet I am refreshed,
to have seen some glimpse here-
of; (as Moses saw the Land
of canan afarr of) my aime
and desire is, to see how
the words, and phrases
lye in the holy texte;
and to dicerne some-
what of the same
for my owne
contente.

———
——
—

J

Then begins the history proper, the first page of which is produced in facsimile in this volume, slightly reduced. The ruled margins end with page thirteen. From that page to the end of the book the writing varies considerably, sometimes being quite coarse and in other places very fine, some pages containing nearly a thousand words each. As a rule, the writing is upon one side of the sheet only, but in entering notes and subsequent thoughts the reverse is sometimes used. The last page number is 270, as appears from the facsimile reproduction in this volume of that page. Page

270 is followed by two blank leaves; then on the second page of the next leaf appears the list of names of those who came over in the "Mayflower," covering four pages and one column on the fifth page. The arrangement of this matter is shown by the facsimile reproduction in this volume of the first page of these names. Last of all there is a leaf of heavy double paper, like the one in the front of the book containing the verses on the death of Mrs. Bradford, and on this last leaf is written an index to a few portions of the history.

For copy, there was used the edition printed in 1856 by the Massachusetts Historical Society. The proof was carefully compared, word for word, with the photographic *facsimile* issued in 1896 in both London and Boston. The value of this comparison is evident in that a total of sixteen lines of the original, omitted in the original first copy, is supplied in this edition. As the work of the Historical Society could not be compared, easily, with the original manuscript in London, these omissions, with sundry minor errors in word and numeral, are not unreasonable. The curious will be pleased to learn that the supplied lines are from the following pages of the manuscript, viz.: page 122, eight lines; page 129, two lines; the obverse of page 201, found on the last page of Appendix A, two lines; page 219, two lines; pages 239 and 258, one line each. The pages of the manuscript are indicated in these printed pages by numerals in parentheses.

There are several errors in the paging of the original manuscript. Pages 105 and 106 are marked 145 and 146, and pages 219 and 220 are marked 119 and 120, respectively. Page 243 is missing.

Such as it is, the book is put forth that the public may know what manner of men the Pilgrims were, through what perils and vicissitudes they passed, and how much we of to-day owe to their devotion and determination.

PROCEEDINGS
OF THE
LEGISLATURE.

JOURNAL OF THE SENATE.

MONDAY, MAY 24, 1897.

The following message from His Excellency the Governor came up from the House, to wit:—

BOSTON, May 22, 1897.

To the Honorable Senate and House of Representatives.

I have the honor to call to your attention the fact that Wednesday, May 26, at 11 A.M., has been fixed as the date of the formal presentation to the Governor of the Commonwealth of the Bradford Manuscript History, recently ordered by decree of the Consistory Court of the Diocese of London to be returned to the Commonwealth of Massachusetts by the hands of the Honorable Thomas F. Bayard, lately Ambassador at the Court of St. James; and to suggest for the favorable consideration of your honorable bodies that the exercises of presentation be held in the House of Representatives on the day and hour above given, in the presence of a joint convention of the two bodies and of invited guests and the public.

ROGER WOLCOTT.

Thereupon, on motion of Mr. Roe,—

Ordered, That, in accordance with the suggestion of His Excellency the Governor, a joint convention of the two branches be held in the chamber of the House of Representatives, on Wednesday, May the twenty-sixth, at eleven o'clock A.M., for the purpose of witnessing the exercises of the formal presentation, to the Governor of the Commonwealth, of the Bradford Manuscript History, recently ordered by decree of the Consistory Court of the Diocese of London to be returned to the Commonwealth of Massachusetts by the hands of the Honorable Thomas F. Bayard, lately Ambassador at the Court of St. James; and further

Ordered, That the clerks of the two branches give notice to His Excellency the Governor of the adoption of this order.

Sent down for concurrence. (It was concurred with same date.)

JOURNAL OF THE SENATE.

WEDNESDAY, MAY 26, 1897.

Joint Convention.

At eleven o'clock A.M., pursuant to assignment, the two branches met in

CONVENTION

in the chamber of the House of Representatives.

On motion of Mr. Roe,—

Ordered, That a committee, to consist of three members of the Senate and eight members of the House of Representatives, be appointed, to wait upon His Excellency the Governor and inform him that the two branches are now in convention for the purpose of witnessing the exercises of the formal presentation, to the Governor of the Commonwealth, of the Bradford Manuscript History.

Messrs. Roe, Woodward and Gallivan, of the Senate, and Messrs. Pierce of Milton, Bailey of Plymouth, Brown of Gloucester, Fairbank of Warren, Bailey of Newbury, Sanderson of Lynn, Whittlesey of Pittsfield and Bartlett of Boston, of the House, were appointed the committee.

Mr. Roe, from the committee, afterwards reported that they had attended to the duty assigned them, and that His Excellency the Governor had been pleased to say that he received the message and should be pleased to wait upon the Convention forthwith for the purpose named.

His Excellency the Governor, accompanied by His Honor the Lieutenant-Governor and the Honorable Council, and by the Honorable Thomas F. Bayard, lately Ambassador of the United States at the Court of St. James's, the Honorable George F. Hoar, Senator from Massachusetts in the Congress of the United States, and other invited guests, entered the chamber.

The decree of the Consistorial and Episcopal Court of London, authorizing the return of the manuscript and its delivery to the Governor, was read.

The President then presented the Honorable George F. Hoar, who gave an account of the manuscript and of the many efforts that had been made to secure its return.

The Honorable Thomas F. Bayard was then introduced by the President, and he formally presented the manuscript to His Excellency the Governor, who accepted it in behalf of the Commonwealth.

On motion of Mr. Bradford, the following order was adopted:—

Whereas, In the presence of the Senate and of the House of Representatives in joint convention assembled, and in accordance with a decree of the Consistorial and Episcopal Court of London, the manuscript of Bradford's "History of the Plimouth Plantation" has this day been delivered to His Excellency the Governor of the Commonwealth by the Honorable Thomas F. Bayard, lately Ambassador of the United States at the Court of St. James's; and

Whereas, His Excellency the Governor has accepted the said manuscript in behalf of the Commonwealth; therefore, be it

Ordered, That the Senate and the House of Representatives of the Commonwealth of Massachusetts place on record their high appreciation of the generous and gracious courtesy that prompted this act of international good-will, and express their grateful thanks to all concerned therein, and especially to the Lord Bishop of London, for the return to the Commonwealth of this precious relic; and be it further

Ordered, That His Excellency the Governor be requested to transmit an engrossed and duly authenticated copy of this order with its preamble to the Lord Bishop of London.

His Excellency, accompanied by the other dignitaries, then withdrew, the Convention was dissolved, and the Senate returned to its chamber.

Subsequently a resolve was passed (approved June 10, 1897) providing for the publication of the history from the original manuscript, together with a report of the proceedings of the joint convention, such report to be prepared by a committee consisting of one member of the Senate and two members of the House of Representatives, and to include, so far as practicable, portraits of His Excellency Governor Roger Wolcott, William Bradford, the Honorable George F. Hoar, the Honorable Thomas F. Bayard, the Archbishop of Canterbury and the Lord Bishop of London; facsimiles of pages from the manuscript history, and a picture of the book itself; copies of the decree of the Consistorial and Episcopal Court of London, the receipt of the Honorable Thomas F. Bayard for the manuscript, and the receipt sent by His Excellency the Governor to the Consistorial and Episcopal Court; an account of the legislative action taken with reference to the presentation and reception of the manuscript; the addresses of the

Honorable George F. Hoar, the Honorable Thomas F. Bayard and His Excellency Governor Roger Wolcott; and such other papers and illustrations as the committee might deem advisable; the whole to be printed under the direction of the Secretary of the Commonwealth, and the book distributed by him according to directions contained in the resolve.

Senator Alfred S. Roe of Worcester and Representatives Francis C. Lowell of Boston and Walter L. Bouvé of Hingham were appointed as the committee.

DECREE
OF THE
CONSISTORIAL AND EPISCOPAL
COURT OF LONDON.

DECREE.

MANDELL by Divine Permission LORD BISHOP OF LONDON—To The Honorable THOMAS FRANCIS BAYARD Ambassador Extraordinary and Plenipotentiary to Her Most Gracious Majesty Queen Victoria at the Court of Saint James's in London and To The Governor and Commonwealth of Massachusetts in the United States of America Greeting— WHEREAS a Petition has been filed in the Registry of Our Consistorial and Episcopal Court of London by you the said Honorable Thomas Francis Bayard as Ambassador Extraordinary and Plenipotentiary to Her Most Gracious Majesty Queen Victoria at the Court of Saint James's in London on behalf of the President and Citizens of the United States of America wherein you have alleged that there is in Our Custody as Lord Bishop of London a certain Manuscript Book known as and entitled "The Log of the Mayflower" containing an account as narrated by Captain William Bradford who was one of the Company of Englishmen who left England in April 1620 in the ship known as "The Mayflower" of the circumstances leading to the prior Settlement of that Company at Leyden in Holland their return to England and subsequent departure for New England their landing at Cape Cod in December 1620 their Settlement at New Plymouth and their later history for several years they being the Company whose Settlement in

America is regarded as the first real Colonisation of the New England States and wherein you have also alleged that the said Manuscript Book had been for many years past and was then deposited in the Library attached to Our Episcopal Palace at Fulham in the County of Middlesex and is of the greatest interest importance and value to the Citizens of the United States of America inasmuch as it is one of the earliest records of their national History and contains much valuable information in regard to the original Settlers in the States their family history and antecedents and that therefore you earnestly desired to acquire possession of the same for and on behalf of the President and Citizens of the said United States of America AND WHEREIN you have also alleged that you are informed that We as Lord Bishop of London had fully recognised the value and interest of the said Manuscript Book to the Citizens of the United States of America and the claims which they have to its possession and that We were desirous of transferring it to the said President and Citizens AND WHEREIN you have also alleged that you are advised and believe that the Custody of documents in the nature of public or ecclesiastical records belonging to the See of London is vested in the Consistorial Court of the said See and that any disposal thereof must be authorised by an Order issued by the Judge of that Honorable Court And that you therefore humbly prayed that the said Honorable Court would deliver to you the said Manuscript Book on your undertaking to use every means in your power for the safe transmission of the said Book to the United States of America and its secure deposit and custody in the Pilgrim Hall at New Plymouth or in such other place as may be selected by the President and Senate of the said United States and upon such conditions as to security and access by and on behalf of the English Nation as that Honorable Court might determine AND WHEREAS the said Petition was set down for hearing on one of the Court days in Hilary Term to wit Thursday the Twenty fifth day of March One thousand eight hundred and ninety seven in Our Consistorial Court in the Cathedral Church of Saint Paul in London before The Right Worshipful Thomas Hutchinson Tristram Doctor of Laws and one of Her Majesty's Counsel learned in the Law Our Vicar General and Official Principal the Judge of the said Court and you at the sitting of the said Court appeared by Counsel in support of the Prayer of the said Petition and during the hearing thereof the said Manuscript Book was produced in the said Court by Our legal Secretary and was then inspected and examined by the said Judge and evidence was also given before the Court by which it appeared that the Registry at Fulham Palace was a Public Registry for Historical and Ecclesiastical Documents relating to the Diocese of London and to the Colonial and other possessions of Great Britain beyond the Seas so long as the same remained by custom within the said Diocese AND WHEREAS it appeared on the face of the said Manuscript Book that the whole of the body thereof with the exception of part of the last page thereof was in the handwriting of the said William Bradford who was elected Governor of New Plymouth in April 1621 and continued Governor thereof from that date excepting between the years 1635 and 1637 up to 1650 and that the last five pages of the said Manuscript which is in the handwriting of the said William Bradford contain what in Law is an authentic Register between 1620 and 1650 of the fact of the Marriages of the Founders of the Colony of New England with the names of their respective wives and the names of their Children the lawful issue of such Marriages and of the fact of the Marriages of many of their Children and Grandchildren and of the names of the issue of such marriages and of the deaths of many of the persons named therein And after hearing Counsel in support of the said application the Judge being of opinion that the said Manuscript Book had been upon the evidence before the Court presumably deposited at Fulham Palace sometime between the year 1729 and the year 1785 during which time the said Colony was by custom within the Diocese of London for purposes Ecclesiastical and the Registry of the said Consistorial Court was a legitimate Registry for the Custody of Registers of Marriages Births and Deaths within the said Colony and that the Registry at Fulham Palace was a Registry for Historical and other Documents connected with the Colonies and possessions of Great Britain beyond the Seas so long as the same remained by custom within the Diocese of London and that on the Declaration of the Independence of the United States of America in 1776 the said Colony had ceased to be within the Diocese of London and the Registry of the Court had ceased to be a public registry for the said Colony and having maturely deliberated on the Cases precedents and practice of the Ecclesiastical Court bearing on the application before him and having regard to the Special Circumstances of the Case Decreed as follows—(1) That a Photographic facsimile reproduction of the said Manuscript Book verified by affidavit as being a true and correct Photographic reproduction of the said Manuscript Book be deposited in the Registry of Our said Court by or on behalf of the Petitioner before the delivery to the Petitioner of the said original Manuscript Book as hereinafter ordered—(2) That the said Manuscript Book be delivered over to the said Honorable Thomas Francis Bayard by the Lord Bishop of London or in his Lordship's absence by the Registrar of the said Court on his giving his undertaking in writing that he will with all due care and diligence on his arrival from England in the United States convey and deliver in person the said Manuscript Book to the Governor of the Commonwealth of Massachusetts in the United States of America at his Official Office in the State House in the City of Boston and that from the time of the delivery of the said Book to him by the said Lord Bishop of London or by the said Registrar until he shall have delivered the same to the Governor of Massachusetts he will retain the same in his own Personal custody—(3) That the said Book be deposited by the Petitioner with the Governor of Massachusetts for the purpose of the same being with all convenient speed finally deposited either in the State Archives of the Commonwealth of Massachusetts in the City of Boston or in the Library of the Historical Society of the said Commonwealth in the City of Boston as the Governor shall determine—(4) That the Governors of the said Commonwealth for all time to come be officially responsible for the safe custody of the said Manuscript Book whether the same be deposited in the State Archives at Boston or in the Historical Library in Boston aforesaid as well as for the performance of the following conditions subject to a compliance wherewith the said Manuscript Book is hereby decreed to be deposited in the Custody of the aforesaid Governor of the Commonwealth of Massachusetts and his Successors to wit:—(a) That all persons have such access to the said Manuscript Book as to the Governor of the said Commonwealth for the time being shall appear to be reasonable and with such safeguard as he shall order—(b) That all persons desirous of searching the said Manuscript Book for the bona fide purpose of establishing or tracing a Pedigree through persons named in the last five pages thereof or in any other part thereof shall be permitted to search the same under such safeguards as the Governor for the time being shall determine on payment of a fee to be fixed by the Governor—(c) That any person applying to the Official having the immediate custody of the said Manuscript Book for a Certified Copy of any entry contained in proof of Marriage Birth or Death of persons named therein or of any other matter of like purport for the purpose of tracing descents shall be furnished with such certificate on the payment of a sum not exceeding one Dollar—(d) That with all convenient speed after the delivery of the said Manuscript Book to the Governor of the Commonwealth of Massachusetts the Governor shall transmit to the Registrar of the Court a Certificate of the delivery of the same to him by the Petitioner and that he accepts the Custody of the same subject to the terms and conditions herein named AND the Judge lastly decreed that the Petitioner on delivering the said Manuscript Book to the Governor aforesaid shall at the same time deliver to him this Our Decree Sealed with the Seal of the Court WHEREFORE WE the Bishop of London aforesaid well weighing and considering the premises DO by virtue of Our Authority Ordinary and Episcopal and as far as in Us lies and by Law We may or can ratify and confirm such Decree of Our Vicar General and Official Principal of Our Consistorial and Episcopal Court of London IN TESTIMONY whereof We have caused the Seal of Our said Vicar General and Official Principal of the Consistorial and Episcopal Court of London which We use in this behalf to be affixed to these Presents DATED AT LONDON this Twelfth day of April One thousand eight hundred and ninety seven and in the first year of Our Translation.

HARRY W. LEE

Exd. H.E.T.

Registrar

(L.S.)

RECEIPT OF AMBASSADOR BAYARD.

In the Consistory Court of London

IN THE MATTER OF THE ORIGINAL MANUSCRIPT OF THE BOOK ENTITLED AND KNOWN AS "THE LOG OF THE MAYFLOWER."

I THE HONOURABLE THOMAS FRANCIS BAYARD lately Ambassador Extraordinary and Plenipotentiary of the United States of America at the Court of Saint James's London Do hereby undertake, in compliance with the Order of this Honourable Court dated the twelfth day of April 1897 and made on my Petition filed in the said Honourable Court, that I will with all due care and diligence on my arrival from England in the United States of America safely convey over the Original Manuscript Book Known as and entitled "The Log of the Mayflower" which has been this twenty ninth day of April 1897 delivered over to me by the Lord Bishop of London, to the City of Boston in the United States of America and on my arrival in the said City deliver the same over in person to the Governor of the Commonwealth of Massachusetts at his Official Office in the State House in the said City of Boston AND I further hereby undertake from the time of the said delivery of the said Book to me by the said Lord Bishop of London until I shall have delivered the same to the Governor of Massachusetts, to retain the same in my own personal custody.

(Signed) T. F. BAYARD

29 April 1897

RECEIPT OF GOVERNOR WOLCOTT.

His Excellency ROGER WOLCOTT, Governor of the Commonwealth of Massachusetts, in the United States of America.

To the Registrar of the Consistorial and Episcopal Court of London.

Whereas, The said Honorable Court, by its decree dated the twelfth day of April, 1897, and made on the petition of the Honorable Thomas Francis Bayard, lately Ambassador Extraordinary and Plenipotentiary of the United States of America at the Court of Saint James in London, did order that a certain original manuscript book then in the custody of the Lord Bishop of London, known as and entitled "The Log of the Mayflower," and more specifically described in said decree, should be delivered over to the said Honorable Thomas Francis Bayard by the Lord Bishop of London, on certain conditions specified in said decree, to be delivered by the said Honorable Thomas Francis Bayard in person to the Governor of the Commonwealth of Massachusetts, thereafter to be kept in the custody of the aforesaid Governor of the Commonwealth of Massachusetts and his successors, subject to a compliance with certain conditions, as set forth in said decree;

And Whereas, The said Honorable Court by its decree aforesaid did further order that, with all convenient speed after the delivery of the said manuscript book to the Governor of the Commonwealth of Massachusetts, the Governor should transmit to the Registrar of the said Honorable Court a certificate of the delivery of the same to him by the said Honorable Thomas Francis Bayard, and his acceptance of the custody of the same, subject to the terms and conditions named in the decree aforesaid;

Now, Therefore, In compliance with the decree aforesaid I do hereby certify that on the twenty-sixth day of May, 1897, the said Honorable Thomas Francis Bayard delivered in person to me, at my official office in the State House in the city of Boston, in the

Commonwealth of Massachusetts, in the United States of America, a certain manuscript book which the said Honorable Thomas Francis Bayard then and there declared to be the original manuscript book known as and entitled "The Log of the Mayflower," which is more specifically described in the decree aforesaid; and I do further certify that I hereby accept the custody of the same, subject to the terms and conditions named in the decree aforesaid.

In witness whereof, I have hereunto signed my name and caused the seal of the Commonwealth to be affixed, at the Capitol in Boston, this twelfth day of July in the year of our Lord one thousand eight hundred and ninety-seven.

ROGER WOLCOTT.

By His Excellency the Governor,

WM. M. OLIN,

Secretary of the Commonwealth.

ADDRESS OF SENATOR HOAR.

The first American Ambassador to Great Britain, at the end of his official service, comes to Massachusetts on an interesting errand. He comes to deliver to the lineal successor of Governor Bradford, in the presence of the representatives and rulers of the body politic formed by the compact on board the "Mayflower," Nov. 11, 1620, the only authentic history of the founding of their Commonwealth; the only authentic history of what we have a right to consider the most important political transaction that has ever taken place on the face of the earth.

Mr. Bayard has sought to represent to the mother country, not so much the diplomacy as the good-will of the American people. If in this anybody be tempted to judge him severely, let us remember what his great predecessor, John Adams, the first minister at the same court, representing more than any other man, embodying more than any other man, the spirit of Massachusetts, said to George III., on the first day of June, 1785, after the close of our long and bitter struggle for independence: "I shall esteem myself the happiest of men if I can be instrumental in restoring an entire esteem, confidence and affection, or, in better words, the old good-nature and the old good-humor between people who, though separated by an ocean and under different governments, have the same language, a similar religion and kindred blood."

And let us remember, too, the answer of the old monarch, who, with all his faults, must have had something of a noble and royal nature stirring in his bosom, when he replied: "Let the circumstances of language, religion and blood have their natural and full effect."

It has long been well known that Governor Bradford wrote and left behind him a history of the settlement of Plymouth. It was quoted by early chroniclers. There are extracts from it in the records at Plymouth. Thomas Prince used it when he compiled his annals. Hubbard depended on it when he wrote his "History of

New England." Cotton Mather had read it, or a copy of a portion of it, when he wrote his "Magnalia." Governor Hutchinson had it when he published the second volume of his history in 1767. From that time it disappeared from the knowledge of everybody on this side of the water. All our historians speak of it as lost, and can only guess what had been its fate. Some persons suspected that it was destroyed when Governor Hutchinson's house was sacked in 1765, others that it was carried off by some officer or soldier when Boston was evacuated by the British army in 1776.

In 1844 Samuel Wilberforce, Bishop of Oxford, afterward Bishop of Winchester, one of the brightest of men, published one of the dullest and stupidest of books. It is entitled "The History of the Protestant Episcopal Church in America." It contained extracts from manuscripts which he said he had discovered in the library of the Bishop of London at Fulham. The book attracted no attention here until, about twelve years later, in 1855, John Wingate Thornton, whom many of us remember as an accomplished antiquary and a delightful gentleman, happened to pick up a copy of it while he was lounging in Burnham's book store. He read the bishop's quotations, and carried the book to his office, where he left it for his friend, Mr. Barry, who was then writing his "History of Massachusetts," with passages marked, and with a note which is not preserved, but which, according to his memory, suggested that the passages must have come from Bradford's long-lost history. That is the claim for Mr. Thornton. On the other hand, it is claimed by Mr. Barry that there was nothing of that kind expressed in Mr. Thornton's note, but in reading the book when he got it an hour or so later, the thought struck him for the first time that the clew had been found to the precious book which had been lost so long. He at once repaired to Charles Deane, then and ever since, down to his death, as President Eliot felicitously styled him, "the master of historical investigators in this country." Mr. Deane saw the importance of the discovery. He communicated at once with Joseph Hunter, an eminent English scholar. Hunter was high authority on all matters connected with the settlement of New England. He visited the palace at Fulham, and established beyond question the identity of the manuscript with Governor Bradford's history, an original letter of Governor Bradford having been sent over for comparison of handwriting.

How the manuscript got to Fulham nobody knows. Whether it was carried over by Governor Hutchinson in 1774; whether it was taken as spoil from the tower of the Old South Church in 1775; whether, with other manuscripts, it was sent to Fulham at the time of the attempts of the Episcopal churches in America, just before the revolution, to establish an episcopate here,—nobody knows. It would seem that Hutchinson would have sent it to the colonial office; that an officer would naturally have sent it to the war office; and a private would have sent it to the war office, unless he had carried it off as mere private booty and plunder,—in which case it would have been unlikely that it would have reached a public place of custody. But we find it in the possession of the church and of the church official having, until independence was declared, special jurisdiction over Episcopal interests in Massachusetts and Plymouth. This may seem to point to a transfer for some ecclesiastical purpose.

The bishop's chancellor conjectures that it was sent to Fulham because of the record annexed to it of the early births, marriages and deaths, such records being in England always in ecclesiastical custody. But this is merely conjecture.

I know of no incident like this in history, unless it be the discovery in a chest in the castle of Edinburgh, where they had been lost for one hundred and eleven years, of the ancient regalia of Scotland,—the crown of Bruce, the sceptre and sword of state. The lovers of Walter Scott, who was one of the commissioners who made the search, remember his intense emotion, as described by his daughter, when the lid was removed. Her feelings were worked up to such a pitch that she nearly fainted, and drew back from the circle.

As she was retiring she was startled by his voice exclaiming, in a tone of the deepest emotion, "something between anger and despair," as she expressed it: "By God, no!" One of the commissioners, not quite entering into the solemnity with which Scott regarded this business, had, it seems, made a sort of motion as if he meant to put the crown on the head of one of the young ladies near him, but the voice and the aspect of the poet were more than sufficient to make this worthy gentleman understand his error; and, respecting the enthusiasm with which he had not been taught to sympathize, he laid down the ancient diadem with an air of painful embarrassment. Scott whispered, "Pray forgive me," and turning round at the moment observed his daughter deadly pale and leaning by the door. He immediately drew her out of the room, and when she had somewhat recovered in the fresh air, walked with her across Mound to Castle Street. "He never spoke all the way home," she says, "but every now and then I felt his arm tremble, and from that time I fancied he began to treat me more like a woman than a child. I thought he liked me better, too, than he had ever done before."

There have been several attempts to procure the return of the manuscript to this country. Mr. Winthrop, in 1860, through the venerable John Sinclair, archdeacon, urged the Bishop of London to give it up, and proposed that the Prince of Wales, then just coming to this country, should take it across the Atlantic and present it to the people of Massachusetts. The Attorney-General, Sir Fitzroy Kelley, approved the plan, and said it would be an exceptional act of grace, a most interesting action, and that he heartily wished the success of the application. But the bishop refused. Again, in 1869, John Lothrop Motley, then minister to England, who had a great and deserved influence there, repeated the proposition, at the suggestion of that most accomplished scholar, Justin Winsor. But his appeal had the same fate. The bishop gave no encouragement, and said, as had been said nine years before, that the property could not be alienated without an act of Parliament. Mr. Winsor planned to repeat the attempt on his visit to England in 1877. When he was at Fulham the bishop was absent, and he was obliged to come home without seeing him in person.

In 1881, at the time of the death of President Garfield, Benjamin Scott, chamberlain of London, proposed again in the newspapers that the restitution should be made. But nothing came of it.

Dec. 21, 1895, I delivered an address at Plymouth, on the occasion of the two hundred and seventy-fifth anniversary of the landing of the Pilgrims upon the rock. In preparing for that duty, I read again, with renewed enthusiasm and delight, the noble and touching story, as told by Governor Bradford. I felt that this precious history of the Pilgrims ought to be in no other custody than that of their children. But the case seemed hopeless. I found myself compelled by a serious physical infirmity to take a vacation, and to get a rest from public cares and duties, which was impossible while I stayed at home. When I went abroad I determined to visit the locality, on the borders of Lincolnshire and Yorkshire, from which Bradford and Brewster and Robinson, the three leaders of the Pilgrims, came, and where their first church was formed, and the places in Amsterdam and Leyden where the emigrants spent thirteen years. But I longed especially to see the manuscript of Bradford at Fulham, which then seemed to me, as it now seems to me, the most precious manuscript on earth, unless we could recover one of the four gospels as it came in the beginning from the pen of the Evangelist.

The desire to get it back grew and grew during the voyage across the Atlantic. I did not know how such a proposition would be received in England. A few days after I landed I made a call upon John Morley. I asked him whether he thought the thing could be done. He inquired carefully into the story, took down from his shelf the excellent though brief life of Bradford in Leslie Stephen's "Biographical Dictionary," and told me he thought the book ought to come back to us, and that he should be glad to do anything in his power to help. It was my fortune, a week or two after, to sit next to Mr. Bayard at a dinner given to Mr. Collins by the American consuls in Great Britain. I took occasion to tell him the story, and he gave me the assurance, which he has since so abundantly and successfully fulfilled, of his powerful aid. I was compelled, by the health of one of the party with whom I was travelling, to go to the continent almost immediately, and was disappointed in the hope of an early return to England. So the matter was delayed until about a week before I sailed for home, when I went to Fulham, in the hope at least of seeing the manuscript. I had supposed that it was a quasi-public library, open to general visitors. But I found the bishop was absent. I asked for the librarian, but there was no such officer, and I was told very politely that the library was not open to the public, and was treated in all respects as that of a private gentleman. So I gave up any hope of doing anything in person. But I happened, the Friday before I sailed for home, to dine with an English friend who had been exceedingly kind to me. As he took leave of me, about eleven o'clock in the evening, he asked me if there was anything more he could do for me. I said, "No, unless you happen to know the Lord Bishop of London. I should like to get a sight at the manuscript of Bradford's history before I go home." He said, "I do not know the bishop myself, but Mr. Grenfell, at whose house you spent a few days in the early summer, married the bishop's niece, and will gladly give you an introduction to his uncle. He is in Scotland. But I will write to him before I go to bed."

Sunday morning brought me a cordial letter from Mr. Grenfell, introducing me to the bishop. I wrote a note to his lordship, saying I should be glad to have an opportunity to see Bradford's history; that I was to sail for the United States the next Wednesday, but would be pleased to call at Fulham Tuesday, if that were agreeable to him.

I got a note in reply, in which he said if I would call on Tuesday he would be happy to show me "The Log of the Mayflower," which is the title the English, without the slightest reason in the world, give the manuscript. I kept the appointment, and found the bishop with the book in his hand. He received me with great courtesy, showed me the palace, and said that that spot had been occupied by a bishop's palace for more than a thousand years.

After looking at the volume and reading the records on the flyleaf, I said: "My lord, I am going to say something which you may think rather audacious. I think this book ought to go back to

Massachusetts. Nobody knows how it got over here. Some people think it was carried off by Governor Hutchinson, the Tory governor; other people think it was carried off by British soldiers when Boston was evacuated; but in either case the property would not have changed. Or, if you treat it as a booty, in which last case, I suppose, by the law of nations ordinary property does change, no civilized nation in modern times applies that principle to the property of libraries and institutions of learning."

"Well," said the bishop, "I did not know you cared anything about it."

"Why," said I, "if there were in existence in England a history of King Alfred's reign for thirty years, written by his own hand, it would not be more precious in the eyes of Englishmen than this manuscript is to us."

"Well," said he, "I think myself it ought to go back, and if it had depended on me it would have gone back before this. But the Americans who have been here—many of them have been commercial people—did not seem to care much about it except as a curiosity. I suppose I ought not to give it up on my own authority. It belongs to me in my official capacity, and not as private or personal property. I think I ought to consult the Archbishop of Canterbury. And, indeed," he added, "I think I ought to speak to the Queen about it. We should not do such a thing behind Her Majesty's back."

I said: "Very well. When I go home I will have a proper application made from some of our literary societies, and ask you to give it consideration."

I saw Mr. Bayard again, and told him the story. He was at the train when I left London for the steamer at Southampton. He entered with great interest into the matter, and told me again he would gladly do anything in his power to forward it.

When I got home I communicated with Secretary Olney about it, who took a kindly interest in the matter, and wrote to Mr. Bayard that the administration desired he should do everything in his power to promote the application. The matter was then brought to the attention of the council of the American Antiquarian Society, the Massachusetts Historical Society, the Pilgrim Society of Plymouth and the New England Society of New York. These bodies appointed committees to unite in the application. Governor Wolcott was also consulted, who gave his hearty approbation to the movement, and a letter was dispatched through Mr. Bayard.

Meantime Bishop Temple, with whom I had my conversation, had himself become Archbishop of Canterbury, and in that capacity Primate of all England. His successor, Rev. Dr. Creighton, had been the delegate of John Harvard's College to the great celebration at Harvard University on the two hundred and fiftieth anniversary of its foundation, in 1886. He had received the degree of doctor of laws from the university, had been a guest of President Eliot, and had received President Eliot as his guest in England.

He is an accomplished historical scholar, and very friendly in sentiment to the people of the United States. So, by great fortune, the two eminent ecclesiastical personages who were to have a powerful influence in the matter were likely to be exceedingly well disposed. Dr. Benjamin A. Gould, the famous mathematician, was appointed one of the committee of the American Antiquarian Society. He died suddenly, just after a letter to the Bishop of London was prepared and about to be sent to him for signing. He took a very zealous interest in the matter. The letter formally asked for the return of the manuscript, and was signed by the following-named gentlemen: George F. Hoar, Stephen Salisbury, Edward Everett Hale, Samuel A. Green, for the American Antiquarian Society; Charles Francis Adams, William Lawrence, Charles W. Eliot, for the Massachusetts Historical Society; Arthur Lord, William M. Evarts, William T. Davis, for the Pilgrim Society of Plymouth; Charles C. Beaman, Joseph H. Choate, J. Pierpont Morgan, for the New England Society of New York; Roger Wolcott, Governor of Massachusetts.

The rarest good fortune seems to have attended every step in this transaction.

I was fortunate in having formed the friendship of Mr. Grenfell, which secured to me so cordial a reception from the Bishop of London.

It was fortunate that the Bishop of London was Dr. Temple, an eminent scholar, kindly disposed toward the people of the United States, and a man thoroughly capable of understanding and respecting the deep and holy sentiment which a compliance with our desire would gratify.

It was fortunate, too, that Bishop Temple, who thought he must have the approbation of the archbishop before his action, when the time came had himself become Archbishop of Canterbury and Primate of all England.

It was fortunate that Dr. Creighton had succeeded to the see of London. He is, himself, as I have just said, an eminent historical scholar. He has many friends in America. He was the delegate of Emmanuel, John Harvard's College, at the great Harvard centennial celebration in 1886. He received the degree of doctor of laws at Harvard and is a member of the Massachusetts Historical Society. He had, as I have said, entertained President Eliot as his guest in England.

It was fortunate, too, that the application came in a time of cordial good-will between the two countries, when the desire of John Adams and the longing of George III. have their ample and complete fulfilment. This token of the good-will of England reached Boston on the eve of the birthday of the illustrious sovereign, who is not more venerated and beloved by her own subjects than by the kindred people across the sea.

THE ARCHBISHOP OF CANTERBURY.

It comes to us at the time of the rejoicing of the English people at the sixtieth anniversary of a reign more crowded with benefit to humanity than any other known in the annals of the race. Upon the power of England, the sceptre, the trident, the lion, the army and the fleet, the monster ships of war, the all-shattering guns, the American people are strong enough now to look with an entire indifference. We encounter her commerce and her manufacture in the spirit of a generous emulation. The inheritance from which England has gained these things is ours also. We, too, are of the Saxon strain.

In our halls is hung

Armory of the invincible knights of old.

Our temple covers a continent, and its porches are upon both the seas. Our fathers knew the secret to lay, in Christian liberty and law, the foundations of empire. Our young men are not ashamed, if need be, to speak with the enemy in the gate.

But to the illustrious lady, type of gentlest womanhood, model of mother and wife and friend, who came at eighteen to the throne of George IV. and William; of purer eyes than to behold iniquity; the maiden presence before which everything unholy shrank; the sovereign who, during her long reign, "ever knew the people that she ruled;" the royal nature that disdained to strike at her kingdom's rival in the hour of our sorest need; the heart which even in the bosom of a queen beat with sympathy for the cause of constitutional liberty; who, herself not unacquainted with grief, laid on the coffin of our dead Garfield the wreath fragrant with a sister's sympathy,—to her our republican manhood does not disdain to bend.

The eagle, lord of land and sea,

Will stoop to pay her fealty.

But I am afraid this application might have had the fate of its predecessors but for our special good fortune in the fact that Mr. Bayard was our ambassador at the Court of St. James. He had been, as I said in the beginning, the ambassador not so much of the diplomacy as of the good-will of the American people. Before his powerful influence every obstacle gave way. It was almost impossible for Englishmen to refuse a request like this, made by him, and in which his own sympathies were so profoundly enlisted.

You are entitled, sir, to the gratitude of Massachusetts, to the gratitude of every lover of Massachusetts and of every lover of the country. You have succeeded where so many others have failed, and where so many others would have been likely to fail. You may be sure that our debt to you is fully understood and will not be forgotten.

The question of the permanent abiding-place of this manuscript will be settled after it has reached the hands of His Excellency. Wherever it shall go it will be an object of reverent care. I do not think many Americans will gaze upon it without a little trembling of the lips and a little gathering of mist in the eyes, as they think of the story of suffering, of sorrow, of peril, of exile, of death and of lofty triumph which that book tells,—which the hand of the great leader and founder of America has traced on those pages.

There is nothing like it in human annals since the story of Bethlehem. These Englishmen and English women going out from their homes in beautiful Lincoln and York, wife separated from husband and mother from child in that hurried embarkation for Holland, pursued to the beach by English horsemen; the thirteen years of exile; the life at Amsterdam "in alley foul and lane obscure;" the dwelling at Leyden; the embarkation at Delfthaven; the farewell of Robinson; the terrible voyage across the Atlantic; the compact in the harbor; the landing on the rock; the dreadful first winter; the death roll of more than half the number; the days of suffering and of famine; the wakeful night, listening for the yell of wild beast and the war-whoop of the savage; the building of the State on those sure foundations which no wave or tempest has ever shaken; the breaking of the new light; the dawning of the new day; the beginning of the new life; the enjoyment of peace with liberty,—of all these things this is the original record by the hand of our beloved father and founder. Massachusetts will preserve it until the time shall come that her children are unworthy of it; and that time shall come,—never.

ADDRESS OF AMBASSADOR BAYARD.

Your Excellency, Gentlemen of the two Houses of the Legislature of Massachusetts, Ladies and Gentlemen, Fellow Countrymen: The honorable and most gratifying duty with which I am charged is about to receive its final act of execution, for I have the book here, as it was placed in my hands by the Lord Bishop of London on April 29, intact then and now; and I am about to deliver it according to the provisions of the decree of the Chancellor of London, which has been read in your presence, and the receipt signed by me and registered in his court that I would obey the provisions of that decree.

I have kept my trust; I have kept the book as I received it; I shall deliver it into the hands of the representative of the people who are entitled to its custody.

And now, gentlemen, it would be superfluous for me to dwell upon the historical features of this remarkable occasion, for it has been done, as we all knew it would be done, with ability, learning, eloquence and impressiveness, by the distinguished Senator who represents you so well in the Congress of the United States.

For all that related to myself, and for every gracious word of recognition and commendation that fell from his lips in relation to the part that I have taken in the act of restoration, I am profoundly grateful. It is an additional reward, but not the reward which induced my action.

To have served your State, to have been instrumental in such an act as this, was of itself a high privilege to me. The Bradford manuscript was in the library of Fulham palace, and if, by lawful means, I could have become possessed of the volume, and have brought it here and quietly deposited it, I should have gone to my home with the great satisfaction of knowing that I had performed an act of justice, an act of right between two countries. Therefore the praise, however grateful, is additional, and I am very thankful for it.

It may not be inappropriate or unpleasing to you should I state in a very simple manner the history of my relation to the return of this book, for it all has occurred within the last twelve months.

I knew of the existence of this manuscript, and had seen the reproduction in facsimile. I knew that attempts had been made, unsuccessfully, to obtain the original book.

At that time Senator Hoar made a short visit to England, and in passing through London I was informed by him of the great interest that he, in common with the people of this State, had in the restoration of this manuscript to the custody of the State.

We discussed the methods by which it might be accomplished, and after two or three concurrent suggestions he returned to the United States, and presently I received, under cover from the Secretary of State,—a distinguished citizen of your own State, Mr. Olney,—a formal note, suggesting rather than instructing that in an informal manner I should endeavor to have carried out the wishes of the various societies that had addressed themselves to the Bishop of London and the Archbishop of Canterbury, in order to obtain the return of this manuscript.

It necessarily had to be done informally. The strict regulations of the office I then occupied forbade my correspondence with any member of the British government except through the foreign office, unless it were informal. An old saying describes the entire case, that "When there's a will there's a way." There certainly was the will to get the book, and there certainly was also a will and a way to give the book, and that way was discovered by the legal custodians of the book itself.

At first there were suggestions of difficulty, some technical questions; and following a very safe rule, the first thought was, What is the law? and the case was submitted to the law officers of the Crown. Then there arose the necessity of a formal act of permission.

There could be entertained no question as to the title to the manuscript in the possession of the British government. There was no authority to grant a claim, founded on adverse title, and the question arose as to the requisite form of law of a permissive rather than of a mandatory nature, in order to be authoritative with those who had charge of the document.

But, as I have said, when there was a will there was found a way. By personal correspondence and interviews with the Bishop of London, I soon discovered that he was as anxious to find the way as I was that he should find it. In March last it was finally agreed that I should employ legal counsel to present a formal petition in the Episcopal Consistorial Court of London, and there before the Chancellor to represent the strong desire of Massachusetts and her people for the return of the record of her early Governor.

Accordingly, the petition was prepared, and by my authority signed as for me by an eminent member of the bar, and it was also signed by the Bishop of London, so that there was a complete consensus. The decree was ordered, as is published in the London "Times" on March 25 last, and nothing after that remained but formalities, in which, as you are well aware, the English law is not lacking, especially in the ecclesiastical tribunals.

These formalities were carried out during my absence from London on a short visit to the Continent, and the decree which you have just heard read was duly entered on April 12 last, consigning the document to my personal custody, to be delivered by me in this city to the high official therein named, subject to those conditions which you have also heard.

Accordingly, on the 29th of April last I was summoned to the court, and there, having signed the receipt, this decree was read in my presence. Then the Bishop of London arose, and, taking the book in his hands, delivered it with a few gracious words into my custody, and here it is to-day.

The records of those proceedings will no doubt be preserved here as accompanying this book, as they are in the Episcopal Consistorial Court in London, and they tell the entire story.

But that is but part. The thing that I wish to impress upon you, and upon my fellow countrymen throughout the United States, is that this is an act of courtesy and friendship by another government—the government of what we once called our "mother country"—to the entire people of the United States.

You cannot limit it to the Governor of this Commonwealth; nor to the Legislature; nor even to the citizens of this Commonwealth. It extends in its courtesy, its kindness and comity to the entire people of the United States. From first to last there was the ready response of courtesy and kindness to the request for the restoration of this manuscript record.

I may say to you that there has been nothing that I have sought more earnestly than to place the affairs of these two great nations in the atmosphere of mutual confidence and respect and good-will. If it be a sin to long for the honor of one's country, for the safety and strength of one's country, then I have been a great sinner, for I have striven to advance the honor and the safety and the welfare of my country, and believed it was best accomplished by treating all with justice and courtesy, and doing those things to others which we would ask to have done to ourselves.

When the Chancellor pronounced his decree in March last, he cited certain precedents to justify him in restoring this volume to Massachusetts. One precedent which powerfully controlled his decision, and which in the closing portion of his judgment he emphasizes, was an act of generous liberality upon the part of the American Library Society in Philadelphia in voluntarily returning to the British government some volumes of original manuscript of the period of James the First, which by some means not very clearly explained had found their way among the books of that institution.

Those books were received by a distinguished man, Lord Romilly, Master of the Rolls, who took occasion to speak of the liberality and kindness which dictated the action of the Philadelphia library. Gentlemen, I am one of those who believe that a generous and kindly act is never unwise between individuals or nations.

The return of this book to you is an echo of the kindly act of your countrymen in the city of Philadelphia in 1866.

It is that, not, as Mr. Hoar has said, any influence or special effort of mine; but it is international good feeling and comity which brought about to you the pleasure and the joy of having this manuscript returned, and so it will ever be. A generous act will beget a generous act; trust and confidence will beget trust and confidence; and so it will be while the world shall last, and well will it be for the man or for the people who shall recognize this truth and act upon it.

Now, gentlemen, there is another coincidence that I may venture to point out. It is history repeating itself. More than three hundred years ago the ancestors from whom my father drew his name and blood were French Protestants, who had been compelled to flee from the religious persecutions of that day, and for the sake of conscience to find an asylum in Holland. Fifty years after they had fled and found safety in Holland, the little congregation of Independents from the English village of Scrooby, under the pastorate of John Robinson, was forced to fly, and with difficulty found its way into the same country of the Netherlands, seeking an asylum for consciences' sake.

Time passed on. The little English colony removed, as this manuscript of William Bradford will tell you, across the Atlantic, and soon after the Huguenot family from whom I drew my name found their first settlement in what was then the New Netherlands, now New York. Both came from the same cause; both came with the same object, the same purpose,—"soul freedom," as Roger Williams well called it. Both came to found homes where they could worship God according to their own conscience and live as free men. They came to these shores, and they have found the asylum, and they have strengthened it, and it is what we see to-day,—a country of absolute religious and civil freedom,—of equal rights and toleration.

And is it not fitting that I, who have in my veins the blood of the Huguenots, should present to you and your Governor the log of the

English emigrants, who left their country for the sake of religious freedom?

They are blended here,—their names, their interests. No man asks and no man has a right to ask or have ascertained by any method authorized by law what is the conscientious religious tenet or opinion of any man, of any citizen, as a prerequisite for holding an office of trust or power in the United States.

I think it well on this occasion to make, as I am sure you are making, acknowledgment to that heroic little country, the Lowlands as they call it, the Netherlands,—the country without one single feature of military defence except the brave hearts of the men who live in it and defend it.

Holland was the anvil upon which religious and civil liberty was beaten out in Europe at a time when the clang was scarcely heard anywhere else. We can never forget our historical debt to that country and to those people. Puritan, Independent, Huguenot, whoever he may be, forced to flee for conscience's sake, will not forget that in the Netherlands there was found in his time of need the asylum where conscience, property and person might be secure.

And now my task is done. I am deeply grateful for the part that I have been enabled to take in this act of just and natural restitution. In Massachusetts or out of Massachusetts there is no one more willing than I to assist this work; and here, sir [addressing Governor Wolcott], I fulfil my trust in placing in your hands the manuscript.

To you, as the honored representative of the people of this Commonwealth, I commit this book, in pursuance of my obligations, gladly undertaken under the decree of the Episcopal Consistorial Court of London.

ADDRESS OF GOVERNOR WOLCOTT.

On receiving the volume, Governor Wolcott, addressing Mr. Bayard, spoke as follows: I thank you, sir, for the diligent and faithful manner in which you have executed the honorable trust imposed upon you by the decree of the Consistorial and Episcopal Court of London, a copy of which you have now placed in my hands. It was fitting that one of your high distinction should be selected to perform so dignified an office.

The gracious act of international courtesy which is now completed will not fail of grateful appreciation by the people of this Commonwealth and of the nation. It is honorable alike to those who hesitated not to prefer the request and to those whose generous liberality has prompted compliance with it. It may be that the story of the departure of this precious relic from our shores may never in its every detail be revealed; but the story of its return will be read of all men, and will become a part of the history of the Commonwealth. There are places and objects so intimately associated with the world's greatest men or with mighty deeds that the soul of him who gazes upon them is lost in a sense of reverent awe, as it listens to the voice that speaks from the past, in words like those which came from the burning bush, "Put off thy shoes from off thy feet, for the place whereon thou standest is holy ground."

On the sloping hillside of Plymouth, that bathes its feet in the waters of the Atlantic, such a voice is breathed by the brooding genius of the place, and the ear must be dull that fails to catch the whispered words. For here not alone did godly men and women suffer greatly for a great cause, but their noble purpose was not doomed to defeat, but was carried to perfect victory. They stablished what they planned. Their feeble plantation became the birthplace of religious liberty, the cradle of a free Commonwealth. To them a mighty nation owns its debt. Nay, they have made the civilized world their debtor. In the varied tapestry which pictures our national life, the richest spots are those where gleam the golden threads of conscience, courage and faith, set in the web by that little band. May God in his mercy grant that the moral impulse which founded this nation may never cease to control its destiny; that no act of any future generation may put in peril the fundamental principles on which it is based,—of equal rights in a free state, equal privileges in a free church and equal opportunities in a free school.

In this precious volume which I hold in my hands—the gift of England to the Commonwealth of Massachusetts—is told the noble, simple story "of Plimoth Plantation." In the midst of suffering and privation and anxiety the pious hand of William Bradford here set down in ample detail the history of the enterprise from its inception to the year 1647. From him we may learn "that all great and honourable actions are accompanied with great difficulties, and must be both enterprised and overcome with answerable courages."

The sadness and pathos which some might read into the narrative are to me lost in victory. The triumph of a noble cause even at a great price is theme for rejoicing, not for sorrow, and the story here told is one of triumphant achievement, and not of defeat.

As the official representative of the Commonwealth, I receive it, sir, at your hands. I pledge the faith of the Commonwealth that for all time it shall be guarded in accordance with the terms of the decree under which it is delivered into her possession as one of her chiefest treasures. I express the thanks of the Commonwealth for the priceless gift. And I venture the prophecy that for countless years to come and to untold thousands these mute pages shall eloquently speak of high resolve, great suffering and heroic endurance made possible by an absolute faith in the over-ruling providence of Almighty God.

THE BISHOP OF LONDON

(Copy)

FULHAM PALACE, S.W.

Oct. 16, 1897.

DEAR SIR,

I would ask you to express to the Convention of the two branches of the General Court of the Commonwealth of Massachusetts my grateful thanks for the copy of their resolution of May 26, which was presented to me by Mr. Adams.[A]

I consider it a great privilege to have been associated with an act of courtesy, which was also an act of justice, in restoring to its proper place a document which is so important in the records of your illustrious Commonwealth.

I am

Yours faithfully,

M. LONDON.

H.D. COOLIDGE, Esq.

Clerk of the Convention.

OF PLIMOTH PLANTATION.

Of Plimoth Plantation.

And first of yᵉ occasion and indũsments ther unto; the which that I may truly unfould, I must begine at yᵉ very roote & rise of yᵉ same. The which I shall endevor to manefest in a plaine stile, with singuler regard unto yᵉ simple trueth in all things, at least as near as my slender judgmente can attaine the same.

1. Chapter.

It is well knowne unto yᵉ godly and judicious, how ever since yᵉ first breaking out of yᵉ lighte of yᵉ gospell in our Honourable Nation of England, (which was yᵉ first of nations whom yᵉ Lord adorned ther with, affter yᵗ grosse darknes of popery which had covered & overspred yᵉ Christian worled,) what warrs & opposissions ever since, Satan hath raised, maintained, and continued against the Saincts, from time to time, in one sorte or other. Some times by bloody death and cruell torments; other whiles imprisonments, banishments, & other hard usages; as being loath his kingdom should goe downe, the trueth prevaile, and yᵉ churches of God reverte to their anciente puritie, and recover their primative order, libertie, & bewtie. But when he could not prevaile by these means, against the maine trueths of yᵉ gospell, but that they began to take rootting in many places, being watered with yᵉ blooud of yᵉ martires, and blessed from heaven with a gracious encrease; He then begane to take him to his anciente strategemes, used of old against the first Christians. That when by ye bloody & barbarous persecutions of ye Heathen Emperours, he could not stoppe & subuerte the course of ye gospell, but that it speedily overspred with a wounderfull celeritie the then best known parts of ye world, He then begane to sow errours, heresies, and wounderfull dissentions amongst ye professours them selves, (working upon their pride & ambition, with other corrupte passions incidente to all mortall men, yea to ye saints them selves in some measure,) by which wofull effects followed; as not only bitter contentions, & hartburnings, schismes, with other horrible confusions, but Satan tooke occasion & advantage therby to foyst in a number of vile ceremoneys, with many unproffitable cannons & decrees, which have since been as snares to many poore & peaceable souls even to this day. So as in ye anciente times, the persecutions[2] by ye heathen & their Emperours, was not greater then of the Christians one against other; the Arians & other their complices against ye orthodoxe & true Christians. As witneseth Socrates in his 2. booke. His words are these;[B] *The violence truly* (saith he) *was no less than that of ould practised towards ye Christians when they were compelled & drawne to sacrifice to idoles; for many indured sundrie kinds of tormente, often rackings, & dismembering of their joynts; confiscating of ther goods; some bereaved of their native soyle; others departed this life under ye hands of ye tormentor; and some died in banishmēte, & never saw ther cuntrie againe, &c.*

The like methode Satan hath seemed to hold in these later times, since ye trueth begane to springe & spread after ye great defection made by Antichrist, y^t man of sine.

For to let pass ye infinite examples in sundrie nations and severall places of ye world, and instance in our owne, when as y^t old serpente could not prevaile by those firie flames & other his cruell tragedies, which he[C] by his instruments put in ure every wher in ye days of queene Mary & before, he then begane an other kind of warre, & went more closly to worke; not only to oppuggen, but even to ruinate & destroy ye kingdom of Christ, by more secrete & subtile means, by kindling ye flames of contention and sowing ye seeds of discorde & bitter enmitie amongst ye proffessors &

seeming reformed them selves. For when he could not prevaile by yᵉ former means against the principall doctrins of faith, he bente his force against the holy discipline & outward regimente of the kingdom of Christ, by which those holy doctrines should be conserved, & true pietie maintained amongest the saints & people of God.

Mr. Foxe recordeth how yᵗ besids those worthy martires & confessors which were burned in queene Marys days & otherwise tormented,[1] *many (both studients & others) fled out of yᵉ land, to yᵉ number of 800. And became severall congregations. At Wesell, Frankford, Bassill, Emden, Markpurge, Strausborugh, & Geneva, &c.* Amongst whom (but especialy those at Frankford) begane yᵗ bitter warr of contention & persecutiō aboute yᵉ ceremonies, & servise-booke, and other popish and antichristian stuffe, the plague of England to this day, which are like yᵉ highplases in Israell, wᶜʰ the prophets cried out against, & were their ruine; [3] which yᵉ better parte sought, according to yᵉ puritie of yᵉ gospell, to roote out and utterly to abandon. And the other parte (under veiled pretences) for their ouwn ends & advancments, sought as stifly to continue, maintaine, & defend. As appeareth by yᵉ discourse therof published in printe, Anᵒ: 1575; a booke yᵗ deserves better to be knowne and considred.

The one side laboured to have yᵉ right worship of God & discipline of Christ established in yᵉ church, according to yᵉ simplicitie of yᵉ gospell, without the mixture of mens inventions, and to have & to be ruled by yᵉ laws of Gods word, dispensed in those offices, & by those officers of Pastors, Teachers, & Elders, &c. according to yᵉ Scripturs. The other partie, though under many colours & pretences, endevored to have yᵉ episcopall dignitie (affter yᵉ popish maner) with their large power & jurisdiction still retained; with all those courts, cannons, & ceremonies, togeather with all such livings, revenues, & subordinate officers, with other such means as formerly upheld their antichristian greatnes, and enabled them with lordly & tyranous power to persecute yᵉ poore servants of God. This contention was so great, as neither yᵉ honour of God, the commone persecution, nor yᵉ mediation of Mr. Calvin & other worthies of yᵉ Lord in those places, could prevaile with those thus episcopally minded, but they proceeded by all means to disturbe yᵉ peace of this poor persecuted church, even so farr as to charge (very unjustly, & ungodlily, yet prelatelike) some of their cheefe opposers, with rebellion & hightreason against yᵉ Emperour, & other such crimes.

And this contētion dyed not with queene Mary, nor was left beyonde yᵉ seas, but at her death these people returning into England under gracious queene Elizabeth, many of them being preferred to bishopricks & other promotions, according to their aimes and desires, that inveterate hatered against yᵉ holy discipline of Christ in his church hath continued to this day. In somuch that for fear [4] it should preveile, all plotts & devices have been used to keepe it out, incensing yᵉ queene & state against it as dangerous for yᵉ comon wealth; and that it was most needfull yᵗ yᵉ fundamentall poynts of Religion should be preached in those ignorante & superstitious times; and to wine yᵉ weake & ignorante, they might retaine diverse harmles ceremoneis; and though it were to be wished yᵗ diverse things were reformed, yet this was not a season for it. And many the like, to stop yᵉ mouthes of yᵉ more godly, to bring them over to yeeld to one ceremoney after another, and one corruption after another; by these wyles begyleing some & corrupting others till at length they begane to persecute all yᵉ zealous professors in yᵉ land (though they knew little what this discipline mente) both by word & deed, if they would not submitte to their ceremonies, & become slaves to them & their popish trash, which have no ground in yᵉ word of God, but are relikes of yᵗ man of sine. And the more yᵉ light of yᵉ gospell grew, yᵉ more yᵉʸ urged their subscriptions to these corruptions. So as (notwithstanding all their former pretences & fair colures) they whose eyes God had not justly blinded might easily see wherto these things tended. And to cast contempte the more upon yᵉ sincere servants of God, they opprobriously & most injuriously gave unto, & imposed upon them, that name of Puritans, which [it] is said the Novatians out of prid did assume & take unto themselves.[E] And lamentable it is to see yᵉ effects which have followed. Religion hath been disgraced, the godly greeved, afflicted, persecuted, and many exiled, sundrie have lost their lives in prisones & otherwayes. On the other hand, sin hath been countenanced, ignorance, profannes, & atheisme increased, & the papists encouraged to hope againe for a day.

This made that holy man Mr. Perkins[F] crie out in his exhortation to repentance, upon Zeph. 2. Religion (saith he) hath been amongst us this 35. years; but the more it is published, the more it is contemned & reproached of many, &c. Thus not prophanes nor wickednes, but Religion it selfe is a byword, a moking-stock, & a matter of reproach; so that in England at this day the man or woman y begines to profes Religion, & to serve God, must resolve with him selfe to sustaine [5] mocks & injueries even as though he lived amongst y enimies of Religion. And this comone experience hath confirmed & made too apparente.

A late observation, as it were by the way, worthy to be Noted.[G]

Full litle did I thinke, y the downfall of y Bishops, with their courts, cannons, & ceremonies, &c. had been so neare, when I first begane these scribled writings (which was aboute y year 1630, and so peeced up at times of leasure afterward), or that I should have lived to have seene or heard of y same; but it is y Lords doing, and ought to be marvelous in our eyes! Every plante which mine heavenly father hath not planted (saith our Saviour) shall be rooted up. Mat: 15. 13.[H] I have snared the, and thou art taken, O Babell (Bishops), and thou wast not aware; thou art found, and also caught, because thou hast striven against the Lord. Jer. 50. 24. But will they needs strive against y truth, against y servants of God; what, & against the Lord him selfe? Doe they provoke the Lord to anger? Are they stronger than he? 1. Cor: 10. 22. No, no, they have mete with their match. Behold, I come unto y, O proud man, saith the Lord God of hosts; for thy day is come, even the time that I will visite the. Jer: 50. 31. May not the people of God now say (and these pore people among y rest), The Lord hath brought forth our righteousnes; come, let us declare in Sion the work of the Lord our God. Jer: 51. 10. Let all flesh be still before the Lord; for he is raised up out of his holy place. Zach: 2. 13.

In this case, these poore people may say (among yᵉ thousands of Israll), When the Lord brougt againe the captivite of Zion, we were like them that dreame. Psa: 126. 1. The Lord hath done greate things for us, wherof we rejoyce. v. 3. They that sow in teares, shall reap in joye. They wente weeping, and carried precious seede, but they shall returne with joye, and bring their sheaves, v. 5, 6.

Doe you not now see yᵉ fruits of your labours, O all yee servants of yᵉ Lord that have suffered for his truth, and have been faithfull witneses of yᵉ same, and yee litle handfull amongst yᵉ rest, yᵉ least amongest yᵉ thousands of Israll? You have not only had a seede time, but many of you have seene yᵉ joyefull harvest; should you not then rejoyse, yea, and againe rejoyce, and say Hallelu-iah, salvation, and glorie, and honour, and power, be to yᵉ Lord our God; for true and righteous are his judgments. Rev. 19. 1, 2.

But thou wilte aske what is yᵉ mater? What is done? Why, art thou a stranger in Israll, that thou shouldest not know what is done? Are not those Jebusites overcome that have vexed the people of Israll so long, even holding Jerusalem till Davids days, and been as thorns in their sids, so many ages; and now begane to scorne that any David should meadle with them; they begane to fortifie their tower, as that of the old Babelonians; but those proud Anakimes are throwne downe, and their glory laid in yᵉ dust. The tiranous bishops are ejected, their courts dissolved, their cannons forceless, their servise casheired, their ceremonies uselese and despised; their plots for popery prevented, and all their superstitions discarded & returned to Roome from whence they came, and yᵉ monuments of idolatrie rooted out of yᵉ land. And the proud and profane suporters, and cruell defenders of these (as bloody papists & wicked athists, and their malignante consorts) marvelously over throwne. And are not these great things? Who can deney it?

But who hath done it? Who, even he that siteth on yͦ white horse, who is caled faithfull, & true, and judgeth and fighteth righteously, Rev: 19. 11. whose garments are dipte in blood, and his name was caled the word of God, v. 13. for he shall rule them with a rode of iron; for it is he that treadeth the winepress of the feircenes and wrath of God almighty. And he hath upon his garmente, and upon his thigh, a name writen, The King of Kings, and Lord of Lords, v. 15, 16.

Hallelu-iah.

Anno Dom: 1646.

But that I may come more near my intendmente; when as by the travell & diligence of some godly & zealous preachers, & Gods blessing on their labours, as in other places of yͦ land, so in yͦ North parts, many became inlightened by the word of God, and had their ignorance & sins discovered unto them, and begane by his grace to reforme their lives, and make conscience of their wayes, the worke of God was no sooner manifest in them, but presently they were both scoffed and scorned by yͦ prophane multitude, and yͦ ministers urged with yͦ yoak of subscription, or els must be silenced; and yͦ poore people were so vexed with apparators, & pursuants, & yͦ comissarie courts, as truly their affliction was not smale; which, notwithstanding, they bore sundrie years with much patience, till they were occasioned (by yͦ continuance & encrease of these troubls, and other means which the Lord raised up in those days) to see further into things by the light of yͦ word of God. How not only these base and beggerly ceremonies were unlawfull, but also that yͦ lordly & tiranous power of yͦ prelats ought not to be submitted unto; which thus, contrary to the freedome of the gospell, would load & burden mens consciences, and by their compulsive power make a prophane mixture of persons & things in the worship of God. And that their offices & calings, courts & cannons, &c. were unlawfull and antichristian; being such as have no warrante in yͦ word of God; but the same yͭ were used in poperie, & still retained. Of which a famous author thus writeth in his Dutch comtaries.[1] At the coming of king James into England; *The new king* (saith he) *found their established yᵉ reformed religion, according to yᵉ reformed religion of king Edward yᵉ 6. Retaining, or keeping still yᵉ spirituall state of yᵉ Bishops, &c. after yᵉ ould maner, much varying & differing from yᵉ reformed churches in Scotland, France, & yᵉ Neatherlands, Embden, Geneva, &c. whose reformation is cut, or shapen much nerer yᵉ first Christian churches, as it was used in yᵉ Apostles times.*[J]

[6] So many therfore of these proffessors as saw yᵉ evill of these things, in thes parts, and whose harts yᵉ Lord had touched wᵗʰ heavenly zeale for his trueth, they shooke of this yoake of antichristian bondage, and as yᵉ Lords free people, joyned them selves (by a covenant of the Lord) into a church estate, in yᵉ felowship of yᵉ gospell, to walke in all his wayes, made known, or to be made known unto them, according to their best endeavours, whatsoever it should cost them, the Lord assisting them. And that it cost them something this ensewing historie will declare.

These people became 2. distincte bodys or churches, & in regarde of distance of place did congregate severally; for they were of sundrie townes & vilages, some in Notingamshire, some of Lincollinshire, and some of Yorkshire, wher they border nearest togeather. In one of these churches (besids others of note) was Mr. John Smith, a man of able gifts, & a good preacher, who afterwards was chosen their pastor. But these afterwards falling into some errours in yᵉ Low Countries, ther (for yᵉ most part) buried them selves, & their names.

But in this other church (wᶜʰ must be yᵉ subjecte of our discourse) besids other worthy men, was Mʳ. Richard Clifton, a grave and reverēd preacher, who by his paines and dilligens had done much good, and under God had ben a means of yᵉ conversion of many. And also that famous and worthy man Mʳ. John Robinson, who afterwards was their pastor for many years, till yᵉ Lord tooke him away by death. Also Mʳ. William Brewster a reverent man, who afterwards was chosen an elder of yᵉ church and lived with them till old age.

But after these things they could not long continue in any peaceable condition, but were hunted & persecuted on every side, so as their former afflictions were but as flea-bitings in comparison of these which now came upon them. For some were taken & clapt up in prison, others had their houses besett & watcht night and day, & hardly escaped their hands; and ye most were faine to flie & leave their howses & habitations, and the means of their livelehood. Yet these & many other sharper things which affterward befell them, were no other then they looked for, and therfore were ye better prepared to bear them by ye assistance of Gods grace & spirite. Yet seeing them selves thus molested, [7] and that ther was no hope of their continuance ther, by a joynte consente they resolved to goe into ye Low-Countries, wher they heard was freedome of Religion for all men; as also how sundrie from London, & other parts of ye land, had been exiled and persecuted for ye same cause, & were gone thither, and lived at Amsterdam, & in other places of ye land. So affter they had continued togeither aboute a year, and kept their meetings every Saboth in one place or other, exercising the worship of God amongst them selves, notwithstanding all ye dilligence & malice of their adverssaries, they seeing they could no longer continue in y^t condition, they resolved to get over into Hollād as they could; which was in ye year 1607. & 1608.; of which more at large in ye next chap.

---

2. Chap.

Of their departure into Holland and their troubls ther aboute, with some of the many difficulties they found and mete withall.

An^o. 1608.

Being thus constrained to leave their native soyle and countrie, their lands & livings, and all their freinds & famillier acquaintance, it was much, and thought marvelous by many. But to goe into a countrie they knew not (but by hearsay), wher they must learne a new language, and get their livings they knew not how, it being a dear place, & subjecte to ye misseries of warr, it was by many thought an adventure almost desperate, a case intolerable, & a misserie worse then death. Espetially seeing they were not aquainted with trads nor traffique, (by which y^t countrie doth subsiste,) but had only been used to a plaine countrie life, & ye inocente trade of husbandrey. But these things did not dismay them (though they did some times trouble them) for their desires were sett on ye ways of God, & to injoye his ordinances; but they rested on his providence, & knew whom they had beleeved. Yet [8] this was not all, for though they could not stay, yet were ye not suffered to goe, but ye ports and havens were shut against them, so as they were faine to seeke secrete means of conveance, & to bribe & fee ye mariners, & give exterordinarie rates for their passages. And yet were they often times betrayed (many of them), and both they & their goods intercepted & surprised, and therby put to great trouble & charge, of which I will give an instance or tow, & omitte the rest.

Ther was a large companie of them purposed to get passage at Boston in Lincoln-shire, and for that end had hired a shipe wholy to them selves, & made agreement with the maister to be ready at a certaine day, and take them and their goods in, at a conveniente place, wher they accordingly would all attende in readines. So after long waiting, & large expences, though he kepte not day with them, yet he came at length & tooke them in, in ye night. But when he had them & their goods abord, he betrayed them, haveing before hand complotted with ye serchers & other officers so to doe; who tooke them, and put them into open boats, & ther rifled & ransaked them, searching them to their shirts for money, yea even ye women furder then became modestie; and then caried them back into ye towne, & made them a spectackle & wonder to the multitude, which came flocking on all sids to behould them. Being thus first, by the chatch-poule officers, rifled, & stripte of their money, books, and much other goods, they were presented to ye magestrates, and messengers sente to informe ye lords of ye Counsell of them; and so they were comited to ward. Indeed yᵉ magestrats used them courteously, and shewed them what favour they could; but could not deliver them, till order came from yᵉ Counsell-table. But yᵉ issue was that after a months imprisonmente, yᵉ greatest parte were dismiste, & sent to yᵉ places from whence they came; but 7. of yᵉ principall were still kept in prison, and bound over to yᵉ Assises.

The nexte spring after, ther was another attempte made by some of these & others, to get over at an other place. And it so fell out, that they light of a Dutchman at Hull, having a ship of his owne belonging to Zealand; they made agreemente with him, and acquainted [9] him with their condition, hoping to find more faithfullnes in him, then in yᵉ former of their owne nation. He bad them not fear, for he would doe well enough. He was by appointment to take them in betweene Grimsbe & Hull, wher was a large comone a good way distante from any towne. Now aganst the prefixed time, the women & children, with yᵉ goods, were sent to yᵉ place in a small barke, which they had hired for yᵗ end; and yᵉ men were to meete them by land. But it so fell out, that they were ther a day before yᵉ shipe came, & yᵉ sea being rough, and yᵉ women very sicke, prevailed with yᵉ seamen to put into a creeke hardby, wher they lay on ground at lowwater. The nexte morning yᵉ shipe came, but they were fast, & could not stir till aboute noone. In yᵉ mean time, yᵉ shipe maister, perceiveing how yᵉ matter was, sente his boate to be getting yᵉ men abord whom he saw ready, walking aboute yᵉ shore. But after yᵉ first boat full was gott abord, & she was ready to goe for more, the mʳ espied a greate company, both horse & foote, with bills, & gunes, & other weapons; for yᵉ countrie was raised to take them. Yᵉ Dutch-man seeing yᵗ, swore his countries oath, "sacremente," and having yᵉ wind faire, waiged his Ancor, hoysed sayles, & away. But yᵉ poore men which were gott abord, were in great distress for their wives and children, which they saw thus to be taken, and were left destitute of their helps; and them selves also, not having a cloath to shifte them with, more then they had on their baks, & some scarce a peney aboute them, all they had being abord yᵉ barke. It drew tears from their eyes, and any thing they had they would have given to have been a shore againe; but all in vaine, ther was no remedy, they must thus sadly part. And afterward endured a fearfull storme at sea, being 14. days or more before yᵉʸ arived at their porte, in 7. wherof they neither saw son, moone, nor stars, & were driven near yᵉ coast of Norway; the mariners them selves often despairing of life; and once with shriks & cries gave over all, as if yᵉ ship had been foundred in yᵉ sea, & they sinking without recoverie. But when mans hope & helpe wholy failed, yᵉ Lords power & mercie appeared in ther recoverie; for yᵉ ship rose againe, & gave yᵉ mariners courage againe to manage her. And if modestie woud suffer me, I might declare with what fervente [10] prayres they cried unto yᵉ Lord in this great distres, (espetialy some of them,) even without any great distraction, when yᵉ water rane into their mouthes & ears; & the mariners cried out, We sinke, we sinke; they cried (if not with mirakelous, yet with a great hight or degree of devine faith), Yet Lord thou canst save, yet Lord thou canst save; with shuch other expressions as I will forbeare. Upon which yᵉ ship did not only recover, but shortly after yᵉ violence of yᵉ storme begane to abate, and yᵉ Lord filed their afflicted minds with shuch comforts as every one canot understand, and in yᵉ end brought them to their desired Haven, wher yᵉ people came flockeing admiring their deliverance, the storme having ben so longe & sore, in which much hurt had been don, as yᵉ masters freinds related unto him in their congrattulations.

But to returne to yᵉ others wher we left. The rest of yᵉ men yᵗ were in greatest danger, made shift to escape away before yᵉ troope could surprise them; those only staying yᵗ best might, to be assistante unto yᵉ women. But pitifull it was to see yᵉ heavie case of these poore women in this distress; what weeping & crying on every side, some for their husbands, that were caried away in yᵉ ship as is before related; others not knowing what should become of them, & their litle ones; others againe melted in teares, seeing their poore litle ones hanging aboute them, crying for feare, and quaking with could. Being thus aprehended, they were hurried from one place to another, and from one justice to another, till in yᵉ ende they knew not what to doe with them; for to imprison so many women & innocent children for no other cause (many of them) but that they must goe with their husbands, semed to be unreasonable and all would crie out of them; and to send them home againe was as difficult, for they aledged, as ye trueth was, they had no homes to goe to, for they had either sould, or otherwise disposed of their houses & livings. To be shorte, after they had been thus turmolyed a good while, and conveyed from one constable to another, they were glad to be ridd of them in ye end upon any termes; for all were wearied & tired with them. Though in ye mean time they (poore soules) indured miserie enough; and thus in the end necessitie forste a way for them.

But y^t I be not tedious in these things, I will omitte ye rest, though I might relate many other notable passages and troubles which they endured & underwente in these their wanderings & travells both at land & sea; but I hast to [11] other things. Yet I may not omitte ye fruite that came hearby, for by these so publick troubls, in so many eminente places, their cause became famouss, & occasioned many to looke into ye same; and their godly cariage & Christian behaviour was such as left a deep impression in the minds of many. And though some few shrunk at these first conflicts & sharp beginings, (as it was no marvell,) yet many more came on with fresh courage, & greatly animated others. And in ye end, notwithstanding all these stormes of oppossition, they all gatt over at length, some at one time & some at an other, and some in one place & some in an other, and mette togeather againe according to their desires, with no small rejoycing.

The 3. Chap.

Of their setling in Holand, & their maner of living, & entertainmente ther.

Being now come into yᵉ Low Countries, they saw many goodly & fortified cities, strongly walled and garded with troopes of armed men. Also they heard a strange & uncouth language, and beheld yᵉ differente maners & customes of yᵉ people, with their strange fashons and attires; all so farre differing from yᵗ of their plaine countrie villages (wherin they were bred, & had so longe lived) as it seemed they were come into a new world. But these were not yᵉ things they much looked on, or long tooke up their thoughts; for they had other work in hand, & an other kind of warr to wage & maintaine. For though they saw faire & bewtifull cities, flowing with abundance of all sorts of welth & riches, yet it was not longe before they saw the grime & grisly face of povertie coming upon them like an armed man, with whom they must bukle & incounter, and from whom they could not flye; but they were armed with faith & patience against him, and all his encounters; and though they were sometimes foyled, yet by Gods assistance they prevailed and got yᵉ victorie.

Now when Mʳ. Robinson, Mʳ. Brewster, & other principall members were come over, (for they were of yᵉ last, & stayed to help yᵉ weakest over before them,) such things were [12] thought on as were necessarie for their setling and best ordering of yᵉ church affairs. And when they had lived at Amsterdam aboute a year, Mʳ. Robinson, their pastor, and some others of best discerning, seeing how Mʳ. John Smith and his companie was allready fallen in to contention with yᵉ church yᵗ was ther before them, & no means they could use would doe any good to cure yᵉ same, and also that yᵉ flames of contention were like to breake out in yᵗ anciente church it selfe (as affterwards lamentably came to pass); which things they prudently foreseeing, thought it was best to remove, before they were any way engaged with yᵉ same; though they well knew it would be much to yᵉ prejudice of their outward estats, both at presente & in licklyhood in yᵉ future; as indeed it proved to be.

Their remoovall to Leyden.

For these & some other reasons they removed to Leyden, a fair & bewtifull citie, and of a sweete situation, but made more famous by yᵉ universitie wherwith it is adorned, in which of late had been so many learned men. But wanting that traffike by sea which Amsterdam injoyes, it was not so beneficiall for their outward means of living & estats. But being now hear pitchet they fell to such trads & imployments as they best could; valewing peace & their spirituall comforte above any other riches whatsoever. And at lenght they came to raise a competente & comforteable living, but with hard and continuall labor.

Being thus setled (after many difficulties) they continued many years in a comfortable condition, injoying much sweete & delightefull societie & spirituall comforte togeather in yᵉ wayes of God, under yᵉ able ministrie, and prudente governmente of Mʳ. John Robinson, & Mʳ. William Brewster, who was an assistante unto him in yᵉ place of an Elder, unto which he was now called & chosen by the church. So as they grew in knowledge & other gifts & graces of yᵉ spirite of God, & lived togeather in peace, & love, and holines; and many came unto them from diverse parts of England, so as they grew a great congregation. And if at any time any differences arose, or offences broak[13] out (as it cannot be, but some time ther will, even amongst yᵉ best of men) they were ever so mete with, and nipt in yᵉ head betims, or otherwise so well composed, as still love, peace, and communion was continued; or els yᵉ church purged of those that were incurable & incorrigible, when, after much patience used, no other means would serve, which seldom came to pass. Yea such was yᵉ mutuall love, & reciprocall respecte that this worthy man had to his flocke, and his flocke to him, that it might be said of them as it once was of yᵗ famouse Emperour Marcus Aurelious,[K] and yᵉ people of Rome, that it was hard to judge wheather he delighted more in haveing shuch a people, or they in haveing such a pastor. His love was greate towards them, and his care was all ways bente for their best good, both for soule and body; for besids his singuler abilities in devine things (wherin he excelled), he was also very able to give directions in civill affaires, and to foresee dangers &

inconveniences; by wch means he was very helpfull to their outward estats, & so was every way as a commone father unto them. And none did more offend him then those that were close and cleaving to them selves, and retired from ye commōe good; as also such as would be stiffe & riged in matters of outward order, and invey against ye evills of others, and yet be remisse in them selves, and not so carefull to express a vertuous conversation. They in like maner had ever a reverente regard unto him, & had him in precious estimation, as his worth & wisdom did deserve; and though they esteemed him highly whilst he lived & laboured amongst them, yet much more after his death, when they came to feele ye wante of his help, and saw (by woefull experience) what a treasure they had lost, to ye greefe of their harts, and wounding of their sowls; yea such a loss as they saw could not be repaired; for it was as hard for them to find such another leader and feeder in all respects, as for ye Taborits to find another Ziska. And though they did not call themselves orphans, as the other did, after his death, yet they had cause as much to lamente, in another regard, their present condition, and after usage. But to returne; I know not but it may be spoken to ye honour of God, & without prejudice [14] to any, that such was ye true pietie, ye humble zeale, & fervent love, of this people (whilst they thus lived together) towards God and his waies, and ye single hartednes & sinceir affection one towards another, that they came as near ye primative patterne of ye first churches, as any other church of these later times have done, according to their ranke & qualitie.

But seeing it is not my purpose to treat of ye severall passages that befell this people whilst they thus lived in ye Low Countries, (which might worthily require a large treatise of it selfe,) but to make way to shew ye begining of this plantation, which is that I aime at; yet because some of their adversaries did, upon ye rumore of their removall, cast out slanders against them, as if that state had been wearie of them, & had rather driven them out (as ye heathen historians did faine of Moyses & ye Isralits when they went out of Egipte), then y^t it was their owne free choyse & motion, I will therfore mention a perticuler or too to shew ye contrary, and the good acceptation they had in yᵉ place wher they lived. And first though many of them weer poore, yet ther was none so poore, but if they were known to be of yͥ congregation, the *Dutch* (either bakers or others) would trust them in any reasonable matter when yᵉʸ wanted money. Because they had found by experience how carfull they were to keep their word, and saw them so painfull & dilligente in their callings; yea, they would strive to gett their custome, and to imploy them above others, in their worke, for their honestie & diligence.

Againe; yᵉ magistrats of yᵉ citie, aboute yᵉ time of their coming away, or a litle before, in yᵉ publick place of justice, gave this comendable testemoney of them, in yᵉ reproofe of the Wallons, who were of yᵉ French church in yͥ citie. These English, said they, have lived amongst us now this 12. years, and yet we never had any sute or accusation came against any of them; but your strifs & quarels are continuall, &c. In these times allso were yᵉ great troubls raised by yᵉ Arminians, who, as they greatly mollested yᵉ whole state, so this citie in particuler, in which was yᵉ cheefe universitie; so as ther were dayly & hote disputs in yᵉ schooles ther aboute; and as yᵉ students & other lerned were devided in their oppinions hearin, so were yᵉ 2. proffessors or devinitie readers them selves; the one daly teaching for it, yᵉ other against it. Which grew to that pass, that few of the discipls of yᵉ one would hear yᵉ other teach. But Mʳ. Robinson, though he taught thrise a weeke him selfe, & write sundrie books, besids his manyfould pains otherwise, yet he went constantly [15] to hear ther readings, and heard yᵉ one as well as yᵉ other; by which means he was so well grounded in yᵉ controversie, and saw yᵉ force of all their arguments, and knew yᵉ shifts of yᵉ adversarie, and being him selfe very able, none was fitter to buckle with them then him selfe, as appered by sundrie disputs; so as he begane to be terrible to yᵉ Arminians; which made Episcopius (yᵉ Arminian professor) to put forth his best stringth, and set forth sundrie Theses, which by publick dispute he would defend against all men. Now Poliander yᵉ other proffessor, and yᵉ cheefe preachers of yᵉ citie, desired Mʳ. Robinson to dispute against him; but he was loath, being a stranger; yet the other did importune him, and tould him yᵗ such was yᵉ abilitie and nimblnes of yᵉ adversarie, that yᵉ truth would suffer if he did not help them. So as he condescended, & prepared him selfe against the time; and when yᵉ day came, the Lord did so help him to defend yᵉ truth & foyle this adversarie, as he put him to an apparent nonplus, in this great & publike audience. And yᵉ like he did a 2. or 3. time, upon such like occasions. The which as it caused many to praise God yᵗ the trueth had so famous victory, so it procured him much honour & respecte from those lerned men & others which loved yᵉ trueth. Yea, so farr were they from being weary of him & his people, or desiring their absence, as it was said by some, of no mean note, that were it not for giveing offence to yᵉ state of England, they would have preferd him otherwise if he would, and alowd them some publike favour. Yea when ther was speech of their remoovall into these parts, sundrie of note & eminencie of yᵗ nation would have had them come under them, and for yᵗ end made them large offers. Now though I might aledg many other perticulers & examples of the like kinde, to shew yᵉ untruth & unlicklyhode of this slander, yet these shall suffice, seeing it was beleeved of few, being only raised by yᵉ malice of some, who laboured their disgrace.

The 4. Chap.

Showing yᵉ reasons & causes of their remoovall.

After they had lived in this citie about some 11. or 12. years, (which is yᵉ more observable being yᵉ whole time of yᵗ famose truce between that state & yᵉ Spaniards,) and sundrie of them were taken away by death, & many others begane to be well striken in years, the grave mistris Experience haveing taught them many things, [16] those prudent governours with sundrie of yᵉ sagest members begane both deeply to apprehend their present dangers, & wisely to foresee yᵉ future, & thinke of timly remedy. In yᵉ agitation of their thoughts, and much discours of things hear aboute, at length they began to incline to this conclusion, of remoovall to some other place. Not out of any newfanglednes, or other such like giddie humor, by which men are oftentimes transported to their great hurt & danger, but for sundrie weightie & solid reasons; some of ye cheefe of which I will hear breefly touch. And first, they saw & found by experience the hardnes of ye place & countrie to be such, as few in comparison would come to them, and fewer that would bide it out, and continew with them. For many y^t came to them, and many more y^t desired to be with them, could not endure y^t great labor and hard fare, with other inconveniences which they underwent & were contented with. But though they loved their persons, approved their cause, and honoured their sufferings, yet they left them as it weer weeping, as Orpah did her mother in law Naomie, or as those Romans did Cato in Utica, who desired to be excused & borne with, though they could not all be Catoes. For many, though they desired to injoye ye ordinances of God in their puritie, and ye libertie of the gospell with them, yet, alass, they admitted of bondage, with danger of conscience, rather then to indure these hardships; yea, some preferred & chose ye prisons in England, rather then this libertie in Holland, with these afflictions. But it was thought that if a better and easier place of living could be had, it would draw many, & take away these discouragments. Yea, their pastor would often say, that many of those w^o both wrate & preached now against them, if they were in a place wher they might have libertie and live comfortably, they would then practise as they did.

2^{ly}. They saw that though ye people generally bore all these difficulties very cherfully, & with a resolute courage, being in ye best & strength of their years, yet old age began to steale on many of them, (and their great & continuall labours, with other crosses and sorrows, hastened it before ye time,) so as it was not only probably thought, but apparently seen, that within a few years more they would be in danger to scatter, by necessities pressing them, or sinke under their burdens, or both. And therfore according to ye devine proverb, y^t a wise man seeth ye plague when it cometh, &

hideth him selfe, Pro. 22. 3., so they like skillfull & beaten souldiers were fearfull either to be intrapped or surrounded by their enimies, so as they should neither be able to fight nor flie; and therfor thought it better to dislodge betimes to some place of better advantage & less danger, if any such could be found. [16] Thirdly; as necessitie was a taskmaster over them, so they were forced to be such, not only to their servants, but in a sorte, to their dearest chilldren; the which as it did not a litle wound yͤ tender harts of many a loving father & mother, so it produced likwise sundrie sad & sorowful effects. For many of their children, that were of best dispositions and gracious inclinations, haveing lernde to bear yͤ yoake in their youth, and willing to bear parte of their parents burden, were, often times, so oppressed with their hevie labours, that though their minds were free and willing, yet their bodies bowed under yͤ weight of yͤ same, and became decreped in their early youth; the vigor of nature being consumed in yͤ very budd as it were. But that which was more lamentable, and of all sorowes most heavie to be borne, was that many of their children, by these occasions, and yͤ great licentiousnes of youth in yͭ countrie, and yͤ manifold temptations of the place, were drawne away by evill examples into extravagante & dangerous courses, getting yͤ raines off their neks, & departing from their parents. Some became souldiers, others tooke upon them farr viages by sea, and other some worse courses, tending to dissolutnes & the danger of their soules, to yͤ great greefe of their parents and dishonour of God. So that they saw their posteritie would be in danger to degenerate & be corrupted.

Lastly, (and which was not least,) a great hope & inward zeall they had of laying some good foundation, or at least to make some way therunto, for yͤ propagating & advancing yͤ gospell of yͤ kingdom of Christ in those remote parts of yͤ world; yea, though they should be but even as stepping-stones unto others for yͤ performing of so great a work.

These, & some other like reasons, moved them to undertake this resolution of their removall; the which they afterward prosecuted with so great difficulties, as by the sequell will appeare.

The place they had thoughts on was some of those vast & unpeopled countries of America, which are frutfull & fitt for habitation, being devoyd of all civill inhabitants, wher ther are only salvage & brutish men, which range up and downe, litle otherwise then yᵉ wild beasts of the same. This proposition being made publike and coming to yᵉ scaning of all, it raised many variable opinions amongst men, and caused many fears & doubts amongst them selves. Some, from their reasons & hops conceived, laboured to stirr up & incourage the rest to undertake & prosecute yᵉ same; others, againe, out of their fears, objected against it, & sought to diverte from it, aledging many things, and those neither unreasonable nor unprobable; as that it was a great designe, and subjecte to many unconceivable perills & dangers; as, besids the casulties of yᵉ seas (which none can be freed from) the length of yᵉ vioage was such, as yᵉ weake bodys of women and other persons worne out with age & traville (as many of them were) could never be able to endure. And yet if they should, the miseries of yᵉ land which they should be [17] exposed unto, would be to hard to be borne; and lickly, some or all of them togeither, to consume & utterly to ruinate them. For ther they should be liable to famine, and nakednes, & yᵉ wante, in a maner, of all things. The chang of aire, diate, & drinking of water, would infecte their bodies with sore sickneses, and greevous diseases. And also those which should escape or overcome these difficulties, should yett be in continuall danger of yᵉ salvage people, who are cruell, barbarous, & most trecherous, being most furious in their rage, and merciles wher they overcome; not being contente only to kill, & take away life, but delight to tormente men in yᵉ most bloodie maner that may be; fleaing some alive with yᵉ shells of fishes, cutting of yᵉ members & joynts of others by peesmeale, and broiling on yᵉ coles, eate yᵉ collops of their flesh in their sight whilst they live; with other cruelties horrible to be related. And surely it could not be thought but yᵉ very hearing of these things could not but move yᵉ very bowels of men to grate within them, and make yᵉ weake to quake & tremble. It was furder objected, that it would require greater sumes of money to furnish such a voiage, and to fitt them with necessaries, then their consumed estats would amounte too; and yett they must as well looke to be seconded with supplies, as presently to be trāsported. Also many presidents of ill success, & lamentable misseries befalne others in the like designes, were easie to be found, and not forgotten to be aledged; besids their owne experience, in their former troubles & hardships in their removall into Holand, and how hard a thing it was for them to live in that strange place, though it was a neighbour countrie, & a civill and rich comone wealth.

It was answered, that all great & honourable actions are accompanied with great difficulties, and must be both enterprised and overcome with answerable courages. It was granted yᵉ dangers were great, but not desperate; the difficulties were many, but not invincible. For though their were many of them likly, yet they were not cartaine; it might be sundrie of yᵉ things feared might never befale; others by providente care & yᵉ use of good means, might in a great measure be prevented; and all of them, through yᵉ help of God, by fortitude and patience, might either be borne, or overcome. True it was, that such atempts were not to be made and undertaken without good ground & reason; not rashly or lightly as many have done for curiositie or hope of gaine, &c. But their condition was not ordinarie; their ends were good & honourable; their calling lawfull, & urgente; and therfore they might expecte yᵉ blessing of God in their proceding. Yea, though they should loose their lives in this action, yet might they have comforte in the same, and their endeavors would be honourable. They lived hear but as men in exile, & in a poore condition; and as great miseries might possibly befale them in this place, for yᵉ 12. years of truce were now out, & ther was nothing but beating of drumes, and preparing for warr, the events wherof are allway uncertaine. Yᵉ Spaniard might prove as cruell as [18] the salvages of America, and yᵉ famine and pestelence as sore hear as ther, & their libertie less to looke out for remedie. After many other perticuler things answered & aledged on both sids, it was fully concluded by yᵉ major parte, to put this designe in execution, and to prosecute it by the best means they could.

The 5. Chap.

Shewing what means they used for preparation to this waightie vioag.

And first after thir humble praiers unto God for his direction & assistance, & a generall conferrence held hear aboute, they consulted what perticuler place to pitch upon, & prepare for. Some (& none of yᵉ meanest) had thoughts & were ernest for Guiana, or some of those fertill places in those hott climats; others were for some parts of Virginia, wher yᵉ English had all ready made enterance, & begining. Those for Guiana aledged that the cuntrie was rich, fruitfull, & blessed with a perpetuall spring, and a florishing greenes; where vigorous nature brought forth all things in abundance & plentie without any great labour or art of man. So as it must needs make yᵉ inhabitants rich, seing less provisions of clothing and other things would serve, then in more coulder & less frutfull countries must be had. As also yᵗ the Spaniards (having much more then they could possess) had not yet planted there, nor any where very near yᵉ same. But to this it was answered, that out of question yᵉ countrie was both frutfull and pleasante, and might yeeld riches & maintenance to yᵉ possessors, more easily then yᵉ other; yet, other things considered, it would not be so fitt for them. And first, yᵗ such hott countries are subject to greevuos diseases, and many noysome impediments, which other more temperate places are freer from, and would not so well agree with our English bodys. Againe, if they should ther live, & doe well, the jealous Spaniard would never suffer them long, but would displante or overthrow them, as he did yᵉ French in Florida, who were seated furder from his richest countries; and the sooner because they should have none to protect them, & their owne strength would be too smale to resiste so potent an enemie, & so neare a neighbor.

On ye other hand, for Virginia it was objected, that if they lived among ye English wch wear ther planted, or so near them as to be under their goverment, they should be in as great danger to be troubled and persecuted for the cause of religion, as if they lived in England, and it might be worse. And if they lived too farr of, they should neither have succour, nor defence from them.

But at length ye conclusion was, to live as a distincte body by them selves, under ye generall Goverment of Virginia; and by their freinds to sue to his majestie that he would be pleased to grant them freedome of Religion; and y^t this might be obtained, they wear putt in good hope by some great persons, of good ranke & qualitie, that were made their freinds. Whereupon 2. were chosen [19] & sent in to England (at ye charge of ye rest) to sollicite this matter, who found the Virginia Company very desirous to have them goe thither, and willing to grante them a patent, with as ample priviliges as they had, or could grant to any, and to give them the best furderance they could. And some of ye cheefe of y^t company douted not to obtaine their suite of ye king for liberty in Religion, and to have it confirmed under ye kings broad seale, according to their desires. But it prooved a harder peece of worke then they tooke it for; for though many means were used to bring it aboute, yet it could not be effected; for ther were diverse of good worth laboured with the king to obtaine it, (amongst whom was one of his cheefe secretaries,[LJ]) and some other wrought with ye archbishop to give way therunto; but it proved all in vaine. Yet thus farr they prevailed, in sounding his majesties mind, that he would connive at them, & not molest them, provided they carried them selves peacably. But to allow or tolerate them by his publick authoritie, under his seale, they found it would not be. And this was all the cheefe of ye Virginia companie or any other of their best freinds could doe in the case. Yet they perswaded them to goe on, for they presumed they should not be troubled. And with this answer ye messengers returned, and signified what diligence had bene used, and to what issue things were come.

But this made a dampe in ye busines, and caused some distraction, for many were afraid that if they should unsetle them selves, & put of their estates, and goe upon these hopes, it might prove dangerous, and but a sandie foundation. Yea, it was thought they might better have presumed hear upon without makeing any suite at all, then, haveing made it, to be thus rejected. But some of yᵉ cheefest thought other wise, and yᵗ they might well proceede hereupon, & that yᵉ kings majestie was willing enough to suffer them without molestation, though for other reasons he would not confirme it by any publick acte. And furdermore, if ther was no securitie in this promise intimated, ther would be no great certainty in a furder confirmation of yᵉ same; for if after wards ther should be a purpose or desire to wrong them, though they had a seale as broad as yᵉ house flore, it would not serve yᵉ turne; for ther would be means enew found to recall or reverse it. Seeing therfore the course was probable, they must rest herein on Gods providence, as they had done in other things.

Upon this resolution, other messengers were dispatched, to end with yᵉ Virginia Company as well as they could. And to procure [20] a patent with as good and ample conditions as they might by any good means obtaine. As also to treate and conclude with such merchants and other freinds as had manifested their forwardnes to provoke too and adventure in this vioage. For which end they had instructions given them upon what conditions they should proceed with them, or els to conclude nothing without further advice. And here it will be requisite to inserte a letter or too that may give light to these proceedings.

A coppie of leter from Sir Edwin Sands, directed to Mr. John Robinson & Mr. William Brewster.

After my hartie salutations. The agents of your congregation, Robert Cushman & John Carver, have been in comunication with diverse selecte gentlemen of his Majesties Counsell for Virginia; and by yᵉ writing of 7. Articles subscribed with your names, have given them yᵗ good degree of satisfaction, which hath caried them on with a resolution to sett forward your desire in yᵉ best sorte yᵗ may be, for your owne & the publick good. Divers perticulers wherof we leave to their faithfull reporte; having carried them selves heere with that good discretion, as is both to their owne and their credite from whence they came. And wheras being to treate for a multitude of people, they have requested further time to conferr with them that are to be interessed in this action, aboute ye severall particularities which in ye prosecution therof will fall out considerable, it hath been very willingly assented too. And so they doe now returne unto you. If therfore it may please God so to directe your desires as that on your parts ther fall out no just impediments, I trust by ye same direction it shall likewise appear, that on our parte, all forwardnes to set you forward shall be found in the best sorte which with reason may be expected. And so I betake you with this designe (wch I hope verily is ye worke of God), to the gracious protection and blessing of the Highest.

Your very loving freind

EDWIN SANDYS.

London, Nov̄b^r 12.

An^o 1617.

Their answer was as foloweth.

Righte Wor^{pl}:

Our humble duties remembred, in our owne, our messengers, and our churches name, with all thankfull acknowledgmente of your singuler love, expressing [21] itselfe, as otherwise, so more spetially in your great care and earnest endeavor of our good in this weightie bussines about Virginia, which ye less able we are to requite, we shall thinke our selves the more bound to commend in our prayers unto God for recompence; whom, as for ye presente you rightly behould in our indeavors, so shall we not be wanting on our parts (the same God assisting us) to returne all answerable fruite, and respecte unto ye labour of your love bestowed upon us. We have with ye best speed and consideration withall that we could, sett downe our requests in writing, subscribed, as you willed, wth the hands of ye greatest parte of our congregation, and have sente ye same unto ye Counsell by our agente, & a deacon of our church, John Carver, unto whom we have also requested a gentleman of our company to adyone him selfe; to the care & discretion of which two, we doe referr ye prosecuting of ye bussines. Now we perswade our selves Right Wor^{pp}: that we need not provoke your godly & loving minde to any further or more tender care of us, since you have pleased so farr to interest us in your selfe, that, under God, above all persons and things in the world, we relye upon you, expecting the care of your love, counsell of your wisdome, & the help & countenance of your authority. Notwithstanding, for your encouragmente in ye worke, so farr as probabilities may leade, we will not forbeare to mention these instances of indusmente.

1. We veryly beleeve & trust ye Lord is with us, unto whom & whose service we have given our selves in many trialls; and that he will graciously prosper our indeavours according to ye simplicitie of our harts therin.

2^{ly}. We are well weaned from ye delicate milke of our mother countrie, and enured to ye difficulties of a strange and hard land, which yet in a great parte we have by patience overcome.

3^{ly}. The people are for the body of them, industrious, & frugall, we thinke we may safly say, as any company of people in the world.

4^{ly}. We are knite togeather as a body in a most stricte & sacred bond and covenante of the Lord, of the violation[M] wherof we make great conscience, and by vertue wherof we doe hould our selves straitly tied to all care of each others good, and of ye whole by every one and so mutually.

5. Lastly, it is not with us as with other men, whom small things can discourage, or small discontentments cause to wish them selves

at home againe. We knowe our entertainmente in England, and in Holand; we shall much prejudice both our arts & means by removall; who, if we should be driven to returne, we should not hope to recover our present helps and comforts, neither indeed looke ever, for our selves, to attaine unto ye like in any other place during our lives, wch are now drawing towards their periods.

[22] These motives we have been bould to tender unto you, which you in your wisdome may also imparte to any other our wor^pp: freinds of ye Counsell with you; of all whose godly dispossition and loving towards our despised persons, we are most glad, & shall not faile by all good means to continue & increase ye same. We will not be further troublesome, but doe, with ye renewed remembrance of our humble duties to your Wor^pp: and (so farr as in modestie we may be bould) to any other of our wellwillers of the Counsell with you, we take our leaves, comiting your persons and counsels to ye guidance and direction of the Almighty.

Yours much bounden in all duty,

JOHN ROBINSON,

WILLIAM BREWSTER.

Leyden, Desem: 15.

An^o: 1617.

For further light in these proceedings see some other letters & notes as followeth.

The coppy of a letter sent to S^r. John Worssenham.

Right Wor^pll: with due acknowledgmente of our thankfullnse for your singular care & pains in the bussines of Virginia, for our, &, we hope, the comone good, we doe remember our humble dutys unto you, and have sent inclosed, as is required, a further explanation of our judgments in the 3. points specified by some of his majesties Hon^bl Privie Counsell; and though it be greevious unto us that such unjust insinuations are made against us, yet we are most glad of ye occasion of making our just purgation unto so honourable personages. The declarations we have sent inclosed, the one more breefe & generall, which we thinke ye fitter to be presented; the other something more large, and in which we express some smale accidentall differances, which if it seeme good unto you and other of our wor^{pl} freinds, you may send in stead of ye former. Our prayers unto God is, y^t your Wor^{pp} may see the frute of your worthy endeaours, which on our parts we shall not faile to furder by all good means in us. And so praing y^t you would please with ye convenientest speed y^t may be, to give us knowledge of ye success of ye bussines with his majesties Privie Counsell, and accordingly what your further pleasure is, either for our direction or furtherance in ye same, so we rest

Your Wor^{pp} in all duty,

JOHN ROBINSON,

WILLIAM BREWSTER.

Leyden, Jan: 27.

An^o: 1617. old stile.

The first breefe note was this.

Touching ye Ecclesiasticall ministrie, namly of pastores for teaching, elders for ruling, & deacons for distributing ye churches contribution, as allso for ye too Sacrements, baptisme, and ye Lords supper, we doe wholy and in all points agree [23] with ye French reformed churches, according to their publick confession of faith.

The oath of Supremacie we shall willingly take if it be required of us, and that conveniente satisfaction be not given by our taking ye oath of Alleagence.

JOHN ROB:

WILLIAM BREWSTER.

Yᵉ 2. was this.

Touching yᵉ Ecclesiasticall ministrie, &c. as in yᵉ former, we agree in all things with the French reformed churches, according to their publick confession of faith; though some small differences be to be found in our practises, not at all in yᵉ substance of the things, but only in some accidentall circumstances.

1. As first, their ministers doe pray with their heads covered; ours uncovered.

2. We chose none for Governing Elders but such as are able to teach; which abilitie they doe not require.

3. Their elders & deacons are anūall, or at most for 2. or 3. years; ours perpetuall.

4. Our elders doe administer their office in admonitions & excommunications for publick scandals, publickly & before yᵉ congregation; theirs more privately, & in their consistories.

5. We doe administer baptisme only to such infants as wherof yᵉ one parente, at yᵉ least, is of some church, which some of ther churches doe not observe; though in it our practice accords with their publick confession and yᵉ judgmente of yᵉ most larned amongst them.

Other differences, worthy mentioning, we know none in these points. Then aboute yᵉ oath, as in yᵉ former.

Subscribed,

JOHN R.

W. B.

Part of another letter from him that delivered these.

London.   Feb: 14.
1617.

Your letter to S[r]. John Worstenholme I delivered allmost as soone
as I had it, to his owne hands, and staid with him y[e] opening &
reading. Ther were 2. papers inclosed, he read them to him selfe, as
also y[e] letter, and in y[e] reading he spake to me & said, Who shall
make them? viz. y[e] ministers; I answered his Wor[pp] that y[e] power of
making was in y[e] church, to be ordained by y[e] imposition of hands,
by y[e] fittest instruments they had. It must either be in y[e] church or
from y[e] pope, & y[e] pope is Antichrist. Ho! said S[r]. John, what y[e]
pope houlds good, (as in y[e] Trinitie,) that we doe well to assente
too; but, said he, we will not enter into dispute now. And as for
your letters he would not show them at any hand, least he should
spoyle all. He expected you should have been of y[e] archbp minde
for y[e] calling of ministers, but it seems you differed. I could have
wished to have known y[e] contents of your tow inclosed, at w[ch] he
stuck so much, espetially y[e] larger. I asked his Wor[p] what good
news he had for me to write to morrow. He tould me very good
news, for both the kings majestie and y[e] bishops have consented.
He said he would goe to M[r]. Chancelor, S[r]. Fulk Grivell, as this
day, & nexte weeke I should know more. I mett S[r]. Edw: Sands on
Wedensday night; he wished me to be at the Virginia Courte y[e]
nexte Wedensday, wher I purpose to be. Thus loath to be
troublsome at present, I hope to have somewhate nexte week of
certentie concerning you. I comitte you to y[e] Lord. Yours,

S. B.

[24] These things being long in agitation, & messengers passing
too and againe aboute them, after all their hopes they were long
delayed by many rubs that fell in y[e] way; for at y[e] returne of these
messengers into England they found things farr otherwise then they
expected. For y[e] Virginia Counsell was now so disturbed with
factions and quarrels amongst them selves, as no bussines could
well goe forward. The which may the better appear in one of the
messengers letters as followeth.

To his loving freinds, &c.

I had thought long since to have write unto you, but could not effecte y^t which I aimed at, neither can yet sett things as I wished; yet, notwithstanding, I doubt not but M^r. B. hath writen to M^r. Robinson. But I thinke my selfe bound also to doe something, least I be thought to neglecte you. The maine hinderance of our proseedings in ye Virginia bussines, is the dissentions and factions, as they terme it, amongs ye Counsell & Company of Virginia; which are such, as that ever since we came up no busines could by them be dispatched. The occasion of this trouble amongst them is, for that a while since S^r. Thomas Smith, repining at his many offices & troubls, wished ye Company of Virginia to ease him of his office in being Treasurer & Gover^r. of ye Virginia Company. Wereupon ye Company tooke occasion to dismisse him, and chose S^r. Edwin Sands Treasure^r & Gover^r of ye Company. He having 60. voyces, S^r. John Worstenholme 16. voices, and Alderman Johnsone 24. But S^r. Thomas Smith, when he saw some parte of his honour lost, was very angrie, & raised a faction to cavill & contend aboute ye election, and sought to taxe S^r. Edwin with many things that might both disgrace him, and allso put him by his office of Governour. In which contentions they yet stick, and are not fit nor readie to intermedle in any bussines; and what issue things will come to we are not yet certaine. It is most like S^r. Edwin will carrie it away, and if he doe, things will goe well in Virginia; if otherwise, they will goe ill enough allways. We hope in some 2. or 3. Court days things will setle. Mean space I thinke to goe downe into Kente, & come up againe aboute 14. days, or 3. weeks hence; except either by these afforesaid contentions, or by ye ille tidings from Virginia, we be wholy discouraged, of which tidings I am now to speake.

Captaine Argoll is come home this weeke (he upon notice of ye intente of ye Counsell, came away before S^r. Georg Yeardley came ther, and so ther is no small dissention). But his tidings are ill, though his person be wellcome. He saith M^r. Blackwells shipe came not ther till March, but going towards winter, they had still norwest winds, which carried them to the southward beyond their course. And yᵉ mʳ of yᵉ ship & some 6. of yᵉ mariners dieing, it seemed they could not find yᵉ bay, till after long seeking & beating aboute. Mʳ. Blackwell is dead, & Mʳ. Maggner, yᵉ Captain; yea, ther are dead, he saith, 130. persons, one & other in yᵗ ship; it is said ther was in all an 180. persons in yᵉ ship, so as they were packed togeather like herings. They had amongst them yᵉ fluxe, and allso wante of fresh water; so as it is hear rather wondred at yᵗ so many are alive, then that so many are dead. The marchants hear say it was Mʳ. Blackwells faulte to pack so many in yᵉ ship; yea, & ther were great mutterings & repinings amongst them, and upbraiding of Mʳ. Blackwell, for his dealing and dispossing of them, when they saw how he had dispossed of them, & how he insulted over them. Yea, yᵉ streets at Gravsend runge of their extreame quarrelings, crying out one of another, Thou hast brought me to this, and, I may thanke the for this. Heavie newes it is, and I would be glad to heare how farr it will discourage. I see none hear discouraged much, [25] but rather desire to larne to beware by other mens harmes, and to amend that wherin they have failed. As we desire to serve one another in love, so take heed of being inthraled by any imperious persone, espetially if they be discerned to have an eye to them selves. It doth often trouble me to thinke that in this bussines we are all to learne and none to teach; but better so, then to depend upon such teachers as Mʳ. Blackwell was. Such a strategeme he once made for Mʳ. Johnson & his people at Emden, wᶜʰ was their subversion. But though he ther clenlily (yet unhonstly) plucked his neck out of yᵉ collar, yet at last his foote is caught. Hear are no letters come, yᵉ ship captain Argole came in is yet in yᵉ west parts; all yᵗ we hear is but his report; it seemeth he came away secretly. The ship yᵗ Mʳ. Blackwell went in will be hear shortly. It is as Mʳ. Robinson once said; he thought we should hear no good of them.

Mʳ. B. is not well at this time; whether he will come back to you or goe into yᵉ north, I yet know not. For my selfe, I hope to see an end of this bussines ere I come, though I am sorie to be thus from you; if things had gone roundly forward, I should have been with you within these 14. days. I pray God directe us, and give us that spirite which is fitting for such a bussines. Thus having sumarily pointed at things wch M^r. Brewster (I thinke) hath more largly write of to M^r. Robinson, I leave you to the Lords protection.

Yours in all readines, &c.   London, May 8.

Robart Cushman.   An^o: 1619.

A word or tow by way of digression touching this M^r. Blackwell; he was an elder of ye church at Amsterdam, a man well known of most of them. He declined from ye trueth wth M^r. Johnson & ye rest, and went with him when y^ey parted assunder in y^t wofull maner, wch brought so great dishonour to God, scandall to ye trueth, & outward ruine to them selves in this world. But I hope, notwithstanding, through ye mercies of ye Lord, their souls are now at rest with him in ye heavens, and y^t they are arrived in ye Haven of hapines; though some of their bodies were thus buried in ye terrable seas, and others sunke under ye burthen of bitter afflictions. He with some others had prepared for to goe to Virginia. And he, with sundrie godly citizens, being at a private meēing (I take it a fast) in London, being discovered, many of them were apprehended, wherof M^r. Blackwell was one; but he so glosed wth ye bps,[N] and either dissembled or flatly denyed ye trueth which formerly he had maintained; and not only so, but very unworthily betrayed and accused another godly man who had escaped, that so he might slip his own neck out of ye collar, & to obtaine his owne freedome brought others into bonds. Wherupon he so wone ye bps favour (but lost ye Lord's) as he was not only dismiste, but in open courte ye arch-bishop gave him great applause and his sollemne blessing to proseed in his vioage. But if such events follow ye bps blessing, happie are they y^t misse ye same; it is much better to keepe a good conscience and have ye Lords blessing, whether in life or death.

But see how ye man thus apprehended by M^r. Blackwells means, writs to a freind of his.

Right dear friend & christian brother, *M^r. Carver*, I salute you & yours in ye Lord, &c. As for my owne presente condition, I doubt not but you well understand it ere this by our brother Maistersone, who should have tasted of ye same cupp, had his place of residence & his person been as well knowne as my selfe. Some what I have written to M^r. *Cushman* how ye matter *still continues*. I have petitioned *twise* to M^r. Sherives, and *once* to my Lord Cooke, and have used such reasons to move them to pittie, that if they were not overruled by some others, I suppose I should soone gaine my libertie; as that I was a yonge man living by my [26] credite, indebted to diverse in our citie, living at more then ordinarie charges in a close & tedious prison; besids great rents abroad, all my bussines lying still, my only servante lying lame in ye countrie, my wife being also great with child. And yet no answer till ye lords of his majesties Counsell gave consente. Howbeit, M^r. Blackwell, a man as deepe in this action as I, was delivered at a cheaper rate, with a great deale less adoe; yea, with an addition of ye Archp: blessing. I am sorie for M^r. Blackwels weaknes, I wish it may prove no worse. But yet he & some others of them, *before their going*, were not sorie, but thought it was for ye best that I was nominated, not because ye Lord sanctifies evill to good, but that ye action was good, yea for ye best. One reason I well remember he used was, because this trouble would encrease ye Virginia plantation, in that now people begane to be more generally inclined to goe; and if he had not nomminated some such as I, he had not bene free, being it was knowne that diverse citizens besids them selves were ther. I expecte an answer shortly what they intende conscerning me; I purpose to write to some others of you, by whom you shall know the certaintie. Thus not haveing further at present to acquaint you withall, comending myselfe to your prairs, I cease, & comitte you and us all to ye Lord.

From my chamber in Wodstreete Compter.

Your freind, & brother in bonds,

SABIN STARESMORE.

Sept^r: 4. An^o: 1618.

But thus much by yᵉ way, which may be of instruction & good use.

But at last, after all these things, and their long attendance, they had a patent granted them, and confirmed under yᵉ Companies seale; but these devissions and distractions had shaken of many of ther pretended freinds, and disappointed them of much of their hoped for & proffered means. By the advise of some freinds this pattente was not taken in yᵉ name of any of their owne, but in yᵉ name of Mr. John Wincob (a religious gentleman then belonging to yᵉ Countess of Lincoline), who intended to goe with them. But God so disposed as he never went, nor they ever made use of this patente, which had cost them so much labour and charge, as by yᵉ sequell will appeare. This patente being sente over for them to veiw & consider, as also the passages aboute yᵉ propossitions between them & such marchants & freinds as should either goe or adventure with them, and espetially with those[o] on whom yᵉʸ did cheefly depend for shipping and means, whose proffers had been large, they were requested to fitt and prepare them selves with all speed. A right emblime, it may be, of yᵉ uncertine things of this world; yᵗ when men have toyld them selves for them, they vanish into smoke.

The 6. Chap.

Conscerning yᵉ agreements and artickles between them, and such marchants & others as adventured moneys; with other things falling out aboute making their provissions.

Upon yᵉ receite of these things by one of their messengers, they had a sollemne meeting and a day of humilliation to seeke yᵉ Lord for his direction; and their pastor tooke this texte, 1 *Sam.* 23. 3, 4. *And David's men said unto him, see, we be afraid hear in Judah, how much more if we come to Keilah against the host of the*

Phillistines? Then David asked counsell of y Lord againe, &c.* From which texte he taught many things very aptly, and befitting ther present occasion and condition, strengthing them against their fears and perplexities, and incouraging them in their resolutions. [27] After which they concluded both what number and what persons should prepare them selves to goe with y* first; for all y* were willing to have gone could not gett ready for their other affairs in so shorte a time; neither if all could have been ready, had ther been means to have trasported them alltogeather. Those that staied being y* greater number required y* pastor to stay with them; and indeede for other reasons he could not then well goe, and so it was y* more easilie yeelded unto. The other then desired y* elder, M*. Brewster, to goe with them, which was also condescended unto. It was also agreed on by mutuall consente and covenante, that those that went should be an absolute church of them selves, as well as those y* staid; seing in such a dangrous vioage, and a removall to such a distance, it might come to pass they should (for y* body of them) never meete againe in this world; yet with this proviso, that as any of y* rest came over to them, or of y* other returned upon occasion, they should be reputed as members without any further dismission or testimoniall. It was allso promised to those y* wente first, by y* body of y* rest, that if y* Lord gave them life, & meās, & opportunitie, they would come to them as soone as they could.

Aboute this time, whilst they were perplexed with y* proseedings of y* Virginia Company, & y* ill news from thence aboute M*. Blackwell & his company, and making inquirey about y* hiring & buying of shiping for their vioage, some Dutchmen made them faire offers aboute goeing with them. Also one M*. Thomas Weston, a m*chant of London, came to Leyden aboute y* same time, (who was well aquainted with some of them, and a furtherer of them in their former proseedings,) haveing much conferance w*th M*. Robinson & other of y* cheefe of them, perswaded them to goe on (as it seems) & not to medle with y* Dutch, or too much to depend on the Virginia Company; for if that failed, if they came to resolution, he and such marchants as were his freinds (togeather with their owne means) would sett them forth; and they should make ready, and neither feare wante of shipping nor money; for what they wanted should be provided. And, not so much for him selfe as for y⁰ satisfing of such frends as he should procure to adventure in this bussines, they were to draw such articls of agreemente, and make such propossitions, as might y⁰ better induce his freinds to venture. Upon which (after y⁰ formere conclusion) articles were drawne & agreed unto, and were showne unto him, and approved by him; and afterwards by their messenger (Mʳ. John Carver) sent into England, who, togeather with Robart Cushman, were to receive y⁰ moneys & make provissione both for shiping & other things for y⁰ vioage; with this charge, not to exseede their comission, but to proseed according to y⁰ former articles. Also some were chossen to doe y⁰ like for such things as were to be prepared there; so those that weare to goe, prepared them selves with all speed, and sould of their estats and (such as were able) put in their moneys into y⁰ commone stock, which was disposed by those appointed, for y⁰ making of generall provissions. Aboute this time also they had heard, both by Mʳ. Weston and others, yᵗ sundrie Honᵇˡ: Lords had obtained a large grante from y⁰ king, for y⁰ more northerly parts of that countrie, derived out of y⁰ Virginia patente, and wholy secluded from their Govermente, and to be called by another name, viz. New-England. Unto which Mʳ. Weston, and y⁰ cheefe of them, begane to incline it was [28] best for them to goe, as for other reasons, so cheefly for y⁰ hope of present profite to be made by y⁰ fishing that was found in yᵗ countrie.

But as in all bussineses y⁰ acting parte is most difficulte, espetially wher y⁰ worke of many agents must concurr, so it was found in this; for some of those yᵗ should have gone in England, fell of & would not goe; other marchants & freinds yᵗ had offered to adventure their moneys withdrew, and pretended many excuses. Some disliking they wente not to Guiana; others againe would adventure nothing excepte they wente to Virginia. Some againe (and those that were most relied on) fell in utter dislike with Virginia, and would doe nothing if they wente thither. In y⁰ midds of these distractions, they of Leyden, who had put of their estats, and laid out their moneys, were brought into a greate streight, fearing what issue these things would come too; but at length y⁰ generalitie was swaid to this latter opinion.

But now another difficultie arose, for Mʳ. Weston and some other that were for this course, either for their better advantage or rather for yᵉ drawing on of others, as they pretended, would have some of those conditions altered yᵗ were first agreed on at Leyden. To which yᵉ 2. agents sent from Leyden (or at least one of them who is most charged with it) did consente; seeing els yᵗ all was like to be dashte, & yᵉ opportunitie lost, and yᵗ they which had put of their estats and paid in their moneys were in hazard to be undon. They presumed to conclude with yᵉ marchants on those termes, in some things contrary to their order & comission, and without giving them notice of yᵉ same; yea, it was conceled least it should make any furder delay; which was yᵉ cause afterward of much trouble & contention.

It will be meete I here inserte these conditions, which are as foloweth.

Anᵒ: 1620. July 1.

1. The adventurers & planters doe agree, that every person that goeth being aged 16. years & upward, be rated at 10ˡⁱ., and ten pounds to be accounted a single share.

2. That he that goeth in person, and furnisheth him selfe out with 10ˡⁱ. either in money or other provissions, be accounted as haveing 20ˡⁱ. in stock, and in yᵉ devission shall receive a double share.

3. The persons transported & yᵉ adventurers shall continue their joynt stock & partnership togeather, yᵉ space of 7. years, (excepte some unexpected impedimente doe cause yᵉ whole company to agree otherwise,) during which time, all profits & benifits that are gott by trade, traffick, trucking, working, fishing, or any other means of any person or persons, remaine still in yᵉ comone stock untill yᵉ division.

4. That at their coming ther, they chose out such a number of fitt persons, as may furnish their ships and boats for fishing upon yᵉ sea; imploying the rest in their severall faculties upon yᵉ land; as building houses, tilling, and planting yᵉ ground, & makeing shuch comodities as shall be most usefull for yᵉ collonie.

5. That at yᵉ end of yᵉ 7. years, yᵉ capitall & profits, viz. the houses, lands, goods and chatles, be equally devided betwixte yᵉ adventurers, and planters; wᶜʰ done, every man shall be free from other of them of any debt or detrimente concerning this adventure.

[29] 6. Whosoever cometh to yᵉ colonie herafter, or putteth any into yᵉ stock, shall at the ende of yᵉ 7. years be alowed proportionably to yᵉ time of his so doing.

7. He that shall carie his wife & children, or servants, shall be alowed for everie person now aged 16. years & upward, a single share in yᵉ devision, or if he provid them necessaries, a duble share, or if they be between 10. year old and 16., then 2. of them to be reconed for a person, both in trāsportation and devision.

8. That such children as now goe, & are under yᵉ age of ten years, have noe other shar in yᵉ devision, but 50. acers of unmanured land.

9. That such persons as die before yᵉ 7. years be expired, their executors to have their parte or sharr at yᵉ devision, proportionably to yᵉ time of their life in yᵉ collonie.

10. That all such persons as are of this collonie, are to have their meate, drink, apparell, and all provissions out of yᵉ comon stock & goods of yᵉ said collonie.

The cheefe & principall differences betwene these & the former conditions, stood in those 2. points; that yᵉ houses, & lands improved, espetialy gardens & home lotts should remaine undevided wholy to yᵉ planters at yᵉ 7. years end. 2ˡʸ, yᵗ they should have had 2. days in a weeke for their owne private imploymente, for yᵉ more comforte of them selves and their families, espetialy such as had families. But because letters are by some wise men counted yᵉ best parte of histories, I shall shew their greevances hereaboute by their owne letters, in which ye passages of things will be more truly discerned.

A letter of M^r. Robinsons to John Carver.

June 14. 1620. N. Stile.

My dear freind & brother, whom with yours I alwaise remember in my best affection, and whose wellfare I shall never cease to comend to God by my best & most earnest praires. You doe throwly understand by our generall letters ye estate of things hear, which indeed is very pitifull; espetialy by wante of shiping, and not seeing means lickly, much less certaine, of having it provided; though withall ther be great want of money & means to doe needfull things. M^r. Pickering, you know before this, will not defray a peny hear; though Robart Cushman presumed of I know not how many 100^{li}. from him, & I know not whom. Yet it seems strange y^t we should be put to him to receive both his & his partners adventer, and yet M^r. Weston write unto him, y^t in regard of it, he hath drawne upon him a 100^{li}. more. But ther is in this some misterie, as indeed it seems ther is in ye whole course. Besids, wheras diverse are to pay in some parts of their moneys yet behinde, they refuse to doe it, till they see shiping provided, or a course taken for it. Neither doe I thinke is ther a man hear would pay any thing, if he had againe his money in his purse. You know right well we depended on M^r. Weston alone, and upon such means as he would procure for this commone bussines; and when we had in hand another course with ye Dutchmen, broke it of at his motion, and upon ye conditions by him shortly after propounded. He did this in his love I know, but things appeare not answerable from him hitherto. That he should have first have put in his moneys, is thought by many to have been but fitt, but y^t I can well excuse, he being a marchante and haveing use of it to his benefite; wheras others, if it had been in their hands, would have consumed it. [30] But y^t he should not but have had either shipping ready before this time, or at least certaine means, and course, and ye same knowne to us for it, or have taken other order otherwise, cannot in my conscience be excused. I have heard y^t when he hath been moved in the bussines, he hath put it of from him selfe, and referred it to ye others;[P] and would come to Georg Morton, & enquire news of him aboute things, as if he had scarce been some accessarie unto it. Wether he hath failed of some helps from others which he expected, and so be not well able to goe through with things, or whether he hath feared least you should be ready too soone & so encrease ye charge of shiping above y^t is meete, or whether he have thought by withhoulding to put us upon straits, thinking y^t therby M^r. Brewer and M^r. Pickering would be drawne by importunitie to doe more, or what other misterie is in it, we know not; but sure we are y^t things are not answerable to such an occasion. M^r. Weston maks himselfe mery with our endeavors about buying a ship, but we have done nothing in this but with good reason, as I am perswaded, nor yet that I know in any thing els, save in those tow; ye one, that we imployed Robart Cushman, who is known (though a good man, & of spetiall abilities in his kind, yet) most unfitt to deale for other men, by reason of his singularitie, and too great indifferancie for any conditions, and for (to speak truly) that[Q] we have had nothing from him but termes & presumptions. The other, y^t we have so much relyed, by implicite faith as it were, upon generalities, without seeing ye perticuler course & means for so waghtie an affaire set down unto us. For shiping, M^r. Weston, it should seeme, is set upon hireing, which yet I wish he may presently effecte; but I see litle hope of help from hence if so it be. Of M^r. Brewer you know what to expecte. I doe not thinke M^r. Pickering will ingage, excepte in ye course of buying, in former letters specified. Aboute ye conditions, you have our reasons for our judgments of what is agreed. And let this spetially be borne in minde, y^t the greatest parte of ye Collonie is like to be imployed constantly, not upon dressing ther perticuler land & building houses, but upon fishing, trading, &c. So as ye land & house will be but a trifell for advantage to ye adventurers, and yet the devission of it a great discouragmente to ye planters, who would with singuler care make it comfortable with borowed houres from their sleep. The same consideration of comone imploymente constantly by the most is a good reason not to have yᵉ 2. daies in a weeke denyed yᵉ few planters for private use, which yet is subordinate to comone good. Consider also how much unfite that you & your liks must serve a new prentishipe of 7. years, and not a daies freedome from taske. Send me word what persons are to goe, who of usefull faculties, & how many, & perticulerly of every thing. I know you wante not a minde. I am sorie you have not been at London all this while, but yᵉ provissions could not wante you. Time will suffer me to write no more; fare you & yours well allways in yᵉ Lord, in whom I rest.

Yours to use,

JOHN ROBINSON.

An other letter from sundrie of them at yᵉ same time.

[31] To their loving freinds John Carver and Robart Cushman, these, &c.

Good bretheren, after salutations, &c. We received diverse letters at yᵉ coming of Mʳ. Nash & our pilott, which is a great incouragmente unto us, and for whom we hop after times will minister occasion of praising God; and indeed had you not sente him, many would have been ready to fainte and goe backe. Partly in respecte of yᵉ new conditions which have bene taken up by you, which all men are against, and partly in regard of our owne inabillitie to doe any one of those many waightie bussineses you referr to us here. For yᵉ former wherof, wheras Robart Cushman desirs reasons for our dislike, promising therupon to alter yᵉ same, or els saing we should thinke he hath no brains, we desire him to exercise them therin, refering him to our pastors former reasons, and them to yᵉ censure of yᵉ godly wise. But our desires are that you will not entangle your selvs and us in any such unreasonable courses as those are, viz. yᵗ the marchants should have yᵉ halfe of mens houses and lands at yᵉ dividente; and that persons should be deprived of yᵉ 2. days in a weeke agreed upon, yea every momente of time for their owne perticuler; by reason wherof we cannot conceive why any should carie servants for their own help and comfort; for that we can require no more of them then all men one of another. This we have only by relation from Mr. Nash, & not from any writing of your owne, & therfore hope you have not proceeded farr in so great a thing without us. But requiring you not to exseed the bounds of your comission, which was to proceed upon yᵉ things or conditions agred upon and expressed in writing (at your going over about it), we leave it, not without marveling, that your selfe, as you write, knowing how smale a thing troubleth our consultations, and how few, as you fear, understands the busnes aright, should trouble us with such matters as these are, &c.

Salute Mr. Weston from us, in whom we hope we are not deceived; we pray you make known our estate unto him, and if you thinke good shew him our letters, at least tell him (yᵗ under God) we much relie upon him & put our confidence in him; and, as your selves well know, that if he had not been an adventurer with us, we had not taken it in hand; presuming that if he had not seene means to accomplish it, he would not have begune it; so we hope in our extremitie he will so farr help us as our expectation be no way made frustrate concerning him. Since therfore, good brethren, we have plainly opened yᵉ state of things with us in this matter, you will, &c. Thus beseeching yᵉ Allmightie, who is allsufficiente to raise us out of this depth of dificulties, to assiste us herein; raising such means by his providence and fatherly care for us, his pore children & servants, as we may with comforte behould yᵉ hand of our God for good towards us in this our bussines, which we undertake in his name & fear, we take leave & remaine

> Your perplexed, yet hopfull
>
> June 10. New Stille, bretheren,
>
> Anᵒ: 1620. S. F. E. W. W. B. J. A.[R]

A letter of Robart Cushmans to them.

Brethern, I understand by letters & passagess y^t have come to me, that ther are great discontents, & dislike of my proceedings amongst you. Sorie I am to hear it, yet contente to beare it, as not doubting but y^t partly by writing, and more principally by word when we shall come togeather, I shall satisfie any reasonable man. I have been perswaded [32] by some, espetialy this bearer, to come and clear things unto you; but as things now stand I canot be absente one day, excepte I should hazard all ye viage. Neither conceive I any great good would come of it. Take then, brethern, this as a step to give you contente. First, for your dislike of ye alteration of one clause in ye conditions, if you conceive it right, ther can be no blame lye on me at all. For ye articles first brought over by John Carver were never seene of any of ye adventurers hear, excepte M^r. Weston, neither did any of them like them because of that clause; nor M^r. Weston him selfe, after he had well considered it. But as at ye first ther was 500^{li}. withdrawne by S^r. Georg Farrer and his brother upon that dislike, so all ye rest would have withdrawne (M^r. Weston excepted) if we had not altered y^t clause. Now whilst we at Leyden conclude upon points, as we did, we reckoned without our host, which was not my falte. Besids, I shewed you by a letter ye equitie of y^t condition, & our inconveniences, which might be sett against all M^r. Rob: inconveniences, that without ye alteration of y^t clause, we could neither have means to gett thither, nor supplie wherby to subsiste when we were ther. Yet notwithstanding all those reasons, which were not mine, but other mens wiser then my selfe, without answer to any one of them, here cometh over many quirimonies, and complaints against me, of lording it over my brethern, and making conditions fitter for theeves & bondslaves then honest men, and that of my owne head I did what I list. And at last a paper of reasons, framed against y^t clause in ye conditions, which as y^{ey} were delivered me open, so my answer is open to you all. And first, as they are no other but inconveniences, such as a man might frame 20. as great on ye other side, and yet prove nor disprove nothing by them, so they misse & mistake both ye very ground of ye article and nature of ye project. For, first, it is said, that if ther had been no divission of houses & lands, it had been better for yᵉ poore. True, and yᵗ showeth yᵉ inequalitie of yᵉ condition; we should more respecte him yᵗ ventureth both his money and his person, then him yᵗ ventureth but his person only.

2. Consider wheraboute we are, not giveing almes, but furnishing a store house; no one shall be porer then another for 7. years, and if any be rich, none can be pore. At yᵉ least, we must not in such bussines crie, Pore, pore, mercie, mercie. Charitie hath it life in wraks, not in venturs; you are by this most in a hopefull pitie of makeing, therfore complaine not before you have need.

3. This will hinder yᵉ building of good and faire houses, contrarie to yᵉ advise of pollitiks. A. So we would have it; our purpose is to build for yᵉ presente such houses as, if need be, we may with litle greefe set a fire, and rune away by the lighte; our riches shall not be in pompe, but in strenght; if God send us riches, we will imploye them to provid more men, ships, munition, &c. You may see it amongst the best pollitiks, that a comonwele is readier to ebe then to flow, when once fine houses and gay cloaths come up.

4. The Goveᵗ may prevente excess in building. A. But if it be on all men beforehand resolved on, to build mean houses, yᵉ Goveʳ laboure is spared.

5. All men are not of one condition. A. If by condition you mean wealth, you are mistaken; if you mean by condition, qualities, then I say he that is not contente his neighbour shall have as good a house, fare, means, &c. as him selfe, is not of a good qualitie. 2ˡʸ. Such retired persons, as have aneie only to them selves, are fitter to come wher catching is, then closing; and are fitter to live alone, then in any societie, either civill or religious.

6. It will be of litle value, scarce worth 5ˡⁱ. A. True, it may be not worth halfe 5ˡⁱ. [33] If then so smale a thing will content them, why strive we thus aboute it, and give them occasion to suspecte us to be worldly & covetous? I will not say what I have heard since these complaints came first over.

7. Our freinds with us yᵗ adventure mind not their owne profite, as did yᵉ old adventurers. A. Then they are better then we, who for a litle matter of profite are readie to draw back, and it is more apparente brethern looke too it, that make profite your maine end; repente of this, els goe not least you be like Jonas to Tarshis. 2ˡʸ. Though some of them mind not their profite, yet others doe mind it; and why not as well as we? venturs are made by all sorts of men, and we must labour to give them all contente, if we can.

8. It will break yᵉ course of comunitie, as may be showed by many reasons. A. That is but said, and I say againe, it will best foster comunion, as may be showed by many reasons.

9. Great profite is like to be made by trucking, fishing, &c. A. As it is better for them, so for us; for halfe is ours, besids our living still upon it, and if such profite in yᵗ way come, our labour shall be yᵉ less on yᵉ land, and our houses and lands must & will be of less value.

10. Our hazard is greater then theirs. A. True, but doe they put us upon it? doe they urge or egg us? hath not yᵉ motion & resolution been always in our selves? doe they any more then in seeing us resolute if we had means, help us to means upon equall termes & conditions? If we will not goe, they are content to keep their moneys. Thus I have pointed at a way to loose those knots, which I hope you will consider seriously, and let me have no more stirre about them.

Now furder, I hear a noise of slavish conditions by me made; but surly this is all that I have altered, and reasons I have sent you. If you mean it of yᵉ 2. days in a week for perticuler, as some insinuate, you are deceived; you may have 3. days in a week for me if you will. And when I have spoken to yᵉ adventurers of times of working, they have said they hope we are men of discretion & conscience, and so fitte to be trusted our selves with that. But indeed yᵉ ground of our proceedings at Leyden was mistaken, and so here is nothing but tottering every day, &c.

As for them of Amsterdam I had thought they would as soone have gone to Rome as with us; for our libertie is to them as ratts bane, and their riggour as bad to us as yᵉ Spanish Inquision. If any practise of mine discourage them, let them yet draw back; I will undertake they shall have their money againe presently paid hear. Or if the company thinke me to be yᵉ Jonas, let them cast me of before we goe; I shall be content to stay with good will, having but the cloaths on my back; only let us have quietnes, and no more of these clamors; full litle did I expecte these things which are now come to pass, &c.

Yours, R. CUSHMAN.

But whether this letter of his ever came to their hands at Leyden I well know not; I rather thinke it was staied by Mʳ. Carver & kept by him, forgiving offence. But this which follows was ther received; both which I thought pertenent to recite.

Another of his to yᵉ aforesaid, June 11. 1620.[S]

Salutations, &c. I received your lẽr. yesterday, by John Turner, with another yᵉ same day from Amsterdam by Mʳ. W. savouring of yᵉ place whenc it came. And indeed the many discouragements I find her, togeather with yᵉ demurrs and retirings ther, had made me to say, I would give up my accounts to John Carver, & at his comeing aquainte him fully with all courses, and so leave it quite, with only yᵉ pore cloaths on my back. But gathering up my selfe by further consideration, [34] I resolved yet to make one triall more, and to aquainte Mʳ. Weston with yᵉ fainted state of our bussines; and though he hath been much discontented at some thing amongst us of late, which hath made him often say, that save for his promise, he would not meadle at all with yᵉ bussines any more, yet considering how farr we were plunged into maters, & how it stood both on our credits & undoing, at yᵉ last he gathered up him selfe a litle more, & coming to me 2. hours after, he tould me he would not yet leave it. And so advising togeather we resolved to hire a ship, and have tooke liking of one till Monday, about 60. laste, for a greater we cannot gett, excepte it be tow great; but a fine ship it is. And seeing our neer freinds ther are so streite lased, we hope to assure her without troubling them any further; and if ye ship fale too small, it fitteth well y^t such as stumble at strawes allready, may rest them ther a while, least worse blocks come in ye way ere 7. years be ended. If you had beaten this bussines so throuly a month agoe, and write to us as now you doe, we could thus have done much more conveniently. But it is as it is; I hope our freinds ther, if they be quitted of the ship hire, will be indusced to venture ye more. All y^t I now require is y^t salt and netts may ther be boughte, and for all ye rest we will here provid it; yet if that will not be, let them but stand for it a month or tow, and we will take order to pay it all. Let M^r. *Reinholds* tarie ther, and bring ye ship to Southampton. We have hired another pilote here, one M^r. *Clarke*, who went last year to Virginia with a ship of kine.

You shall here distinctly by John Turner, who I thinke shall come hence on Tewsday night. I had thought to have come with him, to have answerd to my complaints; but I shal lerne to pass litle for their censurs; and if I had more minde to goe & dispute & expostulate with them, then I have care of this waightie bussines, I were like them who live by clamours & jangling. But neither my mind nor my body is at libertie to doe much, for I am fettered with bussines, and had rather study to be quiet, then to make answer to their exceptions. If men be set on it, let them beat ye eair; I hope such as are my sinceire freinds will not thinke but I can give some reason of my actions. But of your mistaking aboute ye mater, & other things tending to this bussines, I shall nexte informe you more distinctly. Mean space entreate our freinds not to be too bussie in answering matters, before they know them. If I doe such things as I canot give reasons for, it is like you have sett a foole aboute your bussines, and so turne ye reproofe to your selves, & send an other, and let me come againe to my Combes. But setting a side my naturall infirmities, I refuse not to have my cause judged, both of God, & all indifferent men; and when we come togeather I shall give accounte of my actions hear. The Lord, who judgeth justly without respect of persons, see into ye equitie of my cause, and give us quiet, peacable, and patient minds, in all these turmoiles, and sanctifie unto us all crosses whatsoever. And so I take my leave of you all, in all love & affection.

I hope we shall gett all hear ready in 14. days.

Your pore brother,

ROBART CUSHMAN.

June 11. 1620.

Besids these things, ther fell out a differance amongs those 3. that received [35] the moneys & made ye provissions in England; for besids these tow formerly mentioned sent from Leyden for this end, viz. M^r. Carver & Robart Cushman, ther was one chosen in England to be joyned with them, to make ye provisions for ye vioage; his name was M^r. Martin, he came from Billirike in Essexe, from which parts came sundrie others to goe with them, as also from London & other places; and therfore it was thought meete & conveniente by them in Holand that these strangers that were to goe with them, should apointe one thus to be joyned with them, not so much for any great need of their help, as to avoyd all susspition, or jelosie of any partiallitie. And indeed their care for giving offence, both in this & other things afterward, turned to great inconvenience unto them, as in ye sequell will apeare; but however it shewed their equall & honest minds. The provissions were for ye most parte made at Southhamton, contrarie to M^r. Westons & Robert Cushmās mind (whose counsells did most concure in all things). A touch of which things I shall give in a letter of his to M^r. Carver, and more will appear afterward.

To his loving freind M^r. John Carver, these, &c.

Loving freind, I have received from you some letters, full of affection & complaints, and what it is you would have of me I know not; for your crieing out, Negligence, negligence, negligence, I marvell why so negligente a man was used in ye bussines. Yet know you y^t all that I have power to doe hear, shall not be one hower behind, I warent you. You have reference to M^r. Weston to help us with money, more then his adventure; wher he protesteth but for his promise, he would not have done any thing. He saith we take a heady course, and is offended y' our provissions are made so farr of; as also that he was not made aquainted with our quantitie of things; and saith y' in now being in 3. places, so farr remote, we will, with going up & downe, and wrangling & expostulating, pass over y' somer before we will goe. And to speake y' trueth, ther is fallen already amongst us a flatt schisme; and we are redier to goe to dispute, then to sett forwarde a voiage. I have received from Leyden since you wente 3. or 4. letters directed to you, though they only conscerne me. I will not trouble you with them. I always feared y' event of y' Amsterdamers striking in with us. I trow you must excomunicate me, or els you must goe without their companie, or we shall wante no quareling; but let them pass. We have reckoned, it should seeme, without our host; and, counting upon a 150. persons, ther cannot be founde above 1200ʰ. & odd moneys of all y' venturs you can reckone, besids some cloath, stockings, & shoes, which are not counted; so we shall come shorte at least 3. or 400ʰ. I would have had some thing shortened at first of beare & other provissions in hope of other adventurs, & now we could have, both in Amsterd: & Kente, beere inough to serve our turne, but now we cannot accept it without prejudice. You fear we have begune to build & shall not be able to make an end; indeed, our courses were never established by counsell, we may therfore justly fear their standing. Yea, ther was a [36] schisme amongst us 3. at y' first. You wrote to Mr. Martin, to prevente y' making of y' provissions in Kente, which he did, and sett downe his resolution how much he would have of every thing, without respecte to any counsell or exception. Surely he y' is in a societie & yet regards not counsell, may better be a king then a consorte. To be short, if ther be not some other dispossition setled unto then yet is, we y' should be partners of humilitie and peace, shall be examples of jangling & insulting. Yet your money which you ther must have, we will get provided for you instantly. 500ʰ. you say will serve; for y' rest which hear & in Holand is to be used, we may goe scratch for it. For Mr.⁽ᵐ⁾ Crabe, of whom you write, he hath promised to goe with us, yet I tell you I shall not be without feare till I see him shipped, for he is much opposed, yet I hope he will not faile. Thinke ye best of all, and bear with patience what is wanting, and ye Lord guid us all.

Your loving freind,

ROBART CUSHMAN.

London, June 10.

An^o: 1620.

I have bene ye larger in these things, and so shall crave leave in some like passages following, (thoug in other things I shal labour to be more contracte,) that their children may see with what difficulties their fathers wrastled in going throug these things in their first beginings, and how God brought them along notwithstanding all their weaknesses & infirmities. As allso that some use may be made hereof in after times by others in such like waightie imployments; and herewith I will end this chapter.

The 7. Chap.

Of their departure from Leyden, and other things ther aboute, with their arivall at South hamton, were they all mete togeather, and tooke in ther provissions.

At length, after much travell and these debats, all things were got ready and provided. A smale ship[U] was bought, & fitted in Holand, which was intended as to serve to help to transport them, so to stay in ye cuntrie and atend upon fishing and shuch other affairs as might be for ye good & benefite of ye colonie when they came ther. Another was hired at London, of burden about 9. score; and all other things gott in readines. So being ready to departe, they had a day of solleme humiliation, their pastor taking his texte from Ezra

8. 21. *And ther at yᵉ river, by Ahava, I proclaimed a fast, that we might humble ourselves before our God, and seeke of him a right way for us, and for our children, and for all our substance.* Upon which he spente a good parte of yᵉ day very profitably, and suitable to their presente occasion. The rest of the time was spente in powering out prairs to yᵉ Lord with great fervencie, mixed with abundance of tears. And yᵉ time being come that they must departe, they were accompanied with most of their brethren out of yᵉ citie, unto a towne sundrie miles of called Delfes-Haven, wher the ship lay ready to receive them. So they lefte yⁱ goodly & pleasante citie, which had been ther resting place near 12. years; but they knew they were pilgrimes,[V] & looked not much on those things, but lift up their eyes to yᵉ heavens, their dearest cuntrie, and quieted their spirits. When they [37] came to yᵉ place they found yᵉ ship and all things ready; and shuch of their freinds as could not come with them followed after them, and sundrie also came from Amsterdame to see them shipte and to take their leave of them. That night was spent with litle sleepe by yᵉ most, but with freindly entertainmente & christian discourse and other reall expressions of true christian love. The next day, the wind being faire, they wente aborde, and their freinds with them, where truly dolfull was yᵉ sight of that sade and mournfull parting; to see what sighs and sobbs and praires did sound amongst them, what tears did gush from every eye, & pithy speeches peirst each harte; that sundry of yᵉ Dutch strangers yⁱ stood on yᵉ key as spectators, could not refraine from tears. Yet comfortable & sweete it was to see shuch lively and true expressions of clear & unfained love. But the tide (which stays for no man) caling them away yⁱ were thus loath to departe, their Reṽeᵈ: pastor falling downe on his knees, (and they all with him,) with watrie cheeks comended them with most fervente praiers to the Lord and his blessing. And then with mutuall imbrases and many tears, they tooke their leaves one of an other; which proved to be yᵉ last leave to many of them.

Thus hoysing saile,[W] with a prosperus winde they came in short time to Southhamton, wher they found the bigger ship come from London, lying ready, wᵗʰ all the rest of their company. After a joyfull wellcome, and mutuall congratulations, with other frendly entertainements, they fell to parley aboute their bussines, how to dispatch with yᵉ best expedition; as allso with their agents, aboute yᵉ alteration of yᵉ conditions. Mʳ. Carver pleaded he was imployed hear at Hamton, and knew not well what yᵉ other had don at London. Mʳ. Cushman answered, he had done nothing but what he was urged too, partly by yᵉ grounds of equity, and more espetialy by necessitie, other wise all had bene dasht and many undon. And in yᵉ begining he aquainted his felow agents here with, who consented unto him, and left it to him to execute, and to receive yᵉ money at London and send it downe to them at Hamton, wher they made yᵉ provissions; the which he accordingly did, though it was against his minde, & some of yᵉ marchants, yᵗ they were their made. And for giveing them notise at Leyden of this change, he could not well in regarde of yᵉ shortnes of yᵉ time; againe, he knew it would trouble them and hinder yᵉ bussines, which was already delayed overlong in regard of yᵉ season of yᵉ year, which he feared they would find to their cost. But these things gave not contente at presente. Mr. Weston, likwise, came up from London to see them dispatcht and to have yᵉ conditions confirmed; but they refused, and answered him, that he knew right well that these were not according to yᵉ first agreemente, neither could they yeeld to them without yᵉ consente of the rest that were behind. And indeed they had spetiall charge when they came away, from the cheefe of those that were behind, not to doe it. At which he was much offended, and tould them, they must then looke to stand on their owne leggs. So he returned in displeasure, and this was yᵉ first ground of discontent betweene them. And wheras ther wanted well near 100ˡⁱ. to clear things at their going away, he would not take order to disburse a penie, but let them shift as they could. [38] So they were forst to selle of some of their provissions to stop this gape, which was some 3. or 4. score firkins of butter, which comoditie they might best spare, haveing provided too large a quantitie of yᵗ kind. Then they write a leter to yᵉ marchants & adventures aboute yᵉ diferances concerning yᵉ conditions, as foloweth.

Aug. 3. Anᵒ: 1620.

Beloved freinds, sory we are that ther should be occasion of writing at all unto you, partly because we ever expected to see y most of you hear, but espetially because ther should any differance at all be conceived betweene us. But seing it faleth out that we cannot conferr togeather, we thinke it meete (though brefly) to show you y just cause & reason of our differing from those articles last made by Robart Cushman, without our comission or knowledg. And though he might propound good ends to himselfe, yet it no way justifies his doing it. Our maine diference is in y 5. & 9. article, concerning y deviding or holding of house and lands; the injoying wherof some of your selves well know, was one spetiall motive, amongst many other, to provoke us to goe. This was thought so reasonable, y when y greatest of you in adventure (whom we have much cause to respecte), when he propounded conditions to us freely of his owne accorde, he set this downe for one; a coppy wherof we have sent unto you, with some additions then added by us; which being liked on both sids, and a day set for y paimente of moneys, those of Holland paid in theirs. After y, Robart Cushman, M. Peirce, & M. Martine, brought them into a better forme, & write them in a booke now extante; and upon Robarts shewing them and delivering M. Mullins a coppy therof under his hand (which we have), he payd in his money. And we of Holland had never seen other before our coming to Hamton, but only as one got for him selfe a private coppy of them; upon sight wherof we manyfested uter dislike, but had put of our estats & were ready to come, and therfore was too late to rejecte y vioage. Judge therfore we beseech you indiferently of things, and if a faulte have bene comited, lay it wher it is, & not upon us, who have more cause to stand for y one, then you have for y other. We never gave Robart Cushman comission to make any one article for us, but only sent him to receive moneys upon articles before agreed on, and to further y provissions till John Carver came, and to assiste him in it. Yet since you conceive your selves wronged as well as we, we thought meete to add a branch to y end of our 9. article, as will allmost heale that wound of it selfe, which you conceive to be in it. But that it may appeare to all men y we are not lovers of our selves only, but desire also ye good & inriching of our freinds who have adventured your moneys with our persons, we have added our last article to ye rest, promising you againe by leters in ye behalfe of the whole company, that if large profits should not arise within ye 7. years, y^t we will continue togeather longer with you, if ye Lord give a blessing.[X] This we hope is sufficente to satisfie any in this case, espetialy freinds, since we are asured y^t if the whole charge was devided into 4. parts, 3. of them will not stand upon it, nether doe regarde it, &c. We are in shuch a streate at presente, as we are forced to sell away 60^{li}. worth of our provissions to cleare ye Haven, & withall put our selves upon great extremities, scarce haveing any butter, no oyle, not a sole to mend a shoe, [39] nor every man a sword to his side, wanting many muskets, much armoure, &c. And yet we are willing to expose our selves to shuch eminente dangers as are like to insue, & trust to ye good providence of God, rather then his name & truth should be evill spoken of for us. Thus saluting all of you in love, and beseeching the Lord to give a blesing to our endeavore, and keepe all our harts in ye bonds of peace & love, we take leave & rest,

Yours, &c.

Aug. 3. 1620.

It was subscribed with many names of ye cheefest of ye company.

At their parting M^r. Robinson write a leter to ye whole company, which though it hath already bene printed, yet I thought good here likwise to inserte it; as also a breefe leter writ at ye same time to M^r. Carver, in which ye tender love & godly care of a true pastor appears.

My dear Brother,—I received inclosed in your last leter ye note of information, wch I shall carefuly keepe & make use of as ther shall be occasion. I have a true feeling of your perplexitie of mind & toyle of body, but I hope that you who have allways been able so plentifully to administer comforte unto others in their trials, are so well furnished for your selfe as that farr greater difficulties then you have yet undergone (though I conceive them to have been great enough) cannot oppresse you, though they press you, as yᵉ Aspostle speaks. The spirite of a man (sustained by yᵉ spirite of God) will sustaine his infirmitie, I dout not so will yours. And yᵉ beter much when you shall injoye yᵉ presence & help of so many godly & wise bretheren, for yᵉ bearing of part of your burthen, who also will not admitte into their harts yᵉ least thought of suspition of any yᵉ least negligence, at least presumption, to have been in you, what so ever they thinke in others. Now what shall I say or write unto you & your goodwife my loving sister? even only this, I desire (& allways shall) unto you from yᵉ Lord, as unto my owne soule; and assure your selfe yᵗ my harte is with you, and that I will not forslowe my bodily coming at yᵉ first oppertunitie. I have writen a large leter to yᵉ whole, and am sorie I shall not rather speak then write to them; & the more, considering yᵉ wante of a preacher, which I shall also make sume spurr to my hastening after you. I doe ever comend my best affection unto you, which if I thought you made any doubte of, I would express in more, & yᵉ same more ample & full words. And yᵉ Lord in whom you trust & whom you serve ever in this bussines & journey, guid you with his hand, protecte you with his winge, and shew you & us his salvation in yᵉ end, & bring us in yᵉ mean while togeather in yᵉ place desired, if shuch be his good will, for his Christs sake.

Amen.

Yours, &c.

Jo: R.

July 27. 1620.

This was yᵉ last letter yᵗ Mʳ. Carver lived to see from him. The other follows.

[Y]Lovinge Christian friends, I doe hartily & in yᵉ Lord salute you all, as being they with whom I am presente in my best affection, and most ernest longings after you, though I be constrained for a while to be bodily absente from you. I say constrained, God knowing how willingly, & much rather then otherwise, I would

have borne my part with you in this first brunt, were I not by strong
necessitie held back for yᵉ present. Make accounte of me in yᵉ mean
while, as of a man devided in my selfe with great paine, and as
(naturall bonds set a side) having my beter parte with [40] you.
And though I doubt not but in your godly wisdoms, you both
foresee & resolve upon yᵗ which concerneth your presente state &
condition, both severally & joyntly, yet have I thought it but my
duty to add some furder spurr of provocation unto them, who rune
allready, if not because you need it, yet because I owe it in love &
dutie. And first, as we are daly to renew our repentance with our
God, espetially for our sines known, and generally for our
unknowne trespasses, so doth yᵉ Lord call us in a singuler maner
upon occasions of shuch difficultie & danger as lieth upon you, to a
both more narrow search & carefull reformation of your ways in
his sight; least he, calling to remembrance our sines forgotten by us
or unrepented of, take advantage against us, & in judgmente leave
us for yᵉ same to be swalowed up in one danger or other; wheras,
on the contrary, sine being taken away by ernest repentance & yᵉ
pardon therof from yᵉ Lord sealed up unto a mans conscience by
his spirite, great shall be his securitie and peace in all dangers,
sweete his comforts in all distresses, with hapie deliverance from
all evill, whether in life or in death.

Now next after this heavenly peace with God & our owne
consciences, we are carefully to provide for peace with all men
what in us lieth, espetially with our associats, & for yᵉ watchfullnes
must be had, that we neither at all in our selves doe give, no nor
easily take offence being given by others. Woe be unto yᵉ world for
offences, for though it be necessarie (considering yᵉ malice of Satan
& mans corruption) that offences come, yet woe unto yᵉ man or
woman either by whom yᵉ offence cometh, saith Christ, Mat. 18. 7.
And if offences in yᵉ unseasonable use of things in them selves
indifferent, be more to be feared then death itselfe, as yᵉ Apostle
teacheth, 1. Cor. 9. 15. how much more in things simply evill, in
which neither honour of God nor love of man is thought worthy to
be regarded. Neither yet is it sufficiente yᵗ we keepe our selves by
yᵉ grace of God from giveing offence, exepte withall we be armed

against yᵉ taking of them when they be given by others. For how imperfect & lame is yᵉ work of grace in yᵗ person, who wants charritie to cover a multitude of offences, as yᵉ scriptures speake. Neither are you to be exhorted to this grace only upon yᵉ comone grounds of Christianitie, which are, that persons ready to take offence, either wante charitie, to cover offences, of wisdome duly to waigh humane frailtie; or lastly, are grosse, though close hipocrites, as Christ our Lord teacheth, Mat. 7. 1, 2, 3, as indeed in my owne experience, few or none have bene found which sooner give offence, then shuch as easily take it; neither have they ever proved sound & profitable members in societies, which have nurished this touchey humor. But besids these, ther are diverse motives provoking you above others to great care & conscience this way: As first, you are many of you strangers, as to yᵉ persons, so to yᵉ infirmities one of another, & so stand in neede of more watchfullnes this way, least when shuch things fall out in men & women as you suspected not, you be inordinatly affected with them; which doth require at your hands much wisdome & charitie for yᵉ covering & preventing of incident offences that way. And lastly, your intended course of civill comunitie will minister continuall occasion of offence, & will be as fuell for that fire, excepte you dilligently quench it with brotherly forbearance. And if taking of offence causlesly or easilie at mens doings be so carefuly to be avoyded, how much more heed is to be taken yᵗ we take not offence at God him selfe, which yet we certainly doe so oftē as we doe murmure at his providence in our crosses, or beare impatiently shuch afflictions as wherwith he pleaseth to visite us. Store up therfore patience against yᵉ evill day, without which we take offence at yᵉ Lord him selfe in his holy & just works.

A 4. thing ther is carfully to be provided for, to witte, that with your comone imployments you joyne comone affections truly bente upon yᵉ generall good, avoyding as a deadly [41] plague of your both comone & spetiall comfort all retirednes of minde for proper advantage, and all singularly affected any maner of way; let every man represe in him selfe & yᵉ whol body in each person, as so many rebels against yᵉ commone good, all private respects of mens selves, not sorting with yᵉ generall conveniencie. And as men are carfull not to have a new house shaken with any violence before it be well setled & yᵉ parts firmly knite, so be you, I beseech you, brethren, much more carfull, yᵗ the house of God which you are, and are to be, be not shaken with unnecessarie novelties or other oppositions at yᵉ first setling therof.

Lastly, wheras you are become a body politik, using amongst your selves civill govermente, and are not furnished with any persons of spetiall eminencie above yᵉ rest, to be chosen by you into office of goverment, let your wisdome & godlines appeare, not only in chusing shuch persons as doe entirely love and will promote yᵉ comone good, but also in yeelding unto them all due honour & obedience in their lawfull administrations; not behoulding in them yᵉ ordinarinesse of their persons, but Gods ordinance for your good, not being like yᵉ foolish multitud who more honour yᵉ gay coate, then either yᵉ vertuous minde of yᵉ man, or glorious ordinance of yᵉ Lord. But you know better things, & that yᵉ image of yᵉ Lords power & authoritie which yᵉ magistrate beareth, is honourable, in how meane persons soever. And this dutie you both may yᵉ more willingly and ought yᵉ more conscionably to performe, because you are at least for yᵉ present to have only them for your ordinarie governours, which your selves shall make choyse of for that worke.

Sundrie other things of importance I could put you in minde of, and of those before mentioned, in more words, but I will not so farr wrong your godly minds as to thinke you heedless of these things, ther being also diverce among you so well able to admonish both them selves & others of what concerneth them. These few things therfore, & yᵉ same in few words, I doe ernestly comend unto your care & conscience, joyning therwith my daily incessante prayers unto yᵉ Lord, yᵗ he who hath made yᵉ heavens & yᵉ earth, yᵉ sea and all rivers of waters, and whose providence is over all his workes, espetially over all his dear children for good, would so guide & gard you in your wayes, as inwardly by his Spirite, so outwardly by yᵉ hand of his power, as yᵗ both you & we also, for & with you, may have after matter of praising his name all yᵉ days of your and our lives. Fare you well in him in whom you trust, and in whom I rest.

An unfained wellwiller of your hapie
success in this hopefull voyage,

JOHN ROBINSON.

This letter, though large, yet being so frutfull in it selfe, and suitable to their occation, I thought meete to inserte in this place.

All things being now ready, & every bussines dispatched, the company was caled togeather, and this letter read amongst them, which had good acceptation with all, and after fruit with many. Then they ordered & distributed their company for either shipe, as they conceived for y⁰ best. And chose a Governor & 2. or 3. assistants for each shipe, to order y⁰ people by y⁰ way, and see to y⁰ dispossing of there provissions, and shuch like affairs. All which was not only with y⁰ liking of y⁰ maisters of y⁰ ships, but according to their desires. Which being done, they sett sayle from thence aboute y⁰ 5. of August; but what befell them further upon y⁰ coast of England will appeare in y⁰ nexte chapter.

The 8. Chap.

Off the troubls that befell them on the coaste, and at sea being forced, after much trouble, to leave one of ther ships & some of their companie behind them.

[42] Being thus put to sea they had not gone farr, but Mᵣ. Reinolds y⁰ master of y⁰ leser ship complained that he found his ship so leak as he durst not put further to sea till she was mended. So y⁰ mᵣ. of y⁰ biger ship (caled Mᵣ. Jonas) being consulted with, they both resolved to put into Dartmouth & have her ther searched & mended, which accordingly was done, to their great charg &

losse of time and a faire winde. She was hear thorowly searcht from steme to sterne, some leaks were found & mended, and now it was conceived by the workmen & all, that she was sufficiente, & they might proceede without either fear or danger. So with good hopes from hence, they put to sea againe, conceiving they should goe comfortably on, not looking for any more lets of this kind; but it fell out otherwise, for after they were gone to sea againe above 100. leagues without the Lands End, houlding company togeather all this while, the m^r. of ye small ship complained his ship was so leake as he must beare up or sinke at sea, for they could scarce free her with much pumping. So they came to consultation againe, and resolved both ships to bear up backe againe & put into Plimoth, which accordingly was done. But no spetiall leake could be founde, but it was judged to be ye generall weaknes of ye shipe, and that shee would not prove sufficiente for the voiage. Upon which it was resolved to dismise her & parte of ye companie, and proceede with ye other shipe. The which (though it was greevous, & caused great discouragmente) was put in execution. So after they had tooke out such provission as ye other ship could well stow, and concluded both what number and what persons to send bak, they made another sad parting, ye one ship going backe for London, and ye other was to proceede on her viage. Those that went bak were for the most parte such as were willing so to doe, either out of some discontente, or feare they conceived of ye ill success of ye vioage, seeing so many croses befale, & the year time so farr spente; but others, in regarde of their owne weaknes, and charge of many yonge children, were thought least usefull, and most unfite to bear ye brunte of this hard adventure; unto which worke of God, and judgmente of their brethern, they were contented to submite. And thus, like Gedions armie, this small number was devided, as if ye Lord by this worke of his providence thought these few to many for ye great worke he had to doe. But here by the way let me show, how afterward it was found y^t the leaknes of this ship was partly by being over masted, and too much pressed with sayles; for after she was sould & put into her old trime, she made many viages & performed her service very sufficiently, to ye great profite of her owners. But more espetially, by the cuning & deceite of ye m^r. & his company, who were hired to stay a whole year in ye cuntrie, and now fancying dislike & fearing wante of victeles, they ploted this strategem to free them selves; as afterwards was knowne, & by some of them confessed. For they apprehended y^t the greater ship, being of force, & in whom most of ye provissions were stowed, she would retayne enough for her selfe, what soever became of them or ye passengers; & indeed shuch speeches had bene cast out by some of them; and yet, besids other incouragments, ye cheefe of them that came from Leyden wente in this shipe to give ye m^r. contente. But so strong was self love & his fears, as he forgott all duty and [43] former kindnesses, & delt thus falsly with them, though he pretended otherwise. Amongest those that returned was M^r. Cushman & his familie, whose hart & courage was gone from them before, as it seems, though his body was with them till now he departed; as may appear by a passionate letter he write to a freind in London from Dartmouth, whilst ye ship lay ther a mending; the which, besids ye expressions of his owne fears, it shows much of ye providence of God working for their good beyonde man's expectation, & other things concerning their condition in these streats. I will hear relate it. And though it discover some infirmities in him (as who under temtation is free), yet after this he continued to be a spetiall instrumente for their good, and to doe ye offices of a loving freind & faithfull brother unto them, and pertaker of much comforte with them.

The letter is as followth.

To his loving friend Ed: S.[Z] at Henige House in ye Duks Place, these, &c.

Dartmouth, Aug. 17.

Loving friend, my most kind remembrance to you & your wife, with loving E. M. &c. whom in this world I never looke to see againe. For besids ye eminente dangers of this viage, which are no less then deadly, an infirmitie of body hath ceased me, which will not in all lie^clyhoode leave me till death. What to call it I know not, but it is a bundle of lead, as it were, crushing my harte more & more these 14. days, as that allthough I doe ye acctions of a liveing man, yet I am but as dead; but ye will of God be done. Our pinass will not cease leaking, els I thinke we had been halfe way at Virginia, our viage hither hath been as full of crosses, as our selves have been of crokednes. We put in hear to trime her, & I thinke, as others also, if we had stayed at sea but 3. or 4. howers more, shee would have sunke right downe. And though she was twise trimed at Hamton, yet now shee is open and leakie as a seive; and ther was a borde, a man might have puld of with his fingers, 2 foote longe, wher ye water came in as at a mole hole. We lay at Hamton 7. days, in fair weather, waiting for her, and now we lye hear waiting for her in as faire a wind as can blowe, and so have done these 4. days, and are like to lye 4. more, and by y^t time ye wind will happily turne as it did at Hampton. Our victualls will be halfe eaten up, I thinke, before we goe from the coaste of England, and if our viage last longe, we shall not have a months victialls when we come in ye countrie. Neare 700^{li}. hath bene bestowed at Hampton, upon what I know not. Mr. Martin saith he neither can nor will give any accounte of it, and if he be called upon for accounts he crieth out of unthankfullnes for his paines & care, that we are susspitious of him, and flings away, & will end nothing. Also he so insultēh over our poore people, with shuch scorne & contempte, as if they were not good enough to wipe his shoes. It would break your hart to see his dealing,[AA] and ye mourning of our people. They complaine to me, & alass! I can doe nothing for them; if I speake to him, he flies in my face, as mutinous, and saith no complaints shall be heard or received but by him selfe, and saith they are forwarde, & waspish, discontented people, & I doe ill to hear them. Ther are others y^t would lose all they have put in, or make satisfaction for what they have had, that they might departe: but he will not hear them, nor suffer them to goe ashore, least they should rune away. The sailors also are so offended at his ignorante bouldnes, in medling & controuling in things he knows not what belongs too, as y^t some threaten to misscheefe him, others say they will leave ye shipe & goe their way. But at ye best this cometh of it, y^t he maks him selfe a scorne & laughing stock unto them. As for M͡. Weston, excepte grace doe greatly swaye with him, he will hate us ten times more then ever he loved us, for not confirming y͡ᵉ conditions. But now, since some pinches have taken them, they begine to reveile y͡ᵉ trueth, & say M͡. Robinson was in y͡ᵉ falte who charged them never to consente to those conditions, nor chuse me into office, but indeede apointed them to chose them they did chose.[AB] But he & they will rue too late, they may [44] now see, & all be ashamed when it is too late, that they were so ignorante, yea, & so inordinate in their courses. I am sure as they were resolved not to seale those conditions, I was not so resolute at Hampton to have left y͡ᵉ whole bussines, excepte they would seale them, & better y͡ᵉ vioage to have bene broken of then, then to have brought such miserie to our selves, dishonour to God, & detrimente to our loving freinds, as now it is like to doe. 4. or 5. of y͡ᵉ cheefe of them which came from Leyden, came resolved never to goe on those conditions. And M͡. Martine, he said he never received no money on those conditions, he was not beholden to y͡ᵉ marchants for a pine, they were bloudsuckers, & I know not what. Simple man, he indeed never made any conditions w͡ᵗʰ the marchants, nor ever spake with them. But did all that money flie to Hampton, or was it his owne? Who will goe & lay out money so rashly & lavishly as he did, and never know how he comes by it, or on what conditions? 2͡ˡʸ. I tould him of y͡ᵉ alteration longe agoe, & he was contente; but now he dominires, & said I had betrayed them into y͡ᵉ hands of slaves; he is not beholden to them, he can set out 2. ships him selfe to a viage. When, good man? He hath but 50͡ˡⁱ. in, & if he should give up his accounts he would not have a penie left him, as I am persuaded,[AC] &c. Freind, if ever we make a plantation, God works a mirakle; especially considering how scante we shall be of victualls, and most of all ununited amongst our selves, & devoyd of good tutors & regimente. Violence will break all. Wher is y͡ᵉ meek & humble spirite of Moyses? & of Nehemiah who reedified y͡ᵉ wals of Jerusalem, & y͡ᵉ state of Israell? Is not y͡ᵉ sound of Rehoboams braggs daly hear amongst us? Have not y͡ᵉ philosophers and all wise men observed y͡ᵗ, even in setled comone welths, violente governours bring either them selves, or people, or boath, to ruine; how much more in ye raising of comone wealths, when ye morter is yet scarce tempered y^t should bind ye wales. If I should write to you of all things which promiscuously forerune our ruine, I should over charge my weake head and greeve your tender hart; only this, I pray you prepare for evill tidings of us every day. But pray for us instantly, it may be ye Lord will be yet entreated one way or other to make for us. I see not in reason how we shall escape even ye gasping of hunger starved persons; but God can doe much, & his will be done. It is better for me to dye, then now for me to bear it, which I doe daly, & expecte it howerly; haveing received ye sentance of death, both within me & without me. Poore William King & my selfe doe strive[AD] who shall be meate first for ye fishes; but we looke for a glorious resurrection, knowing Christ Jesus after ye flesh no more, but looking unto ye joye y^t is before us, we will endure all these things and accounte them light in comparison of y^t joye we hope for. Remember me in all love to our freinds as if I named them, whose praiers I desire ernestly, & wish againe to see, but not till I can with more comforte looke them in ye face. The Lord give us that true comforte which none can take from us. I had a desire to make a breefe relation of our estate to some freind. I doubte not but your wisdome will teach you seasonably to utter things as here after you shall be called to it. That which I have writen is treue, & many things more which I have forborne. I write it as upon my life, and last confession in England. What is of use to be spoken [45] of presently, you may speake of it, and what is fitt to conceile, conceall. Pass by my weake maner, for my head is weake, & my body feeble, ye Lord make me strong in him, & keepe both you & yours.

Your loving friend,

ROBART CUSHMAN.

Dartmouth, Aug. 17. 1620.

These being his conceptions & fears at Dartmouth, they must needs be much stronger now at Plimoth.

The 9. Chap.

Of their vioage, & how they passed yᵉ sea, and of their safe arrivall at Cape Codd.

SEPTᴿ: 6. These troubls being blowne over, and now all being compacte togeather in one shipe,[AE] they put to sea againe with a prosperus winde, which continued diverce days togeather, which was some incouragmente unto them; yet according to yᵉ usuall maner many were afflicted with sea-sicknes. And I may not omite hear a spetiall worke of Gods providence. Ther was a proud & very profane yonge man, one of yᵉ sea-men, of a lustie, able body, which made him the more hauty; he would allway be contemning yᵉ poore people in their sicknes, & cursing them dayly with greēous execrations, and did not let to tell them, that he hoped to help to cast halfe of them over board before they came to their jurneys end, and to make mery with what they had; and if he were by any gently reproved, he would curse and swear most bitterly. But it plased God before they came halfe seas over, to smite this yong man with a greeveous disease, of which he dyed in a desperate maner, and so was him selfe yᵉ first yᵗ was throwne overbord. Thus his curses light on his owne head; and it was an astonishmente to all his fellows, for they noted it to be yᵉ just hand of God upon him.

After they had injoyed faire winds and weather for a season, they were incountred many times with crosse winds, and mette with many feirce stormes, with which yᵉ shipe was shroudly shaken, and her upper works made very leakie; and one of the maine beames in yᵉ midd ships was bowed & craked, which put them in some fear that yᵉ shipe could not be able to performe yᵉ vioage. So some of yᵉ cheefe of yᵉ company, perceiveing yᵉ mariners to feare yᵉ suffisiencie of yᵉ shipe, as appeared by their mutterings, they entred into serious consulltation with yᵉ mʳ. & other officers of yᵉ ship, to consider in time of yᵉ danger; and rather to returne then to cast them selves into a desperate & inevitable perill. And truly ther was great distraction & differance of opinion amongst yᵉ mariners them selves; faine would they doe what could be done for their wages sake, (being now halfe the seas over,) and on yᵉ other hand they were loath to hazard their lives too desperatly. But in examening of all opinions, the mʳ. & others affirmed they knew yᵉ ship to be stronge & firme under water; and for the buckling of yᵉ maine beame, ther was a great iron scrue yᵉ passengers brought out of Holland, which would raise yᵉ beame into his place; yᵉ which being done, the carpenter & mʳ. affirmed that with a post put under it, set firme in yᵉ lower deck, & otherways bounde, he would make it sufficiente. And as for yᵉ decks & uper workes they would calke them as well as they could, and though with yᵉ workeing of yᵉ ship they [46] would not longe keepe stanch, yet ther would otherwise be no great danger, if they did not overpress her with sails. So they comited them selves to yᵉ will of God, & resolved to proseede. In sundrie of these stormes the winds were so feirce, & yᵉ seas so high, as they could not beare a knote of saile, but were forced to hull, for diverce days togither. And in one of them, as they thus lay at hull, in a mighty storme, a lustie yonge man (called John Howland) coming upon some occasion above yᵉ grattings, was, with a seele of the shipe throwne into [yᵉ] sea; but it pleased God yᵗ he caught hould of yᵉ top-saile halliards, which hunge over board, & rane out at length; yet he held his hould (though he was sundrie fadomes under water) till he was hald up by yᵉ same rope to yᵉ brime of yᵉ water, and then with a boat hooke & other means got into yᵉ shipe againe, & his life saved; and though he was something ill with it, yet he lived many years after, and became a profitable member both in church & comone wealthe. In all this viage ther died but one of yᵉ passengers, which was William Butten, a youth, servant to Samuell Fuller, when they drew near yᵉ coast. But to omite other things, (that I may be breefe,) after longe beating at sea they fell with that land which is called Cape Cod; the which being made & certainly knowne to be it, they were not a litle joyfull. After some deliberation had amongst them selves & with ye m^r. of ye ship, they tacked aboute and resolved to stande for ye southward (ye wind & weather being faire) to finde some place aboute Hudsons river for their habitation. But after they had sailed y^t course aboute halfe ye day, they fell amongst deangerous shoulds and roring breakers, and they were so farr intangled ther with as they conceived them selves in great danger; & ye wind shrinking upon them withall, they resolved to bear up againe for the Cape, and thought them selves hapy to gett out of those dangers before night overtooke them, as by Gods providence they did. And ye next day they gott into ye Cape-harbor wher they ridd in saftie. A word or too by ye way of this cape; it was thus first named by Capten Gosnole & his company,[AF] Anno: 1602, and after by Capten Smith was caled Cape James; but it retains ye former name amongst seamen. Also y^t pointe which first shewed those dangerous shoulds unto them, they called Pointe Care, & Tuckers Terrour; but ye French & Dutch to this day call it Malabarr, by reason of those perilous shoulds, and ye losses they have suffered their.

Being thus arived in a good harbor and brought safe to land, they fell upon their knees & blessed ye God of heaven, who had brought them over ye vast & furious ocean, and delivered them from all ye periles & miseries therof, againe to set their feete on ye firme and stable earth, their proper elemente. And no marvell if they were thus joyefull, seeing wise Seneca was so affected with sailing a few miles on ye coast of his owne Italy; as he affirmed,[AG] that he had rather remaine twentie years on his way by land, then pass by sea to any place in a short time; so tedious & dreadfull was ye same unto him.

But hear I cannot but stay and make a pause, and stand half amased at this poore peoples presente condition; and so I thinke will the reader too, when he well considers [47] ye same. Being thus passed ye vast ocean, and a sea of troubles before in their preparation (as may be remembered by y^t which wente before), they had now no freinds to wellcome them, nor inns to entertaine or refresh their weatherbeaten bodys, no houses or much less townes to repaire too, to seeke for succoure. It is recorded in scripture[AH] as a mercie to yᵉ apostle & his shipwraked company, yᵗ the barbarians shewed them no smale kindnes in refreshing them, but these savage barbarians, when they mette with them (as after will appeare) were readier to fill their sids full of arrows then otherwise. And for yᵉ season it was winter, and they that know yᵉ winters of yᵗ cuntrie know them to be sharp & violent, & subjecte to cruell & feirce stormes, deangerous to travill to known places, much more to serch an unknown coast. Besids, what could they see but a hidious & desolate wildernes, full of wild beasts & willd men? and what multituds ther might be of them they knew not. Nether could they, as it were, goe up to yᵉ tope of Pisgah, to vew from this willdernes a more goodly cuntrie to feed their hops; for which way soever they turnd their eys (save upward to yᵉ heavens) they could have litle solace or content in respecte of any outward objects. For sumer being done, all things stand upon them with a wetherbeaten face; and yᵉ whole countrie, full of woods & thickets, represented a wild & savage heiw. If they looked behind them, ther was yᵉ mighty ocean which they had passed, and was now as a maine barr & goulfe to seperate them from all yᵉ civill parts of yᵉ world. If it be said they had a ship to sucour them, it is trew; but what heard they daly from yᵉ mʳ. & company? but yᵗ with speede they should looke out a place with their shallop, wher they would be at some near distance; for yᵉ season was shuch as he would not stirr from thence till a safe harbor was discovered by them wher they would be, and he might goe without danger; and that victells consumed apace, but he must & would keepe sufficient for them selves & their returne. Yea, it was muttered by some, that if they gott not a place in time, they would turne them & their goods ashore & leave them. Let it also be considred what weake hopes of supply & succoure they left behinde them, yᵗ might bear up their minds in this sade condition and trialls they were under; and they could not but be very smale. It is true, indeed, yᵉ affections & love of their brethren at Leyden was cordiall & entire towards them, but they had litle power to help them, or them selves; and how yᵉ case stode betweene them & yᵉ marchants at their coming away, hath allready been declared. What could now sustaine them but the spirite of God & his grace? May not & ought not the children of these fathers rightly say: *Our faithers were Englishmen which came over this great ocean, and were ready to perish in this willdernes;*[AI] *but they cried unto yᵉ Lord, and he heard their voyce, and looked on their adversitie, &c. Let them therfore praise yᵉ Lord, because he is good, & his mercies endure for ever.*[AJ] *Yea, let them which have been redeemed of yᵉ Lord, shew how he hath delivered them from yᵉ hand of yᵉ oppressour. When they wandered in yᵉ deserte willdernes out of yᵉ way, and found no citie to dwell in, both hungrie, & thirstie, their sowle was overwhelmed in them. Let them confess before yᵉ Lord his loving kindnes, and his wonderfull works before yᵉ sons of men.*

The 10. Chap.

Showing how they sought out a place of habitation, and what befell them theraboute.

[48] Being thus arrived at Cap-Cod yᵉ 11. of November, and necessitie calling them to looke out a place for habitation, (as well as the maisters & mariners importunitie,) they having brought a large shalop with them out of England, stowed in quarters in yᵉ ship, they now gott her out & sett their carpenters to worke to trime her up; but being much brused & shatered in yᵉ shipe wᵗʰ foule weather, they saw she would be longe in mending. Wherupon a few of them tendered them selves to goe by land and discovere those nearest places, whilst yᵉ shallop was in mending; and yᵉ rather because as they wente into yᵗ harbor ther seemed to be an opening some 2. or 3. leagues of, which yᵉ maister judged to be a river. It was conceived ther might be some danger in yᵉ attempte, yet seeing them resolute, they were permited to goe, being 16. of them well armed, under yᵉ conduct of Captain Standish, having shuch instructions given them as was thought meete. They sett forth yᵉ 15. of Noveᵇʳ: and when they had marched aboute the space of a mile

by yᵉ sea side, they espied 5. or 6. persons with a dogg coming towards them, who were salvages; but they fled from them, & rane up into yᵉ woods, and yᵉ English followed them, partly to see if they could speake with them, and partly to discover if ther might not be more of them lying in ambush. But yᵉ Indeans seeing them selves thus followed, they againe forsooke the woods, & rane away on yᵉ sands as hard as they could, so as they could not come near them, but followed them by yᵉ tracte of their feet sundrie miles, and saw that they had come the same way. So, night coming on, they made their randevous & set out their sentinels, and rested in quiete yᵗ *night*, and the next morning followed their tracte till they had headed a great creake, & so left the sands, & turned an other way into yᵉ woods. But they still followed them by geuss, hopeing to find their dwellings; but they soone lost both them & them selves, falling into shuch thickets as were ready to tear their cloaths & armore in peeces, but were most distresed for wante of drinke. But at length they found water & refreshed them selves, being yᵉ first New-England water they drunke of, and was now in thir great thirste as pleasante unto them as wine or bear had been in for-times. Afterwards they directed their course to come to yᵉ other [49] shore, for they knew it was a necke of land they were to crosse over, and so at length gott to yᵉ sea-side, and marched to this supposed river, & by yᵉ way found a pond of clear fresh water, and shortly after a good quantitie of clear ground wher yᵉ Indeans had formerly set corne, and some of their graves. And proceeding furder they saw new-stuble wher corne had been set yᵉ same year, also they found wher latly a house had been, wher some planks and a great ketle was remaining, and heaps of sand newly padled with their hands, which they, digging up, found in them diverce faire Indean baskets filled with corne, and some in eares, faire and good, of diverce collours, which seemed to them a very goodly sight, (haveing never seen any shuch before). This was near yᵉ place of that supposed river they came to seeck; unto which they wente and found it to open it selfe into 2. armes with a high cliffe of sand in yᵉ enterance, but more like to be crikes of salte water then any fresh, for ought they saw; and that ther was good harborige for their shalope; leaving it further to be discovered by their shalop when she was ready. So their time limeted them being expired, they returned to yᵉ ship, least they should be in fear of their saftie; and tooke with them parte of yᵉ corne, and buried up yᵉ rest, and so like yᵉ men from Eshcoll carried with them of yᵉ fruits of yᵉ land, & showed their breethren; of which, & their returne, they were marvelusly glad, and their harts incouraged.

After this, yᵉ shalop being got ready, they set out againe for yᵉ better discovery of this place, & yᵉ mʳ. of yᵉ ship desired to goe him selfe, so ther went some 30. men, but found it to be no harbor for ships but only for boats; ther was allso found 2. of their houses covered with matts, & sundrie of their implements in them, but yᵉ people were rune away & could not be seen; also ther was found more of their corne, & of their beans of various collours. The corne & beans they brought away, purposing to give them full satisfaction when they should meete with any of them (as about some 6. months afterward they did, to their good contente). And here is to be noted a spetiall providence of God, and a great mercie to this poore people, that hear they gott seed to plant them corne yᵉ next year, or els they might have starved, for they had none, nor any liklyhood to get any [50] till yᵉ season had beene past (as yᵉ sequell did manyfest). Neither is it lickly they had had this, if yᵉ first viage had not been made, for the ground was now all covered with snow, & hard frozen. But the Lord is never wanting unto his in their greatest needs; let his holy name have all yᵉ praise.

The month of November being spente in these affairs, & much foule weather falling in, the 6. *of Desemʳ*: they sente out their shallop againe with 10. of their principall men, & some sea men, upon further discovery, intending to circulate that deepe bay of Cap-codd. The weather was very could, & it frose so hard as yᵉ sprea of yᵉ sea lighting on their coats, they were as if they had been glased; yet *that night* betimes they gott downe into yᵉ botome of yᵉ bay, and as they drue nere yᵉ shore they saw some 10. or 12. Indeans very busie aboute some thing. They landed aboute a league or 2. from them, and had much a doe to put a shore any wher, it lay so full of flats. Being landed, it grew late, and they made them selves a barricade with loggs & bowes as well as they could in ye time, & set out their sentenill & betooke them to rest, and saw ye smoake of ye fire ye savages made y^t night. When *morning* was come they devided their company, some to coaste along ye shore in ye boate, and the rest marched throw ye woods to see ye land, if any fit place might be for their dwelling. They came allso to ye place wher they saw the Indans ye night before, & found they had been cuting up a great fish like a grampus, being some 2. inches thike of fate like a hogg, some peeces wher of they had left by ye way; and ye shallop found 2. more of these fishes dead on ye sands, a thing usuall after storms in y^t place, by reason of ye great flats of sand that lye of. So they ranged up and doune all y^t day, but found no people, nor any place they liked. When ye sune grue low, they hasted out of ye woods to meete with their shallop, to whom they made signes to come to them into a *creeke* hardby, the which they did at highwater; of which they were very glad, for they had not seen each other all y^t day, since ye morning. So they made them a barricado (as usually they did every night) with loggs, staks, & thike pine bowes, ye height of a man, leaving it open to leeward, partly to shelter them from ye could & wind (making their fire in ye midle, & lying round aboute it), and partly to defend them from any sudden assaults of ye savags, if they should surround them. So being very weary, they betooke them to rest. But aboute *midnight*, [51] they heard a hideous & great crie, and their sentinell caled, "Arme, arme"; so they bestired them & stood to their armes, & shote of a cupple of moskets, and then the noys seased. They concluded it was a companie of wolves, or such like willd beasts; for one of ye sea men tould them he had often heard shuch a noyse in New-found land. So they rested till about 5. of ye clock in the *morning*; for ye tide, & ther purpose to goe from thence, made them be stiring betimes. So after praier they prepared for breakfast, and it being day dawning, it was thought best to be carring things downe to ye boate. But some said it was not best to carrie ye armes downe, others said they would be the readier, for they had laped them up in their coats from ye dew. But some 3. or 4. would not cary theirs till they wente them selves, yet as it fell out, ye water being not high enough, they layed them downe on yᵉ banke side, & came up to breakfast. But presently, all on yᵉ sudain, they heard a great & strange crie, which they knew to be the same voyces they heard in yᵉ night, though they varied their notes, & one of their company being abroad came runing in, & cried, "Men, Indeans, Indeans"; and wᵗʰall, their arowes came flying amongst them. Their men rane with all speed to recover their armes, as by yᵉ good providence of God they did. In yᵉ mean time, of those that were ther ready, tow muskets were discharged at them, & 2. more stood ready in yᵉ enterance of ther randevoue, but were comanded not to shoote till they could take full aime at them; & yᵉ other 2. charged againe with all speed, for ther were only 4. had armes ther, & defended yᵉ baricado which was first assalted. The crie of yᵉ Indeans was dreadfull, espetially when they saw ther men rune out of yᵉ randevoue towourds yᵉ shallop, to recover their armes, the Indeans wheeling aboute upon them. But some runing out with coats of malle on, & cutlasses in their hands, they soone got their armes, & let flye amongs them, and quickly stopped their violence. Yet ther was a lustie man, and no less valiante, stood behind a tree within halfe a musket shot, and let his arrows flie at them. He was seen shoot 3. arrowes, which were all avoyded. He stood 3. shot of a musket, till one taking full aime at him, and made yᵉ barke or splinters of yᵉ tree fly about his ears, after which he gave an extraordinary shrike, and away they wente all of them. They left some to keep yᵉ shalop, and followed them aboute a quarter of a mille, and shouted once or twise, and shot of 2. or 3. peces, & so returned. This they did, that they might conceive that they were not [52] affrade of them or any way discouraged. Thus it pleased God to vanquish their enimies, and give them deliverance; and by his spetiall providence so to dispose that not any one of them were either hurte, or hitt, though their arrows came close by them, & on every side them, and sundry of their coats, which hunge up in yᵉ barricado, were shot throw & throw. Aterwards they gave God sollamne thanks & praise for their deliverance, & gathered up a bundle of their arrows, & sente them into England afterward by yᵉ mʳ. of yᵉ ship, and called that place yᵉ first encounter. From hence they departed, & costed all along, but discerned no place likly for harbor; & therfore hasted to a place that their pillote, (one Mr. Coppin who had bine in yᵉ cuntrie before) did assure them was a good harbor, which he had been in, and they might fetch it before night; of which they were glad, for it begane to be foule weather. After some houres sailing, it begane to snow & raine, & about yᵉ midle of yᵉ afternoone, yᵉ wind increased, & yᵉ sea became very rough, and they broake their rudder, & it was as much as 2. men could doe to steere her with a cupple of oares. But their pillott bad them be of good cheere, for he saw yᵉ harbor; but yᵉ storme increasing, & night drawing on, they bore what saile they could to gett in, while they could see. But herwith they broake their mast in 3. peeces, & their saill fell over bord, in a very grown sea, so as they had like to have been cast away; yet by Gods mercie they recovered them selves, & having yᵉ floud with them, struck into yᵉ harbore. But when it came too, yᵉ pillott was deceived in yᵉ place, and said, yᵉ Lord be mercifull unto them, for his eys never saw yᵗ place before; & he & the mʳ. mate would have rune her ashore, in a cove full of breakers, before yᵉ winde. But a lusty seaman which steered, bad those which rowed, if they were men, about with her, or ells they were all cast away; the which they did with speed. So he bid them be of good cheere & row lustly, for ther was a faire sound before them, & he doubted not but they should find one place or other wher they might ride in saftie. And though it was *very darke*, and rained sore, yet in yᵉ end they gott under yᵉ lee of a smalle iland, and remained ther all yᵗ night in saftie. But they knew not this to be an iland till morning, but were devided in their minds; some would keepe yᵉ boate for fear they might be amongst yᵉ Indians; others were so weake and could, they could not endure, but got a shore, & with much adoe got fire, (all things being so wett,) and yᵉ rest were glad to come to them; for after midnight yᵉ wind shifted to the [53] north-west, & it frose hard. But though this had been a day & night of much trouble & danger unto them, yet God gave them a *morning* of comforte & refreshing (as usually he doth to his children), for yᵉ next day was a faire sunshinīg day, and they found them sellvs to be on an iland secure from yᵉ Indeans, wher they might drie their stufe, fixe their peeces, & rest them selves, and gave God thanks for his mercies, in their manifould deliverances. And this being the *last day of ye weeke*, they prepared ther to keepe y^e *Sabath*. On *Munday* they sounded ye harbor, and founde it fitt for shipping; and marched into ye land, & found diverse cornfeilds, & litle runing brooks, a place (as they supposed) fitt for situation; at least it was ye best they could find, and ye season, & their presente necessitie, made them glad to accepte of it. So they returned to their shipp againe with this news to ye rest of their people, which did much comforte their harts.

On ye 15. *of Desemr*: they wayed anchor to goe to ye place they had discovered, & came within 2. leagues of it, but were faine to bear up againe; but ye 16. *day* ye winde came faire, and they arrived safe in this harbor. And after wards tooke better view of ye place, and resolved wher to pitch their dwelling; and ye 25. *day* begane to erecte ye first house for comone use to receive them and their goods.

The 2. Booke.

The rest of this History (if God give me life, & opportunitie) I shall, for brevitis sake, handle by way of *annalls*, noteing only the heads of principall things, and passages as they fell in order of time, and may seeme to be profitable to know, or to make use of. And this may be as yᵉ 2. Booke.

The remainder of Anᵒ: 1620.

I shall a litle returne backe and begine with a combination made by them before they came ashore, being yᵉ first foundation of their govermente in this place; occasioned partly by yᵉ discontented & mutinous speeches that some of the strangers amongst them had let fall from them in yᵉ ship—That when they came a shore they would use their owne libertie; for none had power to comand them, the patente they had being for Virginia, and not for New-england, which belonged to an other Goverment, with which yᵉ Virginia Company had nothing to doe. And partly that shuch an [54] acte by them done (this their condition considered) might be as firme as any patent, and in some respects more sure.

The forme was as followeth.

In yᵉ name of God, Amen. We whose names are underwriten, the loyall subjects of our dread soveraigne Lord, King James, by yᵉ grace of God, of Great Britaine, Franc, & Ireland king, defender of yᵉ faith, &c., haveing undertaken, for yᵉ glorie of God, and advancemente of yᵉ Christian faith, and honour of our king & countrie, a voyage to plant yᵉ first colonie in yᵉ Northerne parts of Virginia, doe by these presents solemnly & mutualy in yᵉ presence of God, and one of another, covenant & combine our selves togeather into a civill body politick, for our better ordering & preservation & furtherance of yᵉ ends aforesaid; and by vertue hearof to enacte, constitute, and frame such just & equall lawes, ordinances, acts, constitutions, & offices, from time to time, as shall be thought most meete & convenient for yᵉ generall good of yᵉ Colonie, unto which we promise all due submission and obedience. In witnes wherof we have hereunder subscribed our names at Cap-Codd yᵉ 11. of November, in yᵉ year of yᵉ raigne of our soveraigne lord, King James, of England, France, & Ireland yᵉ eighteenth, and of Scotland yᵉ fiftie fourth. Anᵒ: Dom. 1620.

After this they chose, or rather confirmed, Mʳ. John Carver (a man godly & well approved amongst them) their Governour for that year. And after they had provided a place for their goods, or comone store, (which were long in unlading for want of boats, foulnes of winter weather, and sicknes of diverce,) and begune some small cottages for their habitation, as time would admitte, they mette and consulted of lawes & orders, both for their civill & military Govermente, as yᵉ necessitie of their condition did require, still adding therunto as urgent occasion in severall times, and as cases did require.

In these hard & difficulte beginings they found some discontents & murmurings arise amongst some, and mutinous speeches & carriags in other; but they were soone quelled & overcome by yᵉ wisdome, patience, and just & equall carrage of things by yᵉ Govʳ and better part, wᶜʰ clave faithfully togeather in yᵉ maine. But that which was most sadd & lamentable was, that in 2. or 3. moneths time halfe of their company dyed, espetialy in Jan: & February, being yᵉ depth of winter, and wanting houses & other comforts; being infected with yᵉ scurvie & [55] other diseases, which this long vioage & their inacomodate condition had brought upon them; so as ther dyed some times 2. or 3. of a day, in yᵉ foresaid time; that of 100. & odd persons, scarce 50. remained. And of these in yᵉ time of most distres, ther was but 6. or 7. sound persons, who, to their great comendations be it spoken, spared no pains, night nor day, but with abundance of toyle and hazard of their owne health, fetched them woode, made them fires, drest them meat, made their beads, washed their lothsome cloaths, cloathed & uncloathed them; in a word, did all ye homly & necessarie offices for them wch dainty & quesie stomacks cannot endure to hear named; and all this willingly & cherfully, without any grudging in ye least, shewing herein their true love unto their freinds & bretheren. A rare example & worthy to be remembred. Tow of these 7. were M^r. William Brewster, ther reverend Elder, & Myles Standish, ther Captein & military comander, unto whom my selfe, & many others, were much beholden in our low & sicke condition. And yet the Lord so upheld these persons, as in this generall calamity they were not at all infected either with sicknes, or lamnes. And what I have said of these, I may say of many others who dyed in this generall vissitation, & others yet living, that whilst they had health, yea, or any strength continuing, they were not wanting to any that had need of them. And I doute not but their recompence is with ye Lord.

But I may not hear pass by an other remarkable passage not to be forgotten. As this calamitie fell among ye passengers that were to be left here to plant, and were hasted a shore and made to drinke water, that ye sea-men might have ye more bear, and one[AK] in his sicknes desiring but a small cann of beere, it was answered, that if he were their owne father he should have none; the disease begane to fall amongst them also, so as allmost halfe of their company dyed before they went away, and many of their officers and lustyest men, as ye boatson, gunner, 3. quarter-maisters, the cooke, & others. At wch ye m^r. was something strucken and sent to ye sick a shore and tould ye Govr he should send for beer for them that had need of it, though he drunke water homward bound. But now amongst his company [56] ther was farr another kind of carriage in this miserie then amongst ye passengers; for they that before had been boone companions in drinking & joyllity in ye time of their health & wellfare, begane now to deserte one another in this calamitie, saing they would not hasard ther lives for them, they should be infected by coming to help them in their cabins, and so, after they came to dye by it, would doe litle or nothing for them, but if they dyed let them dye. But shuch of yᵉ passengers as were yet abord shewed them what mercy they could, wᶜʰ made some of their harts relente, as yᵉ boatson (& some others), who was a prowd yonge man, and would often curse & scofe at yᵉ passengers; but when he grew weak, they had compassion on him and helped him; then he confessed he did not deserve it at their hands, he had abused them in word & deed. O! saith he, you, I now see, shew your love like Christians indeed one to another, but we let one another lye & dye like doggs. Another lay cursing his wife, saing if it had not ben for her he had never come this unlucky viage, and anone cursing his felows, saing he had done this & that, for some of them, he had spente so much, & so much, amongst them, and they were now weary of him, and did not help him, having need. Another gave his companion all he had, if he died, to help him in his weaknes; he went and got a litle spise & made him a mess of meat once or twise, and because he dyed not so soone as he expected, he went amongst his fellows, & swore yᵉ rogue would cousen him, he would see him choaked before he made him any more meate; and yet yᵉ pore fellow dyed before morning.

All this while yᵉ Indians came skulking about them, and would sometimes show them selves aloofe of, but when any aproached near them, they would rune away. And once they stoale away their tools wher they had been at worke, & were gone to diner. But about yᵉ 16. *of March* a certaine Indian came bouldly amongst them, and spoke to them in broken English, which they could well understand, but marvelled at it. At length they understood by discourse with him, that he was not of these parts, but belonged to yᵉ eastrene parts, wher some English-ships came to fhish, with whom he was aquainted, & could name sundrie of them by their names, amongst whom he had gott his language. He became proftable to them [57] in aquainting them with many things concerning yᵉ state of yᵉ cuntry in yᵉ east-parts wher he lived, which was afterwards profitable unto them; as also of yᵉ people hear, of their names, number, & strength; of their situation & distance from this place, and who was cheefe amongst them. His name was *Samaset*; he tould them also of another Indian whos name was

Squanto, a native of this place, who had been in England & could speake better English then him selfe. Being, after some time of entertainmente & gifts, dismist, a while after he came againe, & 5. more with him, & they brought againe all yᵉ tooles that were stolen away before, and made way for yᵉ coming of their great Sachem, called *Massasoyt*; who, about *4. or 5. days after*, came with the cheefe of his freinds & other attendance, with the aforesaid *Squanto*. With whom, after frendly entertainment, & some gifts given him, they made a peace with him (which hath now continued this 24. years) in these terms.

1. That neither he nor any of his, should injurie or doe hurte to any of their peopl.

2. That if any of his did any hurte to any of theirs, he should send yᵉ offender, that they might punish him.

3. That if any thing were taken away from any of theirs, he should cause it to be restored; and they should doe yᵉ like to his.

4. If any did unjustly warr against him, they would aide him; if any did warr against them, he should aide them.

5. He should send to his neighbours confederats, to certifie them of this, that they might not wrong them, but might be likewise comprised in yᵉ conditions of peace.

6. That when ther men came to them, they should leave their bows & arrows behind them.

After these things he returned to his place caled *Sowams*, some 40. mile from this place, but *Squanto* continued with them, and was their interpreter, and was a spetiall instrument sent of God for their good beyond their expectation. He directed them how to set their corne, wher to take fish, and to procure other comodities, and was also their pilott to bring them to unknowne places for their profitt, and never left them till he dyed. He was a *native [58] of this place*, & scarce any left alive besids him selfe. He was caried away with diverce others by one *Hunt*, a mʳ. of a ship, who thought to sell them for slaves in Spaine; but he got away for England, and was entertained by a marchante in London, & imployed to Newfoundland & other parts, & lastly brought hither into these parts by one Mr. *Dermer*, a gentle-man imployed by Sr. Ferdinando Gorges & others, for discovery, & other designes in these parts. Of whom I shall say some thing, because it is mentioned in a booke set forth Ano: 1622. by the Presidente & Counsell for New-England,[AL] that he made ye peace betweene ye salvages of these parts & ye English; of which this plantation, as it is intimated, had ye benefite. But what a peace it was, may apeare by what befell him & his men.

This Mr. Dermer was hear the same year that these people came, as apears by a relation written by him, & given me by a friend, bearing date June 30. Ano: 1620. And they came in Novembr: following, so ther was but 4. months differance. In which relation to his honored freind, he hath these passages of this very place.

I will first begine (saith he) wth that place from whence *Squanto*, or *Tisquantem*, was taken away; wch in Cap: *Smiths mape* is called *Plimoth*: and I would that Plimoth had ye like comodities. I would that the first plantation might hear be seated, if ther come to the number of 50. persons, or upward. Otherwise at Charlton, because ther ye savages are lese to be feared. The *Pocanawkits*, which live to ye *west* of *Plimoth*, bear an inveterate malice to ye English, and are of more streingth then all ye savags from thence to Penobscote. Their desire of revenge was occasioned by an English man, who having many of them on bord, made a great slaughter with their murderers & smale shot, when as (they say) they offered no injurie on their parts. Whether they were English or no, it may be douted; yet they beleeve they were, for ye Frenche have so possest them; for which cause *Squanto* canot deney but they would have kiled me when I was at *Namasket*, had he not entreated hard for me. The soyle of ye borders of [59] this great bay, may be compared to most of ye plantations which I have seene in Virginia. The land is of diverce sorts; for *Patuxite* is a hardy but strong soyle, *Nawsel & Saughtughtett* are for ye most part a blakish & deep mould, much like that wher groweth ye best Tobaco in Virginia. In ye botume of yt great bay is store of Codd & basse, or mulett, &c.

But above all he comends *Pacanawkite* for yᵉ richest soyle, and much open ground fitt for English graine, &c.

Massachussets is about 9. leagues from *Plimoth*, & situate in yᵉ mids betweene both, is full of ilands & peninsules very fertill for yᵉ most parte.

With sundrie shuch relations which I forbear to transcribe, being now better knowne then they were to him.

He was taken prisoner by yᵉ Indeans at *Manamoiak* (a place not farr from hence, now well knowne). He gave them what they demanded for his liberty, but when they had gott what they desired, they kept him still & indevored to kill his men; but he was freed by seasing on some of them, and kept them bound till they gave him a cannows load of corne. Of which, see Purch: lib. 9. fol. 1778. But this was Anᵒ: 1619.

After yᵉ writing of yᵉ former relation he came to yᵉ Ile of *Capawack* (which lyes south of this place in yᵉ way to Virginia), and yᵉ foresaid *Squanto* wᵗʰ him, wher he going a shore amongst yᵉ Indans to trad, as he used to doe, was betrayed & assaulted by them, & *all his men slaine, but one that kept the boat*; but him selfe gott abord very sore wounded, & they had cut of his head upon yᵉ cudy of his boat, had not yᵉ man reskued him with a sword. And so they got away, & made shift to gett into Virginia, wher he dyed; whether of his wounds or yᵉ diseases of yᵉ cuntrie, or both togeather, is uncertaine. [60] By all which it may appeare how farr these people were from peace, and with what danger this plantation was begune, save as yᵉ powerfull hand of the Lord did protect them. These things[AM] were partly the reason why they kept aloofe & were so long before they came to the English. An other reason (as after them selvs made know) was how aboute 3. *years before*, a French-ship was cast away at *Cap-Codd*, but yᵉ men gott ashore, & saved their lives, and much of their victails, & other goods; but after yᵉ Indeans heard of it, they geathered togeather from these parts, and never left watching & dogging them till they got advantage, and *kild them all but 3. or 4.* which they kept, & sent from one Sachem to another, to make sporte with, and used them worse then slaves; (of which y⁰ foresaid Mᵣ. Dermer redeemed 2. of them;) and they conceived this ship was now come to revenge it.

Also, (as after was made knowne,) before they came to y⁰ English to make freindship, they gott all the *Powachs* of y⁰ cuntrie, for 3. days togeather, in a horid and divellish maner to curse & execrate them with their cunjurations, which asembly & service they held in a darke & dismale swampe.

But to returne. The spring now approaching, it pleased God the mortalitie begane to cease amongst them, and y⁰ sick and lame recovered apace, which put as it were new life into them; though they had borne their sadd affliction with much patience & contentednes, as I thinke any people could doe. But it was y⁰ Lord which upheld them, and had beforehand prepared them; many having long borne y⁰ yoake, yea from their youth. Many other smaler maters I omite, sundrie of them having been allready published in a Jurnall made by one of the company; and some other passages of jurneys and relations allredy published, to which I referr those that are willing to know them more perticulerly. And being now come to y⁰ 25. of March I shall begine y⁰ year 1621.

[61] Anno. 1621.

They now begane to dispatch y⁰ ship away which brought them over, which lay tille aboute this time, or y⁰ begining of Aprill. The reason on their parts why she stayed so long, was y⁰ necessitie and danger that lay upon them, for it was well towards y⁰ ende of Desember before she could land any thing hear, or they able to receive any thing ashore. Afterwards, y⁰ 14. of Jan: the house which they had made for a generall randevoze by casulty fell afire, and some were faine to retire abord for shilter. Then the sicknes begane to fall sore amongst them, and y⁰ weather so bad as they could not make much sooner any dispatch. Againe, the Govᵣ & cheefe of them, seeing so many dye, and fall downe sick dayly, thought it no wisdom to send away the ship, their condition considered, and y⁰ danger they stood in from y⁰ Indeans, till they could procure some shelter; and therfore thought it better to draw some more charge upon them selves & freinds, then hazard all. The m^r. and sea-men likewise, though before they hasted ye passengers a shore to be goone, now many of their men being dead, & of ye ablest of them, (as is before noted,) and of ye rest many lay sick & weake, ye m^r. durst not put to sea, till he saw his men begine to recover, and ye hart of winter over.

Afterwards they (as many as were able) began to plant ther corne, in which servise Squanto stood them in great stead, showing them both ye maner how to set it, and after how to dress & tend it. Also he tould them excepte they gott fish & set with it (in these old grounds) it would come to nothing, and he showed them y^t in ye midle of Aprill they should have store enough come up ye brooke, by which they begane to build, and taught them how to take it, and wher to get other provissions necessary for them; all which they found true by triall & experience. Some English seed they sew, as wheat & pease, but it came not to good, eather by ye badnes of ye seed, or latenes of ye season, or both, or some other defecte.

[62] In this month of *Aprill* whilst they were bussie about their seed, their Govr (M^r. John Carver) came out of ye feild very sick, it being a hott day; he complained greatly of his head, and lay downe, and within a few howers his sences failed, so as he never spake more till he dyed, which was within a few days after. Whoss death was much lamented, and caused great heavines amongst them, as ther was cause. He was buried in ye best maner they could, with some vollies of shott by all that bore armes; and his wife, being a weak woman, dyed within 5. or 6. weeks after him.

Shortly after William Bradford was chosen Gove^r in his stead, and being not yet recoverd of his ilnes, in which he had been near ye point of death, Isaak Allerton was chosen to be an Asistante unto him, who, by renewed election every year, continued sundry years togeather, which I hear note once for all.

May 12. was ye first mariage in this place, which, according to ye laudable custome of the Low-Cuntries, in which they had lived, was thought most requisite to be performed by the magistrate, as being a civill thing, upon which many questions aboute inheritances doe depende, with other things most proper to their cognizans, and most consonante to ye scripturs, Ruth 4. and no wher found in ye gospell to be layed on ye ministers as a part of their office. "This decree or law about mariage was published by ye Stats of ye Low-Cuntries An^o: 1590. That those of any religion, after lawfull and open publication, coming before ye magistrats, in ye Town or Stat-house, were to be orderly (by them) maried one to another." Petets Hist, fol: 1029. And this practiss hath continued amongst, not only them, but hath been followed by all ye famous churches of Christ in these parts to this time,—An^o: 1646.

Haveing in some sorte ordered their bussines at home, it was thought meete to send some abroad to see their new friend Massasoyet, and to bestow upon him some gratuitie to bind him ye faster unto them; as also that hearby they might veiw ye countrie, and see in what maner he lived, what strength he had aboute him, and how ye ways were to his place, if at any time they should have occasion. So ye 2. *of July* they sente M^r. Edward Winslow & M^r. Hopkins, with ye foresaid Squanto for ther guid, who gave him a suite of cloaths, and a horsemans coate, with some other small things, which were kindly accepted; but they found but short comons, and came both weary & hungrie home. For ye Indeans used then to have nothing [63] so much corne as they have since ye English have stored them with their hows, and seene their industrie in breaking up new grounds therwith. *They found his place to be 40. miles from hence*, ye soyle good, & ye people not many, being dead & abundantly wasted in ye late great mortalitie which fell in all these parts aboute *three years* before ye coming of ye English, wherin thousands of them dyed, they not being able to burie one another; ther sculs and bones were found in many places lying still above ground, where their houses & dwellings had been; a very sad spectackle to behould. But they brought word that ye Narighansets lived but on ye other side of that great bay, & were a strong people, & many in number, living compacte togeather, & had not been at all touched with this wasting plague.

Aboute y^e *later end of this month*, one John Billington lost him selfe in ye woods, & wandered up & downe some 5. days, living on beries & what he could find. At length he light on an Indean plantation, 20. mils south of this place, called *Manamet*, they conveid him furder of, to *Nawsett*, among those peopl that had before set upon yᵉ English when they were costing, whilest yᵉ ship lay at yᵉ Cape, as is before noted. But yᵉ Goveʳ caused him to be enquired for among yᵉ Indeans, and at length Massassoyt sent word wher he was, and yᵉ Goveʳ sent a shalop for him, & had him delivered. Those people also came and made their peace; and they gave full satisfaction to those whose come they had found & taken when they were at Cap-Codd.

Thus ther peace & aquaintance was pretty well establisht wᵗʰ the natives aboute them; and ther was an other Indean called *Hobamack* come to live amongst them, a proper lustie man, and a man of accounte for his vallour & parts amongst yᵉ Indeans, and continued very faithfull and constant to yᵉ English till he dyed. He & Squanto being gone upon bussines amonge yᵉ Indeans, at their returne (whether it was out of envie to them or malice to the English) ther was a Sachem called Corbitant, alyed to Massassoyte, but never any good friend to yᵉ English to this day, mett with them at an Indean towne caled Namassakett 14. miles to yᵉ west of this place, and begane to quarell wᵗʰ [64] them, and offered to stabe Hobamack; but being a lusty man, he cleared him selfe of him, and came runing away all sweating and tould yᵉ Govʳ what had befalne him, and he feared they had killed Squanto, for they threatened them both, and for no other cause but because they were freinds to yᵉ English, and servisable unto them. Upon this yᵉ Goveʳ taking counsell, it was conceivd not fitt to be borne; for if they should suffer their freinds & messengers thus to be wronged, they should have none would cleave unto them, or give them any inteligence, or doe them serviss afterwards; but nexte they would fall upon them selves. Whereupon it was resolved to send yᵉ Captaine & 14. men well armed, and to goe & fall upon them in yᵉ night; and if they found that Squanto was kild, to cut of Corbitants head, but not to hurt any but those that had a hand in it. Hobamack was asked if he would goe & be their guid, & bring them ther before day. He said he would, & bring them to yᵉ house wher the man lay, and show them which was he. So they set forth y⸍ 14. *of August*, and beset y⸍ house round; the Captin giving charg to let none pass out, entred y⸍ house to search for him. But he was goone away that day, so they mist him; but understood y⸍ Squanto was alive, & that he had only threatened to kill him, & made an offer to stabe him but did not. So they withheld and did no more hurte, & y⸍ people came trembling, & brought them the best provissions they had, after they were aquainted by Hobamack what was only intended. Ther was 3. sore wounded which broak out of y⸍ house, and asaid to pass through y⸍ garde. These they brought home with them, & they had their wounds drest & cured, and sente home. After this they had many gratulations from diverce sachims, and much firmer peace; yea, those of y⸍ Iles of Capawack sent to make frendship; and this Corbitant him selfe used y⸍ mediation of Massassoyte to make his peace, but was shie to come neare them a longe while after.

After this, y⸍ 18. of Septemb⸍: they sente out ther shalop to the Massachusets, with 10. men, and Squanto for their guid and [65] interpreter, to discover and veiw that bay, and trade with y⸍ natives; the which they performed, and found kind entertainement. The people were much affraid of y⸍ Tarentins, a people to y⸍ eastward which used to come in harvest time and take away their corne, & many times kill their persons. They returned in saftie, and brought home a good quanty of beaver, and made reporte of y⸍ place, wishing they had been ther seated; (but it seems y⸍ Lord, who assignes to all men y⸍ bounds of their habitations, had apoynted it for an other use). And thus they found the Lord to be with them in all their ways, and to blesse their outgoings & incomings, for which let his holy name have y⸍ praise for ever, to all posteritie.

They begane now to gather in y⸍ small harvest they had, and to fitte up their houses and dwellings against winter, being all well recovered in health & strenght, and had all things in good plenty; for as some were thus imployed in affairs abroad, others were excersised in fishing, aboute codd, & bass, & other fish, of which y⸍y tooke good store, of which every family had their portion. All y⸍ somer ther was no wante. And now begane to come in store of foule, as winter aproached, of which this place did abound when they came first (but afterward decreased by degrees). And besids water foule, ther was great store of wild Turkies, of which they tooke many, besids venison, &c. Besids they had aboute a peck a meale a weeke to a person, or now since harvest, Indean corne to y^t proportion. Which made many afterwards write so largly of their plenty hear to their freinds in England, which were not fained, but true reports.

In Novemb^r, about ye time twelfe month that them selves came, ther came in a small ship to them unexpected or loked for,[AN] in which came Mr. Cushman (so much spoken of before) and with him 35. persons to remaine & live in ye plantation; which did not a litle rejoyce them. And they when they came a shore and found all well, and saw plenty of vitails in every house, were no less glade. For most of them were lusty yonge men, and many of them wild enough, who litle considered whither or aboute what they wente, till they came into ye harbore at Cap-Codd, and ther saw nothing but a naked and barren place. They then begane to thinke what should become of them, if the people here were dead or cut of by ye Indeans. They begane to consulte (upon some speeches that some of ye sea-men had cast out) to take ye sayls from ye yeard least ye ship [66] should gett away and leave them ther. But ye m^r. hereing of it, gave them good words, and tould them if any thing but well should have befallne ye people hear, he hoped he had vitails enough to cary them to Virginia, and whilst he had a bitt they should have their parte; which gave them good satisfaction. So they were all landed; but ther was not so much as bisket-cake or any other victialls[AO] for them, neither had they any beding, but some sory things they had in their cabins, nor pot, nor pan, to drese any meate in; nor overmany cloaths, for many of them had brusht away their coats & cloaks at Plimoth as they came. But ther was sent over some burching-lane suits in ye ship, out of which they were supplied. The plantation was glad of this addition of strenght, but could have wished that many of them had been of beter condition, and all of them beter furnished with provissions; but y^t could not now be helpte.

In this ship M^r. Weston sent a large leter to M^r. Carver, ye late Gove^r, now deseased, full of complaints & expostulations aboute former passagess at Hampton; and ye keeping ye shipe so long in ye country, and returning her without lading, &c., which for brevitie I omite. The rest is as followeth.

Part of Mr. Westons letter.

I durst never aquainte ye adventurers with ye alteration of ye conditions first agreed on betweene us, which I have since been very glad of, for I am well assured had they knowne as much as I doe, they would not have adventured a halfe-peny of what was necesary for this ship. That you sent no lading in the ship is wonderfull, and worthily distasted. I know you^r weaknes was the cause of it, and I beleeve more weaknes of judgmente, then weaknes of hands. A quarter of ye time you spente in discoursing, arguing, & consulting, would have done much more; but that is past, &c. If you mean, bona fide, to performe the conditions agreed upon, doe us ye favore to coppy them out faire, and subscribe them with ye principall of your names. And likwise give us accounte as perticulerly as you can how our moneys were laid out. And then I shall be able to give them some satisfaction, whom I am now forsed with good words to shift of. And consider that ye life of the bussines depends on ye lading of this ship, which, if you doe to any good purpose, that I may be freed from ye great sums I have disbursed for ye former, and must doe for the later, *I promise you I will never quit ye bussines, though all the other adventurers should.*

[67] We have procured you a Charter, the best we could, which is beter then your former, and with less limitation. For any thing y^t is els worth writting, M^r. Cushman can informe you. I pray write instantly for M^r. Robinson to come to you. And so praying God to blesse you with all graces nessessary both for this life & that to come, I rest

Your very loving frend,

THO. WESTON.

London, July 6. 1621.

This ship (caled ye Fortune) was speedily dispatcht away, being laden with good clapbord as full as she could stowe, and 2. hoggsheads of beaver and otter skins, which they gott with a few trifling comodities brought with them at first, being alltogeather unprovided for trade; neither was ther any amongst them that ever saw a beaver skin till they came hear, and were informed by Squanto. The fraight was estimated to be worth near 500^li. M^r. Cushman returned backe also with this ship, for so Mr. Weston & ye rest had apoynted him, for their better information. And he doubted not, nor them selves neither, but they should have a speedy supply; considering allso how by M^r. Cushmans perswation, and letters received from Leyden, wherin they willed them so to doe, they yeelded[AP] to ye afforesaid conditions, and subscribed them with their hands. But it proved other wise, for Mr. Weston, who had made ye large promise in his leter, (as is before noted,) that if all ye rest should fall of, yet he would never quit ye bussines, but stick to them, if they yeelded to ye conditions, and sente some lading in ye ship; and of this M^r. Cushman was confident, and confirmed ye same from his mouth, & serious protestations to him selfe before he came. But all proved but wind, for he was ye first and only man that forsooke them, and that before he so much as heard of ye returne of this ship, or knew what was done; (so vaine is the confidence in man.) But of this more in its place.

A leter in answer to his write to M^r. Carver, was sente to him from ye Govr, of which so much as is pertenente to ye thing in hand I shall hear inserte.

S^r: Your large letter writen to M^r. Carver, and dated ye 6. of July, 1621, I have received ye 10. of Novemb^r, wherin (after ye apologie made for your selfe) you lay many heavie imputations upon him and us all. Touching him, he is departed this life, and now is at rest [68] in ye Lord from all those troubls and incoumbrances with which we are yet to strive. He needs not my appologie; for his care and pains was so great for ye commone good, both ours and yours, as that therwith (it is thought) he oppressed him selfe and shortened his days; of whose loss we cannot sufficiently complaine. At great charges in this adventure, I confess you have beene, and many losses may sustaine; but yᵉ loss of his and many other honest and industrious mens lives, cannot be vallewed at any prise. Of yᵉ one, ther may be hope of recovery, but yᵉ other no recompence can make good. But I will not insiste in generalls, but come more perticulerly to yᵉ things them selves. You greatly blame us for keping yᵉ ship so long in yᵉ countrie, and then to send her away emptie. She lay 5. weks at Cap-Codd, whilst with many a weary step (after a long journey) and the indurance of many a hard brunte, we sought out in the foule winter a place of habitation. Then we went in so tedious a time to make provission to sheelter us and our goods, aboute wᶜʰ labour, many of our armes & leggs can tell us to this day we were not necligent. But it pleased God to vissite us then, with death dayly, and with so generall a disease, that the living were scarce able to burie the dead; and yᵉ well not in any measure sufficiente to tend yᵉ sick. And now to be so greatly blamed, for not fraighting yᵉ ship, doth indeed goe near us, and much discourage us. But you say you know we will pretend weaknes; and doe you think we had not cause? Yes, you tell us you beleeve it, but it was more weaknes of judgmente, then of hands. Our weaknes herin is great we confess, therfore we will bear this check patiently amongst yᵉ rest, till God send us wiser men. But they which tould you we spent so much time in discoursing & consulting, &c., their harts can tell their toungs, they lye. They cared not, so they might salve their owne sores, how they wounded others. Indeed, it is our callamitie that we are (beyound expectation) yoked with some ill conditioned people, who will never doe good, but corrupte and abuse others, &c.

The rest of yᵉ letter declared how they had subscribed those conditions according to his desire, and sente him yᵉ former accounts very perticulerly; also how yᵉ ship was laden, and in what condition their affairs stood; that yᵉ coming of these [69] people would bring famine upon them unavoydably, if they had not supply in time (as Mr. Cushman could more fully informe him & yᵉ rest of yᵉ adventurers). Also that seeing he was now satisfied in all his demands, that offences would be forgoten, and he remember his promise, &c.

After ye departure of this ship, (which stayed not above 14. days,) the Gove^r & his assistante haveing disposed these late comers into severall families, as y^ey best could, tooke an exacte accounte of all their provissions in store, and proportioned ye same to ye number of persons, and found that it would not hould out above 6. months at halfe alowance, and hardly that. And they could not well give less this winter time till fish came in againe. So they were presently put to half alowance, one as well as an other, which begane to be hard, but they bore it patiently under hope of supply.

Sone after this ships departure, ye great people of ye Narigansets, in a braving maner, sente a messenger unto them with a bundl of arrows tyed aboute with a great sneak-skine; which their interpretours tould them was a threatening & a chaleng. Upon which ye Govr, with ye advice of others, sente them a round answere, that if they had rather have warre then peace, they might begine when they would; they had done them no wrong, neither did y^ey fear them, or should they find them unprovided. And by another messenger sente ye sneake-skine back with bulits in it; but they would not receive it, but sent it back againe. But these things I doe but mention, because they are more at large allready put forth in printe, by M^r. Winslow, at ye requeste of some freinds. And it is like ye reason was their owne ambition, who, (since ye death of so many of ye Indeans,) thought to dominire & lord it over ye rest, & conceived ye English would be a barr in their way, and saw that Massasoyt took sheilter allready under their wings.

But this made them ye more carefully to looke to them selves, so as they agreed to inclose their dwellings with a good strong pale, and make flankers in convenient places, with gates to shute, which were every night locked, and a watch kept, and when neede required ther was also warding in ye day time. And ye company was by ye Captaine and ye Govr [70] advise, devided into 4. squadrons, and every one had ther quarter apoynted them, unto which they were to repaire upon any suddane alarme. And if ther should be any crie of fire, a company were appointed for a gard, with muskets, whilst others quenchet yᵉ same, to prevent Indean treachery. This was accomplished very cherfully, and yᵉ towne impayled round by yᵉ begining of March, in which evry family had a prety garden plote secured. And herewith I shall end this year. Only I shall remember one passage more, rather of mirth then of waight. One yᵉ day called Chrismasday, yᵉ Govʳ caled them out to worke, (as was used,) but yᵉ most of this new-company excused them selves and said it wente against their consciences to work on yᵗ day. So yᵉ Govʳ tould them that if they made it mater of conscience, he would spare them till they were better informed. So he led-away yᵉ rest and left them; but when they came home at noone from their worke, he found them in yᵉ streete at play, openly; some pitching yᵉ barr, & some at stoole-ball, and shuch like sports. So he went to them, and tooke away their implements, and tould them that was against his conscience, that they should play & others worke. If they made yᵉ keeping of it mater of devotion, let them kepe their houses, but ther should be no gameing or revelling in yᵉ streets. Since which time nothing hath been atempted that way, at least openly.

Anno 1622.

At yᵉ spring of yᵉ year they had apointed yᵉ Massachusets to come againe and trade with them, and begane now to prepare for that vioag about yᵉ later end of March. But upon some rumors heard, Hobamak, their Indean, tould them upon some jealocies he had, he feared they were joyned wᵗʰ yᵉ Narighansets and might betray them if they were not carefull. He intimated also some jealocie of Squanto, by what he gathered from some private whisperings betweene him and other Indeans. But [71] they resolved to proseede, and sente out their shalop with 10. of their cheefe men aboute yᵉ begining of Aprill, and both Squanto & Hobamake with them, in regarde of yᵉ jelocie betweene them. But they had not bene gone longe, but an Indean belonging to Squantos family came runing in seeming great fear, and tould them that many of yᵉ Narihgansets, with Corbytant, and he thought also Massasoyte, were coming against them; and he gott away to tell them, not without danger. And being examined by y⁰ Gov⁰, he made as if they were at hand, and would still be looking back, as if they were at his heels. At which the Governor caused them to take armes & stand on their garde, and supposing y⁰ boat to be still within hearing (by reason it was calme) caused a warning peece or 2. to be shote of, the which y⁰ʸ heard and came in. But no Indeans apeared; watch was kepte all night, but nothing was scene. Hobamak was confidente for Massasoyt, and thought all was false; yet y⁰ Gov⁰ caused him to send his wife privatly, to see what she could observe (pretening other occasions), but ther was nothing found, but all was quiet. After this they proseeded on their vioge to y⁰ Massachusets, and had good trade, and returned in saftie, blessed be God.

But by the former passages, and other things of like nature, they begane to see yᵗ Squanto sought his owne ends, and plaid his owne game, by putting y⁰ Indeans in fear, and drawing gifts from them to enrich him selfe; making them beleeve he could stur up warr against whom he would, & make peece for whom he would. Yea, he made them beleeve they kept y⁰ plague buried in y⁰ ground, and could send it amongs whom they would, which did much terrifie the Indeans, and made them depend more on him, and seeke more to him then to Massasoyte, which proucured him envie, and had like to have cost him his life. For after y⁰ discovery of his practises, Massasoyt sought it both privatly and openly; which caused him to stick close to y⁰ English, & never durst goe from them till he dyed. They also made good use of y⁰ emulation yᵗ grue betweene Hobamack and him, which made them cary more squarely. And y⁰ Gov⁰ seemed to countenance y⁰ one, and y⁰ Captaine y⁰ other, by which they had better intelligence, and made them both more diligente.

[72] Now in a maner their provissions were wholy spent, and they looked hard for supply, but none came. But about y⁰ *later end of May*, they spied *a boat* at sea, which at first they thought had beene some Frenchman; but it proved a shalop which came from a ship which Mʳ. Weston & an other had set out a fishing, at a place called Damarins-cove, 40. leagues to y⁰ eastward of them, wher

were yᵗ year many more ships come a fishing. This boat brought 7. passengers and some letters, but no vitails, nor any hope of any. Some part of which I shall set downe.

Mʳ. Carver, in my last leters by yᵉ Fortune, in whom Mʳ Cushman wente, and who I hope is with you, for we daly expecte yᵉ shipe back againe. She departed hence, yᵉ begining of July, with 35. persons, though not over well provided with necesaries, by reason of yᵉ parsemonie of yᵉ adventurers.⁽ᴬ🇶⁾ I have solisited them to send you a supply of men and provissions before shee come. They all answer they will doe great maters, when they hear good news. Nothing before; so faithfull, constant, & carefull of your good, are your olde & honest freinds, that if they hear not from you, they are like to send you no supplie, &c. I am now to relate yᵉ occasion of sending *this ship*, hoping if you give credite to my words, you will have a more favourable opinion of it, then some hear, wherof Pickering is one, who taxed me to mind my owne ends, which is in part true, &c. *Mʳ. Beachamp and my selfe* bought *this litle ship*, and have set her out, partly, if it may be, to uphold⁽ᴬᴿ⁾ yᵉ plantation, as well to doe others good as our selves; and partly to gett up what we are formerly out; though we are otherwise censured, &c. This is yᵉ occasion we have sent *this ship* and these passengers, on our owne accounte; whom we desire you will frendly entertaine & supply with shuch necesaries as you cane spare, and they wante, &c. And among other things we pray you lend or sell them some seed corne, and if you have yᵉ salt remaining of yᵉ last year, that yᵘ will let them have it for their presente use, and we will either pay you for it, or give you more when we have set our salt-pan to worke, which we desire may be set up in one of yᵉ litle ilands in your bay, &c. And because we intende, if God plase, [73] (and yᵉ generallitie doe it not,) *to send within a month another shipe*, who, having discharged her passengers, *shal goe to Virginia*, &c. And it may be we shall send a *small ship to abide with you* on yᵉ coast, which I conceive may be a great help to yᵉ plantation. To yᵉ end our desire may be effected, which, I assure my selfe, will be also for your good, we pray you give them entertainmente in your houses yᵉ time they shall be with you, that they may lose no time, but may presently goe in hand to fell trees & cleave them, to y⸰ end lading may be ready and our ship stay not.

Some of y⸰ adventurers have sent you hearwith all some directions for your furtherance in y⸰ comone bussines, who are like those S¹. James speaks of, y¹ bid their brother eat, and warme him, but give him nothing; so they bid you make salt, and uphold y⸰ plantation, but send you no means wherwithall to doe it, &c. By *y⸰ next* we purpose *to send more people on our owne accounte*, and *to take a patente*; that if your peopl should be as unhumane as some of y⸰ adventurers, not to admite us to dwell with them, which were extreme barbarisme, and which will never enter into my head to thinke you have any shuch Pickerings amongst you. Yet to satisfie our passengers I must of force doe it; and for some other reasons not necessary to be writen, &c. I find y⸰ generall so backward, and your freinds at Leyden so could, that I fear you must stand on your leggs, and trust (as they say) to God and your selves.

Subscribed,

your loving freind,

THO: WESTON.

Jan: 12. 1621.

Sundry other things I pass over, being tedious & impertinent.

All this was but could comfort to fill their hungrie bellies, and a slender performance of his former late promiss; and as litle did it either fill or warme them, as those y⸰ Apostle James spake of, by him before mentioned. And well might it make them remember what y⸰ psalmist saith, Psa. 118. 8. *It is better to trust in the Lord, then to have confidence in man.* And Psa. 146. *Put not you trust in princes* (much less in y⸰ marchants) *nor in y⸰ sone of man, for ther is no help in them.* v. 5. *Blesed is he that hath y⸰ God of Jacob for his help, whose hope is in y⸰ Lord his God.* And as they were now fayled of suply by him and others in this their greatest neede and wants, which was caused by him and y⸰ rest, who put so great a company of men upon them, as yᵉ former company were, without any food, and came at shuch a time as they must live almost a whole year before any could [74] be raised, excepte they had sente some; so, upon yᵉ pointe they never had any supply of vitales more afterwards (but what the Lord gave them otherwise); for all yᵉ company sent at any time was allways too short for those people yᵗ came with it.

Ther came allso *by yᵉ same ship* other leters, but of later date, one from Mʳ. Weston, an other from a parte of yᵉ adventurers, as foloweth.

Mʳ. Carver, since my last, to yᵉ end we might yᵉ more readily proceed to help yᵉ generall, at a meeting of some of yᵉ principall adventurers, a proposition was put forth, & alowed by all presente (save Pickering), to adventure each man yᵉ third parte of what he formerly had done. And ther are some other yᵗ folow his example, and will adventure no furder. In regard wherof yᵉ greater part of yᵉ adventurers being willing to uphold yᵉ bussines, finding it no reason that those yᵗ are willing should uphold yᵉ bussines of those that are unwilling, whose backwardnes doth discourage those that are forward, and hinder other new-adventurers from coming in, we having well considered therof, have resolved, according to an article in yᵉ agreemente, (*that it may be lawfull by a generall consente of yᵉ adventurers & planters, upon just occasion, to breake of their joynte stock,*) to breake it of; and doe pray you to ratifie, and confirme yᵉ same on your parts. Which being done, we shall yᵉ more willingly goe forward for yᵉ upholding of you with all things necesarie. But in any case you must agree to yᵉ artickls, and send it by yᵉ first under your hands & seals. So I end

Your loving freind,

THO: WESTON.

Jan: 17. 1621.

Another leter was write from part of yᵉ company of yᵉ adventurers to the same purpose, and subscribed with 9. of their names, wherof M^r. Westons & M^r. Beachamphs were tow. Thes things seemed strang unto them, seeing this unconstancie & shufling; it made them to thinke ther was some misterie in ye matter. And therfore ye Govr concealed these letters from ye publick, only imparted them to some trustie freinds for advice, who concluded with him, that this tended to disband & scater them (in regard of their straits); and if M^r. Weston & others, who seemed to rune in a perticuler way, should come over with shiping so provided as his letters did intimate, they most would fall to him, to ye prejudice of them selves & ye rest of the adventurers,[AS] their freinds, from whom as yet they heard nothing. And it was doubted whether he had not sente [75] over shuch a company in ye former ship, for shuch an end. Yet they tooke compassion of those 7. men which *this ship, which fished to ye eastward, had kept till planting time was over,* and so could set no corne; and allso wanting vitals, (for y^ey turned them off w^thout any, and indeed wanted for them selves,) neither was their salt-pan come, so as y^ey could not performe any of those things which M^r. Weston had apointed, and might have starved if ye plantation had not succoured them; who, in their wants, gave them as good as any of their owne. *The ship wente to Virginia,* wher they sould both ship & fish, of which (it was conceived) M^r. Weston had a very slender accounte.

After this came another of his ships, and brought letters dated ye 10. of Aprill, from M^r. Weston, as followeth.

M^r. Bradford, these, &c. *The Fortune* is arived, of whose good news touching your estate & proceēings, I am very glad to hear. And how soever he was robed on ye way by ye Frenchmen, yet I hope your loss will not be great, for ye conceite of so great a returne doth much animate ye adventurers, so y^t I hope some matter of importance will be done by them, &c. As for my selfe, I have sould my adventure & debts unto them, so as I am quit[AT] of you, & you of me, for that matter, &c. Now though I have nothing to pretend as an adventurer amongst you, yet I will advise you a litle for your good, if you can apprehend it. I perceive & know as well as another, ye dispositions of *your adventurers,* whom ye hope of gaine hath drawne on to this they have done; and yet I fear y^t hope will not draw them much furder. Besids, *most of them are against the sending of them of Leyden, for whose cause this bussines was first begune*, and some of yᵉ most religious (as Mʳ. Greene by name) excepts against them. So yᵗ my advice is (you may follow it if you please) that you forthwith break of your joynte stock, which you have warente to doe, both in law & conscience, for yᵉ most parte of yᵉ adventurers have given way unto it by a former letter. And yᵉ means you have ther, which I hope will be to some purpose by yᵉ trade of this spring, may, with yᵉ help of some freinds hear, bear yᵉ charge of trāsporting those of Leyden; and when they are with you I make no question but by Gods help you will be able to subsist of your selves. But I shall leave you to your discretion.

I desired diverce of yᵉ adventurers, as Mʳ. Peirce, Mʳ. Greene, & others, if they had any thing to send you, either vitails or leters, to send them *by these ships*; and marvelling they sent not so much as a letter, I asked our passengers what leters they had, and with some dificultie one of them tould me he had one, which was delivered him with [76] great charge of secrecie; and for more securitie, to buy a paire of new-shoes, & sow it betweene yᵉ soles for fear of intercepting. I, taking yᵉ leter, wondering what mistrie might be in it, broke it open, and found this treacherous letter subscribed by yᵉ hands of Mʳ. Pickering & Mʳ. Greene. Wich leter had it come to youʳ hands without answer, might have caused yᵉ hurt, if not yᵉ ruine, of us all. For assuredly if you had followed their instructions, and shewed us that unkindness which they advise you unto, to hold us in distruste as enimise, &c., it might have been an occasion to have set us togeather by yᵉ eares, to yᵉ distruction of us all. For I doe beleeve that in shuch a case, they knowing what bussines hath been betweene us, not only my brother, but others also, would have been violent, and heady against you, &c. I mente to have setled yᵉ people I before and now send, with or near you, as well for their as your more securitie and defence, as help on all occasions. But I find yᵉ adventurers so jealous & suspitious, that I have altered my resolution, & given order to my brother & those with him, to doe as they and him selfe shall find fitte. Thus, &c.

Your loving freind,

THO: WESTON.

Aprill 10. 1621.

Some part of Mr. Pickerings letter before mentioned.

To Mʳ. Bradford & Mʳ. Brewster, &c.

My dear love remembred unto you all, &c. The company hath bought out Mʳ. Weston, and are very glad they are freed of him, he being judged a man yᵗ thought him selfe above yᵉ generall, and not expresing so much yᵉ fear of God as was meete in a man to whom shuch trust should have been reposed in a matter of so great importance. I am sparing to be so plaine as indeed is clear against him; but a few words to yᵉ wise.

Mʳ. Weston will not permitte leters to be sent in *his ships*, nor any thing for your good or ours, of which ther is some reason in respecte of him selfe, &c. His brother Andrew, whom he doth send as principall *in one of these ships*, is a heady yong man, & violente, and set against you ther, & yᵉ company hear; ploting with Mʳ. Weston their owne ends, which tend to your & our undooing in respecte of our estates ther, and prevention of our good ends. For by credible testimoney we are informed his purpose is to come to your colonie, pretending he comes for and from yᵉ adventurers, and will seeke to gett what you have in readynes [77] into *his ships*, as if they came from yᵉ company, & possessing all, will be so much profite to him selfe. And further to informe them selves what spetiall places or things you have discovered, to yᵉ end that they may supres & deprive you, &c.

The Lord, who is yᵉ watchman of Israll & slepeth not, preserve you & deliver you from unreasonable men. I am sorie that ther is cause to admonish you of these things concerning this man; so I leave you to God, who bless and multiply you into thousands, to the advancemente of yᵉ glorious gospell of our Lord Jesus. Amen. Fare well.

Your loving freinds,

EDWARD PICKERING.

WILLIAM GREENE.

I pray conceale both yᵉ writing & deliverie of this leter, but make the best use of it. *We hope to sete forth a ship our selves with in this month.*

The heads of his answer.

Mʳ. Bradford, this is yᵉ leter yᵗ I wrote unto you of, which to answer in every perticuler is needles & tedious. My owne conscience & all our people can and I thinke will testifie, yᵗ my end in sending yᵉ *ship Sparrow* was your good, &c. Now I will not deney but ther are many of our people rude fellows, as these men terme them; yet I presume they will be governed by such as I set over them. And I hope not only to be able to reclaime them from yᵗ profanenes that may scandalise yᵉ vioage, but by degrees to draw them to God, &c. I am so farr from sending rude fellows to deprive you either by fraude or violence of what is yours, as I have charged yᵉ mʳ. of yᵉ *ship Sparrow*, not only to leave with you 2000. of bread, but also a good quantitie of fish,⁽ᴬᵁ⁾ &c. But I will leave it to you to consider what evill this leter would or might have done, had it come to your hands & taken yᵉ effecte yᵉ other desired.

Now if you be of yᵉ mind yᵗ these men are, deale plainly with us, & we will seeke our residence els-wher. If you are as freindly as we have thought you to be, give us yᵉ entertainment of freinds, and we will take nothing from you, neither meat, drinke, nor lodging, but what we will, in one kind or other, pay you for, &c. I shall leave in yᵉ countrie *a litle ship* (if God send her safe thither) with mariners & fisher-men to stay ther, who shall coast, & trad with yᵉ savages, & yᵉ old plantation. It may be we shall be as helpfull to you, as you will be to us. I thinke I shall see you yᵉ next spring; and so I comend you to yᵉ protection of God, who ever keep you.

Your loving freind,

THO: WESTON.

[78] Thus all ther hops in regard of M^r. Weston were layed in ye dust, and all his promised helpe turned into an empttie advice, which they apprehended was nether lawfull nor profitable for them to follow. And they were not only thus left destitute of help in their extreme wants, haveing neither vitails, nor any thing to trade with, but others prepared & ready to glean up what ye cuntrie might have afforded for their releefe. As for those harsh censures & susspitions intimated in ye former and following leters, they desired to judg as charitably and wisly of them as they could, waighing them in ye ballance of love and reason; and though they (in parte) came from godly & loveing freinds, yet they conceived many things might arise from over deepe jealocie and fear, togeather with unmeete provocations, though they well saw M^r. Weston pursued his owne ends, and was imbittered in spirite. For after the receit of ye former leters, the Govr received one from M^r. Cushman, who went home in ye ship, and was allway intimate with M^r. Weston, (as former passages declare), and it was much marveled that nothing was heard from him, all this while. But it should seeme it was ye difficulty of sending, for this leter was directed as ye leter of a wife to her husband, who was here, and brought by him to ye Govr. It was as followeth.

Beloved S^r: I hartily salute you, with trust of your health, and many thanks for your love. By Gods providence we got well home ye 17. *of Feb*. Being robbed by ye French-men by ye way, and carried by them into France, and were kepte ther 15. days, and lost all y^t we had that was worth taking; but thanks be to God, we escaped with our lives & ship. I see not y^t it worketh any discouragment hear. I purpose by Gods grace *to see you* shortly, *I hope in June nexte, or before*. In ye mean space know these things, and I pray you be advertised a litle. M^r. Weston hath quite broken of from our company, through some discontents y^t arose betwext him and some of our adventurers, & hath sould all his adventurs, & *hath now sent 3. smale ships for his perticuler plantation*. The *greatest* wherof, *being 100. tune*, M^r. Reynolds goeth m^r. and he with ye rest purposeth to come him selfe; for what end I know not.

The people which they cary are no men for us, wherfore I pray you entertaine them not, neither exchainge man for man with them, excepte it be some of your worst. He hath taken a patente for him selfe. If they offerr to buy any thing of you, let it be shuch as you can spare, and let them give ye worth of it. If they borrow any thing of you, let them leave a good pawne, &c. It is like he [78[AV]] will plant to ye southward of ye Cape, for William Trevore hath lavishly tould but what he knew or imagined of Capewack, Mohiggen, & ye Narigansets. I fear these people will hardly deale so well with ye savages as they should. I pray you therfore signifie to Squanto, that they are a distincte body from us, and we have nothing to doe with them, neither must be blamed for their falts, much less can warrente their fidelitie. We are aboute to recover our losses in France. Our freinds at Leyden are well, and will come to you as many as can *this time*. I hope all will turne to ye best, wherfore I pray you be not discouraged, but gather up your selfe to goe thorow these dificulties cherfully & with courage in y^r place wherin God hath sett you, untill ye day of refreshing come. And ye Lord God of sea & land bring us comfortably togeather againe, if it may stand with his glorie.

Yours,

ROBART CUSHMAN.

On ye other sid of ye leafe, in ye same leter, came these few lines from M^r. John Peirce, in whose name the patente was taken, and of whom more will follow, to be spoken in its place.

Worthy S^r: I desire you to take into consideration that which is writen on ye other side, and not any way to damnifie your owne collony, whos strength is but weaknes, and may therby be more infeebled. And for ye leters of association, by ye next ship we send, I hope you shall receive satisfaction; in ye mean time whom you admite I will approve. But as for M^r. Weston's company, I thinke them so base in condition (for ye most parte) as in all apearance not fitt for an honest mans company. I wish they prove other wise. My purpose is not to enlarge my selfe, but cease in these few lins, and so rest

Your loving freind,

JOHN PEIRCE.

All these things they pondred and well considered, yet concluded to give his men frendly entertainmente; partly in regard of M^r. Weston him selfe, considering what he had been unto them, & done for them, & to some, more espetially; and partly in compassion to ye people, who were now come into a willdernes, (as them selves were,) and were by y^e *ship* to be presently put a shore, (for she was *to cary other passengers to Virginia*, who lay at great charge,) and they were alltogeather unacquainted & knew not what to doe. So as they had received his former company of 7. men, and vitailed them as their owne hitherto, so they also received *these* (being aboute 60. lusty men), and gave [79] housing for them selves and their goods; and many being sicke, they had ye best means ye place could aford them. They stayed hear ye most parte of ye somer till *ye ship came back againe from Virginia*. Then, by his direction, or those whom he set over them, they removed into ye Massachusset Bay, he having got a patente for some part ther, (by light of ther former discovery in leters sent home). Yet they left all ther sicke folke hear till they were setled and housed. But of ther victails they had not any, though they were in great wante, nor any thing els in recompence of any courtecie done them; neither did they desire it, for they saw they were an unruly company, and had no good govermente over them, and by disorder would soone fall into wants if M^r. Weston came not ye sooner amongst them; and therfore, to prevente all after occasion, would have nothing of them.

Amids these streigths, and ye desertion of those from whom they had hoped for supply, and when famine begane now to pinch them sore, they not knowing what to doe, the Lord, (who never fails his,) presents them with an occasion, beyond all expectation. This boat which came from ye eastward brought them a letter from a stranger, of whose name they had never heard before, being a captaine of a ship come ther a fishing. This leter was as followeth. Being thus inscribed.

To all his good freinds at Plimoth, these, &c.

Freinds, cuntrimen, & neighbours: I salute you, and wish you all health and hapines in ye Lord. I make bould with these few lines to trouble you, because unless I were unhumane, I can doe no less. Bad news doth spread it selfe too farr; yet I will so farr informe you that my selfe, with many good freinds in ye south-collonie of Virginia, have received shuch a blow, that 400. persons large will not make good our losses. Therfore I doe intreat you (allthough not knowing you) that ye old rule which I learned when I went to schoole, may be sufficente. That is, Hapie is he whom other mens harmes doth make to beware. And now againe and againe, wishing all those y^t willingly would serve ye Lord, all health and happines in this world, and everlasting peace in ye world to come. And so I rest,

Yours,

JOHN HUDLSTON.

By this boat ye Govr returned a thankfull answer, as was meete, and sent a boate of their owne with them, which was piloted by them, in which M^r. Winslow was sente to procure what provissions he could of ye ships, who was kindly received by ye foresaid gentill-man, who not only spared what he [90^[AW]] could, but writ to others to doe ye like. By which means he gott some good quantitie and returned in saftie, by which ye plantation had a duble benefite, first, a present refreshing by ye food brought, and secondly, they knew ye way to those parts for their benifite hearafter. But what was gott, & this small boat brought, being devided among so many, came but to a litle, yet by Gods blesing it upheld them till harvest. It arose but to a quarter of a pound of bread a day to each person; and ye Govr caused it to be dayly given them, otherwise, had it been in their owne custody, they would have eate it up & then starved. But thus, with what els they could get, they made pretie shift till corne was ripe.

This somer they builte a fort with good timber, both strong & comly, which was of good defence, made with a flate rofe & batllments, on which their ordnance were mounted, and wher they kepte constante watch, espetially in time of danger. It served them allso for a meeting house, and was fitted accordingly for that use. It was a great worke for them in this weaknes and time of wants; but yᵉ deanger of yᵉ time required it, and both yᵉ continuall rumors of yᵉ fears from yᵉ Indeans hear, espetially yᵉ Narigansets, and also yᵉ hearing of that great massacre in Virginia, made all hands willing to despatch yᵉ same.

Now yᵉ wellcome time of harvest aproached, in which all had their hungrie bellies filled. But it arose but to a litle, in comparison of a full years supplie; partly by reason they were not yet well aquainted with yᵉ maner of Indean corne, (and they had no other,) allso their many other imployments, but cheefly their weaknes for wante of food, to tend it as they should have done. Also much was stolne both by night & day, before it became scarce eatable, & much more afterward. And though many were well whipt (when they were taken) for a few ears of corne, yet hunger made others (whom conscience did not restraine) to venture. So as it well appeared yᵉ famine must still insue yᵉ next year allso, if not some way prevented, or supplie should faile, to which they durst not trust. Markets there was none to goe too, but only yᵉ Indeans, and they had no trading comodities. Behold now another providence of God; a ship comes into yᵉ [91] harbor, one Captain Jons being cheefe therin. They were set out by some marchants to discovere all yᵉ harbors betweene this & Virginia, and yᵉ shoulds of Cap-Cod, and to trade along yᵉ coast wher they could. This ship had store of English-beads (which were then good trade) and some knives, but would sell none but at dear rates, and also a good quantie togeather. Yet they weere glad of yᵉ occasion, and faine to buy at any rate; they were faine to give after yᵉ rate of cento per cento, if not more, and yet pay away coat-beaver at 3ˢ. perˡⁱ, which in a few years after yeelded 20ˢ. By this means they were fitted againe to trade for beaver & other things, and intended to buy what corne they could.

But I will hear take liberty to make a litle digression. Ther was in *this ship* a gentle-man by name Mʳ. John Poory; he had been secretarie in Virginia, and was now going home passenger *in this ship*. After his departure he write a leter to yᵉ Govʳ in the postscrite wherof he hath these lines.

To your selfe and Mʳ. Brewster, I must acknowledg my selfe many ways indebted, whose books I would have you thinke very well bestowed on him, who esteemeth them shuch juells. My hast would not suffer me to remember (much less to begg) Mʳ. Ainsworths elaborate worke upon yᵉ 5. books of Moyses. Both his & Mʳ. Robinsons doe highly commend the authors, as being most conversante in yᵉ scripturs of all others. And what good (who knows) it may please God to worke by them, through my hands, (though most unworthy,) who finds shuch high contente in them. God have you all in his keeping.

Your unfained and firme friend,

JOHN PORY.

Aug. 28. 1622.

These things I hear inserte for honour sake of yᵉ authors memorie, which this gentle-man doth thus ingeniusly acknowledg; and him selfe after his returne did this poore-plantation much credite amongst those of no mean ranck. But to returne.

[92] *Shortly after harvest* Mʳ. Westons people who were now seated at yᵉ Massachusets, and by disorder (as it seems) had made havock of their provissions, begane now to perceive that want would come upon them. And hearing that they hear had bought trading comodities & intended to trade for corne, they write to yᵉ Govʳ and desired they might joyne with them, and they would imploy their small ship in yᵉ servise; and furder requested either to

lend or sell them so much of their trading comodities as their part might come to, and they would undertake to make paymente when M^r. Weston, or their supply, should come. The Govr condesended upon equall terms of agreemente, thinkeing to goe aboute ye Cap to ye southward with ye ship, wher some store of corne might be got. Althings being provided, Captaint Standish was apointed to goe with them, and Squanto for a guid & interpreter, about y^e *latter end of September*; but ye winds put them in againe, & putting out ye 2. time, he fell sick of a feavor, so ye Govr wente him selfe. But they could not get aboute ye should of Cap-Cod, for flats & breakers, neither could Squanto directe them better, nor ye m^r. durst venture any further, so they put into Manamoyack Bay and got w^{t[AX]} they could ther. In this place Squanto fell sick of an Indean feavor, bleeding much at ye nose (which ye Indeans take for a simptome of death), and within a few days dyed ther; desiring ye Govr to pray for him, that he might goe to ye Englishmens God in heaven, and bequeathed sundrie of his things to sundry of his English freinds, as remembrances of his love; of whom they had a great loss. They got in this vioage, in one place & other, about 26. or 28. hogsheads of corne & beans, which was more then the Indeans could well spare in these parts, for ye set but a litle till they got English hows. And so were faine to returne, being sory they could not gett about the Cap, to have been better laden. After ward ye Govr tooke a few men & wente to ye inland places, to get what he could, and to fetch it home at ye spring, which did help them something.

[93] After these things, in *Feb*: a messenger came from John Sanders, who was left cheefe over M^r. Weston's men in ye bay of Massachusets, who brought a letter shewing the great wants they were falen into; and he would have borrowed a hh of corne of ye Indeans, but they would lend him none. He desired advice whether he might not take it from them by force to succore his men till he came from ye eastward, whither he was going. The Govr & rest deswaded him by all means from it, for it might so exasperate the Indeans as might endanger their saftie, and all of us might smart for it; for they had already heard how they had so wronged ye Indeans by stealing their corne, &c. as they were much incensed against

them. Yea, so base were some of their own company, as they wente & tould yᵉ Indeans yᵗ their Govʳ was purposed to come and take their corne by force. The which with other things made them enter into a conspiracie against yᵉ English, of which more in yᵉ nexte. Hear with I end this year.

Anno Dom: 1623.

It may be thought strang that these people should fall to these extremities in so short a time, being left competently provided when yᵉ ship left them, and had an addition by that moyetie of corn that was got by trade, besids much they gott of yᵉ Indans wher they lived, by one means & other. It must needs be their great disorder, for they spent excesseivly whilst they had, or could get it; and, it may be, wasted parte away among yᵉ Indeans (for he yᵗ was their cheef was taxed by some amongst them for keeping Indean women, how truly I know not). And after they begane to come into wants, many sould away their cloathes and bed coverings; others (so base were they) became servants to yᵉ Indeans, and would cutt them woode & fetch them water, for a cap full of corne; others fell to plaine stealing, both night & day, from yᵉ Indeans, of which they greevosly complained. In yᵉ end, they came to that misery, that some starved & dyed with could & hunger. One in geathering shell-fish was so weake as he stuck fast in yᵉ mudd, and was found dead in yᵉ place. At last most of them left their dwellings & scatered up & downe in yᵉ [94] woods, & by yᵉ water sids, wher they could find ground nuts & clames, hear 6. and ther ten. By which their cariages they became contemned & scorned of yᵉ Indeans, and they begane greatly to insulte over them in a most insolente maner; insomuch, many times as they lay thus scatered abrod, and had set on a pot with ground nuts or shell-fish, when it was ready the Indeans would come and eate it up; and when night came, wheras some of them had a sorie blanket, or such like, to lappe them selves in, the Indeans would take it and let yᵉ other lye all nighte in the could; so as their condition was very lamentable. Yea, in yᵉ end they were faine to hange one of their men, whom they could not reclaime from stealing, to give yᵉ Indeans contente.

Whilst things wente in this maner with them, yᵉ Govʳ & people hear had notice yᵗ Massasoyte ther freind was sick & near unto death. They sent to vissete him, and withall sente him such comfortable things as gave him great contente, and was a means of his recovery; upon which occasion he discovers yᵉ conspiracie of these Indeans, how they were resolved to cutt of Mʳ. Westons people, for the continuall injuries they did them, & would now take opportunitie of their weaknes to doe it; and for that end had conspired with other Indeans their neighbours their aboute. And thinking the people hear would revenge their death, they therfore thought to doe yᵉ like by them, & had solisited him to joyne with them. He advised them therfore to prevent it, and that speedly by taking of some of yᵉ cheefe of them, before it was to late, for he asured them of yᵉ truth hereof.

This did much trouble them, and they tooke it into serious delibration, and found upon examenation other evidence to give light hear unto, to longe hear to relate. In yᵉ mean time, came one of them from yᵉ Massachucets, with a small pack at his back; and though he knew not a foote of yᵉ way, yet he got safe hither, but lost his way, which was well for him, for he was pursued, and so was mist. He tould them hear how all things stood amongst them, and that he durst stay no longer, he apprehended they (by what he observed) would be all knokt in yᵉ head shortly. This made them make yᵉ more hast, & dispatched a boate away wᵗʰ Capten Standish & some men, who found them in a miserable condition, out of which he rescued them, and helped them to some releef, cut of some few of yᵉ cheefe conspirators, and, according to his order, offered to bring them all hither if they thought good; and they should fare no worse then them selves, till Mʳ. Weston or some supplie came to them. Or, if any other course liked them better, he was to doe them any helpfullnes he could. They thanked him & yᵉ rest. But most of them desired he would help them with some corne, and they would goe with their smale ship to yᵉ eastward, wher hapily they might here of Mʳ. Weston, or some supply from him, seing yᵉ time of yᵉ year was for fishing ships to [95] be in yᵉ land. If not, they would worke among ye fishermen for their liveing, and get ther passage into England, if they heard nothing from M^r. Weston in time. So they shipped what they had of any worth, and he got them all ye corne he could (scarce leaving to bring him home), and saw them well out of the bay, under saile at sea, and so came home, not takeing ye worth of a peny of any thing that was theirs. I have but touched these things breefly, because they have allready been published in printe more at large.

This was ye end of these that some time bosted of their strength, (being all able lustie men,) and what they would doe & bring to pass, in comparison of ye people hear, who had many women & children and weak ons amongst them; and said at their first arivall, when they saw the wants hear, that they would take an other course, and not to fall into shuch a condition, as this simple people were come too. But a mans way is not in his owne power; God can make ye weake to stand; let him also that standeth take heed least he fall.

Shortly after, M^r. Weston came over with some of ye fishermen, under another name, and ye disguise of a blacke-smith, were he heard of ye ruine and disolution of his colony. He got a boat and with a man or 2. came to see how things were. But by ye way, for wante of skill, in a storme, he cast away his shalop in ye botome of ye bay between Meremek river & Pascataquack, & hardly escaped with life, and afterwards fell into the hands of ye Indeans, who pillaged him of all he saved from the sea, & striped him out of all his cloaths to his shirte. At last he got to Pascataquack, & borrowed a suite of cloaths, and got means to come to Plimoth. A strang alteration ther was in him to such as had seen & known him in his former florishing condition; so uncertaine are ye mutable things of this unstable world. And yet men set their harts upon them, though they dayly see ye vanity therof.

After many passages, and much discourse, (former things boyling in his mind, but bit in as was discernd,) he desired to borrow some beaver of them; and tould them he had hope of a ship & good supply to come to him, and then they should have any thing for it they stood in neede of. They gave litle credite to his supplie, but pitied his case, and remembered former curtesies. They tould him he saw their wants, and they knew not when they should have any supply; also how ye case stood betweene them & their adventurers, he well knew; they had not much bever, & if they should let him have it, it were enoughe to make a mutinie among ye people, seeing ther was no other means to procure them foode which they so much wanted, & cloaths allso. Yet they tould him they would help him, considering his necessitie, but must doe it secretly for ye former reasons. So they let him have 100. beaverskins, which waighed 170^li. odd pounds. Thus they helpt him when all ye world faild him, and with this means he went againe to ye ships, and stayed his small ship & some of his men, & bought provissions and fited him selfe; and it was ye only foundation [96] of his after course. But he requited them ill, for he proved after a bitter enimie unto them upon all occasions, and never repayed them any thing for it, to this day, but reproches and evill words. Yea, he divolged it to some that were none of their best freinds, whilst he yet had ye beaver in his boat; that he could now set them all togeather by ye ears, because they had done more then they could answer, in letting him have this beaver, and he did not spare to doe what he could. But his malice could not prevaile.

All this whille no supply was heard of, neither knew they when they might expecte any. So they begane to thinke how they might raise as much corne as they could, and obtaine a beter crope then they had done, that they might not still thus languish in miserie. At length, after much debate of things, the Govr (with ye advise of ye cheefest amongest them) gave way that they should set corne every man for his owne perticuler, and in that regard trust to them selves; in all other things to goe on in ye generall way as before. And so assigned to every family a parcell of land, according to the proportion of their number for that end, only for present use (but made no devission for inheritance), and ranged all boys & youth under some familie. This had very good success; for it made all hands very industrious, so as much more corne was planted then other waise would have bene by any means ye Govr or any other could use, and saved him a great deall of trouble, and gave farr better contente. The women now wente willingly into y᷄ feild, and tooke their litle-ons with them to set corne, which before would aledg weaknes, and inabilitie; whom to have compelled would have bene thought great tiranie and oppression.

The experience that was had in this comone course and condition, tried sundrie years, and that amongst godly and sober men, may well evince the vanitie of that conceite of Platos & other ancients, applauded by some of later times;—that y᷄ taking away of propertie, and bringing in comunitie into a comone wealth, would make them happy and florishing; as if they were wiser then God. For this comunitie (so farr as it was) was found to breed much confusion & discontent, and retard much imploymēt that would have been to their benefite and comforte. For y᷄ yong-men that were most able and fitte for labour & service did repine that they should spend their time & streingth to worke for other mens wives and children, with out any recompence. The strong, or man of parts, had no more in devission of victails & cloaths, then he that was weake and not able to doe a quarter y᷄ other could; this was thought injuestice. The aged and graver men to be ranked and [97] equalised in labours, and victails, cloaths, &c., with y᷄ meaner & yonger sorte, thought it some indignite & disrespect unto them. And for mens wives to be commanded to doe servise for other men, as dresing their meate, washing their cloaths, &c., they deemd it a kind of slaverie, neither could many husbands well brooke it. Upon y᷄ poynte all being to have alike, and all to doe alike, they thought them selves in y᷄ like condition, and one as good as another; and so, if it did not cut of those relations that God hath set amongest men, yet it did at least much diminish and take of y᷄ mutuall respects that should be preserved amongst them. And would have bene worse if they had been men of another condition. Let none objecte this is men's corruption, and nothing to y᷄ course it selfe. I answer, seeing all men have this corruption in them, God in his wisdome saw another course fiter for them.

But to returne. After this course setled, and by that their core was planted, all ther victails were spente, and they were only to rest on Gods providence; at night not many times knowing wher to have a bitt of any thing yᵉ next day. And so, as one well observed, had need to pray that God would give them their dayly brade, above all people in yᵉ world. Yet they bore these wants with great patience & allacritie of spirite, and that for so long a time as for yᵉ most parte of 2. years; which makes me remember what Peter Martire writs, (in magnifying yᵉ Spaniards) in his 5. Decade, pag. 208. *They* (saith he) *led a miserable life for 5. days togeather, with yᵉ parched graine of maize only, and that not to saturitie*; and then concluds, *that shuch pains, shuch labours, and shuch hunger, he thought none living which is not a Spaniard could have endured.* But alass! these, when they had maize (yᵗ is, Indean corne) they thought it as good as a feast, and wanted not only for 5. days togeather, but some time 2. or 3. months togeather, and neither had bread nor any kind of corne. Indeed, in an other place, in his 2. Decade, page 94. he mentions how others of them were worse put to it, wher they were faine to eate doggs, toads, and dead men, and so dyed almost all. From these extremities the[AY] Lord in his goodnes kept these his people, and in their great wants preserved both their lives and healthes; let his name have yᵉ praise. Yet let me hear make use of his conclusion, which in some sorte may be applied to this people: *That with their miseries they opened a way to these new-lands; and after these stormes, with what ease other men came to inhabite in them, in respecte of yᵉ calamities these men suffered; so as they seeme to goe to a bride feaste wher all things are provided for them.*

They haveing but one boat left and she not over well fitted, they were devided into severall companies, 6. or 7. to a gangg or company, and so wente out with a nett they had bought, to take bass & such like fish, by course, every company knowing their turne. No sooner was yᵉ boate discharged [98] of what she brought, but yᵉ next company tooke her and wente out with her. Neither did they returne till they had cauight something, though it were 5. or 6. days before, for they knew ther was nothing at home, and to goe home emptie would be a great discouragemente to yᵉ rest. Yea, they strive who should doe best. If she stayed longe or got litle, then all went to seeking of shel-fish, which at low-water they digged out of yᵉ sands. And this was their living in yᵉ somer time, till God sente yᵐ beter; & in winter they were helped with ground-nuts and foule. Also in yᵉ somer they gott now & then a dear; for one or 2. of yᵉ fitest was apoynted to range yᵉ woods for yᵗ end, & what was gott that way was devided amongst them.

At length they received some leters from yᵉ adventurers, too long and tedious hear to record, by which they heard of their furder crosses and frustrations; begining in this maner.

Loving freinds, as your sorrows & afflictions have bin great, so our croses & interceptions in our proceedings hear, have not been small. For after we had with much trouble & charge sente yᵉ *Parragon* away to sea, and thought all yᵉ paine past, within 14. days after she came againe hither, being dangerously leaked, and brused with tempestious stormes, so as shee was faine to be had into yᵉ docke, and an 100ˡⁱ. bestowed upon her. All yᵉ passengers lying upon our charg for 6. or 7. weeks, and much discontent and distemper was occasioned hereby, so as some dangerous evente had like to insewed. But we trust all shall be well and worke for yᵉ best and your benefite, if yet with patience you can waite, and but have strength to hold in life. Whilst these things were doing, Mʳ. Westons ship came and brought diverce leters from you, &c. It rejoyseth us much to hear of those good reports yᵗ diverce have brought home from you, &c.

These letters were dated Des. 21: 1622.

So farr of this leter.

This ship was brought by Mʳ. John Peirce, and set out at his owne charge, upon hope of great maters. These passengers, & yᵉ goods the company sent in her, he tooke in for fraught, for which they agreed with him to be delivered hear. This was he in whose name their *first patente* was taken, by reason of aquaintance, and some aliance that some of their freinds had with him. But his name was only used in trust. But when he saw they were hear hopfully thus seated, and by yᵉ success God gave them had obtained yᵉ favour of yᵉ Counsell of New-England, he goes and sues to them for *another patent* of much larger extente (in their names), which was easily obtained. But he mente to keep it to him selfe and alow them what he pleased, to hold of him as tenants, and sue to his courts as cheefe Lord, as will appear by that which follows. But yᵉ Lord marvelously crost him; for after this first returne, and yᵉ charge above mentioned, when shee was againe fitted, he pesters him selfe and taks in more passengers, and those not very good to help to bear his losses, and sets out yᵉ 2. time. But [99] what yᵉ event was will appear from another leter from one of yᵉ cheefe of yᵉ company, dated yᵉ 9. of Aprill, 1623. writ to yᵉ Govʳ hear, as followeth.

Loving freind, when I write my last leter, I hope to have received one from you well-nigh by this time. But when I write in Des: I litle thought to have seen Mʳ. John Peirce till he had brought some good tidings from you. But it pleased God, he brought us yᵉ wofull tidings of his returne when he was half-way over, by extraime tempest, werin yᵉ goodnes & mercie of God appeared in sparing their lives, being 109. souls. The loss is so great to Mʳ. Peirce, &c., and yᵉ companie put upon so great charge, as veryly, &c.

Now with great trouble & loss, we have got Mʳ. John Peirce to assigne over yᵉ grand patente to yᵉ companie, which he had taken in his owne name, and made quite voyd our former grante. I am sorie to writ how many hear thinke yᵗ the hand of God was justly against him, both yᵉ first and 2. time of his returne; in regard he, whom you and we so confidently trusted, but only to use his name for yᵉ company, should aspire to be lord over us all, and so make you & us tenants at his will and pleasure, our assurance or patente being quite voyd & disanuled by his means. I desire to judg charitably of him. But his unwillingnes to part with his royall Lordship, and yᵉ high-rate he set it at, which was 500ˡⁱ. which cost him but 50ˡⁱ., maks many speake and judg hardly of him. The company are out for goods in his ship, with charge aboute yᵉ passengers, 640ˡⁱ., &c.

We have agreed with 2. marchants for a ship of 140. tunes, caled yᵉ *Anne*, which is to be ready yᵉ last of this month, to bring 60. passengers & 60. tune of goods, &c.

This was dated Aprill 9. 1623.

These were ther owne words and judgmente of this mans dealing & proceedings; for I thought it more meete to render them in theirs then my owne words. And yet though ther was never got other recompence then the resignation of this patente, and yᵉ shares he had in adventure, for all yᵉ former great sumes, he was never quiet, but sued them in most of yᵉ cheefe courts in England, and when he was still cast, brought it to yᵉ Parlemente. But he is now dead, and I will leave him to yᵉ Lord.

This ship suffered yᵉ greatest extreemitie at sea at her 2. returne, that one shall lightly hear of, to be saved; as I have been informed by Mʳ. William Peirce who was then mʳ. of her, and many others that were passengers in her. It was aboute yᵉ *midle of Feb*: The storme was for yᵉ most parte of 14. days, but for 2. or 3. days & nights togeather in most violent extremitie. After they had cut downe their mast, yᵉ storme beat of their round house and all their uper works; 3. men had worke enough at yᵉ helme, and he that cund yᵉ ship before yᵉ sea, was faine [100] to be bound fast for washing away; the seas did so over-rake them, as many times those upon yᵉ decke knew not whether they were within bord or withoute; and once she was so foundered in yᵉ sea as they all thought she would never rise againe. But yet yᵉ Lord preserved them, and brought them at last safe to *Ports-mouth*, to yᵉ wonder of all men yᵗ saw in what a case she was in, and heard what they had endured.

About yᵉ later end of *June* came in a ship, with Captaine Francis West, who had a comission to be admirall of New-England, to restraine interlopers, and shuch fishing ships as came to fish & trade without a licence from yᵉ Counsell of New-England, for which they should pay a round sume of money. But he could doe no good of them, for they were to stronge for him, and he found yᵉ fisher men to be stuberne fellows. And their owners, upon complainte made to yᵉ Parlemente, procured an order yᵗ fishing should be free. He tould ye Govr they spooke with a ship at sea, and were abord her, y^t was coming for this plantation, in which were sundrie passengers, and they marvelled she was not arrived, fearing some miscariage; for they lost her in a storme that fell shortly after they had been abord. Which relation filled them full of fear, yet mixed with hope. The m^r. of this ship had some 2. hh of pease to sell, but seeing their wants, held them at 9^li. sterling a hoggshead, & under 8^li. he would not take, and yet would have beaver at an under rate. But they tould him they had lived so long with out, and would doe still, rather then give so unreasonably. So they went from hence to Virginia.[AZ]

About 14. days after came in this ship, caled y^e *Anne*, wherof M^r. William Peirce was m^r., and aboute a weeke or 10. days after came in ye pinass which in foule weather they lost at sea, a fine new vessell of about 44. tune, which ye company had builte to stay in the cuntrie. They brought about 60. persons for ye generall, some of them being very usefull persons, and became good members to ye body, and some were ye wives and children of shuch as were hear allready. And some were so bad, as they were faine to be at charge to send them home againe ye next year. Also, besids these ther came a company, that did not belong to ye generall body, but came one[BA] their perticuler, and were to have lands assigned them, and be for them selves, yet to be subjecte to ye generall Goverment; which caused some diferance and disturbance [101] amongst them, as will after appeare. I shall hear againe take libertie to inserte a few things out of shuch leters as came in this shipe, desiring rather to manefest things in ther words and apprehentions, then in my owne, as much as may be, without tediousness.

Beloved freinds, I kindly salute you all, with trust of your healths & wellfare, being right sorie y^t no supplie hath been made to you all this while; for defence wher of, I must referr you to our generall leters. Naitheir indeed have we now sent you many things, which we should & would, for want of money. But persons, more then inough, (though not all we should,) for people come flying in upon us, but monys come creeping in to us. Some few of your old freinds are come, as, &c. So they come droping to you, and by degrees, I hope ere long you shall enjoye them all. And because people press so hard upon us to goe, and often shuch as are none of ye fitest, I pray you write ernestly to ye Treasurer and directe what persons should be sente. It greeveth me to see so weake a company sent you, and yet had I not been hear they had been weaker. You must still call upon the company hear to see y^t honest men be sente you, and threaten to send them back if any other come, &c. We are not any way so much in danger, as by corrupte an noughty persons. Shuch, and shuch, came without my consente; but ye importunitie of their freinds got promise of our Treasurer in my absence. Neither is ther need we should take any lewd men, for we may have honest men enew, &c.

Your assured freind,

R. C.

The following was from ye genrall.

Loving freinds, we most hartily salute you in all love and harty affection; being yet in hope y^t the same God which hath hithertoo preserved you in a marvelous maner, doth yet continue your lives and health, to his owne praise and all our comforts. Being right sory that you have not been sent unto all this time, &c. We have in this ship sent shuch women, as were willing and ready to goe to their husbands and freinds, with their children, &c. We would not have you discontente, because we have not sent you more of your old freinds, and in speciall, him[BB] on whom you most depend. Farr be it from us to neclecte you, or contemne him. But as ye intente was at first, so ye evente at last shall shew it, that we will deal fairly, and squarly answer your expectations to the full. Ther are also come unto you, some honest men to plant upon their particulers besids you. A thing which if we should not give way unto, we should wrong both them and you. Them, by puting them on things more inconveniente, and you, for that being honest men, they will be a strengthening to y⁻ place, and good neighbours [102] unto you. Tow things we would advise you of, which we have likwise signified them hear. First, y⁻ trade for skins to be retained for the generall till y⁻ devidente; 2ˡʸ. yᵗ their setling by you, be with shuch distance of place as is neither inconvenient for y⁻ lying of your lands, nor hurtfull to your speedy & easie assembling togeather.

We have sente you diverse fisher men, with salte, &c. Diverse other provissions we have sente you, as will appear in your bill of lading, and though we have not sent all we would (because our cash is small), yet it is yᵗ we could, &c.

And allthough it seemeth you have discovered many more rivers and fertill grounds then yᵗ wher you are, yet seeing by Gods providence yᵗ place fell to youʳ lote, let it be accounted as your portion; and rather fixe your eyes upon that which may be done ther, then languish in hops after things els-wher. If your place be not y⁻ best, it is better, you shall be y⁻ less envied and encroached upon; and shuch as are earthly minded, will not setle too near your border.[BC] If y⁻ land afford you bread, and y⁻ sea yeeld you fish, rest you a while contented, God will one day afford you better fare. And all men shall know you are neither fugetives nor discontents. But can, if God so order it, take y⁻ worst to your selves, with content,[BD] & leave y⁻ best to your neighbours, with cherfullnes.

Let it not be greeveous unto you yᵗ you have been instruments to breake y⁻ ise for others who come after with less dificulty, the honour shall be yours to y⁻ worlds end, &c.

We bear you always in our brests, and our harty affection is towards you all, as are y⁻ harts of hundreds more which never saw your faces, who doubtles pray for your saftie as their owne, as we our selves both doe & ever shall, that y⁻ same God which hath so marvelously preserved you from seas, foes, and famine, will still preserve you from all future dangers, and make you honourable amongst men, and glorious in blise at y⁻ last day. And so y⁻ Lord be with you all & send us joyfull news from you, and inable us with one shoulder so to accomplish & perfecte this worke, as much glorie may come to Him yᵗ confoundeth y⁻ mighty by the weak, and maketh small thinges great. To whose greatnes, be all glorie for ever & ever.

This leter was subscribed with 13. of their names.

These passengers, when they saw their low & poore condition a shore, were much danted and dismayed, and according to their diverse humores were diversly affected; some wished them selves in England againe; others fell a weeping, fancying their own miserie in what y^ey saw now in others; other some pitying the distress they saw their freinds had been long in, and still were under; in a word, all were full of sadnes. Only some of their old freinds rejoysed to see them, and y^t it was no worse with them, for they could not expecte it should be better, and now hoped they should injoye better days togeather. And truly it was [103] no marvell they should be thus affected, for they were in a very low condition, many were ragged in aparell, & some litle beter then halfe naked; though some y^t were well stord before, were well enough in this regard. But for food they were all alike, save some y^t had got a few pease of ye ship y^t was last hear. The best dish they could presente their freinds with was a lobster, or a peece of fish, without bread or any thing els but a cupp of fair spring water. And ye long continuance of this diate, and their labours abroad, had something abated ye freshnes of their former complexion. But God gave them health and strength in a good measure; and shewed them by experience ye truth of y^t word, Deut. 8. 3. *Y^t man liveth not by bread only, but by every word y^t proceedeth out of ye mouth of ye Lord doth a man live.*

When I think how sadly ye scripture speaks of the famine in Jaakobs time, when he said to his sonns, Goe buy us food, that we may live and not dye. Gen. 42. 2. and 43. 1, that the famine was great, or heavie in the land; and yet they had such great herds, and store of catle of sundrie kinds, which, besids flesh, must needs produse other food, as milke, butter & cheese, &c., and yet it was counted a sore affliction; theirs hear must needs be very great, therfore, who not only wanted the staffe of bread, but all these things, and had no Egipte to goe too. But God fedd them out of ye sea for yᵉ most parte, so wonderfull is his providence over his in all ages; for his mercie endureth for ever.

On yᵉ other hand the old planters were affraid that their corne, when it was ripe, should be imparted to yᵉ new-comers, whose provissions wᶜʰ they brought with them they feared would fall short before yᵉ year wente aboute (as indeed it did). They came to yᵉ Govʳ and besought him that as it was before agreed that they should set corne for their perticuler, and accordingly they had taken extraordinary pains ther aboute, that they might freely injoye the same, and they would not have a bitte of yᵉ victails now come, but waite till harvest for their owne, and let yᵉ new-comers injoye what they had brought; they would have none of it, excepte they could purchase any of it of them by bargaine or exchainge. Their requeste was granted them, for it gave both sides good contente; for yᵉ new-comers were as much afraid that yᵉ hungrie planters would have eat up yᵉ provissions brought, and they should have fallen into yᵉ like condition.

This ship was in a shorte time laden with clapbord, by yᵉ help of many hands. Also they sente in her all yᵉ beaver and other furrs they had, & Mʳ. Winslow was sent over with her, to informe of all things, and procure such things as were thought needfull for their presente condition. By this time harvest was come, and in stead of famine, now God gave them plentie, and yᵉ face of things was changed, to yᵉ rejoysing of yᵉ harts of many, for which they blessed God. And yᵉ effect of their particuler planting was well seene, for all had, one way & other, pretty well to bring yᵉ year aboute, and some of yᵉ abler sorte and more [104] industrious had to spare, and sell to others, so as any generall wante or famine hath not been amongst them since to this day.

Those that come on their perticuler looked for greater matters then they found or could attaine unto, aboute building great houses, and such pleasant situations for them, as them selves had fancied; as if they would be great men & rich, all of a sudaine; but they proved castls in yᵉ aire. These were yᵉ conditions agreed on betweene yᵉ colony and them.

First, that yᵉ Govʳ, in yᵉ name and with yᵉ consente of yᵉ company, doth in all love and frendship receive and imbrace them; and is to allote them competente places for habitations within yᵉ towne. And promiseth to shew them all such other curtesies as shall be reasonable for them to desire, or us to performe.

2. That they, on their parts, be subjecte to all such laws & orders as are already made, or hear after shall be, for yᵉ publick good.

3. That they be freed and exempte from yᵉ generall imployments of the said company, (which their presente condition of comunitie requireth,) excepte commune defence, & such other imployments as tend to yᵉ perpetuall good of yᵉ collony.

4ˡʸ. Towards yᵉ maintenance of Goṽⁿ, & publick officers of yᵉ said collony, every male above yᵉ age of 16. years shall pay a bushell of Indean wheat, or yᵉ worth of it, into yᵉ commone store.

5ˡʸ. That (according to yᵉ agreemente yᵉ marchants made with yᵐ before they came) they are to be wholy debared from all trade with the Indeans for all sorts of furrs, and such like commodities, till yᵉ time of yᵉ comunallitie be ended.

About yᵉ midle of September arrived Captaine Robart Gorges in yᵉ Bay of yᵉ Massachusets, with sundrie passengers and families, intending ther to begine a plantation; and pitched upon yᵉ place Mʳ. Weston's people had forsaken. He had a comission from yᵉ Counsell of New-England, to be generall Goveʳ of yᵉ cuntrie, and they appoynted for his counsell & assistance, Captaine Francis West, yᵉ aforesaid admirall, Christopher Levite, Esquire, and yᵉ Govʳ of Plimoth for yᵉ time beeing, etc. Allso, they gave him authoritie to chuse such other as he should find fit. Allso, they gave (by their comission) full power to him and his assistants, or any 3. of them, wherof him selfe was allway to be one, to doe and execute what to them should seeme good, in all cases, Capitall, Criminall, and Civill, etc., with diverce other instructions. Of which, and his comission, it pleased him to suffer yᵉ Govʳ hear to take a coppy.

He gave them notice of his arivall by letter, but before they could visite him he went to yᵉ eastward with yᵉ ship he came in; but a storme arising, (and they wanting a good pilot to harbor them in those parts,) they bore up for this harbor. He and his men were hear kindly entertained; he stayed hear 14. days. In y⁵ mean time came in Mʳ. Weston with his small ship, which he had now recovered. [105[BE]] Captaine Gorges tooke hold of y⁵ opportunitie, and acquainted y⁵ Govʳ hear, that one occasion of his going to y⁵ eastward was to meete with Mʳ. Weston, and call him to accounte for some abuses he had to lay to his charge. Wherupon he called him before him, and some other of his assistants, with y⁵ Govʳ of this place; and charged him, first, with y⁵ ille carriage of his men at y⁵ Massachusets; by which means the peace of y⁵ cuntrie was disturbed, and him selfe and the people which he had brought over to plante in that bay were therby much prejudised. To this Mʳ. Weston easily answered, that what was that way done, was in his absence, and might have befalen any man; he left them sufficently provided, and conceived they would have been well governed; and for any errour comitted he had sufficiently smarted. This particuler was passed by. A 2ᵈ. was, for an abuse done to his father, Sʳ. Ferdenando Gorges, and to y⁵ State. The thing was this; he used him & others of y⁵ Counsell of New-England, to procure him a licence for y⁵ transporting of many peeces of great ordnance for New-England, pretending great fortification hear in y⁵ countrie, & I know not what shipping. The which when he had obtained, he went and sould them beyond seas for his private profite; for which (he said) y⁵ State was much offended, and his father suffered a shrowd check, and he had order to apprehend him for it. Mʳ. Weston excused it as well as he could, but could not deney it; it being one maine thing (as was said) for which he with-drew himself. But after many passages, by y⁵ mediation of y⁵ Govʳ and some other freinds hear, he was inclined to gentlnes (though he aprehended y⁵ abuse of his father deeply); which, when Mʳ. Weston saw, he grew more presumptuous, and gave such provocking & cutting speches, as made him rise up in great indignation & distemper, and vowed yᵗ he would either curb him, or send him home for England. At which Mʳ. Weston was something danted, and came privatly to y⁵ Govʳ hear, to know whether they would suffer Captaine Gorges to apprehend him. He was tould they could not hinder him, but much blamed him, yᵗ after they had pacified things, he should thus breake out, by his owne folly & rashnes, to bring trouble upon him selfe & them too. He confest it was his passion, and prayd yᵉ Govʳ to entreat for him, and pacifie him if he could. The which at last he did, with much adoe; so he was called againe, and yᵉ Govʳ was contente to take his owne bond to be ready to make further answer, when either he or yᵉ lords should send for him. And at last he tooke only his word, and ther was a freīdly parting on all hands.

But after he was gone, Mʳ. Weston in lue of thanks to yᵉ Govʳ and his freinds hear, gave them this quib (behind their baks) for all their pains. That though they were but yonge justices, yet they wear good beggers. Thus they parted at this time, and shortly after yᵉ Govʳ tooke his leave and went to yᵉ Massachusets by land, being very thankfull for his kind entertainemente. The ship stayed hear, and fitted her selfe to goe for Virginia, having some passengers ther to deliver; and with her returned sundrie of those from hence which came over on their perticuler, some out of discontente and dislike of yᵉ cuntrie; others by reason of a fire that broke out, and burnt yᵉ houses they lived in, and all their provisions [106[BF]] so as they were necessitated therunto. This fire was occasioned by some of yᵉ sea-men that were roystering in a house wher it first begane, makeing a great fire in very could weather, which broke out of yᵉ chimney into yᵉ thatch, and burnte downe 3. or 4. houses, and consumed all yᵉ goods & provissions in yᵐ. The house in which it begane was right against their store-house, which they had much adoe to save, in which were their comone store & all their provissions; yᵉ which if it had been lost, yᵉ plantation had been over-throwne. But through Gods mercie it was saved by yᵉ great dilligence of yᵉ people, & care of the Govʳ & some aboute him. Some would have had yᵉ goods throwne out; but if they had, ther would much have been stolne by the rude company yᵗ belonged to these 2. ships, which were allmost all ashore. But a trusty company was plased within, as well as those that with wet-cloaths & other means kept of yᵉ fire without, that if necessitie required they might have them out with all speed. For y^{ey} suspected some malicious dealling, if not plaine treacherie, and whether it was only suspition or no, God knows; but this is certaine, that when ye tumulte was greatest, ther was a voyce heard (but from whom it was not knowne) that bid them looke well aboute them, for all were not freinds y^t were near them. And shortly after, when the vemencie of ye fire was over, smoke was seen to arise within a shed y^t was joynd to ye end of ye storehouse, which was watled up with bowes, in ye withered leaves wherof ye fire was kindled, which some, runing to quench, found a longe firebrand of an ell longe, lying under ye wale on ye inside, which could not possibly come their by cassualtie, but must be laid ther by some hand, in ye judgmente of all that saw it. But God kept them from this deanger, what ever was intended.

Shortly after Captaine Gorges, ye generall Govr, was come home to ye Massachusets, he sends a warrante to arrest M^r. Weston & his ship, and sends a m^r. to bring her away thither, and one Captain Hanson (that belonged to him) to conducte him along. The Govr & others hear were very sory to see him take this course, and tooke exception at ye warrante, as not legall nor sufficiente; and withall write to him to disswade him from this course, shewing him y^t he would but entangle and burthen him selfe in doing this; for he could not doe M^r. Weston a better turne, (as things stood with him); for he had a great many men that belonged to him in this barke, and was deeply ingaged to them for wages, and was in a maner out of victails (*and now winter*); all which would light upon him, if he did arrest his barke. In ye mean time M^r. Weston had notice to shift for him selfe; but it was conceived he either knew not whither to goe, or how to mend him selfe, but was rather glad of ye occasion, and so stirred not. But ye Govr would not be perswaded, but [107] sent a very formall warrente under his hand & seall, with strict charge as they would answere it to ye state; he also write that he had better considered of things since he was hear, and he could not answer it to let him goe so; besids other things that were come to his knowledg since, which he must answer too. So he was suffered to proceede, but he found in the end that to be true that was tould him; for when an inventorie was taken of what was in ye ship, ther was not vitailes found for above 14. days, at a pare allowance, and not much else of any great worth, & the men did so crie out of him for wages and diate, in ye mean time, as made him soone weary. So as in conclusion it turned to his loss, and ye expence of his owne provissions; and *towards the spring* they came to agreement, (after they had bene to ye eastward,) and ye Govr restord him his vessell againe, and made him satisfaction, in bisket, meal, and such like provissions, for what he had made use of that was his, or what his men had any way wasted or consumed. So M^r. Weston came hither againe, and afterward shaped his course for Virginie, & so for present I shall leave him.[BG]

The Govr and some y^t depended upon him returned for England, haveing scarcly saluted ye cuntrie in his Govermente, not finding the state of things hear to answer his quallitie & condition. The peopl dispersed them selves, some went for England, others for Virginia, some few remained, and were helped with supplies from hence. The Govr brought over a minister with him, one M^r. Morell, who, about a year after ye Govr returned, tooke shipping from hence. He had I know not what power and authority of superintendancie over other churches granted him, and sundrie instructions for that end; but he never shewed it, or made any use of it; (it should seeme he saw it was in vaine;) he only speake of it to some hear at his going away. This was in effect ye end of a 2. plantation in that place. Ther were allso this year some scatering beginings made in other places, as at Paskataway, by M^r. David Thomson, at Monhigen, and some other places by sundrie others.

It rests now y^t I speake a word aboute ye pinass spoken of before, which was sent by ye adventurers to be imployed in ye cuntrie. She was a fine vessell, and bravely set out,[BH] and I fear ye adventurers did over pride them selves in her, for she had ill success. How ever, they erred grosly in tow things aboute her; first, though she had a sufficiente maister, yet she was rudly maned, and all her men were upon shars, and none was to have any wages but ye m^r. 2^{ly}, wheras they mainly lookt at trade, they had sent nothing of any value to trade with. When the men came hear, and mette with ill counsell from M^r. Weston & his crue, with others of ye same stampe, neither m^r. nor Govr could scarce rule [108] them, for they exclaimed that they were abused & deceived, for they were tould they should goe for a man of warr, and take I know not whom, French & Spaniards, &c. They would neither trade nor fish, excepte they had wages; in fine, they would obey no comand of ye maisters; so it was apprehended they would either rune away with ye vessell, or get away wth ye ships, and leave her; so as M^r. Peirce & others of their freinds perswaded the Govr to chaing their condition, and give them wages; which was accordingly done. And she was sente about ye Cape to ye Narigansets to trade, but they made but a poore vioage of it. Some corne and beaver they got, but ye Dutch used to furnish them with cloath & better comodities, they haveing only a few beads & knives, which were not ther much esteemed. Allso, in her returne home, at ye very entrance into ther owne harbore, she had like to have been cast away in a storme, and was forced to cut her maine mast by ye bord, to save herselfe from driving on ye flats that lye without, caled Browns Ilands, the force of y^e wind being so great as made her anchors give way and she drive right upon them; but her mast & takling being gone, they held her till y^e wind shifted.

Anno Dom: 1624.

The time of new election of ther officers for this year being come, and$^{[B1]}$ y^e number of their people increased, and their troubls and occasions therwith, the Govr desired them to chainge y^e persons, as well as renew y^e election; and also to adde more Assistans to y^e Govr for help & counsell, and y^e better carrying on of affairs. Showing that it was necessarie it should be so. If it was any honour or benefite, it was fitte others should be made pertakers of it; if it was a burthen, (as doubtles it was,) it was but equall others should help to bear it; and y^t this was ye end of Anuall Elections. The issue was, that as before ther was but one Assistante, they now chose 5. giving the Govr a duble voyce; and aftwards they increased them to 7. which course hath continued to this day.

They having with some truble & charge new-masted and rigged their pinass, in ye begining of March they sent her well vitaled to the eastward on fishing. She arrived safly at a place near Damarins cove, and was there well harbored in a place wher ships used to ride, ther being also some ships allready arived out of England. But shortly after ther [109] arose such a violent & extraordinarie storme, as yᵉ seas broak over such places in yᵉ harbor as was never seene before, and drive her against great roks, which beat such a hole in her bulke, as a horse and carte might have gone in, and after drive her into deep-water, wher she lay sunke. The mʳ. was drowned, the rest of yᵉ men, all save one, saved their lives, with much a doe; all her provision, salt, and what els was in her, was lost. And here I must leave her to lye till afterward.

Some of those that still remained hear on their perticuler, begane privatly to nurish a faction, and being privie to a strong faction that was among yᵉ adventurers in England, on whom sundry of them did depend, by their private whispering they drew some of the weaker sorte of yᵉ company to their side, and so filld them with discontente, as nothing would satisfie them excepte they might be suffered to be in their perticuler allso; and made great offers, so they might be freed from yᵉ generall. The Govʳ consulting with yᵉ ablest of yᵉ generall body what was best to be done hear in, it was resolved to permitte them so to doe, upon equall conditions. The conditions were the same in effect with yᵉ former before related. Only some more added, as that they should be bound here to remaine till yᵉ generall partnership was ended. And also that they should pay into yᵉ store, yᵉ on halfe of all such goods and comodities as they should any waise raise above their food, in consideration of what charg had been layed out for them, with some such like things. This liberty granted, soone stopt this gape, for ther was but a few that undertooke this course when it came too; and they were as sone weary of it. For the other had perswaded them, & Mʳ. Weston togeather, that ther would never come more supply to yᵉ generall body; but yᵉ perticulers had such freinds as would carry all, and doe for them I know not what.

Shortly after, Mʳ. Winslow came over, and brought a pretty good supply, and the ship came on fishing, a thing fatall to this plantation. He brought 3. heifers & a bull, the first begining of any catle of that kind in ye land, with some cloathing & other necessaries, as will further appear; but withall ye reporte of a strong faction amongst ye adventurers[BJ] against them, and espetially against ye coming of ye rest from Leyden, and with what difficulty this supply was procured, and how, by their strong & long opposision, bussines was so retarded as not only they were now falne too late for ye fishing season, but the best men were taken up of ye fishermen in the west countrie, and he was forct to take such a m^r. & company for that imployment as he could procure upon ye present. Some letters from them shall beter declare these things, being as followeth.

[110] Most worthy & loving freinds, your kind & loving leters I have received, and render you many thanks, &c. It hath plased God to stirre up ye harts of our adventurers[BJ] to raise a new stock for the seting forth of this shipe, caled the Charitie, with men & necessaries, both for the plantation and the fishing, though accomplished with very great difficulty; in regard we have some amongst us which undoubtedly aime more at their owne private ends, and the thwarting & opposing of some hear, and other worthy instruments,[BK] of Gods glory elswher, then at the generall good and furtherance of this noble & laudable action. Yet againe we have many other, and I hope the greatest parte, very honest Christian men, which I am perswaded their ends and intents are wholy for the glory of our Lord Jesus Christ, in the propagation of his gospell, and hope of gaining those poore salvages to the knowledg of God. But, as we have a proverbe, One scabed sheep may marr a whole flock, so these malecontented persons, & turbulente spirits, doe what in them lyeth to withdraw mens harts from you and your freinds, yea, even from the generall bussines; and yet under show and pretence of godlynes and furtherance of the plantation. Wheras the quite contrary doth plainly appeare; as some of the honester harted men (though of late of their faction) did make manifest at our late meeting. But what should I trouble you or my selfe with these restles opposers of all goodnes, and I doubte will be continuall disturbers of our frendly meetings & love. On Thurs-day

the 8. of Jan: we had a meeting aboute the artickls betweene you & us; wher they would rejecte that, which we in our late leters prest you to grante, (an addition to the time of our joynt stock). And their reason which they would make known to us was, it trobled their conscience to exacte longer time of you then was agreed upon at the first. But that night they were so followed and crost of their perverse courses, as they were even wearied, and offered to sell their adventurs; and some were willing to buy. But I, doubting they would raise more scandale and false reports, and so diverse waise doe us more hurt, by going of in such a furie, then they could or can by continuing adventurers amongst us, would not suffer them. But on ye 12. of Jan: we had another meting, but in the interime diverse of us had talked with most of them privatly, and had great combats & reasoning, pro & con. But at night when we mete to read y^e generall letter, we had y^e loveingest and frendlyest meeting that ever I knew[BL] and our greatest enemise offered to lend us 50$_{li}$. So I sent for a potle of wine, (I would you could[BM] doe y^e like,) which we dranke freindly together. Thus God can turne y^e harts of men when it pleaseth him, &c. Thus loving freinds, I hartily salute you all in y^e Lord, hoping ever to rest,

Yours to my power,

JAMES SHERLEY.

Jan: 25. 1623.

[111] Another leter.

Beloved S^r., &c. We have now sent you, we hope, men & means, to setle these 3. things, viz. fishing, salt making, and boat making; if you can bring them to pass to some perfection, your wants may be supplyed. I pray you bend you selfe what you can to setle these bussinesses. Let ye ship be fraught away as soone as you can, and sent to Bilbow. You must send some discreete man for factore, whom, once more, you must also authorise to confirme ye conditions. If M^r. Winslow could be spared, I could wish he came againe. This ship carpenter is thought to be the fittest man for you in the land, and will no doubte doe you much good. Let him have an absolute comand over his servants & such as you put to him. Let him build you 2. catches, a lighter, and some 6. or 7. shalops, as soone as you can. The salt-man is a skillfull & industrious man, put some to him, that may quickly apprehende yᵉ misterie of it. The preacher we have sent is (we hope) an honest plaine man, though none of yᵉ most eminente and rare. Aboute chusing him into office use your owne liberty & discretion; he knows he is no officer amongst you, though perhaps custome & universalitie may make him forget him selfe. Mʳ. Winslow & my selfe gave way to his going, to give contente to some hear, and we see no hurt in it, but only his great charge of children.

We have tooke a patente for Cap Anne, &c. I am sory ther is no more discretion used by some in their leters hither.[BN] Some say you are starved in body & soule; others, yᵗ you eate piggs & doggs, that dye alone; others, that yᵉ things hear spoaken of, yᵉ goodnes of yᵉ cuntry, are gross and palpable lyes; that ther is scarce a foule to be seene, or a fish to be taken, and many such like. I would such discontented men were hear againe, for it is a miserie when yᵉ whole state of a plantation shall be thus exposed to yᵉ passionate humors of some discontented men. And for my selfe I shall hinder for hearafter some yᵗ would goe, and have not better composed their affections; mean space it is all our crosses, and we must bear them.

I am sorie we have not sent you more and other things, but in truth we have rune into so much charge, to victaile yᵉ ship, provide salte & other fishing implements, &c. as we could not provid other comfortable things, as buter, suger, &c. I hope the returne of this ship, and the James, will put us in cash againe. The Lord make you full of courage in this troublesome bussines, which now must be stuck unto, till God give us rest from our labours. Fare well in all harty affection.

Your assured friend,

R. C.

Jan: 24. 1623.

With yᵉ former letter write by Mʳ. Sherley, there were sente sundrie objections concerning which he thus writeth. "These are the cheefe objections which they [112] that are now returned make against you and the countrie. I pray you consider them, and answer them by the first conveniencie." These objections were made by some of those that came over on their perticuler and were returned home, as is before mentioned, and were of yᵉ same suite with those yᵗ this other letter mentions.

I shall here set them downe, with yᵉ answers then made unto them, and sent over at yᵉ returne of this ship; which did so confound yᵉ objecters, as some confessed their falte, and others deneyed what they had said, and eate their words, & some others of them have since come over againe and heere lived to convince them selves sufficiently, both in their owne & other mens judgments.

1. obj. was diversitie aboute Religion. Ans: We know no such matter, for here was never any controversie or opposition, either publicke or private, (to our knowledg,) since we came.

2. ob: Neglecte of familie duties, one yᵉ Lords day.

Ans. We allow no such thing, but blame it in our selves & others; and they that thus reporte it, should have shewed their Christian love the more if they had in love tould yᵉ offenders of it, rather then thus to reproach them behind their baks. But (to say no more) we wish them selves had given better example.

3. ob: Wante of both the sacrements.

Ans. The more is our greefe, that our pastor is kept from us, by whom we might injoye them; for we used to have the Lords Supper every Saboth, and baptisme as often as ther was occasion of children to baptise.

4. ob: Children not catechised nor taught to read.

Ans: Neither is true; for diverse take pains with their owne as they can; indeede, we have no comone schoole for want of a fitt person, or hithertoo means to maintaine one; though we desire now to begine.

5. ob: Many of yᵉ perticuler members of yᵉ plantation will not work for yᵉ generall.

Ans: This allso is not wholy true; for though some doe it not willingly, & other not honestly, yet all doe it; and he that doth worst gets his owne foode & something besids. But we will not excuse them, but labour to reforme them yᵉ best we cane, or else to quitte yᵉ plantation of them.

6. ob: The water is not wholsome.

Ans: If they mean, not so wholsome as yᵉ good beere and wine in London, (which they so dearly love,) we will not dispute with them; but els, for water, it is as good as any in the world, (for ought we knowe,) and it is wholsome enough to us that can be contente therwith.

7. ob: The ground is barren and doth bear no grasse.

[113] Ans: It is hear (as in all places) some better & some worse; and if they well consider their words, in England they shall not find such grasse in them, as in their feelds & meadows. The catle find grasse, for they are as fatt as need be; we wish we had but one for every hundred that hear is grase to keep. Indeed, this objection, as some other, are ridiculous to all here which see and know yᵉ contrary.

8. ob: The fish will not take salt to keepe sweete.

Ans: This is as true as that which was written, that ther is scarce a foule to be seene or a fish to be taken. Things likly to be true in a cuntrie wher so many sayle of ships come yearly a fishing; they might as well say, there can no aile or beere in London be kept from sowering.

9. ob: Many of them are theevish and steale on from an other.

Ans: Would London had been free from that crime, then we should not have been trobled with these here; it is well knowne sundrie have smarted well for it, and so are yᵉ rest like to doe, if they be taken.

10. ob: The countrie is anoyed with foxes and woules.

Ans: So are many other good cuntries too; but poyson, traps, and other such means will help to destroy them.

11. ob: The Dutch are planted nere Hudsons Bay, and are likely to overthrow the trade.

Ans: They will come and plante in these parts, also, if we and others doe not, but goe home and leave it to them. We rather commend them, then condemne them for it.

12. ob: The people are much anoyed with muskeetoes.

Ans: They are too delicate and unfitte to begine new-plantations and collonies, that cannot enduer the biting of a muskeeto; we would wish such to keepe at home till at least they be muskeeto proofe. Yet this place is as free as any, and experience teacheth that yᵉ more yᵉ land is tild, and yᵉ woods cut downe, the fewer ther will be, and in the end scarse any at all.

Having thus dispatcht these things, that I may handle things togeather, I shall here inserte 2. other letters from Mʳ. Robinson their pastor; the one to yᵉ Govʳ, yᵉ other to Mʳ. Brewster their Elder, which will give much light to yᵉ former things, and express the tender love & care of a true pastor over them.

His leter to yᵉ Govʳ.

My loving & much beloved friend, whom God hath hithertoo preserved, preserve and keepe you still to his glorie, and yᵉ good of many; that his blessing may make your godly and wise endeavours answerable to yᵉ valuation which they ther have, & set upon yᵉ same. Of your love too and care for us here, we never doubted; so are we glad to take knowledg of it in that fullnes we doe. Our love & care to and for you, is mutuall, though our hopes of coming [114] unto you be small, and weaker then ever. But of this at large in Mr. Brewsters letter, with whom you, and he with you, mutualy, I know, comunicate your letters, as I desire you may doe these, &c.

Concerning ye killing of those poor Indeans, of which we heard at first by reporte, and since by more certaine relation, oh! how happy a thing had it been, if you had converted some, before you had killed any; besids, wher bloud is one begune to be shed, it is seldome stanched of a long time after. You will say they deserved it. I grant it; but upon what provocations and invitments by those heathenish Christians?[BO] Besids, you, being no magistrats over them, were to consider, not what they deserved, but what you were by necessitie constrained to inflicte. Necessitie of this, espetially of killing so many, (and many more, it seems, they would, if they could,) I see not. Methinks on or tow principals should have been full enough, according to that approved rule, The punishmente to a few, and ye fear to many. Upon this occasion let me be bould to exhorte you seriouly to consider of ye dispossition of your Captaine, whom I love, and am perswaded ye Lord in great mercie and for much good hath sent you him, if you use him aright. He is a man humble and meek amongst you, and towards all in ordinarie course. But now if this be meerly from an humane spirite, ther is cause to fear that by occasion, espetially of provocation, ther may be wanting y^t tendernes of ye life of man (made after Gods image) which is meete. It is also a thing more glorious in mens eyes, then pleasing in Gods, or conveniente for Christians, to be a terrour to poore barbarous people; and indeed I am afraid least, by these occasions, others should be drawne to affecte a kind of rufling course in the world. I doubt not but you will take in good part these things which I write, and as ther is cause make use of them. It were to us more comfortable and convenient, that we comunicated our mutuall helps in presence, but seeing that canot be done, we shall always long after you, and love you, and waite Gods apoynted time. The adventurers it seems have neither money nor any great mind of us, for ye most parte. They deney it to be any part of ye covenants betwixte us, that they should trāsporte us, neither doe I looke for any further help from them, till means come from you. We hear are strangers in effecte to ye whole course, and so both we and you (save as your owne wisdoms and worths have intressed you further) of principals intended in this bussines, are scarce accessaries, &c. My wife, with me, resalute you & yours. Unto him who is ye same to his in all places, and nere to them which are farr from one an other, I comend you and all with you, resting,

Yours truly loving,

JOHN ROBINSON.

Leyden, Des: 19. 1623.

His to M^r. Brewster.

Loving and dear friend and brother: That which I most desired of God in regard of you, namly, ye continuance of your life and health, and the safe coming of these sent unto you, that I most gladly hear of, and praise God for the same. And I hope M^rs. Brewsters weake and decayed state of body will have some reparing by the coming of her daughters, and the provissions in this and former ships, I hear is made for you; which maks us with more patience bear our languishing state, and ye deferring of our desired trāsportation; wch I call desired, rather than hoped for, whatsoever you are borne in hand by any others. For first, ther is no hope at all, that I know, or can conceive of, of any new stock to be raised for that end; so that all must depend [115] upon returns from you, in which are so many uncertainties, as that nothing with any certaintie can thence be concluded. Besids, howsoever for ye presente the adventurers aledg nothing but want of money, which is an invincible difculty, yet if that be taken away by you, others without doubte will be found. For the beter clearing of this, we must dispose ye adventurers into 3. parts; and of them some 5. or 6. (as I conceive) are absolutly bent for us, above any others. Other 5. or 6. are our bitter professed adversaries. The rest, being the body, I conceive to be honestly minded, & loveingly also towards us; yet such as have others (namly ye forward preachers) nerer unto them, then us, and whose course so farr as ther is any differance, they would rather advance then ours. Now what a hanck these men have over yᵉ professors, you know. And I perswade my selfe, that for me, they of all others are unwilling I should be transported, espetially such of them as have an eye that way them selves; as thinking if I come ther, ther market will be mard in many regards. And for these adversaries, if they have but halfe yᵉ witte to their malice, they will stope my course when they see it intended, for which this delaying serveth them very opportunly. And as one restie jade can hinder, by hanging back, more then two or 3. can (or will at least, if they be not very free) draw forward, so will it be in this case. A notable[BP] experimente of this, they gave in your messengers presence, constraining yᵉ company to promise that none of the money now gathered should be expended or imployed to yᵉ help of any of us towards you. Now touching yᵉ question propounded by you, I judg it not lawfull for you, being a ruling Elder, as Rom. 12. 7. 8. & 1. Tim. 5. 17. opposed to the Elders that teach & exhorte and labore in yᵉ word and doctrine, to which yᵉ sacrements are anexed, to administer them, nor convenient if it were lawfull. Whether any larned man will come unto you or not, I know not; if any doe, you must *Consiliū capere in arena.* Be you most hartily saluted, & yourʳ wife with you, both from me & mine. Your God & ours, and yᵉ God of all his, bring us together if it be his will, and keep us in the mean while, and allways to his glory, and make us servisable to his majestic, and faithfull to the end. Amen.

Your very loving brother,

JOHN ROBINSON.

Leyden, Des: 20. 1623.

These things premised, I shall now prosecute yᵉ procedings and afairs here. And before I come to other things I must speak a word of their planting this year; they having found yᵉ benifite of their last years harvest, and setting corne for their particuler, having therby with a great deale of patience overcome hunger & famine. Which maks me remember a saing of Senecas, *Epis: 123. That a great parte of libertie is a well governed belly, and to be patiente in all wants.* They begane now highly to prise corne as more pretious then silver, and those that had some to spare begane to trade one with another for smale things, by y͏ᵉ quarte, potle, & peck, &c.; for money they had none, and if any had, corne was prefered before it. That they might therfore encrease their tillage to better advantage, they made suite [116] to the Gov͏ʳ to have some portion of land given them for continuance, and not by yearly lotte, for by that means, that which y͏ᵉ more industrious had brought into good culture (by much pains) one year, came to leave it y͏ᵉ nexte, and often another might injoye it; so as the dressing of their lands were the more sleighted over, & to lese profite. Which being well considered, their request was granted. And to every person was given only one acrre of land, to them & theirs, as nere y͏ᵉ towne as might be, and they had no more till y͏ᵉ 7. years were expired. The reason was, that they might be kept close together both for more saftie and defence, and y͏ᵉ better improvement of y͏ᵉ generall imployments. Which condition of theirs did make me often thinke, of what I had read in Plinie[30] of y͏ᵉ Romans first beginings in Romulus time. *How every man contented him selfe with 2. Acres of land, and had no more assigned them. And chap. 3. It was thought a great reward, to receive at y͏ᵉ hands of y͏ᵉ people of Rome a pinte of corne. And long after, the greatest presente given to a Captaine y͏ᵗ had gotte a victory over their enemise, was as much ground as they could till in one day. And he was not counted a good, but a dangerous man, that would not contente him selfe with 7. Acres of land. As also how they did pound their corne in morters,* as these people were forcte to doe many years before they could get a mille.

The ship which brought this supply, was speedily discharged, and with her m͏ʳ & company sente to Cap-Anne (of which place they had gott a patente, as before is shewed) on fishing, and because the season was so farr spente some of y͏ᵉ planters were sent to help to build their stage, to their owne hinderance. But partly by y͏ᵉ latenes of y͏ᵉ year, and more espetialy by y͏ᵉ basnes of y͏ᵉ m͏ʳ, one Baker, they made a poore viage of it. He proved a very drunken beast, and did nothing (in a maner) but drink, & gusle, and consume away yᵉ time & his victails; and most of his company followed his example; and though Mʳ. William Peirce was to over see the busines, & to be mʳ. of yᵉ ship home, yet he could doe no good amongst them, so as yᵉ loss was great, and would have bene more to them, but that they kept one a trading ther, which in those times got some store of skins, which was some help unto them.

The ship-carpenter that was sent them, was an honest and very industrious man, and followed his labour very dilligently, and made all that were imployed with him doe yᵉ like; he quickly builte them 2. very good & strong shalops (which after did them greate service), and a great and strong lighter, and had hewne timber for 2. catches; but that was lost, for he fell into a feaver in yᵉ hote season of the year, and though he had the best means yᵉ place could aforde, yet he dyed; of whom they had a very [117] great loss, and were very sorie for his death. But he whom they sent to make salte was an ignorante, foolish, self-willd fellow; he bore them in hand he could doe great matters in making salt-works, so he was sente to seeke out fitte ground for his purpose; and after some serch he tould yᵉ Govʳ that he had found a sufficente place, with a good botome to hold water, and otherwise very conveniente, which he doubted not but in a short time to bring to good perfection, and to yeeld them great profite; but he must have 8. or ten men to be constantly imployed. He was wisht to be sure that yᵉ ground was good, and other things answerable, and yᵗ he could bring it to perfection; otherwise he would bring upon them a great charge by imploying him selfe and so many men. But he was, after some triall, so confidente, as he caused them to send carpenters to rear a great frame for a large house, to receive yᵉ salte & such other uses. But in yᵉ end all proved vaine. Then he layed fault of yᵉ ground, in which he was deceived; but if he might have the lighter to cary clay, he was sure then he could doe it. Now though yᵉ Govʳ & some other foresaw that this would come to litle, yet they had so many malignant spirits amongst them, that would have laid it upon them, in their letters of complainte to the adventurers, as to be their falte yᵗ would not suffer him to goe on to bring his work to perfection; for as he by his bould confidence & large promises deceived them in England that sente him, so he had wound him selfe in to these mens high esteeme hear, so as they were faine to let him goe on till all men saw his vanity. For he could not doe any thing but boyle salt in pans, & yet would make them yᵗ were joynd with him beleeve ther was so grat a misterie in it as was not easie to be attained, and made them doe many unnecessary things to blind their eys, till they discerned his sutltie. The next yere he was sente to Cap-Anne, and yᵉ pans were set up ther wher the fishing was; but before somer was out, he burte the house, and the fire was so vehemente as it spoyld the pans, at least some of them, and this was the end of that chargable bussines.

The 3ᵈ. eminente person (which yᵉ letters before mention) was yᵉ minister which they sent over, by name Mᵣ. John Lyford, of whom & whose doing I must be more large, though I shall abridg things as much as I can. When this man first came a shore, he saluted them with that reverence & humilitie as is seldome to be seen, and indeed made them ashamed, he so bowed and cringed unto them, and would have kissed their hands if they would have [118] suffered him;[BR] yea, he wept & shed many tears, blessing God that had brought him to see their faces; and admiring yᵉ things they had done in their wants, &c. as if he had been made all of love, and yᵉ humblest person in the world. And all the while (if we may judg by his after cariags) he was but like him mentioned in Psa: 10. 10. That croucheth & boweth, that heaps of poore may fall by his might. Or like to that dissembling Ishmaell,[BS] who, when he had slaine Gedelia, went out weeping and mette them yᵗ were coming to offer incence in yᵉ house of yᵉ Lord; saing, Come to Gedelia, when he ment to slay them. They gave him yᵉ best entertainment yᵉʸ could, (in all simplisitie,) and a larger alowans of food out of yᵉ store then any other had, and as the Govᵣ had used in all waightie affairs to consulte with their Elder, Mᵣ. Brewster, (togeither with his assistants,) so now he caled Mᵣ. Liford also to counsell with them in their waightiest bussineses. Ater some short time he desired to joyne himselfe a member to yᵉ church hear, and was accordingly received. He made a large confession of his faith, and an acknowledgemente of his former disorderly walking, and his being intangled with many corruptions, which had been a burthen to his conscience, and blessed God for this opportunitie of freedom & libertie to injoye yᵉ ordinances of God in puritie among his people, with many more such like expressions. I must hear speake a word also of Mʳ. John Oldom, who was a copartner with him in his after courses. He had bene a cheefe sticler in yᵉ former faction among yᵉ perticulers, and an intelligencer to those in England. But now, since the coming of this ship and he saw the supply that came, he tooke occasion to open his minde to some of yᵉ cheefe amongst them heere, and confessed he had done them wrong both by word & deed, & writing into England; but he now saw the eminente hand of God to be with them, and his blesing upon them, which made his hart smite him, neither should those in England ever use him as an instrumente any longer against them in any thing; he also desired former things might be forgotten, and that they would looke upon him as one that desired to close with them in all things, with such like expressions. Now whether this was in hipocrisie, or out of some sudden pange of conviction (which I rather thinke), God only knows. Upon it they shew all readynes to imbrace his love, and carry towards him in all frendlynes, and called him to counsell with them in all cheefe affairs, as yᵉ other, without any distrust at all.

Thus all things seemed to goe very comfortably and smothly on amongst them, at which they did much rejoyce; but this lasted not [119] long, for both Oldom and he grew very perverse, and shewed a spirite of great malignancie, drawing as many into faction as they could; were they never so vile or profane, they did nourish & back them in all their doings; so they would but cleave to them and speak against yᵉ church hear; so as ther was nothing but private meetings and whisperings amongst them; they feeding themselves & others with what they should bring to pass in England by the faction of their freinds their, which brought others as well as them selves into a fools paradise. Yet they could not cary so closly but much of both their doings & sayings were discovered, yet outwardly they still set a faire face of things.

At lenght when ye ship was ready to goe, it was observed Liford was long in writing, & sente many letters, and could not forbear to comunicate to his intimats such things as made them laugh in their sleeves, and thought he had done ther errand sufficiently. The Govr and some other of his freinds knowing how things stood in England, and what hurt these things might doe, tooke a shalop and wente out with the ship a league or 2. to sea, and caled for all Lifords & Oldums letters. Mr. William Peirce being m^r. of ye ship, (and knew well their evill dealing both in England & here,) afforded him all ye assistance he could. He found above 20. of Lyfords letters, many of them larg, and full of slanders, & false accusations, tending not only to their prejudice, but to their ruine & utter subversion. Most of the letters they let pas, only tooke copys of them, but some of ye most materiall they sent true copyes of them, and kept ye originalls, least he should deney them, and that they might produce his owne hand against him. Amongst his letters they found ye coppyes of tow letters which he sent inclosed in a leter of his to M^r. John Pemberton, a minster, and a great opposite of theirs. These 2. letters of which he tooke the coppyes were one of them write by a gentle-man in England to M^r. Brewster here, the other by M^r. Winslow to M^r. Robinson, in Holand, at his coming away, as ye ship lay at Gravsend. They lying sealed in ye great cabin, (whilst M^r. Winslow was bussie aboute the affairs of ye ship,) this slye marchante taks & opens them, taks these coppys, & seals them up againe; and not only sends the coppyes of them thus to his friend and their adversarie, but adds thertoo in ye margente many scurrilous and flouting anotations. This ship went out *towards eving*, and *in the night* ye Govr retured. They were somwaht blanke at it, but after some weeks, when they heard nothing, they then were as briske as ever, thinking nothing had been knowne, but all was gone currente, and that the Govr went but to dispatch his owne letters. The reason why the Govr & rest concealed these things the longer, was to let things ripen, that they [120] might ye better discover their intents and see who were their adherents. And ye rather because amongst ye rest they found a letter of one of their confederats, in wch was writen that M^r. Oldame & M^r. Lyford intended a reformation in church and commone wealth; and, as soone as the ship was gone, they intended to joyne togeather, and have the sacrements, &c.

For Oldame, few of his leters were found, (for he was so bad a scribe as his hand was scarce legible,) yet he was as deepe in yᵉ mischeefe as the other. And thinking they were now strong enough, they begane to pick quarells at every thing. Oldame being called to watch (according to order) refused to come, fell out with yᵉ Capten, caled him raskell, and beggerly raskell, and resisted him, drew his knife at him; though he offered him no wrong, nor gave him no ille termes, but with all fairnes required him to doe his duty. The Govʳ, hearing yᵉ tumulte, sent to quiet it, but he ramped more like a furious beast then a man, and cald them all treatours, and rebells, and other such foule language as I am ashamed to remember; but after he was clapt up a while, he came to him selfe, and with some slight punishmente was let goe upon his behaviour for further censure.

But to cutt things shorte, at length it grew to this esseue, that Lyford with his complicies, without ever speaking one word either to yᵉ Govʳ, Church, or Elder, withdrewe them selves & set up a publick meeting aparte, on yᵉ Lord's day; with sundry such insolente cariages, too long here to relate, begining now publikly to acte what privatly they had been long plotting.

It was now thought high time (to prevent further mischeefe) to calle them to accounte; so yᵉ Govʳ called a courte and sumoned the whol company to appeare. And then charged Lyford & Oldom with such things as they were guilty of. But they were stiffe, & stood resolutly upon yᵉ deneyall of most things, and required proofe. They first alledged what was write to them out of England, compared with their doings & pactises hear; that it was evident they joyned in plotting against them, and disturbing their peace, both in respecte of their civill & church state, which was most injurious; for both they and all yᵉ world knew they came hither to injoye yᵉ libertie of their conscience and yᵉ free use of Gods ordinances; and for y[t] end had ventured their lives and passed throwgh so much hardshipe hithertoo, and they and their freinds had borne the charg of these beginings, which was not small. And that Lyford for his parte was sent over on this charge, and that both he and his great family was maintained on y[e] same, and also was joyned to y[e] church, & a member of them; and for him to plote against them & seek their ruine, was most unjust & perfidious. And for [121] Oldam or any other that came over at their owne charge, and were on ther perticuler, seeing they were received in curtesie by the plantation, when they came only to seeke shelter & protection under their wings, not being able to stand alone, that they, (according to y[e] fable,) like the Hedghogg whom y[e] conny in a stormy day in pittie received into her borrow, would not be content to take part with her, but in the end with her sharp pricks forst the poore conny to forsake her owne borrow; so these men with the like injustice indevored to doe y[e] same to thos that entertained them.

Lyford denyed that he had any thing to doe with them in England, or knew of their courses, and made other things as strange that he was charged with. Then his letters were prodused & some of them read, at which he was struck mute. But Oldam begane to rage furiously, because they had intercepted and opened his letters, threatening them in very high language, and in a most audacious and mutinous maner stood up & caled upon y[e] people, saying, My maisters, wher is your harts? now shew your courage, you have oft complained to me so & so; now is y[e] time, if you will doe any thing, I will stand by you, &c. Thinking y[t] every one (knowing his humor) that had soothed and flattered him, or other wise in their discontente uttered any thing unto him, would now side wth him in open rebellion. But he was deceived, for not a man opened his mouth, but all were silent, being strucken with the injustice of y[e] thing. Then y[e] Gov[r] turned his speech to M[r]. Lyford, and asked him if he thought they had done evill to open his letters; but he was silente, & would not say a word, well knowing what they might reply. Then y[e] Gov[r] shewed the people he did it as a magistrate, and was bound to it by his place, to prevent y[e] mischeefe & ruine that this conspiracie and plots of theirs would bring on this poor colony. But he, besids his evill dealing hear, had delte trecherusly with his freinds yᵗ trusted him, & stole their letters & opened them, and sent coppies of them, with disgracefull anotations, to his freinds in England. And then yᵉ Govᵣ produced them and his other letters under his owne hand, (which he could not deney,) and caused them to be read before all yᵉ people; at which all his freinds were blanke, and had not a word to say.

It would be too long & tedious here to inserte his letters (which would almost fill a volume), though I have them by me. I shall only note a few of yᵉ cheefe things collected out of them, with yᵉ answers to them as they were then given; and but a few of those many, only for instance, by which the rest may be judged of.

[121⁽ᴮᵀ⁾] 1. First, he saith, the church would have none to live hear but them selves. 2ˡʸ. Neither are any willing so to doe if they had company to live elswher.

Ans: Their answer was, that this was false, in both yᵉ parts of it; for they were willing & desirous yᵗ any honest men may live with them, that will cary them selves peacably, and seek yᵉ comone good, or at least doe them no hurte. And againe, ther are many that will not live els wher so long as they may live with them.

2. That if ther come over any honest men that are not of yᵉ seperation, they will quickly distast them, &c.

A. Ther answer was as before, that it was a false callumniation, for they had many amongst them that they liked well of, and were glad of their company; and should be of any such like that should come amongst them.

3. That they excepted against him for these 2. doctrins raised from 2. Sam: 12. 7. First, that ministers must sume times perticulerly apply their doctrine to spetiall persons; 2ˡʸ, that great men may be reproved as well as meaner.

A. Their answer was, that both these were without either truth or colour of yᵉ same (as was proved to his face), and that they had taught and beleeved these things long before they knew Mʳ. Liford.

4. That they utterly sought yᵉ ruine of yᵉ perticulers; as appeareth by this, that they would not suffer any of yᵉ generall either to buy or sell with them, or to exchaing one comoditie for another.

Ans: This was a most malicious slander and voyd of all truth, as was evidently proved to him before all men; for any of them did both buy, sell, or exchaing with them as often as they had any occation. Yea, and allso both lend & give to them when they wanted; and this the perticuler persons them selves could not deney, but freely confest in open court. But yᵉ ground from whence this arose made it much worse, for he was in counsell with them. When one was called before them, and questioned for receiving powder and bisket from yᵉ guner of the small ship, which was yᵉ companys, and had it put in at his window in the night, and allso for buying salt of one, that had no right to it, he not only stood to back him (being one of these perticulers) by excusing & extenuating his falte, as long as he could, but upon this builds this mischecous & most false slander: That because they would not suffer them to buy stolne goods, ergo, they sought their utter ruine. Bad logick for a devine.

5. Next he writs, that he chocked them with this; that they turned [122] men into their perticuler, and then sought to starve them, and deprive them of all means of subsistance.

A. To this was answered, he did them manifest wrong, for they turned none into their perticuler; it was their owne importunitie and ernest desire that moved them, yea, constrained them to doe it. And they apealed to yᵉ persons them selves for yᵉ truth hereof. And they testified the same against him before all present, as allso that they had no cause to complaine of any either hard or unkind usage.

6. He accuseth them with unjust distribution, and writeth, that it was a strang difference, that some have bene alowed 16ˡⁱ. of meale by yᵉ weeke, and others but 4ˡⁱ. And then (floutingly) saith, it seems some mens mouths and bellies are very litle & slender over others.

Ans: This might seeme strange indeed to those to whom he write his leters in England, which knew not yᵉ reason of it; but to him and others hear, it could not be strange, who knew how things stood.

For the first comers had none at all, but lived on their corne. Those wᶜʰ *came in yᵉ Anne, yᵉ August before*, & were to live 13. months of the provissions they brought, had as good alowance in meal & pease as it would extend too, yᵉ most part of yᵉ year; but a litle before harvest, when they had not only fish, but other fruits began to come in, they had but 4ˡⁱ. having their libertie to make their owne provisions. But some of these which came last, as yᵉ ship carpenter, and samiers, the salte-men & others that were to follow constante imployments, and had not an howers time, from their hard labours, to looke for any thing above their alowance; they had at first, 16ˡⁱ. alowed them, and afterwards as fish, & other food coued be gott, they had as balemente, to 14. &. 12. yea some of them to 8. as the times & occasions did vary. And yet those which followed planting and their owne occasions, and had but 4ˡⁱ. of meall a week, lived better then yᵉ other, as was well knowne to all. And yet it must be remembered that Lyford & his had allwais the highest alowance.

Many other things (in his letters) he accused them of, with many aggravations; as that he saw exseeding great wast of tools & vesseles; & this, when it came to be examened, all yᵉ instance he could give was, that he had seen an old hogshed or too fallen to peeces, and a broken how or tow lefte carlesly in yᵉ feilds by some. Though he also knew that a godly, honest man was appointed to looke to these things. But these things & such like was write of by him, to cast disgrace & prejudice upon them; as thinking what came from a [123] minister would pass for currente. Then he tells them that Winslow should say, that ther was not above 7. of yᵉ adventurers yᵗ souight yᵉ good of yᵉ collony. That Mʳ. Oldam & him selfe had had much to doe with them, and that yᵉ faction here might match yᵉ Jesuits for politie. With many yᵉ like greevious complaints & accusations.

1. Then, in the next place, he comes to give his freinds counsell and directtion. And first, that yᵉ Leyden company (Mʳ. Robinson & yᵉ rest) must still be kepte back, or els all will be spoyled. And least any of them should be taken in privatly somewher on yᵉ coast of

England, (as it was feared might be done,) they must chaing the m^r. of ye ship (M^r. William Peirce), and put another allso in Winslows stead, for marchante, or els it would not be prevented.

2. Then he would have such a number provided as might oversway them hear. And that ye perticulers should have voyces in all courts & elections, and be free to bear any office. And that every perticuler should come over as an adventurer, if he be but a servante; some other venturing 10^{li}., ye bill may be taken out in ye servants name, and then assigned to ye party whose money it was, and good covenants drawn betweene them for ye clearing of ye matter; and this (saith he) would be a means to strengthen this side ye more.

3. Then he tells them that if that Capten they spoake of should come over hither as a generall, he was perswaded he would be chosen Capten; for this Captaine Standish looks like a silly boy, and is in utter contempte.

4. Then he shows that if by ye forementioned means they cannot be strengthened to cary & overbear things, it will be best for them to plant els wher by them selves; and would have it artickled by them that they might make choyse of any place that they liked best within 3. or 4. myls distance, shewing ther were farr better places for plantation then this.

5. And lastly he concluds, that if some number came not over to bear them up here, then ther would be no abiding for them, but by joyning with these hear. Then he adds: Since I begane to write, ther are letters come from your company, wherin they would give sole authoritie in diverce things unto the Govr here; which, if it take place, then, *Ve nobis.* But I hope you will be more vigilante hereafter, that nothing may pass in such a maner. I suppose (saith he) M^r. Oldame will write to you further of these things. I pray you conceall me in the discovery of these things, &c.

Thus I have breefly touched some cheefe things in his leters, and shall now returne to their procceeding with him. After the reading of his leters before the whole company, he was demanded what he could say to these things. [124] But all ye answer he made was, that

Billington and some others had informed him of many things, and made sundrie complaints, which they now deneyed. He was againe asked if that was a sufficiente ground for him thus to accuse & traduse them by his letters, and never say word to them, considering the many bonds betweene them. And so they went on from poynte to poynte; and wisht him, or any of his freinds & confederats, not to spare them in any thing; if he or they had any proofe or witnes of any corrupte or evill dealing of theirs, his or their evidence must needs be ther presente, for ther was the whole company and sundery strangers. He said he had been abused by others in their informations, (as he now well saw,) and so had abused them. And this was all the answer they could have, for none would take his parte in any thing; but Billington, & any whom he named, deneyed the things, and protested he wronged them, and would have drawne them to such & such things which they could not consente too, though they were sometimes drawne to his meetings. Then they delte with him aboute his dissembling with them aboute y church, and that he professed to concur with them in all things, and what a large confession he made at his admittance, and that he held not him selfe a minister till he had a new calling, &c. And yet now he contested against them, and drew a company aparte, & sequestred him selfe; and would goe minister the sacrements (by his Episcopall caling) without ever speaking a word unto them, either as magistrats or bretheren. In conclusion, he was fully convicted, and burst out into tears, and "confest he feared he was a reprobate, his sinns were so great that he doubted God would not pardon them, he was unsavorie salte, &c.; and that he had so wronged them as he could never make them amends, confessing all he had write against them was false & nought, both for matter & maner." And all this he did with as much fullnes as words & tears could express.

After their triall & conviction, the court censured them to be expeld the place; Oldame presently, though his wife & family had liberty to stay all winter, or longer, till he could make provission to remove them comfortably. Lyford had liberty to stay 6. months. It was, indeede, with some eye to his release, if he caried him selfe well in the meane time, and that his repentance proved sound. Lyford acknowledged his censure was farr less then he deserved.

Afterwards, he confest his sin publikly in yᵉ church, with tears more largly then before. I shall here put it downe as I find it recorded by some who tooke it from his owne words, as him selfe utered them. Acknowledging [125] "That he had don very evill, and slanderously abused them; and thinking most of yᵉ people would take parte with him, he thought to cary all by violence and strong hand against them. And that God might justly lay inocente blood to his charge, for he knew not what hurt might have come of these his writings, and blest God they were stayed. And that he spared not to take knowledg from any, of any evill that was spoaken, but shut his eyes & ears against all the good; and if God should make him a vacabund in yᵉ earth, as was Caine, it was but just, for he had sined in envie & malice against his brethren as he did. And he confessed 3. things to be yᵉ ground & causes of these his doings: pride, vaine-glorie, & selfe love." Amplifying these heads with many other sade expressions, in the perticulers of them.

So as they begane againe to conceive good thoughts of him upon this his repentance, and admited him to teach amongst them as before; and Samuell Fuller (a deacon amongst them), and some other tender harted men amongst them, were so taken with his signes of sorrow & repentance, as they professed they would fall upon their knees to have his censure released.

But that which made them all stand amased in the end, and may doe all others that shall come to hear yᵉ same, (for a rarer president can scarse be showne,) was, that after a month or 2. notwithstand all his former conffessions, convictions, and publick acknowledgments, both in yᵉ face of yᵉ church and whole company, with so many tears & sadde censures of him selfe before God & men, he should goe againe to justifie what he had done.

For secretly he write a 2ᵈ. leter to yᵉ adventurers in England, in wᶜʰ he justified all his former writings, (save in some things which tended to their damage,) the which, because it is brefer then yᵉ former, I shall here inserte.

Worthy S^rs: Though the filth of mine owne doings may justly be cast in my face, and with blushing cause my perpetuall silence, yet that ye truth may not herby be injuried, your selves any longer deluded, nor injurious[BU] dealing caried out still, with bould out facings, I have adventured once more to write unto you. Firest, I doe freely confess I delte very indiscreetly in some of my perticuler leters wch I wrote to private freinds, for ye courses in coming hither & the like; which I doe in no sorte seeke to justifie, though stired up ther unto in the beholding ye indirecte courses held by others, both hear, & ther with you, for effecting their designes. But am hartily sory for it, and doe to ye glory of God & mine owne shame acknowledg it. Which leters being intercepted by the Govr, I have for ye same undergone ye censure [126] of banishmente. And had it not been for ye respecte I have unto you, and some other matters of private regard, I had returned againe at this time by ye pinass for England; for hear I purpose not to abide, unless I receive better incouragmente from you, then from ye church (as they call them selves) here I doe receive. I purposed before I came, to undergoe hardnes, therfore I shall I hope cherfully bear ye conditions of ye place, though very mean; and they have chainged my wages ten times allready. I suppose my letters, or at least ye coppies of them, are come to your hands, for so they hear reporte; which, if it be so, I pray you take notice of this, that I have writen nothing but what is certainly true, and I could make so apeare planly to any indifferente men, whatsoever colours be cast to darken ye truth, and some ther are very audatious this way; besids many other matters which are farre out of order hear. My mind was not to enlarge my selfe any further, but in respecte of diverse poore souls here, ye care of whom in parte belongs to you, being here destitute of the meās of salvation. For how so ever ye church are provided for, to their contente, who are ye smalest number in ye collony, and doe so appropriate ye ministrie to them selves, houlding this principle, that ye Lord hath not appointed any ordinary ministrie for ye conversion of those y^t are without, so y^t some of ye poor souls have wth tears complained of this to me, and I was taxed for preaching to all in generall. Though in truth they have had no ministrie here since they came, but such as may be performed by any of you, by their owne possition, what soever great pretences they make; but herin they equivocate, as in many other things they doe. But I exceede ye bounds I set my selfe, therfore resting thus, untill I hear further from you, so it be within ye time limited me. I rest, &c.,

Remaining yours ever,

JOHN LYFORD, Exille.

Dated Aug: 22. An^o: 1624.

They made a breefe answer to some things in this leter, but referred cheefly to their former. The effecte was to this purpose: That if God in his providence had not brought these things to their hands (both ye former & later), they might have been thus abused, tradused, and calumniated, overthrowne, & undone; and never have knowne by whom, nor for what. They desired but this equall favoure, that they would be pleased to hear their just defence, as well as his accusations, and waigh them in ye balance of justice & reason, and then censure as they pleased. They had write breefly to ye heads of things before, and should be ready to give further [127] answer as any occasion should require; craving leave to adde a word or tow to this last.

1. And first, they desire to examene what filth that was y^t he acknowledgeth might justly be throwne in his face, and might cause blushing & perpetuall silence; some great mater sure! But if it be looked into, it amounts to no more then a poynte of indiscretion, and thats all; and yet he licks of y^t too with this excuse, that he was stired up therunto by beholding ye indirecte course here. But this point never troubled him here, it was counted a light matter both by him & his freinds, and put of with this,—that any man might doe so, to advise his private freinds to come over for their best advantage. All his sorrow & tears here was for ye wrong & hurt he had done us, and not at all for this he pretends to be done to you: it was not counted so much as indiscretion.

2. Having thus payed you full satisfaction, he thinks he may lay load of us here. And first complains that we have changed his wages ten times. We never agreed with him for any wages, nor made any bargen at all with him, neither know of any that you have made. You sent him over to teach amongst us, and desired he might be kindly used; and more then this we know not. That he hath beene kindly used, (and farr beter then he deserves from us,) he shall be judged first of his owne mouth. If you please to looke upon that writing of his, that was sent you amongst his leters, which he cals a generall relation, in which, though he doth otherwise traduse us, yet in this he him selfe clears us. In y latter end therof he hath these words. *I speak not this* (saith he) *out of any ill affection to the men, for I have found them very kind & loving to me.* You may ther see these to be his owne words under his owne hand. 2ly. It will appere by this that he hath ever had a larger alowance of food out of y store for him and his then any, and clothing as his neede hath required; a dwelling in one of our best houses, and a man wholy at his owne comand to tend his private affairs. What cause he hath therfore to complaine, judge ye; and what he means in his speech we know not, except he aluds to y of Jaacob & Laban. If you have promised him more or other wise, you may doe it when you please.

3. Then with an impudente face he would have you take notice, that (in his leters) he hath write nothing but what is certainly true, yea, and he could make it so appeare plainly to any indifferente men. This indeed doth astonish us and causeth us to tremble at y deceitfullnes [128] and desperate wickednes of mans harte. This is to devoure holy things, and after voues to enquire. It is admirable that after such publick confession, and acknowledgmente in court, in church, before God, & men, with such sadd expressions as he used, and with such melting into teares, that after all this he shoud now justifie all againe. If things had bene done in a corner, it had been some thinge to deney them; but being done in y open view of y cuntrie & before all men, it is more then strange now to avow to make them plainly appear to any indifferente men; and here wher things were done, and all y evidence that could be were presente,

and yet could make nothing appear, but even his freinds condemnd him & gave their voyce to his censure, so grose were they; we leave your selves to judge herein. Yet least this man should triumph in his wikednes, we shall be ready to answer him, when, or wher you will, to any thing he shall lay to our charg, though we have done it sufficiently allready.

4. Then he saith he would not inlarge, but for some poore souls here who are destiute of yᵉ means of salvation, &c. But all his soothing is but that you would use means, that his censure might be released that he might here continue; and under you (at least) be sheltered, till he sees what his freinds (on whom he depends) can bring about & effecte. For such men pretend much for poor souls, but they will looke to their wages & conditions; if that be not to their content, let poor souls doe what they will, they will shift for them selves, and seek poore souls some wher els among richer bodys.

Next he fals upon yᵉ church, that indeed is yᵉ burthensome stone that troubls him. First, he saith they hold this principle, that the Lord hath not apointed any ordinarie ministrie for yᵉ converssion of those without. The church needs not be ashamed of what she houlds in this, haveing Gods word for her warrente; that ordinarie officers are bound cheefly to their flocks, Acts 20. 28. and are not to be extravagants, to goe, come, and leave them at their pleasurs to shift for them selves, or to be devoured of wolves. But he perverts yᵉ truth in this as in other things, for yᵉ Lord hath as well appoynted them to converte, as to feede in their severall charges; and he wrongs yᵉ church to say other wise. Againe, he saith he was taxed for preaching to all in generall. This is a meere untruth, for this dissembler knows that every Lords day some are appointed to visite suspected places, & if any be found idling and neglecte yᵉ hearing of yᵉ word, (through idlnes or profanes,) they are punished for yᵉ same. Now to procure all to come to hear, and then to blame him for preaching to all, were to play yᵉ mad men.

[129] 6. Next (he saith) they have had no ministrie since they came, what soever pretences they make, &c. We answer, the more

is our wrong, that our pastor is kept from us by these mens means, and then reproach us for it when they have done. Yet have we not been wholy distitute of ye means of salvation, as this man would make ye world beleeve; for our reve^d Elder hath laboured diligently in dispencing the word of God unto us, before he came; and since hath taken equalle pains with him selfe in preaching the same; and, be it spoaken without ostentation, he is not inferriour to M^r. Lyford (& some of his betters) either in gifts or larning, though he would never be perswaded to take higher office upon him. Nor ever was more pretended in this matter. For equivocating, he may take it to him selfe; what ye church houlds, they have manifested to ye world, in all plaines, both in open confession, doctrine, & writing.

This was ye sume of ther answer, and hear I will let them rest for ye presente. I have bene longer in these things then I desired, and yet not so long as the things might require, for I pass many things in silence, and many more deserve to have been more largly handled. But I will returne to other things, and leave ye rest to its place.

The pinass that was left sunck & cast away near Damarins-cove, as is before showed, some of ye fishing maisters said it was a pity so fine a vessell should be lost, and sent them word that, if they would be at ye cost, they would both directe them how to waygh her, and let them have their carpenters to mend her. They thanked them, & sente men aboute it, and beaver to defray ye charge, (without which all had been in vaine). So they gott coopers to trime, I know not how many tune of cask, and being made tight and fastened to her at low-water, they boyed her up; and then with many hands hald her on shore in a conveniente place wher she might be wrought upon; and then hired sundrie carpenters to work upon her, and other to saw planks, and at last fitted her & got her home. But she cost a great deale of money, in thus recovering her, and buying riging & seails for her, both now and when before she lost her mast; so as she proved a chargable vessell to ye poor plantation. So they sent her home, and with her Lyford sent his last letter, in great secrecie; but ye party intrusted with it gave it ye Govr.

The winter was passed over in ther ordinarie affairs, without any spetiall mater worth noteing; saveing that many who before stood something of from yᵉ church, now seeing Lyfords unrighteous dealing, and malignitie against yᵉ church, now tendered them selves to yᵉ church, and were joyned to yᵉ same; proffessing that it was not out of yᵉ dislike of any thing that they had stood of so long, but a desire to fitte them selves beter for such a state, and they saw now yᵉ Lord cald for their help. [130] And so these troubls prodused a quite contrary effecte in sundrie hear, then these adversaries hoped for. Which was looked at as a great worke of God, to draw on men by unlickly means; and that in reason which might rather have set them further of. And thus I shall end this year.

Anno Dom: 1625.

At yᵉ spring of yᵉ year, about yᵉ time of their Election Court, Oldam came againe amongst them; and though it was a part of his censure for his former mutinye and miscariage, not to returne without leave first obtained, yet in his dareing spirite, he presumed without any leave at all, being also set on & hardened by yᵉ ill counsell of others. And not only so, but suffered his unruly passion to rune beyond yᵉ limits of all reason and modestie; in so much that some strangers which came with him were ashamed of his outrage, and rebuked him; but all reprofes were but as oyle to yᵉ fire, and made yᵉ flame of his coller greater. He caled them all to nought, in this his mad furie, and a hundred rebells and traytors, and I know not what. But in conclusion they comited him till he was tamer, and then apointed a gard of musketers wᶜʰ he was to pass throw, and ever one was ordered to give him a thump on yᵉ brich, with yᵉ but end of his musket, and then was conveied to yᵉ water side, wher a boat was ready to cary him away. Then they bid him goe & mende his maners.

Whilst this was a doing, Mʳ. William Peirce and Mʳ. Winslow came up from yᵉ water side, being come from England; but they were so busie with Oldam, as they never saw them till they came thus upon them. They bid them not spare either him or Liford, for they had played yᵉ vilans with them. But that I may hear make an end with him, I shall hear once for all relate what befell concerning him in yᵉ future, & yᵗ breefly. After yᵉ removall of his familie from hence, he fell into some straits, (as some others did,) and aboute a year or more afterwards, towards winter, he intended a vioage for Virginia; but it so pleased God that yᵉ barke that caried him, and many other passengers, was in that danger, as they dispaired of life; so as many of them, as they fell to prayer, so also did they begine to examine their consciences [131] and confess such sins as did most burthen them. And Mʳ. Ouldame did make a free and large confession of yᵉ wrongs and hurt he had done to yᵉ people and church here, in many perticulers, that as he had sought their ruine, so God had now mette with him and might destroy him; yea, he feared they all fared yᵉ worce for his sake; he prayed God to forgive him, and made vowes that, if yᵉ Lord spard his life, he would become otherwise, and yᵉ like. This I had from some of good credite, yet living in yᵉ Bay, and were them selves partners in the same dangers on yᵉ shoulds of Cap-Codd, and heard it from his owne mouth. It pleased God to spare their lives, though they lost their viage; and in time after wards, Ouldam caried him selfe fairly towards them, and acknowledged yᵉ hand of God to be with them, and seemed to have an honourable respecte of them; and so farr made his peace with them, as he in after time had libertie to goe and come, and converse with them, at his pleasure. He went after this to Virginia, and had ther a great sicknes, but recovered and came back againe to his familie in yᵉ Bay, and ther lived till some store of people came over. At lenght going a trading in a smale vessell among yᵉ Indians, and being weakly mand, upon some quarell they knockt him on yᵉ head with a hatched, so as he fell downe dead, & never spake word more. 2. litle boys that were his kinsmen were saved, but had some hurte, and yᵉ vessell was strangly recovered from yᵉ Indeans by another that belonged to yᵉ Bay of Massachusets; and this his death was one ground of the Pequente warr which followed.

I am now come to Mʳ. Lyford. His time being now expired, his censure was to take place. He was so farre from answering their hopes by amendmente in yᵉ time, as he had dubled his evill, as is before noted. But first behold yᵉ hand of God conceiring him, wherin that of yᵉ Psalmist is verified. Psa: 7. 15. He hath made a pitte, & digged it, and is fallen into the pitte he made. He thought to bring shame and disgrace upon them, but in stead therof opens his owne to all yᵉ world. For when he was delte with all aboute his second letter, his wife was so affected with his doings, as she could no longer conceaill her greefe and sorrow of minde, but opens yᵉ same to one of their deacons & some other of her freinds, & after uttered yᵉ same to Mʳ. Peirce upon his arrivall. Which was to this purpose, that she feared some great judgment of God would fall upon them, and upon her, for her husbands cause; now that they were to remove, she feared to fall into yᵉ Indeans hands, and to be defiled by them, as he had defiled other women; or some shuch like [132] judgmente, as God had threatened David, 2. Sam. 12. 11. I will raise up evill against yᵉ, and will take thy wives & give them, &c. And upon it showed how he had wronged her, as first he had a bastard by another before they were maried, & she having some inkling of some ill cariage that way, when he was a suitor to her, she tould him what she heard, & deneyd him; but she not certainly knowing yᵉ thing, other wise then by some darke & secrete muterings, he not only stifly denied it, but to satisfie her tooke a solemne oath ther was no shuch matter. Upon which she gave consente, and maried with him; but afterwards it was found true, and yᵉ bastard brought home to them. She then charged him with his oath, but he prayed pardon, and said he should els not have had her. And yet afterwards she could keep no maids but he would be medling with them, and some time she hath taken him in yᵉ maner, as they lay at their beds feete, with shuch other circumstances as I am ashamed to relate. The woman being a grave matron, & of good cariage all yᵉ while she was hear, and spoake these things out of yᵉ sorrow of her harte, sparingly, and yet wᵗʰ some further intimations. And that which did most seeme to affecte her (as they conceived) was, to see his former cariage in his repentance, not only hear with yᵉ church, but formerly about these things; sheding tears, and using great & sade expressions, and yet eftsone fall into the like things.

Another thing of y⁼ same nature did strangly concurr herewith. When M͏ʳ. Winslow & M͏ʳ. Peirce were come over, M͏ʳ. Winslow informed them that they had had y⁼ like bickering with Lyfords freinds in England, as they had with him selfe and his freinds hear, aboute his letters & accusations in them. And many meetings and much clamour was made by his freinds theraboute, crying out, a minister, a man so godly, to be so esteemed & taxed they held a great skandale, and threated to prosecute law against them for it. But things being referred to a further meeting of most of y⁼ adventurers, to heare y⁼ case and decide y⁼ matters, they agreed to chose 2. eminente men for moderators in the bussines. Lyfords faction chose M͏ʳ. White, a counselor at law, the other parte chose Reṽe͏ᵈ. M͏ʳ. Hooker, the minister, and many freinds on both sids were brought in, so as ther was a great assemblie. In y⁼ mean time, God in his providence had detected Lyford's evill cariage in Ireland to some freinds amongst y⁼ company, who made it knowne to M͏ʳ. Winslow, and directed him to 2. godly and grave witnesses, who would testifie y⁼ same (if caled therunto) upon their oath. The thing was this; he being gott into Ireland, had wound him selfe into y⁼ esteeme of sundry godly & zelous professours in those parts, who, having been burthened with y⁼ ceremonies in England, found ther some more liberty to their consciences; amongst whom were these 2. men, which gave [133] this evidence. Amongst y⁼ rest of his hearers, ther was a godly yonge man that intended to marie, and cast his affection on a maide which lived their aboute; but desiring to chose in y⁼ Lord, and preferred y⁼ fear of God before all other things, before he suffered his affection to rune too farr, he resolved to take M͏ʳ. Lyfords advise and judgmente of this maide, (being y⁼ minister of y⁼ place,) and so broak y⁼ matter unto him; & he promised faithfully to informe him, but would first take better knowledg of her, and have private conferance with her; and so had sundry times; and in conclusion comended her highly to y⁼ yong man as a very fitte wife for him. So they were maried togeather; but some time after mariage the woman was much troubled in mind, and afflicted in conscience, and did nothing but weepe and mourne, and long it was before her husband could get of her what was yᵉ cause. But at length she discovered yᵉ thing, and prayed him to forgive her, for Lyford had overcome her, and defiled her body before marriage, after he had comended him unto her for a husband, and she resolved to have him, when he came to her in that private way. The circumstances I forbear, for they would offend chast ears to hear them related, (for though he satisfied his lust on her, yet he indeaoured to hinder conception.) These things being thus discovered, yᵉ womās husband tooke some godly freinds with him, to deale with Liford for this evill. At length he confest it, with a great deale of seeming sorrow & repentance, but was forct to leave Irland upon it, partly for shame, and partly for fear of further punishmente, for yᵉ godly withdrew them selves from him upon it; and so coming into England unhapily he was light upon & sente hither.

But in this great assembly, and before yᵉ moderators, in handling yᵉ former matters aboute yᵉ letters, upon provocation, in some heate of replie to some of Lyfords defenders, Mʳ. Winslow let fall these words, That he had delte knavishly; upon which on of his freinds tooke hold, & caled for witneses, that he cald a minister of yᵉ gospell knave, and would prosecute law upon it, which made a great tumulte, upon which (to be shorte) this matter broke out, and the witnes were prodused, whose persons were so grave, and evidence so plaine, and yᵉ facte so foule, yet delivered in such modest & chast terms, and with such circumstances, as strucke all his freinds mute, and made them all ashamed; insomuch as yᵉ moderators with great gravitie declared that yᵉ former matters gave them cause enough to refuse him & to deal with him as they had done, but these made him unmeete for ever to bear ministrie any more, what repentance soever he should pretend; with much more to like effecte, and so wisht his freinds to rest quiete. Thus was this matter ended.

From hence Lyford wente to Natasco, in yᵉ Bay of yᵉ Massachusets, with some other of his freinds with him, wher Oldom allso lived. From thence he removed to Namkeke, since called Salem; but after ther came some people over, wheather for hope of greater profite, or what ends els I know not, he left his freinds that followed him, and went from thence to Virginia, wher he shortly after dyed, and so I leave him to yᵉ Lord. His wife afterwards returned againe to this cuntry, and thus much of this matter.

[134] This storme being thus blowne over, yet sundrie sad effects followed yᵉ same; for the Company of Adventurers broake in peeces here upon, and yᵉ greatest parte wholy deserted yᵉ colony in regarde of any further supply, or care of their subsistance. And not only so, but some of Lyfords & Oldoms freinds, and their adherents, set out a shipe on fishing, on their owne accounte, and getting yᵉ starte of yᵉ ships that came to the plantation, they tooke away their stage, & other necessary provisions that they had made for fishing at Cap-Anne yᵉ year before, at their great charge, and would not restore yᵉ same, excepte they would fight for it. But yᵉ Govʳ sent some of yᵉ planters to help yᵉ fisher men to build a new one, and so let them keepe it. This shipe also brought them some small supply, of little value; but they made so pore a bussines of their fishing, (neither could these men make them any returne for yᵉ supply sente,) so as, after this year, they never looked more after them.

Also by this ship, they, some of them, sent (in yᵉ name of yᵉ rest) certaine reasons of their breaking of from yᵉ plantation, and some tenders, upon certaine conditions, of reuniting againe. The which because they are longe & tedious, and most of them aboute the former things already touched, I shall omite them; only giveing an instance in one, or tow. 1. reason, they charged them for dissembling with his majestie in their petition, and with yᵉ adventurers about yᵉ French discipline, &c. 2ˡʸ, for receiving[BV] a man[BW] into their church, that in his conffession renownced all, universall, nationall, and diocessan churches, &c., by which (say they) it appears, that though they deney the name of Browists, yet they practiss yᵉ same, &c. And therfore they should sine against God in building up such a people.

Then they adde: Our dislikes thus laid downe, that we may goe on in trade wᵗʰ better contente & credite, our desires are as followeth. First, that as we are partners in trade, so we may be in Goῦⁿ ther, as the patente doth give us power, &c.

2. That the French discipline may be practised in the plantation, as well in the circumstances theirof, as in yᵉ substance; wherby yᵉ scandallous name of yᵉ Brownists, and other church differences, may be taken away.

3. Lastly, that Mʳ. Robinson and his company may not goe over to our plantation, unless he and they will reconcile themselves to our church by a recantation under their hands, &c.

Their answer in part to these things was then as foloweth.

Wheras you taxe us for dissembling with his majestie & yᵉ adventurers aboute yᵉ French discipline, you doe us wrong, for we both hold & practice yᵉ discipline of yᵉ French & other reformed churches, (as they have published yᵉ same in yᵉ Harmony of Confessions,) according to our means, in effecte & substance. But wheras you would tye us to the French discipline in every circumstance, you derogate from yᵉ libertie we have in Christ Jesus. The Apostle Paule would have none to follow him in any thing but wherin he follows Christ, much less ought any Christian or church in yᵉ world to doe it. The French may erre, we may erre, and other churches may erre, and doubtless doe in many circumstances. That honour therfore belongs only to yᵉ infallible word of God, and pure Testamente of Christ, to be propounded and followed as yᵉ only rule and pattern for direction herin to all churches & Christians. And it is too great arrogancie for any man, or church [135] to thinke yᵗ he or they have so sounded yᵉ word of God to yᵉ bottome, as precislie to sett downe yᵉ churches discipline, without error in substance or circumstance, as yᵗ no other without blame may digress or differ in any thing from yᵉ same. And it is not difficulte to shew, yᵗ the reformed churches differ in many circumstances amongest them selves.

The rest I omitte, for brevities sake, and so leave to prosecute these men or their doings any further, but shall returne to yᵉ rest of their freinds of ye company, wch stuck to them. And I shall first inserte some part of their letters as followeth; for I thinke it best to render their minds in ther owne words.

To our loving freinds, &c.

Though the thing we feared be come upon us, and ye evill we strove against have overtaken us, yet we cannot forgett you, nor our freindship and fellowship which togeather we have had some years; wherin though our expressions have been small, yet our harty affections towards you (unknown by face) have been no less then to our nearest freinds, yea, to our owne selves. And though this your friend M^r. Winslow can tell you ye state of things hear, yet least we should seeme to neglecte you, to whom, by a wonderfull providence of God, we are so nearly united, we have thought good once more to write unto you, to let you know what is here befallen, and ye resons of it; as also our purposes & desirs toward you for hereafter.

The former course for the generalitie here is wholy dissolved from what it was; and wheras you & we were formerly sharers and partners, in all viages & deallings, this way is now no more, but you and we are left to bethinke our sellves what course to take in ye future, that your lives & our monies be not lost.

The reasons and causes of this allteration have been these. First and mainly, ye many losses and crosses at sea, and abuses of sea-men, wch have caused us to rune into so much charge, debts, & ingagements, as our estats & means were not able to goe on without impoverishing our selves, except our estats had been greater, and our associats cloven beter unto us. 2^ly, as here hath been a faction and siding amongst us now more then 2. years, so now there is an uter breach and sequestration amongst us, and in too parts of us a full dissertion and forsaking of you, without any intente or purpose of medling more with you. And though we are perswaded the maine cause of this their doing is wante of money, (for neede wherof men use to make many excuses,) yet other things are pretended, as that you are Brownists, &c. Now what use you or we ought to make of these things, it remaineth to be considered, for we know yᵉ hand of God to be in all these things, and no doubt he would admonish some thing therby, and to looke what is amise. And allthough it be now too late for us or you to prevent & stay these things, yet it is[BX] not to late to exercise patience, wisdom, and conscience in bearing them, and in caring our selves in & under them for yᵉ time to come.

[136] And as we our selves stand ready to imbrace all occasions that may tend to yᵉ furthrance of so hopefull a work, rather admiring of what is, then grudging for what is not; so it must rest in you to make all good againe. And if in nothing else you can be approved, yet let your honestie & conscience be still approved, & lose not one jote of youʳ innocencie, amids your crosses & afflictions. And surly if you upon this allteration behave your selves wisly, and goe on fairly, as men whose hope is not in this life, you shall need no other weapon to wound your adversaries; for when your righteousnes is revealled as yᵉ light, they shall cover their faces with shame, that causlesly have sought your overthrow.

Now we thinke it but reason, that all such things as ther apertaine to the generall, be kept & preserved togeather, and rather increased dayly, then any way be dispersed or imbeseled away for any private ends or intents whatsoever. And after your necessities are served, you gather togeather such comodities as yᵉ cuntrie yeelds, & send them over to pay debts & clear ingagements hear, which are not less then 1400ˡⁱ. And we hope you will doe your best to free our ingagements, &c. Let us all indeavor to keep a faire & honest course, and see what time will bring forth, and how God in his providence will worke for us. We still are perswaded you are yᵉ people that must make a plantation in those remoate places when all others faile and returne. And your experience of Gods providence and preservation of you is such as we hope your harts will not faile you, though your freinds should forsake you (which we our selves shall not doe whilst we live, so long as your honestie so well appereth). Yet surly help would arise from some other place whilst you waite on God, with uprightnes, though we should leave you allso.

And lastly be you all intreated to walke circumspectly, and carry your selves so uprightly in all your ways, as y' no man may make just exceptions against you. And more espetially that y⁰ favour and countenance of God may be so toward you, as y' you may find abundante joye & peace even amids tribulations, that you may say with David, Though my father & mother should forsake me, yet y⁰ Lord would take me up.

We have sent you hear some catle, cloath, hose, shoes, leather, &c., but in another nature then formerly, as it stood us in hand to doe; we have comitted them to y⁰ charge & custody of Mʳ. Allerton and Mʳ. Winslow, as our factours, at whose discretion they are to be sould, and comodities to be taken for them, as is fitting. And by how much y⁰ more they will be chargable unto you, the better[BY] they had need to be husbanded, &c. Goe on, good freinds, comfortably, pluck up your spirits, and quitte your selves like men in all your difficulties, that notwithstanding all displeasure and threats of men, yet y⁰ work may goe on you are aboute, and not be neglected. Which is so much for y⁰ glorie of God, and the furthrance of our countrie-men, as that a man may with more comforte [137] spend his life in it, then live y⁰ life of Mathusala, in wasting y⁰ plentie of a tilled land, or eating y⁰ fruite of a growne tree. Thus with harty salutations to you all, and harty prayers for you all, we lovingly take our leaves, this 18. of Des: 1624.

Your assured freinds to our powers,

J. S. W. C. T. F. R. H. &c.

By this leter it appears in what state y⁰ affairs of y⁰ plantation stood at this time. These goods they bought, but they were at deare rates, for they put 40. in y⁰ hundred upon them, for profite and adventure, outward bound; and because of y⁰ vnture of y⁰ paiment homeward, they would have 30.[BZ] in y⁰ 100. more, which was in all 70. pʳ. cent; a thing thought unreasonable by some, and too great an oppression upon y⁰ poore people, as their case stood. The catle were y⁰ best goods, for y⁰ other being ventured ware, were neither at y⁰ best (some of them) nor at y⁰ best prises. Sundrie of their freinds disliked these high rates, but coming from many hands, they could not help it.

They sent over also 2. ships on fishing on their owne acounte; the one was yᵉ pinass that was cast away yᵉ last year hear in yᵉ cuntrie, and recovered by yᵉ planters, (as was before related,) who, after she came home, was attached by one of yᵉ company for his perticuler debte, and now sent againe on this accounte. The other was a great ship, who was well fitted with an experienced mʳ. & company of fisher-men, to make a viage, & to goe to Bilbo or Sabastians with her fish; the lesser, her order was to load with cor-fish, and to bring the beaver home for England, yᵗ should be received for yᵉ goods sould to yᵉ plantation. This bigger ship made a great viage of good drie fish, the which, if they had gone to a market wᵗʰ, would have yeelded them (as such fish was sould yᵗ season) 1800ˡⁱ. which would have enriched them. But because ther was a bruite of warr with France, yᵉ mʳ. neglected (through timerousnes) his order, and put first into Plimoth, & after into Portsmouth, and so lost their opportunitie, and came by the loss. The lesser ship had as ill success, though she was as hopfull as yᵉ other for yᵉ marchants profite; for they had fild her with goodly cor-fish taken upon yᵉ banke, as full as she could swime; and besids she had some 800ˡⁱ. weaight of beaver, besids other furrs to a good value from yᵉ plantation. The mʳ. seeing so much goods come, put it abord yᵉ biger ship, for more saftie; but Mʳ. Winslow (their factor in this busines) was bound in a bond of 500ˡⁱ. to send it to London in yᵉ smale ship; ther was some contending between yᵉ mʳ, & him aboute it. But he tould yᵉ mʳ. he would follow his order aboute it; if he would take it out afterward, it should be at his perill. So it went in yᵉ smale ship, and he sent bills of lading in both. The mʳ. was so carfull being both so well laden, as they went joyfully home togeather, for he towed yᵉ leser ship at his sterne all yᵉ way over bound, and they had such fayr weather as he never cast her of till they were shott deep in to yᵉ English Chanell, almost within yᵉ sight of Plimoth; and yet ther she was unhaply taken by a Turks man of warr, and carried into Saly, wher yᵉ mʳ. and men were made slaves, and many of yᵉ beaver skins were sould for 4ᵈ. a peece. [138] Thus was all their hops dasht, and the joyfull news they ment to cary home turned to heavie tidings. Some thought this a hand of God for their too great exaction of yᵉ poore plantation, but Gods judgments are unseerchable, neither dare I be bould therwith: but however it shows us yᵉ uncertainty of all humane things, and what litle cause ther is of joying in them or trusting to them.

In yᵉ bigger of these ships was sent over Captine Standish from yᵉ plantation, wᵗʰ leters & instructions, both to their freinds of yᵉ company which still clave to them, and also to yᵉ Honourable Counsell of New-England. To yᵉ company to desire yᵗ seeing that they ment only to let them have goods upon sale, that they might have them upon easier termes, for they should never be able to bear such high intrest, or to allow so much per cent; also that what they would doe in yᵗ way that it might be disburst in money, or such goods as were fitte and needfull for them, & bought at best hand; and to aquainte them with yᵉ contents of his leters to yᵉ Counsell above said, which was to this purpose, to desire their favour & help; that such of yᵉ adventurers as had thus forsaken & deserted them, might be brought to some order, and not to keepe them bound, and them selves be free. But that they might either stand to ther former covenants, or ells come to some faire end, by dividente, or composition. But he came in a very bad time, for yᵉ Stat was full of trouble, and yᵉ plague very hote in London, so as no bussines could be done; yet he spake with some of yᵉ Honourd Counsell, who promised all helpfullnes to yᵉ plantation which lay in them. And sundrie of their freinds yᵉ adventurers were so weakened with their losses yᵉ last year, by yᵉ losse of yᵉ ship taken by the Turks, and yᵉ loss of their fish, wᶜʰ by reason of yᵉ warrs they were forcte to land at Portsmouth, and so came to litle; so as, though their wills were good, yet theyʳ power was litle. And ther dyed such multituds weekly of yᵉ plague, as all trade was dead, and litle money stirring. Yet with much adooe he tooke up 150ˡⁱ. (& spent a good deal of it in expences) at 50. per cent, which he bestowed in trading goods & such other most needfull comodities as he knew requiset for their use; and so returned passenger in a fhishing ship, haveing prepared a good way for yᵉ compossition that was afterward made.

In yᵉ mean time it pleased yᵉ Lord to give yᵉ plantation peace and health and contented minds, and so to blese ther labours, as they had corne sufficient, (and some to spare to others,) with other foode; neither ever had they any supply of foode but what they first brought with them. After harvest this year, they sende out a boats load of corne 40. or 50. leagues to yᵉ eastward, up a river called Kenibeck; it being one of those 2. shalops which their carpenter had built them yᵉ year before; for bigger vessell had they none. They had laid a litle deck over her midships to keepe yᵉ corne drie, but yᵉ men were faine to stand it out all weathers without shelter; and yᵗ time [139] of yᵉ year begins to growe tempestious. But God preserved them, and gave them good success, for they brought home 700ˡⁱ. of beaver, besids some other furrs, having litle or nothing els but this corne, which them selves had raised out of yᵉ earth. This viage was made by Mʳ. Winslow & some of yᵉ old standards,[CA] for seamen they had none.

Anno Dom: 1626.

About yᵉ begining of Aprill they heard of Captain Standish his arrivall, and sent a boat to fetch him home, and yᵉ things he had brought. Welcome he was, but yᵉ news he broughte was sadd in many regards; not only in regarde of the former losses, before related, which their freinds had suffered, by which some in a maner were undon, others much disabled from doing any further help, and some dead of yᵉ plague, but also yᵗ Mʳ. Robinson, their pastor, was dead, which struck them with much sorrow & sadnes, as they had cause. His and their adversaries had been long & continually plotting how they might hinder his coming hither, but yᵉ Lord had appointed him a better place; concerning whose death & the maner therof, it will appere by these few lines write to Govʳ & Mʳ. Brewster.

Loving & kind frinds, &c. I know not whether this will ever come to your hands, or miscarie, as other my letters have done; yet in regard of yᵉ Lords dealing with us hear, I have had a great desire to write unto you, knowing your desire to bear a parte with us, both in our joyes, & sorrows, as we doe wᵗʰ you. These are therfore to give you to understand, that it hath pleased the Lord to take out of this vaell of tears, your and our loving & faithfull pastor, and my dear & Reveᵈ brother, Mʳ. John Robinson, who was sick some 8. days. He begane to be sick on Saturday in yᵉ morning, yet yᵉ next day (being the Lords day) he taught us twise. And so yᵉ weeke after grew weaker, every day more then other; yet he felt no paine but weaknes all yᵉ time of his sicknes. The phisick he tooke wrought kindly in mans judgmente, but he grew weaker every day, feeling litle or no paine, and sensible to yᵉ very last. He fell sicke yᵉ 22. of Feb: and departed this life yᵉ 1. of March. He had a continuall inwarde ague, but free from infection, so yᵗ all his freinds came freely to him. And if either prayers, tears, or means, would have saved his life, he had not gone hence. But he having faithfully finished his course, and performed his worke which yᵉ Lord had appointed him here to doe, he now resteth with yᵉ Lord in eternall hapines. We wanting him & all Church Govʳˢ, yet we still (by yᵉ mercie of God) continue & hould close togeather, in peace and quietnes; and so hope we shall doe, though we be very weake. Wishing (if such were yᵉ will of God) that you & we were againe united togeather in one, either ther or here; but seeing it is yᵉ will of yᵉ Lord thus to dispose of things, we must labour wᵗʰ patience to rest contented, till it please yᵉ Lord otherwise to dispose. For [140] news, is here not much; only as in England we have lost our old king James, who departed this life aboute a month agoe, so here they have lost yᵉ old prince, Grave Mourise; who both departed this life since my brother Robinson. And as in England we have a new-king Charls, of whom ther is great hope, so hear they have made prince Hendrick Generall in his brothers place, &c. Thus with my love remembred, I take leave & rest,

Your assured loving friend,

ROGER WHITE.

Leyden, Aprill 28.
An°: 1625.

Thus these too great princes, and their pastor, left this world near aboute one time. Death maks no difference.

He further brought them notice of yᵉ death of their anciente friend, Mr. Cush-man, whom yᵉ Lord tooke away allso this year, & aboute this time, who was as their right hand with their freinds yᵉ adventurers, and for diverce years had done & agitated all their bussines with them to ther great advantage. He had write to yᵉ Goveʳ but some few months before, of yᵉ sore sicknes of Mʳ. James Sherley, who was a cheefe friend to yᵉ plantation, and lay at yᵉ pointe of death, declaring his love & helpfullnes, in all things; and much bemoned the loss they should have of him, if God should now take him away, as being yᵉ stay & life of yᵉ whole bussines. As allso his owne purposs this year to come over, and spend his days with them. But he that thus write of anothers sicknes, knew not yᵗ his owne death was so near. It shows allso that a mās ways are not in his owne power, but in his hands who hath yᵉ issues of life and death. Man may purpose, but God doth dispose.

Their other freinds from Leyden writ many leters to them full of sad laments for ther heavie loss; and though their wills were good to come to them, yet they saw no probabilitie of means, how it might be effected, but concluded (as it were) that all their hopes were cutt of; and many, being aged, begane to drop away by death.

All which things (before related) being well weighed and laied togither, it could not but strick them with great perplexitie; and to looke humanly on yᵉ state of things as they presented them selves at this time, it is a marvell it did not wholy discourage them, and sinck them. But they gathered up their spirits, and yᵉ Lord so helped them, whose worke they had in hand, as now when they were at lowest[CB] they begane to rise againe, and being striped (in a maner) of all humane helps and hops, he brought things aboute other wise, in his devine providence, as they were not only upheld & sustained, but their proceedings both honoured and imitated by others; as by yᵉ sequell will more appeare, if yᵉ Lord spare me life & time to declare yᵉ same.

Haveing now no fishing busines, or other things to intend, but only their trading & planting, they sett them selves to follow the same with ye best industrie they could. The planters finding their corne, what they could spare from ther necessities, to be a comoditie, (for they sould it at 6^s. a bushell,) used great dilligence in planting ye same. And ye Gove^r and such as were designed to manage the trade, (for it was retained for ye generall good, [141] and none were to trade in perticuler,) they followed it to the best advantage they could; and wanting trading goods, they understoode that a plantation which was at Monhigen, & belonged to some marchants of Plimoth was to breake up, and diverse usefull goods was ther to be sould; the Gove^r and M^r. Winslow tooke a boat and some hands and went thither. But M^r. David Thomson, who lived at Pascataway, understanding their purpose, tooke oppertunitie to goe with them, which was some hinderance to them both; for they, perceiveing their joynte desires to buy, held their goods at higher rates; and not only so, but would not sell a parcell of their trading goods, excepte they sould all. So, lest they should further prejudice one an other, they agreed to buy all, & devid them equally between them. They bought allso a parcell of goats, which they distributed at home as they saw neede & occasion, and tooke corne for them of ye people, which gave them good content. Their moyety of ye goods came to above 400^{li}. starling. Ther was allso that spring a French ship cast away at Sacadahock, in wch were many Biscaie ruggs & other comodities, which were falen into these mens hands, & some other fisher men at Damerins-cove, which were allso bought in partnership, and made their parte arise to above 500^{li}. This they made shift to pay for, for ye most part, with ye beaver & comodities they had gott ye winter before, & what they had gathered up y^t somer. M^r. Thomson having some thing overcharged him selfe, desired they would take some of his, but they refused except he would let them have his French goods only; and ye marchant (who was one of Bristol) would take their bill for to be paid ye next year. They were both willing, so they became ingaged for them & tooke them. By which means they became very well furnished for trade; and tooke of therby some other ingagments wch lay upon them, as the money taken up by Captaine Standish, and yᵉ remains of former debts. With these goods, and their corne after harvest, they gott good store of trade, so as they were enabled to pay their ingagements against yᵉ time, & to get some cloathing for yᵉ people, and had some comodities before hand. But now they begane to be envied, and others wente and fild yᵉ Indeans with corne, and beat downe yᵉ prise, giveing them twise as much as they had done, and under traded them in other comodities allso.

This year they sent Mʳ. Allerton into England, and gave him order to make a composition with yᵉ adventurers, upon as good termes as he could (unto which some way had ben made yᵉ year before by Captaine Standish); but yet injoyned him not to conclud absolutly till they knew yᵉ termes, and had well considered of them; but to drive it to as good an issew as he could, and referr yᵉ conclusion to them. Also they gave him a comission under their hands & seals to take up some money, provided it exeeded not such a sume specified, for which they engaged them selves, and gave him order how to lay out yᵉ same for yᵉ use of yᵉ plantation.

And finding they rane a great hazard to goe so long viages in a smale open boat, espetialy yᵉ winter season, they begane to thinke how they might gett a small pinass; as for yᵉ reason afforesaid, so also because others had raised yᵉ prise with yᵉ Indeans above yᵉ halfe of what they had formerly given, so as in such a boat they could not [143[ᶜᶜ]] carry a quantity sufficient to answer their ends. They had no ship-carpenter amongst them, neither knew how to get one at presente; but they having an ingenious man that was a house carpenter, who also had wrought with yᵉ ship carpenter (that was dead) when he built their boats, at their request he put forth him selfe to make a triall that way of his skill; and tooke one of yᵉ bigest of ther shalops and sawed her in yᵉ midle, and so lenthened her some 5. or 6. foote, and strengthened her with timbers, and so builte her up, and laid a deck on her; and so made her a conveniente and wholsome vessell, very fitt & comfortable for their use, which did them servise 7. years after; and they gott her finished, and fitted with sayles & anchors, yᵉ insuing year. And thus passed yᵉ affairs of this year.

Anno Dom: 1627.

At yᵉ usuall season of yᵉ coming of ships Mʳ. Allerton returned, and brought some usfull goods with him, according to yᵉ order given him. For upon his commission he tooke up 200ˡⁱ. which he now gott at 30. per cent. The which goods they gott safly home, and well conditioned, which was much to the comfort & contente of yᵉ plantation. He declared unto them, allso, how, with much adoe and no small trouble, he had made a composition with yᵉ adventurers, by the help of sundrie of their faithfull freinds ther, who had allso tooke much pains ther about. The agreement or bargen he had brought a draught of, with a list of ther names ther too annexed, drawne by the best counsell of law they could get, to make it firme. The heads wherof I shall here inserte.

To all Christian people, greeting, &c. Wheras at a meeting yᵉ 26. of October last past, diverse & sundrie persons, whose names to yᵉ one part of these presents are subscribed in a schedule hereunto annexed, Adventurers to New-Plimoth in New-England in America, were contented and agreed, in consideration of the sume of one thousand and eight hundred pounds sterling to be paid, (in maner and forme folling,) to sell, and make sale of all & every yᵉ stocks, shares, lands, marchandise, and chatles, what soever, to yᵉ said adventurers, and other ther fellow adventurers to New Plimoth aforesaid, any way accruing, or belonging to yᵉ generalitie of yᵉ said adventurers aforesaid; as well by reason of any sume or sumes of money, or marchandise, at any time heretofore adventured or disbursed by them, or other wise howsoever; for yᵉ better expression and setting forth of which said agreemente, the parties to these presents subscribing, doe for [144] them selves severally, and as much as in them is, grant, bargan, alien, sell, and transfere all & every yᵉ said shares, goods, lands, marchandice, and chatles to them belonging as aforesaid, unto Isaack Alerton, one of yᵉ planters resident at Plimoth afforesaid, assigned, and sent over as agente for yᵉ rest of yᵉ planters ther, and to such other planters at Plimoth afforesaid as yᵉ said Isack, his heirs, or assignes, at his or ther arrivall, shall by writing or otherwise thinke fitte to joyne or partake in y⁹ premisses, their heirs, & assignes, in as large, ample, and beneficiall maner and forme, to all intents and purposes, as y⁹ said subscribing adventurers here could or may doe, or performe. All which stocks, shares, lands, &c. to the said adven: in severallitie alloted, apportioned, or any way belonging, the said adven: doe warrant & defend unto the said Isaack Allerton, his heirs and assignes, against them, their heirs and assignes, by these presents. And therfore y⁹ said Isaack Allerton doth, for him, his heirs & assigns, covenant, promise, & grant too & with y⁹ adven: whose names are here unto subscribed, ther heirs, &c. well & truly to pay, or cause to be payed, unto y⁹ said adven: or 5. of them which were, at y¹ meeting afforsaid, nominated & deputed, viz. *John Pocock, John Beachamp, Robart Keane, Edward Base,* and *James Sherley,* marchants, their heirs, &c. too and for y⁹ use of y⁹ generallitie of them, the sume of 1800ˡⁱ. of lawfull money of England, at y⁹ place appoynted for y⁹ receipts of money, on the west side of y⁹ Royall Exchaing in London, by 200ˡⁱ. yearly, and every year, on y⁹ feast of St. Migchell, the first paiment to be made Anᵒ: 1628. &c. Allso y⁹ said Isaack is to indeavor to procure & obtaine from the planters of N. P. aforesaid, securitie, by severall obligations, or writings obligatory, to make paiment of y⁹ said sume of 1800ˡⁱ. in forme afforsaid, according to y⁹ true meaning of these presents. In testimonie wherof to this part of these presents remaining with y⁹ said Isaack Allerton, y⁹ said subscribing adven: have sett to their names,[CD] &c. And to y⁹ other part remaining with y⁹ said adven: the said Isaack Allerton hath subscribed his name, y⁹ *15. Novᵇʳ Anᵒ: 1626. in y⁹ 2. year of his Majesties raigne.*

This agreemente was very well liked of, & approved by all y⁹ plantation, and consented unto; though they knew not well how to raise y⁹ payment, and discharge their other ingagements, and supply the yearly wants of y⁹ plantation, seeing they were forced for their necessities to take up money or goods at so high intrests. Yet they undertooke it, and 7. or 8. of y⁹ cheefe of y⁹ place became joyntly bound for y⁹ paimente of this 1800ˡⁱ. (in y⁹ behalfe of y⁹ rest) at y⁹ severall days. In which they rane a great adventure, as their present state stood, having many other heavie burthens allready upon them, and all things in an uncertaine condition amongst them. So yᵉ next returne it was absolutly confirmed on both sids, and yᵉ bargen fairly ingrossed in partchmente and in many things put into better forme, by yᵉ advice of yᵉ learnedest counsell they could gett; and least any forfeiture should fall on yᵉ whole for none paimente at any of yᵉ days, it rane thus: to forfite 30ˢ. a weeke if they missed yᵉ time; and was concluded under their hands & seals, as may be seen at large by yᵉ deed it selfe.

[145] Now though they had some untowarde persons mixed amongst them from the first, which came out of England, and more afterwards by some of yᵉ adventurers, as freindship or other affections led them,—though sundrie were gone, some for Virginia, and some to other places,—yet diverse were still mingled amongst them, about whom yᵉ Goveʳ & counsell with other of their cheefe freinds had serious consideration, how to setle things in regard of this new bargen or purchas made, in respecte of yᵉ distribution of things both for yᵉ presente and future. For yᵉ present, excepte peace and union were preserved, they should be able to doe nothing, but indanger to over throw all, now that other tyes & bonds were taken away. Therfore they resolved, for sundrie reasons, to take in all amongst them, that were either heads of families, or single yonge men, that were of abillity, and free, (and able to governe them selvs with meete descretion, and their affairs, so as to be helpfull in yᵉ comone-welth,) into this partnership or purchass. First, yᵉʸ considered that they had need of men & strength both for defence and carrying on of bussinesses. 2ˡʸ, most of them had borne ther parts in former miseries & wants with them, and therfore (in some sort) but equall to partake in a better condition, if yᵉ Lord be pleased to give it. But cheefly they saw not how peace would be preserved without so doing, but danger & great disturbance might grow to their great hurte & prejudice other wise. Yet they resolved to keep such a mean in distribution of lands, and other courses, as should not hinder their growth in others coming to them.

So they caled yᵉ company togeather, and conferred with them, and came to this conclusion, that yᵉ trade should be managed as before, to help to pay the debts; and all such persons as were above named should be reputed and inrouled for purchasers; single free men to have a single share, and every father of a familie to be alowed to purchass so many shares as he had persons in his family; that is to say, one for him selfe, and one for his wife, and for every child that he had living with him, one. As for servants, they had none, but what either their maisters should give them out of theirs, or their deservings should obtaine from yᵉ company afterwards. Thus all were to be cast into single shares according to the order abovesaid; and so every one was to pay his part according to his proportion towards yᵉ purchass, & all other debts, what yᵉ profite of yᵉ trade would not reach too; viz. a single man for a single share, a maister of a famalie for so many as he had. This gave all good contente. And first accordingly the few catle which they had were devided, which arose to this proportion; a cowe to 6. persons or shars, & 2. goats to yᵉ same, which were first equalised for age & goodnes, and then lotted for; single persons consorting with others, as they thought good, & smaler familys likwise; and swine though more [146] in number, yet by yᵉ same rule. Then they agreed that every person or share should have 20. acres of land devided unto them, besids yᵉ single acres they had allready; and they appoynted were to begin first on yᵉ one side of yᵉ towne, & how farr to goe; and then on yᵉ other side in like maner; and so to devid it by lotte; and appointed sundrie by name to doe it, and tyed them to certaine ruls to proceed by; as that they should only lay out settable or tillable land, at least such of it as should butt on yᵉ water side, (as yᵉ most they were to lay out did,) and pass by yᵉ rest as refuse and comune; and what they judged fitte should be so taken. And they were first to agree of yᵉ goodnes & fitnes of it before the lott was drawne, and so it might as well prove some of ther owne, as an other mans; and this course they were to hould throwout. But yet seekeing to keepe yᵉ people togither, as much as might be, they allso agreed upon this order, by mutuall consente, before any lots were cast: that whose lotts soever should fall next yᵉ towne, or most conveninte for nearnes, they should take to them a neigboure or tow, whom they best liked; and should suffer them to plant corne with them for 4. years; and afterwards they might use as much of theirs for as long time, if they would. Allso every share or 20. acers was to be laid out 5. acres in breadth by yᵉ water side, and 4. acres in lenght, excepting nooks & corners, which were to be measured as yᵉʸ would bear to best advantage. But no meadows were to be laid out at all, nor were not of many years after, because they were but streight of meadow grounds; and if they had bene now given out, it would have hindred all addition to them afterwards; but every season all were appoynted wher they should mowe, according to yᵉ proportion of catle they had. This distribution gave generally good contente, and setled mens minds. Also they gave yᵉ Goveʳ & 4. or 5. of yᵉ spetiall men amongst them, yᵉ houses they lived in; yᵉ rest were valued & equalised at an indiferent rate, and so every man kept his owne, and he that had a better alowed some thing to him that had a worse, as yᵉ valuation wente.

Ther is one thing that fell out in yᵉ begining of yᵉ winter before, which I have refferred to this place, that I may handle yᵉ whole matter togeither. Ther was a ship, with many passengers in her and sundrie goods, bound for Virginia. They had lost them selves at sea, either by yᵉ insufficiencie of yᵉ maister, or his ilnes; for he was sick & lame of yᵉ scurvie, so that he could but lye in yᵉ cabin dore, & give direction; and it should seeme was badly assisted either wᵗʰ mate or mariners; or else yᵉ fear and unrulines of yᵉ passengers were such, as they made them stear a course betweene yᵉ southwest & yᵉ norwest, that they might fall with some land, what soever it was they cared not. For they had been 6. weeks at sea, and had no water, nor beere, nor any woode left, but had burnt up all their emptie caske; only one of yᵉ company had a hogshead of wine or 2. which was allso allmost spente, so as they feared they should be starved at sea, or consumed with diseases, which made them rune this desperate course. But it plased God that though they came so neare yᵉ shoulds of Cap-Codd [147] or else ran stumbling over them in yᵉ night, they knew not how, they came right before a small blind harbore, that lyes about yᵉ midle of Manamoyake Bay, to yᵉ southward of Cap-Codd, with a small gale of wind; and about highwater toucht upon a barr of sand that lyes before it, but had no hurte, yᵉ sea being smoth; so they laid out an anchore. But towards the evening the wind sprunge up at sea, and was so rough, as broake their cable, & beat them over the barr into yᵉ harbor, wher they saved their lives & goods, though much were hurte with salt water; for wᵗʰ beating they had sprung yᵉ but end of a planke or too, & beat out ther occome; but they were soone over, and ran on a drie flate within the harbor, close by a beach; so at low water they gatt out their goods on drie shore, and dried those that were wette, and saved most of their things without any great loss; neither was yᵉ ship much hurt, but shee might be mended, and made servisable againe. But though they were not a litle glad that they had thus saved their lives, yet when they had a litle refreshed them selves, and begane to thinke on their condition, not knowing wher they were, nor what they should doe, they begane to be strucken with sadnes. But shortly after they saw some Indians come to them in canows, which made them stand upon their gard. But when they heard some of yᵉ Indeans speake English unto them, they were not a litle revived, especially when they heard them demand if they were the Goveʳ of Plimoths men, or freinds; and yᵗ they would bring them to yᵉ English houses, or carry their letters.

They feasted these Indeans, and gave them many giftes; and sente 2. men and a letter with them to yᵉ Goveʳ, and did intreat him to send a boat unto them, with some pitch, and occume, and spiks, wᵗʰ divers other necessaries for yᵉ mending of ther ship (which was recoverable). Allso they besought him to help them with some corne and sundrie other things they wanted, to enable them to make their viage to Virginia; and they should be much bound to him, and would make satisfaction for any thing they had, in any comodities they had abord. After yᵉ Goveʳ was well informed by yᵉ messengers of their condition, he caused a boate to be made ready, and such things to be provided as they write for; and because others were abroad upon trading, and such other affairs, as had been fitte to send unto them, he went him selfe, and allso carried some trading comodities, to buy them corne of yᵉ Indeans. It was no season of yᵉ year to goe withoute yᵉ Cape, but understanding wher yᵉ ship lay, he went into yᵉ bottom of yᵉ bay, on yᵉ inside, and put into a crick called Naumskachett, wher it is not much above 2. mile over [148] land to yᵉ bay wher they were, wher he had yᵉ Indeans ready to cary over any thing to them. Of his arrivall they were very glad, and received the things to mend ther ship, and other necessaries. Allso he bought them as much corne as they would have; and wheras some of their sea-men were rune away amonge the Indeans, he procured their returne to yᵉ ship, and so left them well furnished and contented, being very thankfull for yᵉ curtesies they receaved. But after the Governor thus left them, he went into some other harbors ther aboute and loaded his boat with corne, which he traded, and so went home. But he had not been at home many days, but he had notice from them, that by the violence of a great storme, and yᵉ bad morring of their ship (after she was mended) she was put a shore, and so beatten and shaken as she was now wholy unfitte to goe to sea. And so their request was that they might have leave to repaire to them, and soujourne with them, till they could have means to convey them selves to Virginia; and that they might have means to trāsport their goods, and they would pay for yᵉ same, or any thing els wher with yᵉ plantation should releeve them. Considering their distres, their requests were granted, and all helpfullnes done unto them; their goods transported, and them selves & goods sheltered in their houses as well as they could.

The cheefe amongst these people was one Mʳ. Fells and Mʳ. Sibsie, which had many servants belonging unto them, many of them being Irish. Some others ther were yᵗ had a servante or 2. a peece; but yᵉ most were servants, and such as were ingaged to the former persons, who allso had yᵉ most goods. Affter they were hither come, and some thing setled, the maisters desired some ground to imploye ther servants upon; seing it was like to be yᵉ latter end of yᵉ year before they could have passage for Virginia, and they had now yᵉ winter before them; they might clear some ground, and plant a crope (seeing they had tools, & necessaries for yᵉ same) to help to bear their charge, and keep their servants in imployment; and if they had opportunitie to departe before the same was ripe, they would sell it on yᵉ ground. So they had ground appointed them in convenient places, and Fells & some other of them raised a great deall of corne, which they sould at their departure. This Fells, amongst his other servants, had a maid servante which kept his house & did his household affairs, and by the intimation of some that belonged unto him, he was suspected to keep her, as his concubine; and both of them were examined ther upon, but nothing could be proved, and they stood upon their justification; so with admonition they were dismiste. But afterward it appeard she was with child, so he gott a small boat, & ran away with her, for fear of punishmente. First he went to Cap-Anne, and after into yᵉ bay of yᵉ Massachussets, but could get no passage, and had like to have been cast away; and was forst to come againe and submite him selfe; but they pact him away & those that belonged unto him by the first oppertunitie, and dismiste all the rest as soone as could, being many untoward people amongst them; though ther were allso some that caried them selves very orderly all yᵉ time they stayed. And the [149] plantation had some benefite by them, in selling them corne & other provisions of food for cloathing; for they had of diverse kinds, as cloath, perpetuanes, & other stuffs, besids hose, & shoes, and such like comodities as yᵉ planters stood in need of. So they both did good, and received good one from another; and a cuple of barks caried them away at yᵉ later end of somer. And sundrie of them have acknowledged their thankfullnes since from Virginia.

That they might yᵉ better take all convenient opportunitie to follow their trade, both to maintaine them selves, and to disingage them of those great sumes which they stood charged with, and bound for, they resoloved to build a smale pinass at Manamet, a place 20. mile from yᵉ plantation, standing on yᵉ sea to yᵉ southward of them, unto which, by an other creeke on this side, they could cary their goods, within 4. or 5. miles, and then trāsport them over land to their vessell; and so avoyd the compasing of Cap-Codd, and those deangerous shoulds, and so make any vioage to yᵉ southward in much shorter time, and with farr less danger. Also for yᵉ saftie of their vessell & goods, they builte a house their, and kept some servants, who also planted corne, and reared some swine, and were allwayes ready to goe out with yᵉ barke when ther was occasion. All which tooke good effecte, and turned to their profite.

They now sent (with yᵉ returne of yᵉ ships) Mʳ. Allerton againe into England, giveing him full power, under their hands & seals, to conclude the former bargaine with yᵉ adventurers; and sent ther bonds for yᵉ paimente of the money. Allso they sent what beaver they could spare to pay some of their ingagementes, & to defray his chargs; for those deepe interests still kepte them low. Also he had order to procure a patente for a fitt trading place in yᵉ river of Kenebec; for being emulated both by the planters at Pascataway &, other places to yᵉ eastward of them, and allso by yᵉ fishing ships, which used to draw much profite from yᵉ Indeans of those parts, they threatened to procure a grante, & shutte them out from thence; espetially after they saw them so well furnished with comodities, as to carie the trade from them. They thought it but needfull to prevente such a thing, at least that they might not be excluded from free trade ther, wher them selves had first begune and discovered the same, ād brought it to so good effecte. This year allso they had letters, and messengers from yᵉ Dutch-plantation, sent unto them from yᵉ Govʳ ther, writen both in Dutch & French. The Dutch had traded in these southerne parts, diverse years before they came; but they begane no plantation hear till 4. or 5. years after their coming, and here begining. Ther letters were as followeth. It being their maner to be full of complementall titles.

Eedele, Eerenfeste Wyse Voorsinnige Heeren, den Gŏveerneŭr, ende Raeden in Nieu-Pliemŭen residerende; onse seer Goede vrinden den directeŭr ende Raed van Nieu-Nederlande, wensen vwe Edn: eerenfesten, ende wijse voorsinnige gelŭck salichitt [gelukzaligheid?], In Christi Jesu onsen Heere; met goede voorspoet, ende gesonthijt, naer siele, ende lichaem. Amen.[CF]

The rest I shall render in English, leaving out the repetition of superfluous titles.

[150] We have often before this wished for an opportunitie or an occasion to congratulate you, and your prosperous and praise-worthy undertakeings, and Government of your colony ther. And the more, in that we also have made a good begining to pitch yᵉ foundation of a collonie hear; and seeing our native countrie lyes not farr from yours, and our forefathers (diverse hundred years agoe) have made and held frendship and alliance with your ancestours, as sufficently appears by yᵉ old contractes, and entrecourses, confirmed under yᵉ hands of kings & princes, in yᵉ pointe of warr & trafick; as may be seene and read by all yᵉ world in yᵉ old chronakles. The which are not only by the king now reigning confirmed, but it hath pleased his majesty, upon mature deliberation, to make a new covenante, (and to take up armes,) with yᵉ States Generall of our dear native country, against our commone enemie the Spaniards, who seeke nothing else but to usurpe and overcome other Christian kings and princes lands, that so he might obtaine and possess his pretended monarchic over all Christendom; and so to rule and comand, after his owne pleasure, over yᵉ consciences of so many hundred thousand sowles, which God forbid.

And also seeing it hath some time since been reported unto us, by some of our people, that by occasion came so farr northward with their shalop, and met with sundry of yᵉ Indeans, who tould them that they were within halfe a days journey of your plantation, and offered ther service to cary letters unto you; therfore we could not forbear to salute you with these few lines, with presentation of our good will and servise unto you, in all frendly-kindnes &

neighbourhood. And if it so fall out that any goods that comes to our hands from our native countrie, may be serviceable unto you, we shall take our selves bound to help and accomadate you ther with; either for beaver or any other wares or marchandise that you should be pleased to deale for. And if in case we have no comodity at present that may give you contente, if you please to sell us any beaver, or otter, or such like comodities as may be usefull for us, for ready money, and let us understand therof by this bearer in writing, (whom we have apoynted to stay 3. or 4. days for your answer,) when we understand your minds therin, we shall depute one to deale with you, at such place as you shall appointe. In y⁰ mean time we pray the Lord to take you, our honoured good freinds and neighbours, into his holy protection.

By the appointment of yᵉ Govʳ and Counsell, &c.

ISAAK DE RASIER, Secrectaris.

From yᵉ Manhatas, in yᵉ fort Amsterdam,

March 9. Anᵒ: 1627.

To this they returned answer as followeth, on yᵉ other side.

[151] To the Honoured, &c.

The Goveʳ & Counsell of New-Plim: wisheth, &c. We have received your leters, &c. wherin appeareth your good wills & frendship towards us; but is expresed wᵗʰ over high titls, more then belongs to us, or is meete for us to receive. But for your good will, and congratulations of our prosperitie in these smale beginings of our poore colonie, we are much bound unto you, and with many thanks doe acknowledg yᵉ same; taking it both for a great honour done unto us, and for a certaine testimoney of your love and good neighbourhood.

Now these are further to give your Worᵖᵖˢ to understand, that it is to us no smale joye to hear, that his majestie hath not only bene pleased to confirme y^t ancient amitie, aliance, and frendship, and other contracts, formerly made & ratified by his predecessors of famous memorie, but hath him selfe (as you say) strengthened the same with a new-union the better to resist ye prid of y^t comone enemy ye Spaniard, from whose cruelty the Lord keep us both, and our native countries. Now forasmuch as this is sufficiente to unite us togeather in love and good neighbourhood, in all our dealings, yet are many of us further obliged, by the good and curteous entreaty which we have found in your countrie; haveing lived ther many years, with freedome, and good contente, as also many of our freinds doe to this day; for which we, and our children after us, are bound to be thankfull to your Nation, and shall never forgett ye same, but shall hartily desire your good & prosperity, as our owne, for ever.

Likwise for your freindly tender, & offer to acomodate and help us with any comodities or marchandise you have, or shall come to you, either for beaver, otters, or other wares, it is to us very acceptable, and we doubte not but in short time we may have profitable comerce & trade togeather. But for this year we are fully supplyed with all necessaries, both for cloathing and other things; but hereafter it is like we shall deale with you, if your rates be reasonable. And therfore when you please to send to us againe by any of yours, we desire to know how you will take beaver, by ye pounde, & otters, by ye skine; and how you will deale per cent. for other comodities, and what you can furnishe us with. As likwise what other commodities from us may be acceptable unto you, as tobaco, fish, corne, or other things, and what prises you will give, &c.

Thus hoping that you will pardon & excuse us for our rude and imperfecte writing in your language, and take it in good parte, because [152] for wante of use we cannot so well express that we understand, nor hapily understand every thing so fully as we should. And so we humbly pray the Lord for his mercie sake, that he will take both us and you into his keeping & gratious protection.

By ye Gove^r and Counsell of New-Plimoth,

Your Wor^pps very good freinds & neigbours, &c.

New-Plim: March 19.

After this ther was many passages betweene them both by letters and other entercourse; and they had some profitable commerce togither for diverce years, till other occasions interrupted ye same, as may happily appear afterwards, more at large.

Before they sent M^r. Allerton away for England this year, ye Gove^r and some of their cheefe freinds had serious consideration, not only how they might discharge those great ingagments which lay so heavily upon them, as is affore mentioned, but also how they might (if possiblie they could) devise means to help some of their freinds and breethren of Leyden over unto them, who desired so much to come to them, ād they desired as much their company. To effecte which, they resolved to rune a high course, and of great adventure, not knowing otherwise how to bring it aboute. Which was to hire ye trade of ye company for certaine years, and in that time to undertake to pay that 1800^li. and all ye rest of ye debts that then lay upon ye plantation, which was aboute some 600^li. more; and so to set them free, and returne the trade to ye generalitie againe at ye end of ye terme. Upon which resolution they called ye company togeither, and made it clearly appear unto all what their debts were, and upon what terms they would undertake to pay them all in such a time, and sett them clear. But their other ends they were faine to keepe secrete, haveing only privatly acquaynted some of their trusty freinds therwith; which were glad of ye same, but doubted how they would be able to performe it. So after some agitation of the thing wth ye company, it was yeelded unto, and the agreemente made upon ye conditions following.

Articles of agreemente betweene ye collony of New-Plimoth of ye one partie, and William Bradford, Captein Myles Standish, Isaack Allerton, &c. one ye other partie; and shuch others as they shall thinke good to take as partners and undertakers with them, concerning the trade for beaver & other furrs & comodities, &c.; made July, 1627.

First, it is agreed and covenanted betweexte yᵉ said parties, that yᵉ afforsaid William Bradford, Captain Myl Standish, & Isaack Allerton, &c. have undertaken, and doe by these presents, covenante and agree to pay, discharge, and acquite yᵉ said collony of all yᵉ debtes both due for yᵉ purchass, or any other belonging to them, at yᵉ day of yᵉ date of these presents.

[153] Secondly, yᵉ above-said parties are to have and freely injoye yᵉ pinass latly builte, the boat at Manamett, and yᵉ shalop, called yᵉ Bass-boat, with all other implements to them belonging, that is in yᵉ store of yᵉ said company; with all yᵉ whole stock of furrs, fells, beads, corne, wampampeak, hatchets, knives, &c. that is now in yᵉ storre, or any way due unto yᵉ same uppon accounte.

3ˡʸ. That yᵉ above said parties have yᵉ whole trade to them selves, their heires and assignes, with all yᵉ privileges therof, as yᵉ said collonie doth now, or may use the same, for 6. full years, to begine yᵉ last of September next insuing.

4ˡʸ. In furder consideration of yᵉ discharge of yᵉ said debtes, every severall purchaser doth promise and covenante yearly to pay, or cause to be payed, to the above said parties, during yᵉ full terme of yᵉ said 6. years, 3. bushells of corne, or 6ˡⁱ. of tobaco, at yᵉ undertakers choyse.

5ˡʸ. The said undertakers shall dureing yᵉ afforesaid terme bestow 50ˡⁱ. per annum, in hose and shoese, to be brought over for yᵉ collonies use, to be sould unto them for corne at 6ˢ. per bushell.

6ˡʸ. That at yᵉ end of yᵉ said terme of 6. years, the whole trade shall returne to yᵗ use and benefite of yᵉ said collonie, as before.

Lastly, if yᵉ afforesaid undertakers, after they have aquainted their freinds in England with these covenants, doe (upon yᵉ first returne) resolve to performe them, and undertake to discharge yᵉ debtes of yᵉ said collony, according to yᵉ true meaning & intente of these presents, then they are (upon such notice given) to stand in full force; otherwise all things to remaine as formerly they were, and a true accounte to be given to yᵉ said collonie, of the disposing of all things according to the former order.

M[r]. Allerton carried a coppy of this agreemente with him into England, and amongst other his instructions had order given him to deale with some of their speciall freinds, to joyne with them in this trade upon y[e] above recited conditions; as allso to imparte their further ends that moved them to take this course, namly, the helping over of some of their freinds from Leyden, as they should be able; in which if any of them would joyne with them they should thankfully acceptt of their love and partnership herein. And with all (by their letters) gave them some grounds of their hops of the accomplishmente of these things with some advantage.

Anno Dom: 1628.

After M[r]. Allertons arivall in England, he aquainted them with his comission and full power to conclude y[e] forementioned bargan & purchas; upon [154] the veiw wherof, and y[e] delivery of y[e] bonds for y[e] paymente of y[e] money yearly, (as is before mentioned,) it was fully concluded, and a deede[CF] fairly ingrossed in partchmente was delivered him, under their hands & seals confirming the same. Morover he delte with them aboute other things according to his instructions. As to admitt some of these their good freinds into this purchass if they pleased, and to deale with them for moneys at better rates, &c. Touching which I shall hear inserte a letter of M[r]. Sherleys, giving light to what followed therof, writ to y[e] Gov[r] as followeth.

S[r]: I have received yours of y[e] 26. of May by M[r]. Gibs, & M[r]. Goffe, with y[e] barrell of otter skins, according to y[e] contents; for which I got a bill of store, and so tooke them up, and sould them togeather at 78[li]. 12[s]. sterling; and since, M[r]. Allerton hath received y[e] money, as will apear by the accounte. It is true (as you write) that your ingagments are great, not only the purchass, but you are yet necessitated to take up y[e] stock you work upon; and y[t] not at 6. or 8. p[r] cent. as it is here let out, but at 30. 40. yea, & some at 50. p[r] cent. which, were not your gaines great, and Gods blessing on your honest indeaours more then ordinarie, it could not be y[t] you should longe subsiste in y[e] maintaining of, & upholding of your worldly affaires. And this your honest & discreete agente, M[r]. Allerton, hath seriously considered, & deeply laid to mind, how to ease you of it. He tould me you were contented to accepte of me & some few others, to joyne with you in ye purchass, as partners; for which I kindly thanke you and all ye rest, and doe willingly accepte of it. And though absente, shall willingly be at shuch charge as you & ye rest shall thinke meete; and this year am contented to forbear my former 50^{li}. and 2. years increase for ye venture, both which now makes it 80^{li}. without any bargaine or condition for ye profite, you (I mean ye generalitie) stand to ye adventure, outward, and homeward. I have perswaded M^r. Andrews and M^r. Beachamp to doe ye like, so as you are eased of ye high rate, you were at ye other 2. yeares; I say we leave it freely to your selves to alow us what you please, and as God shall blesse. What course I rune, M^r. Beachamp desireth to doe ye same; and though he have been or seemed somwhat harsh heretofore, yet now you shall find he is new moulded. I allso see by your letter, you desire I should be your agente or factore hear. I have ever found you so faithfull, honest, and upright men, as I have even resolved with my selfe (God assisting me) to doe you all ye good lyeth in my power; and therfore if you please to make choyse of so weak a man, both for abillities and body, to performe your bussines, I promise (ye Lord enabling me) to doe ye best I can according to those abillities he hath given me; and wherin I faile, blame your selves, y^t you made no better choyce. Now, because I am sickly, and we are all mortall, I have advised M^r. Allerton to joyne M^r. Beachamp with me in your deputation, which I conceive to be very necessary & good for you; your charge shall be no more, for it is not your salarie maks me undertake your [156^[CG]] bussines. Thus contending you & yours, and all Gods people, unto ye guidance and protection of ye Allmightie, I ever rest,

Your faithfull loving freind,

JAMES SHERLEY.[CH]

London, Nov. 17. 1628.

With this leter they sent a draught of a formall deputation to be hear sealed and sent back unto them, to authorise them as their agents, according to what is mentioned in y above said letter; and because some inconvenience grue therby afterward I shall here inserte it.

To all to whom these prēts shall come greeting; know yee that we, William Bradford, Gov of Plimoth, in N.E. in America, Isaak Allerton, Myles Standish, William Brewster, & Ed: Winslow, of Plimoth aforesaid, marchants, doe by these presents for us & in our names, make, substitute, & appointe James Sherley, Goldsmith, & John Beachamp, Salter, citizens of London, our true & lawfull agents, factors, substitutes, & assignes; as well to take and receive all such goods, wares, & marchandise what soever as to our said substitutes or either of them, or to y citie of London, or other place of y Relme of Engl: shall be sente, transported, or come from us or any of us, as allso to vend, sell, barter, or exchaing y said goods, wares, and marchandise so from time to time to be sent to such person or persons upon credite, or other wise in such maner as to our said agents & factors joyently, or to either of them severally shall seeme meete. And further we doe make & ordaine our said substituts & assignes joyntly & severally for us, & to our uses, & accounts, to buy and consigne for and to us into New-Engl: aforesaid, such goods and marchandise to be provided here, and to be returned hence, as by our said assignes, or either of them, shall be thought fitt. And to recover, receive, and demand for us & in our names all such debtes & sumes of money, as now are or hereafter shall be due incidente accruing or belonging to us, or any of us, by any wayes or means; and to acquite, discharge, or compound for any debte or sume of money, which now or hereafter shall be due or oweing by any person or persons to us, or any of us. And generally for us & in our names to doe, performe, and execute every acte & thing which to our said assignes, or either of them, shall seeme meete to be done in or aboute y premissies, as fully & effectually, to all intents & purposes, as if we or any of us were in person presente. And whatsoever our said agents & factors joyntly or severally shall doe, or cause to be done, in or aboute ye premisses, we will & doe, & every of us doth ratife, alow, & confirme, by these presents. In wittnes wherof we have here unto put our hands & seals. Dated 18. Nov^br 1628.

This was accordingly confirmed by the above named, and 4. more of the cheefe of them under their hands & seals, and delivered unto them. Also M^r. Allerton formerly had authoritie under their hands & seals for ye transacting of ye former bussines, and taking up of moneys, &c. which still he retained whilst he was imployed in these affaires; they mistrusting neither him nor any of their freinds faithfullnes, which made them more remisse in looking to shuch acts as had passed under their hands, as necessarie for ye time; but letting them rune on to long unminded or recaled, it turned to their harme afterwards, as will appere in its place.

[157] M^r. Allerton having setled all things thus in a good and hopfull way, he made hast to returne in ye first of ye spring to be hear with their supply for trade, (for ye fishermen with whom he came used to sett forth in winter & be here betimes.) He brought a resonable supply of goods for ye plantation, and without those great interests as before is noted; and brought an accounte of ye beaver sould, and how ye money was disposed for goods, & ye paymente of other debtes, having paid all debts abroad to others, save to M^r. Sherley, M^r. Beachamp, & M^r. Andrews; from whom likwise he brought an accounte which to them all amounted not to above 400^li. for which he had passed bonds. Allso he had payed the first paymente for ye purchass, being due for this year, viz. 200^li. and brought them ye bonde for ye same canselled; so as they now had no more foreine debtes but ye abovesaid 400^li. and odde pownds, and ye rest of ye yearly purchass monie. Some other debtes they had in ye cuntrie, but they were without any intrest, & they had wherwith to discharge them when they were due. To this pass the Lord had brought things for them. Also he brought them further notice that their freinds, the abovenamed, & some others that would joyne with them in ye trad & purchass, did intend for to send over to Leyden, for a competente number of them, to be hear the next year without fayle, if ye Lord pleased to blesse their journey. He allso

brought them a patente for Kenebeck, but it was so straite & ill bounded, as they were faine to renew & inlarge it the next year, as allso that which they had at home, to their great charge, as will after appeare. Hithertoo M^r. Allerton did them good and faithfull service; and well had it been if he had so continued, or els they had now ceased for imploying him any longer thus into England. But of this more afterwards.

Having procured a patente (as is above said) for Kenebeck, they now erected a house up above in ye river in ye most convenientest place for trade, as they conceived, and furnished the same with comodities for y^t end, both winter & somer, not only with corne, but also with such other commodities as ye fishermen had traded with them, as coats, shirts, ruggs, & blankets, biskett, pease, prunes, &c.; and what they could not have out of England, they bought of the fishing ships, and so carried on their bussines as well as they could.

This year the Dutch sent againe unto them from their plantation, both kind leterss, and also diverse comodities, as suger, linen cloth, Holand finer & courser stufes, &c. They came up with their barke to Manamete, to their house ther, in which came their Secretarie Rasier; who was accompanied with a noyse of trumpeters, and some other attendants; and desired that they would send a boat for him, for he could not travill so farr over land. So they sent a boat to Manonscussett, and brought him to ye plantation, with ye cheefe of his company. And after some few days entertainmente, he returned to his barke, and some of them wente with him, and bought sundry of his goods; after which begining thus made, they sente often times to ye same place, and had entercourse togeather for diverce years; and amongst other comodities, they vended [158] much tobaco for linen cloath, stuffs, &c., which was a good benefite to ye people, till the Virginians found out their plantation. But that which turned most to their profite, in time, was an entrance into the trade of Wampampeake; for they now bought aboute 50^li. worth of it of them; and they tould them how vendable it was at their forte Orania; and did perswade them they would find it so at Kenebeck; and so it came to pass in time, though at first it stuck, & it was 2.

years before they could put of this small quantity, till ye inland people knew of it; and afterwards they could scarce ever gett enough for them, for many years togeather. And so this, with their other provissions, cutt of they trade quite from ye fisher-men, and in great part from other of ye stragling planters. And strange it was to see the great allteration it made in a few years amonge ye Indeans them selves; for all the Indeans of these parts, & ye Massachussets, had none or very litle of it,[CI] but ye sachems & some spetiall persons that wore a litle of it for ornamente. Only it was made & kepte amonge ye Nariganssets, & Pequents, which grew rich & potent by it, and these people were poore & begerly, and had no use of it. Neither did the English of this plantation, or any other in ye land, till now that they had knowledg of it from ye Dutch, so much as know what it was, much less yt it was a comoditie of that worth & valew. But after it grue thus to be a comoditie in these parts, these Indeans fell into it allso, and to learne how to make it; for ye Narigansets doe geather ye shells of which yey make it from their shors. And it hath now continued a current comoditie aboute this 20. years, and it may prove a drugg in time. In ye mean time it maks ye Indeans of these parts rich & power full and also prowd therby; and fills them with peeces, powder, and shote, which no laws can restraine, by reasone of ye bassnes of sundry unworthy persons, both English, Dutch, & French, which may turne to ye ruine of many. Hithertoo ye Indeans of these parts had no peeces nor other armes but their bowes & arrowes, nor of many years after; nether durst they scarce handle a gune, so much were they affraid of them; and ye very sight of one (though out of kilter) was a terrour unto them. But those Indeans to ye east parts, which had comerce with ye French, got peces of them, and they in the end made a commone trade of it; and in time our English fisher-men, led with ye like covetoussnes, followed their example, for their owne gaine; but upon complainte against them, it pleased the kings majestie to prohibite ye same by a stricte proclaimation, commanding that no sorte of armes, or munition, should by any of his subjects be traded with them.

Aboute some 3. or 4. years before this time, ther came over one
Captaine Wolastone, (a man of pretie parts,) and with him 3. or 4.
more of some eminencie, who brought with them a great many
servants, with provissions & other implments for to begine a
plantation; and pitched them selves in a place within the
Massachusets, which they called, after their Captains name,
Mount-Wollaston. Amongst whom was one M͏ͬ. Morton, who, it
should seeme, had some small adventure (of his owne or other
mens) amongst them; but had litle respecte [159] amongst them,
and was sleghted by y͏ᵉ meanest servants. Haveing continued ther
some time, and not finding things to answer their expectations, nor
profite to arise as they looked for, Captaine Wollaston takes a great
part of y͏ᵉ sarvants, and transports them to Virginia, wher he puts
them of at good rates, selling their time to other men; and writs
back to one M͏ͬ. Rassdall, one of his cheefe partners, and accounted
their marchant, to bring another parte of them to Verginia likewise,
intending to put them of ther as he had done y͏ᵉ rest. And he, w͏ᵗʰ y͏ᵉ
consente of y͏ᵉ said Rasdall, appoynted one Fitcher to be his
Livetenante, and governe y͏ᵉ remaines of y͏ᵉ plantation, till he or
Rasdall returned to take further order theraboute. But this Morton
abovesaid, haveing more craft then honestie, (who had been a kind
of petie-fogger, of Furnefells Inne,) in y͏ᵉ others absence, watches
an oppertunitie, (commons being but hard amongst them,) and gott
some strong drinck & other junkats, & made them a feast; and after
they were merie, he begane to tell them, he would give them good
counsell. You see (saith he) that many of your fellows are carried
to Virginia; and if you stay till this Rasdall returne, you will also be
carried away and sould for slaves with y͏ᵉ rest. Therfore I would
advise you to thruste out this Levetenant Fitcher; and I, having a
parte in the plantation, will receive you as my partners and
consociats; so may you be free from service, and we will converse,
trad, plante, & live togeather as equalls, & supporte & protecte one
another, or to like effecte. This counsell was easily received; so
they tooke oppertunitie, and thrust Levetenante Fitcher out a dores,
and would suffer him to come no more amongst them, but forct
him to seeke bread to eate, and other releefe from his neigbours, till

he could gett passages for England. After this they fell to great licenciousnes, and led a dissolute life, powering out them selves into all profanenes. And Morton became lord of misrule, and maintained (as it were) a schoole of Athisme. And after they had gott some good into their hands, and gott much by trading with yᵉ Indeans, they spent it as vainly, in quaffing & drinking both wine & strong waters in great exsess, and, as some reported, 10ˡⁱ. worth in a morning. They allso set up a May-pole, drinking and dancing aboute it many days togeather, inviting the Indean women, for their consorts, dancing and frisking togither, (like so many fairies, or furies rather,) and worse practises. As if they had anew revived & celebrated the feasts of yᵉ Roman Goddes Flora, or yᵉ beasly practieses of yᵉ madd Bacchinalians. Morton likwise (to shew his poetrie) composed sundry rimes & verses, some tending to lasciviousnes, and others to yᵉ detraction & scandall of some persons, which he affixed to this idle or idoll May-polle. They chainged allso the name of their place, and in stead of calling it Mounte Wollaston, they call it Merie-mounte, [160] as if this joylity would have lasted ever. But this continued not long, for after Morton was sent for England, (as follows to be declared,) shortly after came over that worthy gentlman, Mʳ. John Indecott, who brought over a patent under yᵉ broad seall, for yᵉ govermente of yᵉ Massachusets, who visiting those parts caused yⁱ May-polle to be cutt downe, and rebuked them for their profannes, and admonished them to looke ther should be better walking; so they now, or others, changed yᵉ name of their place againe, and called it Mounte-Dagon.

Now to maintaine this riotous prodigallitie and profuse excess, Morton, thinking him selfe lawless, and hearing what gaine yᵉ French & fisher-men made by trading of peeces, powder, & shotte to yᵉ Indeans, he, as yᵉ head of this consortship, begane yᵉ practise of yᵉ same in these parts; and first he taught them how to use them, to charge, & discharg, and what proportion of powder to give yᵉ peece, according to yᵉ sise or bignes of yᵉ same; and what shotte to use for foule, and what for deare. And having thus instructed them, he imployed some of them to hunte & fowle for him, so as they became farr more active in that imploymente then any of yᵉ English, by reason of ther swiftnes of foote, & nimblnes of body, being also quick-sighted, and by continuall exercise well knowing yᵉ hants of all sorts of game. So as when they saw yᵉ execution that a peece would doe, and yᵉ benefite that might come by yᵉ same, they became madd, as it were, after them, and would not stick to give any prise they could attaine too for them; accounting their bowes & arrowes but bables in comparison of them.

And here I may take occasion to bewaile yᵉ mischefe that this wicked man began in these parts, and which since base covetousnes prevailing in men that should know better, has now at length gott yᵉ upper hand, and made this thing comone, notwithstanding any laws to yᵉ contrary; so as yᵉ Indeans are full of peeces all over, both fouling peeces, muskets, pistols, &c. They have also their moulds to make shotte, of all sorts, as muskett bulletts, pistoll bullets, swane & gose shote, & of smaler sorts; yea, some have seen them have their scruplats to make scrupins them selves, when they wante them, with sundery other implements, wherwith they are ordinarily better fited & furnished then yᵉ English them selves. Yea, it is well knowne that they will have powder & shot, when the English want it, nor cannot gett it; and yᵗ in a time of warr or danger, as experience hath manifested, that when lead hath been scarce, and men for their owne defence would gladly have given a groat a l which is dear enoughe, yet hath it bene bought up & sent to other places, and sould to shuch as trade it with yᵉ Indeans, at 12. pence yᵉ li.; and it is like they give 3. or 4.ˢ yᵉ pound, for they will have it at any rate. And these things have been done in yᵉ same times, when some of their neigbours & freinds are daly killed by yᵉ Indeans, or are in deanger therof, and live but at yᵉ Indeans mercie. [161] Yea, some (as they have aquainted them with all other things) have tould them how gunpowder is made, and all yᵉ materialls in it, and that they are to be had in their owne land; and I am confidente, could they attaine to make saltpeter, they would teach them to make powder. O the horiblnes of this vilanie! how many both Dutch & English have been latly slaine by those Indeans, thus furnished; and no remedie provided, nay, yᵉ evill more increased, and yᵉ blood of their brethren sould for gaine, as is to be feared; and in what danger all these colonies are in is too well known. Oh! that princes & parlements would take some timly order to prevente this mischeefe, and at length to suppress it, by some exemplerie punishmente upon some of these gaine thirstie murderers, (for they deserve no better title,) before their collonies in these parts be over throwne by these barbarous savages, thus armed with their owne weapons, by these evill instruments, and traytors to their neigbors and cuntrie. But I have forgott my selfe, and have been to longe in this digression; but now to returne. This Morton having thus taught them yᵉ use of peeces, he sould them all he could spare; and he and his consorts detirmined to send for many out of England, and had by some of yᵉ ships sente for above a score. The which being knowne, and his neigbours meeting yᵉ Indeans in yᵉ woods armed with guns in this sorte, it was a terrour unto them, who lived straglingly, and were of no strenght in any place. And other places (though more remote) saw this mischeefe would quietly spread over all, if not prevented. Besides, they saw they should keep no servants, for Morton would entertaine any, how vile soever, and all yᵉ scume of yᵉ countrie, or any discontents, would flock to him from all places, if this nest was not broken; and they should stand in more fear of their lives & goods (in short time) from this wicked & deboste crue, then from yᵉ salvages them selves.

So sundrie of yᵉ cheefe of yᵉ stragling plantations, meeting togither, agreed by mutuall consente to sollissite those of Plimoth (who were then of more strength then them all) to joyne with them, to prevente yᵉ further grouth of this mischeefe, and suppress Morton & his consortes before yᵉʸ grewe to further head and strength. Those that joyned in this acction (and after contributed to the charge of sending him for England) were from Pascataway, Namkeake, Winisimett, Weesagascusett, Natasco, and other places wher any English were seated. Those of Plimoth being thus sought too by their messengers & letters, and waying both their reasons, and the comone danger, were willing to afford them their help; though them selves had least cause of fear or hurte. So, to be short, they first resolved joyntly to write to him, and in a freindly & neigborly way to admonish him to forbear these courses, & sent a messenger with their letters to bring his answer. But he was so highe as he scorned all advise, and asked who had to doe with him; he had and would trade peeces with yᵉ Indeans in dispite of all, with many other scurillous termes full of disdaine. They sente to him a second time, and bad him be better advised, and more temperate in his termes, for yᵉ countrie could not beare yᵉ injure he did; it was against their comone saftie, and against yᵉ king's proclamation. He answerd in high terms as before, and that yᵉ kings proclamation was no law; demanding what penaltie was upon it. It was answered, more then he could [162] bear, his majesties displeasure. But insolently he persisted, and said yᵉ king was dead and his displeasure with him, & many yᵉ like things; and threatened withall that if any came to molest him, let them looke to them selves, for he would prepare for them. Upon which they saw ther was no way but to take him by force; and having so farr proceeded, now to give over would make him farr more hautie & insolente. So they mutually resolved to proceed, and obtained of yᵉ Govᵣ of Plimoth to send Captaine Standish, & some other aide with him, to take Morton by force. The which accordingly was done; but they found him to stand stifly in his defence, having made fast his dors, armed his consorts, set diverse dishes of powder & bullets ready on yᵉ table; and if they had not been over armed with drinke, more hurt might have been done. They somaned him to yeeld, but he kept his house, and they could gett nothing but scofes & scorns from him; but at length, fearing they would doe some violence to yᵉ house, he and some of his crue came out, but not to yeeld, but to shoote; but they were so steeld with drinke as their peeces were to heavie for them; him selfe with a carbine (over charged & allmost halfe fild with powder & shote, as was after found) had thought to have shot Captaine Standish; but he stept to him, & put by his peece, & tooke him. Neither was ther any hurte done to any of either side, save yᵗ one was so drunke yᵗ he rane his owne nose upon yᵉ pointe of a sword yᵗ one held before him as he entred yᵉ house; but he lost but a litle of his hott blood. Morton they brought away to Plimoth, wher he was kepte, till a ship went from yᵉ Ile of Shols for England, with which he was sente to yᵉ Counsell of New-England; and letters writen to give them information of his course & cariage; and also one was sent at their comone charge to informe their Hoⁿˢ more perticulerly, & to prosecute against him. But he foold of yᵉ messenger, after he was gone from hence, and though he wente for England, yet nothing was done to him, not so much as rebukte, for ought was heard; but returned yᵉ nexte year. Some of yᵉ worst of yᵉ company were disperst, and some of yᵉ more modest kepte yᵉ house till he should be heard from. But I have been too long aboute so un-worthy a person, and bad a cause.

This year Mʳ. Allerton brought over a yonge man for a minister to yᵉ people hear, wheather upon his owne head, or at yᵉ motion of some freinds ther, I well know not, but it was without yᵉ churches sending; for they had bene so bitten by Mʳ. Lyford, as they desired to know yᵉ person well whom they should invite amongst them. His name was Mʳ. Rogers; but they perceived, upon some triall, that he was crased in his braine; so they were faine to be at further charge to send him back againe yᵉ nexte year, and loose all yᵉ charge that was expended in his hither bringing, which was not smalle by Mʳ. Allerton's accounte, in provissions, aparell, bedding, &c. After his returne he grue quite distracted, and Mʳ. Allerton was much blamed yᵗ he would bring such a man over, they having charge enough otherwise.

Mʳ. Allerton, in yᵉ years before, had brought over some small quantie of goods, upon his owne perticuler, and sould them for his owne private benefite; which was more then any man had yet hithertoo attempted. But because he had other wise done them good service, and also he sould them among yᵉ people at yᵉ plantation, by which their wants were supplied, and he aledged it was the [163] love of Mʳ. Sherley and some other freinds that would needs trust him with some goods, conceiveing it might doe him some good, and none hurte, it was not much lookt at, but past over. But this year he brought over a greater quantitie, and they were so intermixte with yᵉ goods of yᵉ generall, as they knew not which were theirs, & wᶜʰ was his, being pact up together; so as they well saw that, if any casualty had beefalne at sea, he might have laid yᵉ whole on them, if he would; for ther was no distinction. Allso what was most vendible, and would yeeld presente pay, usualy that was his; and he now begane allso to sell abroad to others of forine places, which, considering their comone course, they began to dislike. Yet because love thinkes no evill, nor is susspitious, they tooke his faire words for excuse, and resolved to send him againe this year for England; considering how well he had done yᵉ former bussines, and what good acceptation he had with their freinds ther; as also seeing sundry of their freinds from Leyden were sente for, which would or might be much furthered by his means. Againe, seeing the patente for Kenebeck must be inlarged, by reason of yᵉ former mistaks in the bounding of it, and it was conceived, in a maner, yᵉ same charge would serve to inlarge this at home with it, and he that had begane yᵉ former yᵉ last year would be yᵉ fittest to effecte this; so they gave him instructions and sente him for England this year againe. And in his instructions bound him to bring over no goods on their accounte, but 50ˡⁱ. in hose & shoes, and some linen cloth, (as yᵉʸ were bound by covenante when they tooke yᵉ trad;) also some trading goods to such a value; and in no case to exseed his instructions, nor rune them into any further charge; he well knowing how their state stood. Also yᵗ he should so provide yᵗ their trading goods came over betimes, and what so ever was sent on their accounte should be pact up by it selfe, marked with their marke, and no other goods to be mixed with theirs. For so he prayed them to give him such instructions as they saw good, and he would folow them, to prevente any jellocie or farther offence, upon the former forementioned dislikes. And thus they conceived they had well provided for all things.

Anno Dom: 1629.

Mʳ. Allerton safly arriving in England, and delivering his leters to their freinds their, and aquainting them with his instructions, found good acceptation with them, and they were very forward & willing to joyne with them in yᵉ partnership of trade, & in yᵉ charge to send over yᵉ Leyden people; a company wherof were allready come out of Holand, and prepared to come over, and so were sent away before Mʳ. Allerton could be ready to come. They had passage with yᵉ ships that came to Salem, that brought over many godly persons to begine yᵉ plantations & churches of Christ ther, & in yᵉ Bay of Massachussets; so their long stay & keeping back [164] was recompensed by yᵉ Lord to ther freinds here with a duble blessing, in that they not only injoyed them now beyond ther late expectation, (when all their hops seemed to be cutt of,) but, with them, many more godly freinds & Christian breethren, as yᵉ begining of a larger harvest unto yᵉ Lord, in yᵉ increase of his churches & people in these parts, to yᵉ admiration of many, and allmost wonder of yᵉ world; that of so small beginings so great things should insue, as time after manifested; and that here should be a resting place for so many of yᵉ Lords people, when so sharp a scourge came upon their owne nation. But it was yᵉ Lords doing, & it ought to be marvellous in our eyes.

But I shall hear inserte some of their freinds letters, which doe best expresse their owne minds in these thir proceedings.

A leter of Mʳ. Sherleys to yᵉ Govʳ.

May 25, 1629.[C]

Sʳ: &c. Here are now many of your and our freinds from Leyden coming over, who, though for yᵉ most parte be but a weak company, yet herein is a good parte of that end obtained which was aimed at, and which hath been so strongly opposed by some of our former adventurers. But God hath his working in these things, which man cannot frustrate. With them we have allso sent some servants in yᵉ ship called the Talbut, that wente hence latly; but these come in yᵉ May-flower. Mʳ. Beachamp & my selfe, with Mʳ. Andrews & Mʳ. Hatherly, are, with your love and liking, joyned partners with you, &c.

Your deputation we have received, and ye goods have been taken up & sould by your friend & agente, M^r. Allerton, my selfe having bine nere 3. months in Holland, at Amsterdam & other parts in ye Low-Countries. I see further the agreemente you have made with ye generallitie, in which I cannot understand but you have done very well, both for them & you, and also for your freinds at Leyden. M^r. Beachamp, M^r. Andrews, M^r. Hatherley, & my selfe, doe so like and approve of it, as we are willing to joyne with you, and, God directing and inabling us, will be assisting and helpfull to you, ye best y^t possiblie we can. Nay, had you not taken this course, I doe not see how you should accomplish ye end you first aimed at, and some others indevored these years past. We know it must keep us from ye profite, which otherwise by ye blessing of God and your indeaours, might be gained; for most of those that came in May, & these now sente, though I hope honest & good people, yet not like to be helpfull to raise profite, but rather, ney, certaine must, some while, be chargable to you & us; at which it is lickly, had not this wise & discreete course been taken, many of your generalitie would have grudged. Againe, you say well in your letter, and I make no doubte but you will performe it, that now being but a few, on whom ye burthen must be, you will both menage it ye beter, and sett too it more cherfully, haveing no discontente nor contradiction, but so lovingly to joyne togeither, in affection and counsell, as God no doubte will blesse and prosper your honest labours & indeavors. And therfore in all respects I doe not see but you have done marvelously discreetly, & advisedly, and no doubt but it gives all parties good contente; I mean y^t are reasonable & honest men, such as make conscience of giving ye best satisfaction they be able for their debts, and y^t regard not their owne perticuler so much as ye accomplishing of y^t good end for which this bussines was first intended, &c. Thus desiring ye Lord to blese & prosper you, & all yours, and all our honest endeavors, I rest

Your unfained & ever loving friend,

JAMES SHERLEY.

Lon: March 8. 1629.[CK]

[165] That I may handle things together, I have put these 2. companies that came from Leyden in this place; though they came at 2. severall times, yet they both came out of England this year. The former company, being 35. persons, were shiped in May, and arived here aboute August. The later were shiped in ye begining of March, and arived hear ye later end of May, 1630. M^r. Sherleys 2. letters, ye effect wherof I have before related, (as much of them as is pertinente,) mentions both. Their charge, as M^r. Allerton brought it in afterwards on accounte, came to above 550^{li}. besids ther fetching hither from Salem & ye Bay, wher they and their goods were landed; viz. their transportation from Holland to England, & their charges lying ther, and passages hither, with clothing provided for them. For I find by accounte for ye one company, 125. yeards of karsey, 127. ellons of linen cloath, shoes, 66. p^r, with many other perticulers. The charge of ye other company is reckoned on ye severall families, some 50^{li}., some 40^{li}., some 30^{li}., and so more or less, as their number & expencess were. And besids all this charg, their freinds & bretheren here were to provid corne & other provissions for them, till they could reap a crope which was long before. Those that came in May were thus maintained upward of 16. or 18. months, before they had any harvest of their owne, & ye other by proportion. And all they could doe in ye mean time was to gett them some housing, and prepare them grounds to plant on, against the season. And this charg of maintaining them all this while was litle less then ye former sume. These things I note more perticulerly, for sundry regards. First, to shew a rare example herein of brotherly love, and Christian care in performing their promises and covenants to their bretheren, too, & in a sorte beyonde their power; that they should venture so desperatly to ingage them selves to accomplish this thing, and bear it so cheerfully; for they never demanded, much less had, any repaymente of all these great sumes thus disbursed. 2^{ly}. It must needs be that ther was more then of man in these acheevements, that should thus readily stire up ye harts of shuch able frinds to

joyne in partnership with them in shuch a case, and cleave so faithfullie to them as these did, in so great adventures; and the more because the most of them never saw their faces to this day; ther being neither kindred, aliance, or other acquaintance or relations betweene any of them, then hath been before mentioned; it must needs be therfore the spetiall worke and hand of God. 3^{ly}. That these poore people here in a wilderness should, notwithstanding, be inabled in time to repay all these ingagments, and many more unjustly brought upon them through the unfaithfullnes of some, and many other great losses which they sustained, which will be made manifest, if ye Lord be pleased to give life and time. In ye mean time, I cannot but admire his ways and workes towards his servants, and humbly desire to blesse his holy name for his great mercies hithertoo.

[166] The Leyden people being thus come over, and sundry of ye generalitie seeing & hearing how great ye charg was like to be that was that way to be expended, they begane to murmure and repine at it, notwithstanding ye burden lay on other mens shoulders; espetially at ye paying of ye 3. bushells of corne a year, according to ye former agreemente, when ye trad was lett for ye 6. years aforesaid. But to give them contente herein allso, it was promised them, that if they could doe it in ye time without it, they would never demand it of them; which gave them good contente. And indeed it never was paid, as will appeare by ye sequell.

Concerning M^r. Allertons proceedings about ye inlarging & confirming of their patent, both y^t at home & Kenebeck, will best appere by another leter of M^r. Sherleys; for though much time & money was expended aboute it, yet he left it unaccomplisht this year, and came without it. See M^r. Sherleys letter.

Most worthy & loving freinds, &c.

Some of your letters I received in July, & some since by M^r. Peirce, but till our maine bussines, ye patent, was granted, I could not setle my mind nor pen to writing. M^r. Allerton was so turrmoyled about it, as verily I would not nor could not have undergone it, if I might have had a thousand pounds; but ye Lord so blessed his labours (even beyond expectation in these evill days) as he obtained yᵉ love & favore of great men in repute & place. He got granted from yᵉ Earle of Warwick & Sʳ. Ferdinando Gorge all that Mʳ. Winslow desired in his letters to me, & more also, which I leave to him to relate. Then he sued to yᵉ king to confirme their grante, and to make you a corporation, and so to inable you to make & execute lawes, in such large & ample maner as yᵉ Massachusett plantation hath it; which yᵉ king graciously granted, referring it to yᵉ Lord Keeper to give order to yᵉ solisiter to draw it up, if ther were a presidente for it. So yᵉ Lord Keeper furthered it all he could, and allso yᵉ solissiter; but as Festus said to Paule, With no small sume of money obtained I this freedom; for by yᵉ way many ridells must be resolved, and many locks must be opened with yᵉ silver, ney, yᵉ golden key. Then it was to come to yᵉ Lord Treasurer, to have his warrente for freeing yᵉ custume for a certaine time; but be would not doe it, but refferd it to yᵉ Counsell table. And ther Mʳ. Allerton atended day by day, when they sate, but could not gett his petition read. And by reason of Mʳ. Peirce his staying with all yᵉ passengers at Bristoll, he was forct to leave yᵉ further prosecuting of it to a solissiter. But ther is no fear nor doubte but it will be granted, for he hath yᵉ cheefe of them to freind; yet it will be marvelously needfull for him to returne by yᵉ first ship yᵗ comes from thence; for if you had this confirmed, then were you compleate, and might bear such sway & goverment as were fitt for your ranke & place yᵗ God hath called you unto; and stope yᵉ moueths of base and scurrulous fellowes, yᵗ are ready to question & threaten you in every action you [167] doe. And besids, if you have yᵉ custome free for 7. years inward, & 21. outward, yᵉ charge of yᵉ patent will be soone recovered, and ther is no fear of obtaining[CL] it. But such things must work by degrees; men cannot hasten it as they would; werefore we (I write in behalfe of all our partners here) desire you to be ernest with Mʳ. Allerton to come, and his wife to spare him this one year more, to finish this great & waighty bussines, which we conceive will be much for your good, & I hope for your posteritie, and for many generations to come.

Thus much of this letter. It was dated yᵉ 19. March, 1629.

By which it appears what progress was made herein, & in part what charge it was, and how left unfinished, and some reason of yᵉ same; but in truth (as was afterwards appehended) the meaine reason was Mʳ. Allerton's policie, to have an opportunitie to be sent over againe, for other regards; and for that end procured them thus to write. For it might then well enough have been finshed, if not with yᵗ clause aboute yᵉ custumes, which was Mʳ. Allertons & Mʳ. Sherleys device, and not at all thought on by yᵉ colony here, nor much regarded, yet it might have been done without it, without all queston, having passed yᵉ kings hand; nay it was conceived it might then have beene done with it, if he had pleased; but covetousnes never brings ought home, as yᵉ proverb is, for this oppertunytie being lost, it was never accomplished, but a great deale of money veainly & lavishly cast away aboute it, as doth appear upon their accounts. But of this more in its place.

Mʳ. Alerton gave them great and just ofence in this (which I had omited[CM] and almost forgotten),—in bringing over this year, for base gaine, that unworthy man, and instrumente of mischeefe, Morton, who was sent home but yᵉ year before for his misdemenors. He not only brought him over, but to yᵉ towne (as it were to nose them), and lodged him at his owne house, and for a while used him as a scribe to doe his bussines, till he was caused to pack him away. So he wente to his old nest in yᵉ Massachusets, wher it was not long but by his miscariage he gave them just occation to lay hands on him; and he was by them againe sent prisoner into England, wher he lay a good while in Exeter Jeole. For besids his miscariage here, he was vemently suspected for yᵉ murder of a man that had adventured moneys with him, when he came first into New-England. And a warrente was sente from yᵉ Lord Cheefe Justice to apprehend him, by vertue wherof he was by the Govʳ of yᵉ Massachusets sent into England; and for other his misdemenors amongst them, they demolisht his house, that it might be no longer a roost for shuch unclaine birds to nestle in. Yet he got free againe, and write an infamouse & scurillous booke against many godly & cheefe men of yᵉ cuntrie; full of lyes & slanders, and fraight with profane callumnies against their names and persons, and yᵉ ways of God. After sundry years, when yᵉ warrs were hott in England, he came againe into yᵉ cuntrie, and was imprisoned at Boston for this booke and other things, being grown old in wickednes.

Concerning yᵉ rest of Mʳ. Allertons instructions, in which they strictly injoyned him not to exceed above yᵗ 50ˡⁱ. in yᵉ goods before mentioned, not to bring any but trading comodities, he followed them not at all, but did the quite contrarie; bringing over many other sorts of retaile goods, selling what he could by the way on his owne accounte, and delivering the rest, which he said to be theirs, into yᵉ store; and for trading goods brought but litle in comparison; excusing the matter, they had laid out much about yᵉ Laiden people, & patent, &c. And for other goods, they had much of them of ther owne dealings, without present disbursemente, & to like effect. And as for passing his bounds & instructions, he laid it on Mʳ. Sherley, &c., who, he said, they might see his mind in his leters; also that they had sett out Ashley at great charg; but next year they should have what trading goods they would send for, if things were now well setled, &c. And thus were they put off; indeed Mʳ. Sherley write things tending this way, but it is like he was overruled by Mʳ. Allerton, and harkened more to him then to their letters from hence.

Thus he further writs in yᵉ former leter.

I see what you write in your leters concerning yᵉ over-coming & paying of our debts, which I confess are great, and had need be carfully looked unto; yet no doubt but we, joyning in love, may soone over-come them; but we must follow it roundly & to purposs, for if we pedle out yᵉ time of our trad, others will step in and nose us. But we know yᵗ you have yᵗ aquaintance & experience in yᵉ countrie, as none have the like; wherfore, freinds & partners, be no way discouraged with yᵉ greatnes of yᵉ debt, &c., but let us not fulfill yᵉ proverbe, to bestow 12ᵈ. on a purse, and put 6ᵈ. [168] in it; but as you and we have been at great charg, and undergone much for setling you ther, and to gaine experience, so as God shall enable us, let us make use of it. And think not with 50ˡⁱ. pound a yeare sent you over, to rayse shuch means as to pay our debts. We see a possibillitie of good if you be well supplied, and fully furnished; and cheefly if you lovingly agree. I know I write to godly and wise men, such as have lerned to bear one an others infirmities, and rejoyce at any ones prosperities; and if I were able I would press this more, because it is hoped by some of your enimies, that you will fall out one with another, and so over throw your hopfull bussines. Nay, I have heard it crediblie reported, y[t] some have said, that till you be disjoynted by discontents & factions[CN] amongst your sellves, it bootes not any to goe over, in hope of getting or doing good in those parts. But we hope beter things of you, and that you will not only bear one with another, but banish such thoughts, and not suffer them to lodg in your brests. God grant you may disappointe y[e] hopes of your foes, and procure y[e] hartie desire of your selves & freinds in this perticuler.

By this it appears that ther was a kind of concurrance betweene M[r]. Allerton and them in these things, and that they gave more regard to his way & course in these things, then to y[e] advise from hence; which made him bould to presume above his instructions, and to rune on in y[e] course he did, to their greater hurt afterwards, as will appear. These things did much trouble them hear, but they well knew not how to help it, being loath to make any breach or contention hear aboute; being so premonished as before in y[e] leter above recited. An other more secrete cause was herewith concurrente; M[r]. Allerton had maried y[e] daughter of their Reverend Elder, M[r]. Brewster (a man beloved & honoured amongst them, and who tooke great paines in teaching & dispenceing y[e] word of God unto them), whom they were loath to greeve or any way offend, so as they bore with much in that respecte. And with all M[r]. Allerton carried so faire with him, and procured such leters from M[r]. Sherley to him, with shuch applause of M[r]. Allertons wisdom, care, and faithfullnes, in y[e] bussines; and as things stood none were so fitte to send aboute them as he; and if any should suggest other wise, it was rather out of envie, or some other sinister respecte then other wise. Besids, though private gaine, I doe perswade my selfe, was some cause to lead M[r]. Allerton aside in these beginings, yet I thinke, or at least charitie caries me to hope, that he intended to deale faithfully with them in yᵉ maine, and had such an opinion of his owne abillitie, and some experience of yᵉ benefite that he had made in this singuler way, as he conceived he might both raise him selfe an estate, and allso be a means to bring in such profite to Mʳ. Sherley, (and it may be yᵉ rest,) as might be as lickly to bring in their moneys againe with advantage, and it may be sooner then from the generall way; or at least it was looked upon by some of them to be a good help ther unto; and that neither he nor any other did intend to charge yᵉ generall accounte with any thing that rane in perticuler; or yᵗ Mʳ. Sherley or any other did purposs but yᵗ yᵉ generall should be first & fully supplyed. I say charitie makes me thus conceive; though things fell out other wise, and they missed of their aimes, and yᵉ generall suffered abundantly hereby, as will afterwards apear.

[169] Togeither herewith sorted an other bussines contrived by Mʳ. Allerton and them ther, wᵗʰout any knowledg of yᵉ partners, and so farr proceeded in as they were constrained to allow therof, and joyne in yᵉ same, though they had no great liking of it, but feared what might be yᵉ evente of yᵉ same. I shall relate it in a further part of Mʳ. Sherley's leter as foloweth.

I am to aquainte you that we have thought good to joyne with one Edward Ashley (a man I thinke yᵗ some of you know); but it is only of yᵗ place wherof he hath a patente in Mʳ. Beachamps name; and to that end have furnished him with larg provissions, &c. Now if you please to be partners with us in this, we are willing you shall; for after we heard how forward Bristoll men (and as I hear some able men of his owne kindrid) have been to stock & supply him, hoping of profite, we thought it fitter for us to lay hould of such an opportunitie, and to keep a kind of runing plantation, then others who have not borne yᵉ burthen of setling a plantation, as we have done. And he, on yᵉ other side, like an understanding yonge man, thought it better to joyne with those yᵗ had means by a plantation to supply & back him ther, rather then strangers, that looke but only after profite. Now it is not knowne that you are partners with him; but only we 4., Mʳ. Andrews, Mʳ. Beachamp, my selfe, & Mʳ.

Hatherley, who desired to have ye patente, in consideration of our great loss we have allready sustained in setling ye first plantation ther; so we agreed togeather to take it in our names. And now, as I said before, if you please to joyne with us, we are willing you should. M^r. Allerton had no power from you to make this new contracte, neither was he willing to doe any thing therin without your consente & approbation. M^r. William Peirce is joyned with us in this, for we thought it very conveniente, because of landing Ashley and his goods ther, if God please; and he will bend his course accordingly. He hath a new boate with him, and boards to make another, with 4. or 5. lustie fellowes, wherof one is a carpenter. Now in case you are not willing in this perticuler to joyne with us, fearing ye charge & doubting ye success, yet thus much we intreate of you, to afford him all the help you can, either by men, commodities, or boats; yet not but y^t we will pay you for any thing he hath. And we desire you to keep ye accounts apart, though you joyne with us; becase ther is, as you see, other partners in this then ye other; so, for all mens wages, boats-hire, or comodities, which we shall have of you, make him debtore for it; and what you shall have of him, make ye plantation or your selves debtore for it to him, and so ther will need no mingling of ye accounts.

And now, loving freinds & partners, if you joyne in Ashles patent & bussines, though we have laid out ye money and taken up much to stock this bussines & the other, yet I thinke it conscionable and reasonable y^t you should beare your shares and proportion of ye stock, if not by present money, yet by securing us for so much as it shall come too; for it is not barly ye interest that is to be alowed & considered of, but allso ye adventure; though I hope in God, by his blessing & your honest indeavors, it may soon be payed; yet ye years y^t this partnership holds is not long, nor many; let all therfore lay it to harte, and make ye best use of ye time that possiblie we cann, and let every man put too his shoulder, and ye burthen will be the lighter. I know you are so honest & conscionable men, as you will consider hereof, [170] and returne shuch an answer as may give good satisfaction. Ther is none of us that would venture as we have done, were it not to strengthen & setle you more then our owne perticuler profite.

Ther is no liclyhood of doing any good in buying ye debte for ye purchas. I know some will not abate ye interest, and therfore let it rune its course; they are to be paied yearly, and so I hope they shall, according to agreemente. The Lord grant y^t our loves & affections may still be united, and knit togeither; and so we rest your ever loving friends,

JAMES SHERLEY.

TIMOTHY HATHERLEY.

Bristoll, March 19. 1629.

This mater of ye buying ye debts of ye purchass was parte of M^r. Allertons instructions, and in many of them it might have been done to good profite for ready pay (as some were); but M^r. Sherley had no mind to it. But this bussines aboute Ashley did not a litle trouble them; for though he had wite & abillitie enough to menage ye bussines, yet some of them knew him to be a very profane yonge man; and he had for some time lived amonge ye Indeans as a savage, & wente naked amongst them, and used their maners (in wch time he got their language), so they feared he might still rune into evill courses (though he promised better), and God would not prosper his ways. As soone as he was landed at ye place intended, caled Penobscote, some 4 score leagues from this place, he write (& afterwards came) for to desire to be supplyed with Wampampeake, corne against winter, and other things. They considered these were of their cheefe comodities, and would be continually needed by him, and it would much prejudice their owne trade at Kenebeck if they did not joyne with him in ye ordering of things, if thus they should supply him; and on ye other hand, if they refused to joyne with him, and allso to afford any supply unto him, they should greatly offend their above named friends, and might hapily lose them hereby; and he and M^r. Allerton, laying their craftie wits togither, might gett supplies of these things els wher; besids, they considered that if they joyned not in ye bussines, they knew M^r. Allerton would be with them in it, & so would swime, as it were, betweene both, to ye prejudice of boath, but of them selves espetially. For they had reason to thinke this bussines was cheefly of his contriving, and Ashley was a man fitte for his turne and dealings. So they, to prevente a worse mischeefe, resolved to joyne in ye bussines, and gave him supplies in what they could, & overlooked his proceedings as well as they could; the which they did ye better, by joyning an honest yonge man,[co] that came from Leyden, with him as his fellow (in some sorte), and not merely as a servante. Which yonge man being discreete, and one whom they could trust, they so instructed as keept Ashley in some good mesure within bounds. And so they returned their answer to their freinds in England, that they accepted of their motion, and joyned with them in Ashleys bussines; and yet withall tould them what their fears were concerning him.

But when they came to have full notice of all ye goods brought them that year, they saw they fell very short of trading goods, and Ashley farr better suppleyed then [171] themselves; so as they were forced to buy of the fisher men to furnish them selves, yea, & cottens & carseys & other such like cloath (for want of trading cloath) of M^r. Allerton himselfe, and so to put away a great parte of their beaver, at under rate, in the countrie, which they should have sente home, to help to discharge their great ingagementes; which was to their great vexation; but M^r. Allerton prayed them to be contente, and ye nexte yere they might have what they would write for. And their ingagmentes of this year were great indeed when they came to know them, (which was not wholy till 2. years after); and that which made them ye more, M^r. Allerton had taken up some large sumes at Bristoll at 50. p^r cent. againe, which he excused, that he was forcte to it, because other wise he could at ye spring of year get no goods transported, such were their envie against their trade. But wheither this was any more then an excuse, some of them doubted; but however, ye burden did lye on their backs, and they must bear it, as they did many heavie loads more in ye end.

This paying of 50. p^r cent. and dificulty of having their goods trāsported by the fishing ships at ye first of ye year, (as was beleeved,) which was ye cheefe season for trade, put them upon another projecte. M^r. Allerton, after ye fishing season was over, light of a bargan of salte, at a good fishing place, and bought it; which came to aboute 113^{li}.; and shortly after he might have had 30^{li}. cleare profite for it, without any more trouble aboute it. But M^r. Winslow coming that way from Kenebeck, & some other of ther partners with him in ye barke, they mett with M^r. Allerton, and falling into discourse with him, they stayed him from selling ye salte; and resolved, if it might please ye rest, to keep it for them selves, and to hire a ship in ye west cuntrie to come on fishing for them, on shares, according to ye coustome; and seeing she might have her salte here ready, and a stage ready builte & fitted wher the salt lay safely landed & housed. In stead of bringing salte, they might stowe her full of trading goods, as bread, pease, cloth, &c., and so they might have a full supply of goods without paing fraight, and in due season, which might turne greatly to their advantage. Coming home, this was propounded, and considered on, and aproved by all but ye Govr, who had no mind to it, seeing they had allway lost by fishing; but ye rest were so ernest, as thinkeing that they might gaine well by ye fishing in this way; and if they should but save, yea, or lose some thing by it, ye other benefite would be advantage inough; so, seeing their ernestnes, he gave way, and it was referd to their freinds in England to alow, or disalow it. Of which more in its place.

Upon ye consideration of ye bussines about ye paten, & in what state it was left, as is before remembred, and M^r. Sherleys ernest pressing to have M^r. Allertō to come over againe to finish it, & perfect ye accounts, &c., it was concluded to send him over this year againe; though it was with some fear & jeolocie; yet he gave them fair words and promises of well performing all their bussineses according to their directions, and to mend his former errors. So he was accordingly sent with full instructions for all things, with large letters to M^r. Sherley & ye rest, both aboute Ashleys bussines and their owne suply with trading comodities, and how much it did concerne them to be furnished therwith, & what yᵉ had suffered for wante therof; and of what litle use other goods were [172] in comparison therof; and so likewise aboute this fishing ship, to be thus hired, and fraught with trading goods, which might both supply them & Ashley, and yᵉ benefite therof; which was left to their consideration to hire & set her out, or not; but in no case not to send any, exepte she was thus fraighte with trading goods. But what these things came too will appere in yᵉ next years passages.

I had like to have omited an other passage that fell out yᵉ begining of this year. Ther was one Mʳ. Ralfe Smith, & his wife & familie, yᵗ came over into yᵉ Bay of yᵉ Massachusets, and sojourned at presente with some stragling people that lived at Natascoe; here being a boat of this place putting in ther on some occasion, he ernestly desired that they would give him & his, passage for Plimoth, and some such things as they could well carrie; having before heard yᵗ ther was liklyhood he might procure house-roome for some time, till he should resolve to setle ther, if he might, or els-wher as God should disposs; for he was werie of being in yᵗ uncoth place, & in a poore house yᵗ would neither keep him nor his goods drie. So, seeing him to be a grave man, & understood he had been a minister, though they had no order for any such thing, yet they presumed and brought him. He was here accordingly kindly entertained & housed, & had yᵉ rest of his goods & servants sente for, and exercised his gifts amongst them, and afterwards was chosen into yᵉ ministrie, and so remained for sundrie years.

It was before noted that sundry of those that came from Leyden, came over in the ships yᵗ came to Salem, wher Mʳ. Endecott had cheefe comand; and by infection that grue amonge yᵉ passengers at sea, it spread also among them a shore, of which many dyed, some of yᵉ scurvie, other of an infectious feaoure, which continued some time amongst them (though our people, through Gods goodnes, escaped it). Upon which occasion he write hither for some help, understanding here was one that had some skill yᵗ way, & had cured diverse of yᵉ scurvie, and others of other diseases, by letting blood, & other means. Upon which his request yᵉ Govʳ hear sent him unto them, and also write to him, from whom he received an answere; the which, because it is breefe, and shows ye begining of their aquaintance, and closing in ye truth & ways of God, I thought it not unmeete, nor without use, hear to inserte it; and an other showing ye begining of their fellowship & church estate ther.

Being as followeth.

Right worthy S^r:

It is a thing not usuall, that servants to one m^r and of ye same houshold should be strangers; I assure you I desire it not, nay, to speake more plainly, I cannot be so to you. Gods people are all marked with one and ye same marke, and sealed with one and ye same seale, and have for ye maine, one & ye same harte, guided by one & same spirite of truth; and wher this is, ther can be no discorde, nay, here must needs be sweete harmonie. And ye same request (with you) I make unto ye Lord, that we may, as Christian breethren, be united by a heavenly & unfained love; bending all our harts and forces in furthering a worke beyond our strength, with reverence & fear, fastening our eyse allways on him that only is able to directe and prosper all our ways. I acknowledge my selfe much bound to you for your kind love and care in sending M^r. Fuller among us, and rejoyce much y^t I am by him satisfied touching your judgments of ye outward forme of Gods worshipe. It is, as farr as [173] I can yet gather, no other then is warrented by ye evidence of truth, and ye same which I have proffessed and maintained ever since ye Lord in mercie revealed him selfe unto me; being farr from ye commone reporte that hath been spread of you touching that perticuler. But Gods children must not looke for less here below, and it is ye great mercie of God, that he strengthens them to goe through with it. I shall not neede at this time to be tedious unto you, for, God willing, I purpose to see your face shortly. In ye mean time, I humbly take my leave of you, comiting you to ye Lords blessed protection, & rest.

Your assured loving friend,

JO: ENDECOTT.

Naumkeak, May 11. An⁰. 1629.

This second leter sheweth ther proceedings in their church affaires at Salem, which was yᵉ 2. church erected in these parts; and afterwards yᵉ Lord established many more in sundrie places.

Sʳ: I make bould to trouble you with a few lines, for to certifie you how it hath pleased God to deale with us, since you heard from us. How, notwithstanding all opposition that hath been hear, & els wher, it hath pleased God to lay a foundation, the which I hope is agreeable to his word in every thing. The 20. of July, it pleased yᵉ Lord to move yᵉ hart of our Govʳ to set it aparte for a solemne day of humilliation for yᵉ choyce of a pastor & teacher. The former parte of yᵉ day being spente in praier & teaching, the later parte aboute yᵉ election, which was after this maner. The persons thought on (who had been ministers in England) were demanded concerning their callings; they acknowledged ther was a towfould calling, the one an inward calling, when yᵉ Lord moved yᵉ harte of a man to take yᵗ calling upon him, and fitted him with guiftes for yᵉ same; the second was an outward calling, which was from yᵉ people, when a company of beleevers are joyned togither in covenante, to walke togither in all yᵉ ways of God, and every member (being men) are to have a free voyce in yᵉ choyce of their officers, &c. Now, we being perswaded that these 2. men were so quallified, as yᵉ apostle speaks to Timothy, wher he saith, A bishop must be blamles, sober, apte to teach, &c., I thinke I may say, as yᵉ eunuch said unto Philip, What should let from being baptised, seeing ther was water? and he beleeved. So these 2. servants of God, clearing all things by their answers, (and being thus fitted,) we saw noe reason but we might freely give our voyces for their election, after this triall. So Mʳ. Skelton was chosen pastor, and Mʳ. Higgison to be teacher; and they accepting yᵉ choyce, Mʳ. Higgison, with 3. or 4. of yᵉ gravest members of yᵉ church, laid their hands on Mʳ. Skelton, using prayer therwith. This being done, ther was imposission of hands on Mʳ. Higgison also. And since that time, Thursday (being, as I take it, yᵉ 6. of August) is appoynted for another day of humilliation, for y� choyce of elders & deacons, & ordaining of them.

And now, good Sʳ, I hope yᵗ you & yᵉ rest of Gods people (who are aquainted with the ways of God) with you, will say that hear was a right foundation layed, and that these 2. blessed servants of yᵉ Lord came in at yᵉ dore, and not at yᵉ window. Thus I have made bould to trouble you with these few lines, desiring you to remember us, &c. And so rest,

At your service in what I may,

CHARLES GOTT.

Salem, July 30. 1629.

[174] *Anno Dom*: 1630.

Ashley, being well supplyed, had quickly gathered a good parcell of beaver, and like a crafty pate he sent it all home, and would not pay for yᵉ goods he had had of yᵉ plantation hear, but lett them stand still on yᵉ score, and tooke up still more. Now though they well enough knew his aime, yet they let him goe on, and write of it into England. But partly yᵉ beaver they received, & sould, (of which they weer sencible,) and partly by Mʳ. Allertons extolling of him, they cast more how to supplie him then yᵉ plantation, and something to upbraid them with it. They were forct to buy him a barke allso, and to furnish her wᵗʰ a mʳ. & men, to transports his corne & provissions (of which he put of much); for yᵉ Indeans of those parts have no corne growing, and at harvest, after corne is ready, yᵉ weather grows foule, and yᵉ seas dangerous, so as he could doe litle good with his shallope for yᵗ purposs.

They looked ernestly for a timely supply this spring, by the fishing ship which they expected, and had been at charg to keepe a stage for her; but none came, nor any supply heard of for them. At length they heard sume supply was sent to Ashley by a fishing ship, at which they something marvelled, and the more yᵗ they had no letters either from Mʳ. Allerton or Mʳ. Sherley; so they went on in their bussines as well as ye could. At last they heard of M^r. Peirce his arivall in ye Bay of ye Massachusetts, who brought passengers & goods thither. They presently sent a shallop, conceiving they should have some thing by him. But he tould them he had none; and a ship was sett out on fishing, but after 11. weeks beating at sea, she mett with shuch foull weather as she was forcte back againe for England, and, ye season being over, gave off ye vioage. Neither did he hear of much goods in her for ye plantation, or y^t she did belong to them, for he had heard some thing from M^r. Allerton tending that way. But M^r. Allerton had bought another ship, and was to come in her, and was to fish for bass to ye eastward, and to bring goods, &c. These things did much trouble them, and half astonish them. M^r. Winslow haveing been to ye eastward, brought nuese of the like things, wth some more perticulers, and y^t it was like M^r. Allerton would be late before he came. At length they, having an oppertunitie, resolved to send M^r. Winslow, with what beaver they had ready, into England, to see how ye squars wente, being very jeolouse of these things, & M^r. Allertons courses; and writ shuch leters, and gave him shuch instructions, as they thought meet; and if he found things not well, to discharge M^r. Allerton for being any longer agent for them, or to deal any more in ye bussines, and to see how ye accounts stood, &c.

Aboute ye midle of somer arrives M^r. Hatherley in ye Bay of ye Massachusetts, (being one of ye partners,) and came over in ye same ship that was set out on fhishing (called ye Frendship). They presently sent to him, making no question but now they had goods come, and should know how all things stood. But they found [175] the former news true, how this ship had been so long at sea, and spente and spoyled her provissions, and overthrowne ye viage. And he being sent over by ye rest of ye partners, to see how things wente hear, being at Bristoll with M^r. Allerton, in ye shipe bought (called ye White-Angell), ready to set sayle, over night came a messenger from Bastable to M^r. Allerton, and tould him of ye returne of ye ship, and what had befallen. And he not knowing what to doe, having a great chareg under hand, ye ship lying at his rates, and now ready to set sayle, got him to goe and discharg ye ship, and take order for ye goods. To be short, they found M^r. Hatherley some thing reserved, and troubled in him selfe, (M^r. Allerton not being ther,) not knowing how to dispose of ye goods till he came; but he heard he was arived with ye other ship to ye eastward, and expected his coming. But he tould them ther was not much for them in this ship, only 2. packs of Bastable ruggs, and 2. hoggsheads of meatheglin, drawne out in wooden flackets (but when these flackets came to be received, ther was left but 6. gallons of ye 2. hogsheads, it being drunke up under ye name leackage, and so lost). But the ship was filled with goods for sundrie gentlemen, & others, that were come to plant in ye Massachusets, for which they payed fraight by ye tun. And this was all the satisfaction they could have at presente, so they brought this small parcell of goods & returned with this nues, and a letter as obscure; which made them much to marvell therat. The letter was as followeth.

Gentle-men, partners, and loving friends, &c.

Breefly thus: wee have this year set forth a fishing ship, and a trading ship, which later we have bought; and so have disbursed a great deale of money, as may and will appeare by ye accounts. And because this ship (called ye White Angell) is to acte 2. parts, (as I may say,) fishing for bass, and trading; and that while M^r. Allerton was imployed aboute ye trading, the fishing might suffer by carlesnes or neglecte of ye sailors, we have entreated your and our loving friend, M^r. Hatherley, to goe over with him, knowing he will be a comforte to M^r. Allerton, a joye to you, to see a carfull and loving friend, and a great stay to ye bussines; and so great contente to us, that if it should please God ye one should faile, (as God forbid,) yet ye other would keepe both recconings, and things uprighte. For we are now out great sumes of money, as they will acquainte you withall, &c. When we were out but 4. or 5. hundred pounds a peece, we looked not much after it, but left it to you, & your agente, (who, without flaterie, deserveth infinite thanks & comendations, both of you & us, for his pains, &c.); but now we are out double, nay, trible a peece, some of us, &c.; which maks us both write, and send over our friend, M^r. Hatherley, whom we pray you to entertaine kindly, of which we doubte not of. The main end of sending him is to see yᵉ state and accounte of all yᵉ bussines, of all which we pray you informe him fully, though yᵉ ship & bussines wayte for it and him. For we should take it very unkindly that we should intreat him to take such a journey, and that, when it pleaseth God he returnes, he could not give us contente & satisfaction in this perticuler, through defaulte of any of you. [176] But we hope you will so order bussines, as neither he nor we shall have cause to complaine, but to doe as we ever have done, thinke well of you all, &c. I will not promise, but shall indeaour & hope to effecte yᵉ full desire and grant of your patente, & that ere it be longe. I would not have you take any thing unkindly. I have not write out of jeolocie of any unjuste dealing. Be you all kindly saluted in yᵉ Lord, so I rest,

Yours in what I may,

JAMES SHERLEY.

March 25. 1630.

It needs not be thought strange, that these things should amase and trouble them; first, that this fishing ship should be set out, and fraight with other mens goods, & scarce any of theirs; seeing their maine end was (as is before remembred) to bring them a full supply, and their speatiall order not to sett out any excepte this was done. And now a ship to come on their accounte, clean contrary to their both end & order, was a misterie they could not understand; and so much yᵉ worse, seeing she had shuch ill success as to lose both her vioage & provissions. The 2. thing, that another ship should be bought and sente out on new designes, a thing not so much as once thought on by any here, much less, not a word intimated or spoaken of by any here, either by word or letter, neither could they imagine why this should be. Bass fishing was never lookt at by them, but as soone as ever they heard on it, they looked at it as a vaine thing, that would certainly turne to loss. And for Mʳ. Allerton to follow any trade for them, it was never in their thoughts. And 3ˡʸ, that their friēds should complaine of disbursements, and yet rune into such great things, and charge of shiping & new projects of their owne heads, not only without, but against, all order & advice, was to them very strang. And 4ly, that all these matters of so great charg & imployments should be thus wrapped up in a breefe and obscure letter, they knew not what to make of it. But amids all their doubts they must have patience till Mr. Allerton & Mr. Hatherley should come. In ye mean time Mr. Winslow was gone for England; and others of them were forst to folow their imployments with ye best means they had, till they could hear of better.

At length Mr. Hatherley & Mr. Allerton came unto them, (after they had delivered their goods,) and finding them strucken with some sadnes aboute these things, Mr. Allerton tould them that ye ship Whit-Angele did not belong to them, nor their accounte, neither neede they have any thing to doe with her, excepte they would. And Mr. Hatherley confirmed ye same, and said that they would have had him to have had a parte, but he refused; but he made question whether they would not turne her upon ye generall accounte, if ther came loss (as he now saw was like), seeing Mr. Allerton laid downe this course, and put them on this projecte. But for ye fishing ship, he tould them they need not be so much troubled, for he had her accounts here, and showed them that her first seting out came not much to exceed 600li. as they might see by ye accounte, which he showed them; and for this later viage, it would arrise to profite by ye fraight of the goods, and ye salle of some katle which he shiped and had allready sould, & was to be paid for partly here & partly by bills into England, so as they should not have this put on their acounte at all, except they [178][CP] would. And for ye former, he had sould so much goods out of her in England, and imployed ye money in this 2. viage, as it, togeither with such goods & implements as Mr. Allerton must need aboute his fishing, would rise to a good parte of ye money; for he must have ye sallt and nets, allso spiks, nails, &c.; all which would rise to nere 400li; so, with ye bearing of their parts of ye rest of the loses (which would not be much above 200li.), they would clear them of this whole accounte. Of which motion they were glad, not being willing to have any accounts lye upon them; but aboute their trade, which made them willing to harken therunto, and demand of Mr. Hatherley how he could make this good, if they should agree their unto, he tould them he was sent over as their agente, and had this order from them, that whatsoever he and Mr. Allerton did togeather, they would stand to it; but they would not alow of what Mr. Allerton did alone, except they liked it; but if he did it alone, they would not gaine say it. Upon which they sould to him & Mr. Allerton all ye rest of ye goods, and gave them present possession of them; and a writing was made, and confirmed under both Mr. Hatherleys and Mr. Allertons hands, to ye effecte afforesaide. And Mr. Allertone, being best aquainted wth ye people, sould away presenly all shuch goods as he had no need of for ye fishing, as 9. shallop sails, made of good new canvas, and ye roads for them being all new, with sundry such usefull goods, for ready beaver, by Mr. Hatherleys allowance. And thus they thought they had well provided for them selvs. Yet they rebuked Mr. Allerton very much for runing into these courses, fearing ye success of them. Mr. Allerton & Mr. Hatherley brought to ye towne with them (after he had sould what he could abroad) a great quantity of other goods besids trading comodities; as linen cloath, bedticks, stockings, tape, pins, ruggs, &c., and tould them they were to have them, if they would; but they tould Mr. Allerton that they had forbid him before for bringing any such on their accounte; it would hinder their trade and returnes. But he & Mr. Hatherley said, if they would not have them, they would sell them, them selves, and take corne for what they could not otherwise sell. They tould them they might, if they had order for it. The goods of one sorte & other came to upward of 500li.

After these things, Mr. Allerton wente to ye ship aboute his bass fishing; and Mr. Hatherley, (according to his order,) after he tooke knowledg how things stood at ye plantation, (of all which they informed him fully,) he then desired a boate of them to goe and visite ye trading houeses, both Kenebeck, and Ashley at Penobscote; for so they in England had injoyned him. They accordingly furnished him with a boate & men for ye viage, and aquainted him plainly & thorowly with all things; by which he had good contente and satisfaction, and saw plainly that M^r. Allerton plaid his owne game, and rane a course not only to ye great wrong & detrimente of ye plantation, who imployed & trusted him, but abused them in England also, in possessing them with prejudice against ye plantation; as y^t, they would never be able to repaye their moneys (in regard of their great charge), but if [179] they would follow his advice and projects, he & Ashley (being well supplyed) would quickly bring in their moneys with good advantage. Mr. Hatherley disclosed also a further projecte aboute ye setting out of this ship, ye White-angell; how, she being wel fitted with good ordnance, and known to have made a great fight at sea (when she belongd to Bristoll) and caried away the victory, they had agreed (by M^r. Allerton's means) that, after she had brought a fraight of goods here into the countrie, and fraight her selfe with fish, she should goe from hence to Port of porte,^[CQ] and ther be sould, both ship, goods, and ordenance; and had, for this end, had speech with a factore of those parts, beforehand, to whom she should have been consigned. But this was prevented at this time, (after it was known,) partly by ye contrary advice given by their freinds hear to M^r. Allerton & M^r. Hatherley, showing how it might insnare their friends in England, (being men of estate,) if it should come to be knowne; and for ye plantation, they did and would disalow it, and protest against it; and partly by their bad viage, for they both came too late to doe any good for fishing, and allso had such a wicked and drunken company as neither M^r. Allerton nor any els could rule; as M^r. Hatherley, to his great greefe & shame, saw, & beheld, and all others that came nere them.

Ashley likwise was taken in a trape, (before M^r. Hatherley returned,) for trading powder & shote with ye Indeans; and was ceased upon by some in authoritie, who allso would have confiscated above a thousand weight of beaver; but ye goods were freed, for ye Governer here made it appere, by a bond under Ashleys hand, wherin he was bound to them in 500^li. not to trade any munition with the Indeans, or other wise to abuse him selfe; it was also manifest against him that he had comited uncleannes with

Indean women, (things that they feared at his first imployment, which made them take this strict course with him in yᵉ begining); so, to be shorte, they gott their goods freed, but he was sent home prisoner. And that I may make an end concerning him, after some time of imprisonmente in yᵉ Fleet, by yᵉ means of friends he was set at liberty, and intended to come over againe, but yᵉ Lord prevented it; for he had a motion made to him, by some marchants, to goe into Russia, because he had such good skill in yᵉ beaver trade, the which he accepted of, and in his returne home was cast away at sea; this was his end.

Mʳ. Hatherley, fully understanding yᵉ state of all things, had good satisfaction, and could well informe them how all things stood betweene Mʳ. Allerton and yᵉ plantation. Yea, he found that Mʳ. Allerton had gott within him, and [180] got all the goods into his owne hands, for which Mʳ. Hatherley stood joyntly ingaged to them hear, aboute yᵉ ship-Freīdship, as also most of yᵉ fraigte money, besids some of his owne perticuler estate; about wᶜʰ more will appear here after. So he returned into England, and they sente a good quantity of beaver with him to yᵉ rest of yᵉ partners; so both he and it was very wellcome unto them.

Mʳ. Allerton followed his affaires, & returned with his White Angell, being no more imployed by yᵉ plantation; but these bussinesses were not ended till many years after, nor well understood of a longe time, but foulded up in obscuritie, & kepte in yᵉ clouds, to yᵉ great loss & vexation of yᵉ plantation, who in yᵉ end were (for peace sake) forced to bear yᵉ unjust burthen of them, to their allmost undoing, as will appear, if God give life to finish this history.

They sent their letters also by Mʳ. Hatherley to yᵉ partners ther, to show them how Mʳ. Hatherley & Mʳ. Allerton had discharged them of yᵉ Friendships accounte, and that they boath affirmed yᵗ the White-Angell did not at all belong to them; and therfore desired that their accounte might not be charged therwith. Also they write to Mʳ. Winslow, their agente, that he in like maner should (in their names) protest against it, if any such thing should be intended, for they would never yeeld to yᵉ same. As allso to signifie to them that they renounsed Mʳ. Allerton wholy, for being their agente, or to have any thing to doe in any of their bussines.

This year John Billinton yᵉ elder (one that came over with yᵉ first) was arrained, and both by grand & petie jurie found guilty of willfull murder, by plaine & notorious evidence. And was for the same accordingly executed.[CR] This, as it was yᵉ first execution amongst them, so was it a mater of great sadnes unto them. They used all due means about his triall, and tooke yᵉ advice of Mʳ. Winthrop and other yᵉ ablest gentle-men in yᵉ Bay of yᵉ Massachusets, that were then new-ly come over, who concured with them yᵗ he ought to dye, and yᵉ land to be purged from blood. He and some of his had been often punished for miscariags before, being one of the profanest families amongst them. They came from London, and I know not by what freinds shufled into their company. His facte was, that he way-laid a yong-man, one John New-comin, (about a former quarell,) and shote him with a gune, wherof he dyed.[CS]

Having by a providence a letter or to yᵗ came to my hands concerning the proceedings of their Reᵈ freinds in yᵉ Bay of yᵉ Massachusets, who were latly come over, I thought it not amise here to inserte them, (so farr as is pertenente, and may be usefull for after times,) before I conclude this year.

Sʳ: Being at Salem the 25. of July, being yᵉ saboath, after yᵉ evening exercise, Mʳ. Johnson received a letter from yᵉ Governor, Mr. John Winthrop, manifesting yᵉ hand of God to be upon them, and against them at Charles-towne, in visiting them with sicknes, and taking diverse from amongst them, not sparing yᵉ righteous, but partaking with yᵉ wicked in these bodily judgments. It was therfore by his desire taken into yᵉ Godly consideration of yᵉ best hear, what was to be done to pacifie yᵉ Lords wrath, &c. Wher it was concluded, that the Lord was to be sought in righteousnes; and to that end, yᵉ 6. day (being Friday) of this present weeke, is set aparte, that they may humble them selves before God, and seeke him in his ordenances; and that then also such godly persons that are amongst them, and know each to other, may publickly, at ye end of their exercise, make known their Godly desire, and practise ye same, viz. solemly to enter into [181] covenante with ye Lord to walke in his ways. And since they are so disposed of in their outward estats, as to live in three distinct places, each having men of abilitie amongst them, ther to observe ye day, and become 3. distincte bodys; not then intending rashly to proceed to ye choyce of officers, or ye admitting of any other to their societie then a few, to witte, such as are well knowne unto them; promising after to receive in such by confession of faith, as shall appeare to be fitly qualified for y estate. They doe ernestly entreate that ye church of Plimoth would set apparte ye same day, for ye same ends, beseeching ye Lord, as to withdraw his hand of correction from them, so also to establish and direct them in his wayes. And though ye time be shorte, we pray you be provocked to this godly worke, seing ye causes are so urgente; wherin God will be honoured, and they & we undoubtedly have sweete comforte. Be you all kindly saluted, &c.

Your brethren in Christ, &c.

Salem, July 26. 1630.

S^r: etc. The sadd news here is, that many are sicke, and many are dead; ye Lord in mercie looke upon them. Some are here entered into church covenante; the first were 4. namly, ye Govr, M^r. John Winthrop, M^r. Johnson, M^r. Dudley, and M^r. Willson; since that 5. more are joyned unto them, and others, it is like, will adde them selves to them dayly; the Lord increase them, both in number and in holines for his mercie sake. Here is a gentleman, one M^r. Cottington, (a Boston man,) who tould me, that M^r. Cottons charge at Hamton was, that they should take advise of them at Plimoth, and should doe nothing to offend them. Here are diverce honest Christians that are desirous to see us, some out of love which they bear to us, and ye good perswasion they have of us; others to see whether we be so ill as they have heard of us. We have a name of holines, and love to God and his saincts; the Lord make us more and more answerable, and that it may be more then a name, or els it will doe us no good. Be you lovingly saluted, and all the rest of our friends. The Lord Jesus blese us, and yᵉ whole Israll of God. Amen.

Your loving brother, &c.

Charles-towne, Aug. 2. 1630.

Thus out of smalle beginings greater things have been prodused by his hand yᵗ made all things of nothing, and gives being to all things that are; and as one small candle may light a thousand, so yᵉ light here kindled hath shone to many, yea in some sorte to our whole nation; let yᵉ glorious name of Jehova have all yᵉ praise.

[182] *Anno Dom*: 1631.

Ashley being thus by yᵉ hand of God taken away, and Mʳ. Allerton discharged of his imploymente for them, their bussines began againe to rune in one chanell, and them selves better able to guide the same, Penobscote being wholy now at their disposing. And though Mʳ. William Peirce had a parte ther as is before noted, yet now, as things stood, he was glad to have his money repayed him, and stand out. Mʳ. Winslow, whom they had sent over, sent them over some supply as soone as he could; and afterwards when he came, which was something longe by reason of bussines, he brought a large supply of suitable goods with him, by which ther trading was well carried on. But by no means either he, or yᵉ letters yᵉʸ write, could take off Mʳ. Sherley & yᵉ rest from putting both yᵉ Friendship and Whit-Angell on yᵉ generall accounte; which caused continuall contention betweene them, as will more appeare.

I shall inserte a leter of Mʳ. Winslow's about these things, being as foloweth.

Sʳ: It fell out by Gods providence, yᵗ I received and brought your leters pʳ Mʳ. Allerton from Bristoll, to London; and doe much feare what will be yᵉ event of things. Mʳ. Allerton intended to prepare yᵉ ship againe, to set forth upon fishing. Mʳ. Sherley, Mʳ. Beachamp,

& M^r. Andrews, they renounce all perticulers, protesting but for us they would never have adventured one penie into those parts; M^r. Hatherley stands inclinable to either. And wheras you write that he and M^r. Allerton have taken ye Whit-Angell upon them, for their partners here, they professe they neiver gave any such order, nor will make it good; if them selves will cleare ye accounte & doe it, all shall be well. What ye evente of these things will be, I know not. The Lord so directe and assiste us, as he may not be dishonoured by our divissions. I hear (p^r a friend) that I was much blamed for speaking w^[CT] I heard in ye spring of ye year, concerning ye buying & setting forth of y^t ship;^[CU] sure, if I should not have tould you what I heard so peremtorly reported (which report I offered now to prove at Bristoll), I should have been unworthy my imploymente. And concerning ye commission so long since given to M^r. Allerton, the truth is, the thing we feared is come upon us; for M^r. Sherley & ye rest have it, and will not deliver it, that being ye ground of our agents credite to procure shuch great sumes. But I looke for bitter words, hard thoughts, and sower looks, from sundrie, as well for writing this, as reporting ye former. I would I had a more thankfull imploymente; but I hope a good conscience shall make it comefortable, &c.

Thus farr he. Dated Nov: 16. 1631.

The comission above said was given by them under their hand and seale, when M^r. Allerton was first imployed by them, and redemanded of him in ye year 29. when they begane to suspecte his course. He tould them it was amongst his papers, but he would seeke it out & give it them before he wente. But he being ready to goe, it was demanded againe. He said he could not find it, but it was amongst his papers, which he must take wth him, [183] and he would send it by ye boat from ye eastward; but ther it could not be had neither, but he would seeke it up at sea. But whether M^r. Sherley had it before or after, it is not certaine; but having it, he would not let it goe, but keeps it to this day. Wherfore, even amongst freinds, men had need be carfull whom they trust, and not lett things of this nature lye long unrecaled.

Some parts of M^r. Sherley's letters aboute these things, in which ye truth is best manifested.

Sir: Yours I have received by our loving friends, M^r. Allerton & M^r. Hatherley, who, blesed be God, after a long & dangerous passage with ye ship Angell, are safely come to Bristoll. M^r. Hatherley is come up, but M^r. Allerton I have not yet seen. We thanke you, and are very glad you have disswaded him from his Spanish viage, and y^t he did not goe on in these designes he intended; for we did all uterly dislick of that course, as allso of ye fishing y^t ye Freindship should have performed; for we wished him to sell ye salte, and were unwilling to have him undertake so much bussines, partly for ye ill success we formerly had in those affairs, and partly being loath to disburse so much money. But he perswaded us this must be one way y^t must repay us, for ye plantation would be long in doing of it; ney, to my rememberance, he doubted you could not be able, with ye trade ther, to maintaine your charge & pay us. And for this very cause he brought us on y^t bussines with Ed: Ashley, for he was a stranger to us, &c.

For ye fishing ship, we are sorie it proves so heavie, and will be willing to bear our parts. What M^r. Hatherley & M^r. Allerton have done, no doubt but them selves will make good;[CV] we gave them no order to make any composition, to seperate you and us in this or any other. And I thinke you have no cause to forsake us, for we put you upon no new thing, but what your agent perswaded us to, & you by your letters desired. If he exceede your order, I hope you will not blame us, much less cast us of, when our moneys be layed out, &c. But I fear neither you nor we have been well delte withall, for sure, as you write, halfe 4000^li.?, nay, a quarter, in fitting comodities, and in seasonable time, would have furnished you beter then you were. And yet for all this, and much more I might write, I dare not but thinke him honest, and that his desire and intente was good; but ye wisest may faile. Well, now y^t it hath pleased God to give us hope of meeting, doubte not but we will all indeavore to perfecte these accounts just & right, as soone as possibly we can. And I suppose you sente over M^r. Winslow, and we Mr. Hatherley, to certifie each other how ye state of things stood. We have received some contente upon Mr. Hatherley's returne, and I hope you will receive good contente upon Mr. Winslow's returne. Now I should come to answer more perticulerly your letter, but herin I shall be very breefe. The coming of ye White Angele on your accounte could not be more strang to you, then ye buying of her was to us; for you gave him commission[CW] that what he did you would stand too; we gave him none, and yet for his credite, and your saks, payed what bills he charged on us, &c. For yi I write she was to acte tow parts, fishing & trade; beleeve me, I never so much as thought of any perticuler trade, nor will side with any yt doth, if I conceive it may wrong you; for I ever was against it, useing these words: They will eate up and destroy ye generall.

Other things I omite as tedious, and not very pertenente. This was dated Novr. 19. 1631.

In an other leter bearing date ye 24. of this month, being an answer to ye generall order, he hath these words:—

[184] For ye White Angell, against which you write so ernestly, and say we thrust her upon you, contrary to ye intente of ye buyer, herin we say you forgett your selves, and doe us wrong. We will not take uppon us to devine what ye thougts or intents of ye buyer was, but what he spack we heard, and that we will affirme, and make good against any yt oppose it; which is, yt unles shee were bought, and shuch a course taken, Ashley could not be supplyed; and againe, if he weer not supplyed, we could not be satisfied what we were out for you. And further, you were not able to doe it; and he gave some reasons which we spare to relate, unless by your unreasonable refusall you will force us, and so, hasten yt fire which is a kindling too fast allready, &c.

Out of another of his, bearing date Jan. 2. 1631.

We purpose to keep ye Freindship and ye Whit Angell, for ye last year viages, on the generall accounte, hoping togeither they will rather produse profite then loss, and breed less confution in our accounts, and less disturbance in our affections. As for ye White

Angell, though we layed out ye money, and tooke bills of salle in our owne names, yet none of us had so much as a thought (I dare say) of deviding from you in any thing this year, because we would not have ye world (I may say Bristoll) take notice of any breach betwixte M^r. Allerton and you, and he and us; and so disgrace him in his proceedings on^[CX] in his intended viage. We have now let him ye ship at 30^{li}. p^r month, by charter-partie, and bound him in a bond of a 1000^{li}. to performe covenants, and bring her to London (if God please). And what he brings in her for you, shall be marked wth your marke, and bils of laden taken, & sent in M^r. Winslows letter, who is this day riding to Bristoll about it. So in this viage, we deale & are with him as strangers. He hath brought in 3. books of accounts, one for ye company, an other for Ashley's bussines, and ye third for ye Whit-Angell and Freindship. The books, or coppies, we purpose to send you, for you may discover ye errours in them better then we. We can make it appear how much money he hath had of us, and you can charg him with all ye beaver he hath had of you. The totall sume, as he hath put it, is 7103. 17. 1. Of this he hath expended, and given to Mr. Vines & others, aboute 543^{li}. ode money, and then by your books you will find whether you had such, & so much goods, as he chargeth you with all; and this is all that I can say at presente concerning these accounts. He thought to dispatch them in a few howers, but he and Straton & Fogge were above a month aboute them; but he could not stay till we had examined them, for losing his fishing viage, which I fear he hath allready done, &c.

We blese God, who put both you & us in mind to send each to other, for verily had he rune on in that desperate & chargable course one year more, we had not been able to suport him; nay, both he and we must have lyen in ye ditch, and sunck under ye burthen, &c. Had ther been an orderly course taken, and your bussines better managed, assuredly (by ye blessing of God) you had been ye ablest plantation that, as we think, or know, hath been undertaken by Englishmen, &c.

Thus farr of these letters of M^r. Sherley's.^[CY]

[185] A few observations from ye former letters, and then I shall set downe the simple truth of ye things (thus in controversie betweene them), at least as farr as by any good evidence it could be made to appeare; and so laboure to be breefe in so tedious and intricate a bussines, which hunge in expostulation betweene them many years before ye same was ended. That though ther will be often occasion to touch these things about other passages, yet I shall not neede to be large therin; doing it hear once for all.

First, it seemes to appere clearly that Ashley's bussines, and ye buying of this ship, and ye courses framed ther upon, were first contrived and proposed by Mr. Allerton, as also yt the pleaes and pretences which he made, of ye inablitie of ye plantation to repaye their moneys, &c., and ye hops he gave them of doing it with profile, was more beleeved & rested on by them (at least some of them) then any thing ye plantation did or said.

2. It is like, though Mr. Allerton might thinke not to wrong ye plantation in ye maine, yet his owne gaine and private ends led him a side in these things: for it came to be knowne, and I have it in a letter under Mr. Sherley's hand, that in ye first 2. or 3. years of his imploymente, he had cleared up 400li. and put it into a brew-house of Mr. Colliers in London, at first under Mr. Sherley's name, &c.; besids what he might have other wise. Againe, Mr. Sherley and he had perticuler dealings in some things; for he bought up ye beaver that sea-men & other passengers brought over to Bristoll, and at other places, and charged ye bills to London, which Mr. Sherley payed; and they got some time 50li. a peece in a bargen, as was made knowne by Mr. Hatherley & others, besids what might be other wise; which might make Mr. Sherley harken unto him in many things; and yet I beleeve, as he in his forementioned leter write, he never would side in any perticuler trade wch he conceived would wrong ye plantation, and eate up & destroy ye generall.

3ly. It may be perceived that, seeing they had done so much for ye plantation, both in former adventures and late disbursements, and allso that Mr. Allerton was ye first occasioner of bringing them upon these new designes, which at first seemed faire & profitable unto them, and unto which they agreed; but now, seeing them to turne to loss, and decline to greater intanglments, they thought it more meete for yᵉ plantation to bear them, then them selves, who had borne much in other things allready, and so tooke advantage of such comission & power as Mʳ. Allerton had formerly had as their agente, to devolve these things upon them.

4ˡʸ. With pitie and compassion (touching Mʳ. Allerton) I may say with yᵉ apostle to Timothy, 1. Tim. 6. 9. *They that will be rich fall into many temtations and snares, &c., and pearce them selves throw with many sorrows, &c.; for the love of money is yᵉ roote of all evill,* v. 10. God give him to see yᵉ evill in his failings, that he may find mercie by repentance for yᵉ wrongs he hath done to any, and this pore plantation in spetiall. They that doe such things doe not only bring them selves into snares, and sorrows, but many with them, (though in an other kind,) as lamentable experience shows; and is too manifest in this bussines.

[186] Now about these ships & their setting forth, the truth, as farr as could be learned, is this. The motion aboute setting forth yᵉ fishing ship (caled yᵉ Frindship) came first from yᵉ plantation, and yᵉ reasons of it, as is before remembered; but wholy left to them selves to doe or not to doe, as they saw cause. But when it fell into consideration, and yᵉ designe was held to be profitable and hopefull, it was propounded by some of them, why might not they doe it of them selves, seeing they must disburse all yᵉ money, and what need they have any refferance to yᵉ plantation in yᵗ; they might take yᵉ profile them selves, towards other losses, & need not let yᵉ plantation share therin; and if their ends were other wise answered for their supplyes to come too them in time, it would be well enough. So they hired her, & set her out, and fraighted her as full as she could carry with passengers goods yᵗ belonged to yᵉ Massachussets, which rise to a good sume of money; intending to send yᵉ plantations supply in yᵉ other ship. The effecte of this Mʳ. Hatherley not only declared afterward upon occasion, but affirmed upon othe, taken before yᵉ Govʳ & Dep: Govʳ of the Massachusets, Mʳ. Winthrop & Mʳ. Dudley: That this ship-Frindship was not sett

out nor intended for yᵉ joynt partnership of yᵉ plantation, but for yᵉ perticuler accounte of Mʳ. James Sherley, Mʳ. Beachampe, Mʳ. Andrews, Mʳ. Allerton, & him selfe. This deposition was taken at Boston yᵉ 29. of Aug: 1639. as is to be seen under their hands; besids some other concurente testimonies declared at severall times to sundrie of them.

About yᵉ Whit-Angell, though she was first bought, or at least the price beaten, by Mʳ. Allerton (at Bristoll), yet that had been nothing if Mʳ. Sherley had not liked it, and disbursed yᵉ money. And that she was not intended for yᵉ plantation appears by sundrie evidences;[CZ] as, first, yᵉ bills of sale, or charter-parties, were taken in their owne names, without any mention or refferance to yᵉ plantation at all; viz. Mʳ. Sherley, Mʳ. Beachampe, Mʳ. Andrews, Mʳ. Denison, and Mʳ. Allerton; for Mʳ. Hatherley fell off, and would not joyne with them in this. That she was not bought for their accounte, Mʳ. Hatherley tooke his oath before yᵉ parties afforesaid, yᵉ day and year above writen.

Mʳ. Allerton tooke his oath to like effecte concerning this ship, the Whit-Angell, before yᵉ Govʳ & Deputie, the 7. of Sep: 1639. and likewise deposed, yᵉ same time, that Mʳ. Hatherley and him selfe did, in the behalfe of them selves and yᵉ said Mʳ. Sherley, Mʳ. Andrews, & Mʳ. Beachamp, agree and undertake to discharge, and save harmless, all yᵉ rest of yᵉ partners & purchasers, of and from yᵉ said losses of Freindship for 200ˡⁱ., which was to be discounted therupon; as by ther depossitions (which are in writing) may appeare more at large, and some other depositions & other testemonies by Mʳ. Winslow,[DA] &c. But I suppose these may be sufficente to evince the truth in these things, against all pretences to yᵉ contrary. And yet the burthen lay still upon yᵉ plantation; or, to speake more truly and rightly, upon those few that were ingaged for all, for they were faine to wade through these things without any help from any.

[187] Concerning Mʳ. Allerton's accounts, they were so larg and intrecate, as they could not well understand them, much less

examine & correcte them, without a great deale of time & help, and his owne presence, which was now hard to gett amongst them; and it was 2. or 3. years before they could bring them to any good pass, but never make them perfecte. I know not how it came to pass, or what misterie was in it, for he tooke upon him to make up all accounts till this time, though M^r. Sherley was their agente to buy & sell their goods, and did more then he therin; yet he past in accounts in a maner for all disbursments, both concerning goods bought, which he never saw, but were done when he was hear in ye cuntrie or at sea; and all ye expences of ye Leyden people, done by others in his absence; the charges aboute ye patente, &c. In all which he made them debtore to him above 300^{li}. and demanded paimente of it. But when things came to scaning, he was found above 2000^{li}. debtore to them, (this wherin M^r. Hatherley & he being joyntly ingaged, which he only had, being included,) besids I know not how much y^t could never be cleared; and interest moneys which ate them up, which he never accounted. Also they were faine to alow such large bills of charges as were intolerable; the charges of ye patent came to above 500^{li}. and yet nothing done in it but what was done at first without any confirmation; 30^{li}. given at a clape, and 50^{li}. spent in a journey. No marvell therfore if M^r. Sherley said in his leter, if their bussines had been better managed, they might have been ye richest plantation of any English at y^t time. Yea, he scrued up his poore old father in law's accounte to above 200^{li}. and brought it on ye generall accounte, and to befreind him made most of it to arise out of those goods taken up by him at Bristoll, at 50. per cent., because he knew they would never let it lye on ye old man, when, alass! he, poore man, never dreamte of any such thing, nor y^t what he had could arise nere y^t valew; but thought that many of them had been freely bestowed on him & his children by M^r. Allerton. Nither in truth did they come nere y^t valew in worth, but y^t sume was blowne up by interest & high prises, which ye company did for ye most parte bear, (he deserving farr more,) being most sory that he should have a name to have much, when he had in effecte litle.

This year also M^r. Sherley sent over an accounte, which was in a maner but a cash accounte what M^r. Allerton had had of them, and disbursed, for which he referd to his accounts; besids an account of beaver sould, which M^r. Winslow & some others had carried over, and a large supply of goods which M^r. Winslow had sent & brought over, all which was comprised in that accounte, and all ye disbursments aboute ye Freindship, & Whit-Angell, and what concerned their accounts from first to last; or any thing else he could charg ye partners with. So they were made debtor in ye foote of that accounte 4770^li 19. 2.[DB] besids 1000^li. still due for ye purchase yet unpayed; notwithstanding all ye beaver, and returnes that both Ashley & they had made, which were not small.

[188] In these accounts of M^r. Sherley's some things were obscure, and some things twise charged, as a 100. of Bastable ruggs which came in ye Freindship, & cost 75^li., charged before by M^r. Allerton, and now by him againe, with other perticulers of like nature doubtfull, to be twise or thrise charged; as also a sume of 600^li. which M^r. Allerton deneyed, and they could never understand for what it was. They sent a note of these & such like things afterward to M^r. Sherley by M^r. Winslow; but (I know not how it came to pass) could never have them explained.

Into these deepe sumes had M^r. Allerton rune them in tow years, for in ye later end of ye year 1628. all their debts did not amounte to much above 400^li., as was then noted; and now come to so many thousands. And wheras in ye year 1629. M^r. Sherley & M^r. Hatherley being at Bristoll, and write a large letter from thence, in which they had given an account of ye debts, and what sumes were then disbursed, M^r. Allerton never left begging & intreating of them till they had put it out. So they bloted out 2. lines in y^t leter in which ye sumes were contained, and write upon it so as not a word could be perceived; as since by them was confessed, and by ye leters may be seene. And thus were they kept hoodwinckte, till now they were so deeply ingaged. And wheras M^r. Sherley did so ernestly press y^t M^r. Allerton might be sent over to finish ye great bussines aboute ye patente, as may be seen in his leter write 1629. as is before recorded, and y^t they should be ernest wth his wife to suffer him to goe, &c., he hath since confessed by a letter under my hands, that it was Mʳ. Allerton's owne doings, and not his, and he made him write his words, & not his owne. The patent was but a pretence, and not yᵉ thing. Thus were they abused in their simplicitie, and no beter then bought & sould, as it may seeme.

And to mend yᵉ matter, Mʳ. Allerton doth in a sorte wholy now deserte them; having brought them into yᵉ briers, he leaves them to gett out as they can. But God crost him mightily, for he having hired yᵉ ship of Mʳ. Sherly at 30ˡⁱ., a month, he set forth againe with a most wicked and drunken crue, and for covetousnes sake did so over lade her, not only filling her hould, but so stufed her betweene decks, as she was walte, and could not bear sayle, and they had like to have been cast away at sea, and were forced to put for Millford Havene, and new-stow her, & put some of ther ordnance & more heavie goods in yᵉ botome; which lost them time, and made them come late into yᵉ countrie, lose ther season, and made a worse viage then yᵉ year before. But being come into yᵉ countrie, he sells trading comodities to any yᵗ will buy, to yᵉ great prejudice of yᵉ plantation here; but that which is worse, what he could not sell, he trustes; and sets up a company of base felows and maks them traders, to rune into every hole, & into yᵉ river of Kenebeck, to gleane away yᵉ trade from yᵉ house ther, aboute yᵉ patente & priviledge wherof he had dasht away so much money of theirs here; [189] and now what in him lay went aboute to take away yᵉ benefite therof, and to overthrow them. Yea, not only this, but he furnishes a company, and joyns with some consorts, (being now deprived of Ashley at Penobscote,) and sets up a trading house beyoned Penobscote, to cute of yᵉ trade from thence also. But yᵉ French perceiving that that would be greatly to their damage allso, they came in their begining before they were well setled, and displanted them, slue 2. of their men, and tooke all their goods to a good valew, yᵉ loss being most, if not all, Mʳ. Allerton's; for though some of them should have been his partners, yet he trusted them for their partes; the rest of yᵉ men were sent into France, and this was the end of yᵗ projecte. The rest of those he trusted, being lose and drunken fellows, did for yᵉ most parte but coussen & cheate him of all they got into their hands; that howsoever he did his friends some hurte hereby for yᵉ presente, yet he gate litle good, but wente by yᵉ loss by Gods just hand. After in time, when he came to Plimoth, yᵉ church caled him to accounte for these, and other his grosse miscarrages; he confessed his faulte, and promised better walking, and that he would wind him selfe out of these courses as soone as he could, &c.

This year also Mr. Sherley would needs send them over a new-acountante; he had made mention of such a thing yᵉ year before, but they write him word, that their charge was great allready, and they neede not increase it, as this would; but if they were well delte with, and had their goods well sent over, they could keep their accounts hear them selves. Yet he now sente one, which they did not refuse, being a yonger brother of Mʳ. Winslows, whom they had been at charge to instructe at London before he came. He came over in the White Angell with Mʳ. Allerton, and ther begane his first imploymente; for though Mʳ. Sherley had so farr befreinded Mr. Allerton, as to cause[DC] Mʳ. Winslow to ship yᵉ supply sente to yᵉ partners here in this ship, and give him 4ˡⁱ. per tune, wheras others carried for 3. and he made them pay their fraight ready downe, before yᵉ ship wente out of yᵉ harbore, wheras others payed upon certificate of yᵉ goods being delivered, and their fraight came to upward of 6. score pounds, yet they had much adoe to have their goods delivered, for some of them were chainged, as bread & pease; they were forced to take worse for better, neither could they ever gett all. And if Josias Winslow had not been ther, it had been worse; for he had yᵉ invoyce, and order to send them to yᵉ trading houses.

This year their house at Penobscott was robed by yᵉ French, and all their goods of any worth they carried away, to yᵉ value of 400. or 500ˡⁱ. as yᵉ cost first peny worth; in beaver 300ˡⁱ. waight; and yᵉ rest in trading goods, as coats, ruggs, blankett, biskett, &c. It was in this maner. The mʳ. of yᵉ house, and parte of yᵉ company with him, were come with their vessell to yᵉ westward to fecth a supply of goods which was brought over for them. In yᵉ mean time comes a smale French ship into yᵉ harbore (and amongst yᵉ company was a false Scott); they pretended they were nuly come from yᵉ sea, and knew not wher they were, and that their vesell was very leake, and desired they might hale her a shore and stop their leaks. And many French complements they used, and congees they made; and in ye ende, seeing but 3. or 4. simple men, y^t were servants, and by this Scoth-man understanding that ye maister & ye rest of ye company were gone from home, they fell of comending their gunes and muskets, that lay upon racks by ye wall side, and tooke them downe to looke on them, asking if they were charged. And when they were possesst of them, one presents a peece ready charged against ye servants, and another a pistoll; and bid them not sturr, but quietly deliver them their goods, and carries some of ye men aborde, & made ye other help to carry away ye goods. And when they had tooke what they pleased, they sett them at liberty, and wente their way, with this mocke, biding them tell their m^r. when he came, that some of ye Ile of Rey gentlemen had been ther.[DD]

[DE] This year, on Sr Christopher Gardener, being, as him selfe said, descended of y^t house y^t the Bishop of Winchester came of (who was so great a persecutor of Gods saincts in Queene Maries days), and being a great traveler, received his first honour of knighthood at Jerusalem, being made Knight of ye Sepulcher ther. He came into these parts under pretence of forsaking ye world, and to live a private life, in a godly course, not unwilling to put him selfe upon any meane imployments, and take any paines for his living; and some time offered him selfe to joyne to ye churchs in sundry places. He brought over with him a servante or 2. and a comly yonge woman, whom be caled his cousin, but it was suspected, she (after ye Italian maner) was his concubine. Living at ye Massachusets, for some miscariages which he should have answered, he fled away from authority, and gott amonge ye Indeans of these parts; they sent after him, but could not gett him, and promissed some reward to those y^t should find him. The Indeans came to ye Govr here, and tould wher he was, and asked if they might kill him; he tould them no, by no means, but if they could take him and bring him hither, they should be payed for their paines. They said he had a gune & a rapier, & he would kill them if y^ey went aboute it; and ye Massachuset Indeans said they might kille him. But yᵉ Govʳ tould them no, they should not kill him, but watch their opportunitie, & take him. And so they did, for when they light of him by a river side, he got into a canowe to get from them, & when they came nere him, whilst he presented his peece at them to keep them of, the streame carried yᵉ canow against a rock, and tumbled both him & his peece & rapier into yᵉ water; yet he got out, and having a litle dagger by his side, they durst not close with him, but getting longe pols they soone beat his dagger out of his hand, so he was glad to yeeld; and they brought him to yᵉ Govʳ. But his hands and armes were swolen & very sore with yᵉ blowes they had given him. So he used him kindly, & sent him to a lodging wher his armes were bathed and anoynted, and he was quickly well againe, and blamed yᵉ Indeans for beating him so much. They said that they did but a litle whip him with sticks. In his lodging, those yᵗ made his bed found a litle note booke that by accidente had slipt out of his pockett, or some private place, in which was a memoriall what day he was reconciled to yᵉ pope & church of Rome, and in what universitie he tooke his scapula, and such & such degrees. It being brought to yᵉ Govʳ, he kept it, and sent yᵉ Govʳ of yᵉ Massachusets word of his taking, who sent for him. So yᵉ Govʳ sent him and these notes to yᵉ Govʳ ther, who tooke it very thankfuly; but after he gott for England, he shewed his malice, but God prevented him.

See yᵉ Govʳ leter on yᵉ other side.[DF]

Sʳ: It hath pleased God to bring Sʳ. Christopher Gardener safe to us, with thos that came with him. And howsoever I never intended any hard measure to him, but to respecte and use him according to his qualitie, yet I let him know your care of him, and yᵗ he shall speed yᵉ better for your mediation. It was a spetiall providence of God to bring those notes of his to our hands; I desire yᵗ you will please to speake to all yᵗ are privie to them, not to discovere them to any one, for yᵗ may frustrate yᵉ means of any further use to be made of them. The good Lord our God who hath allways ordered things for yᵉ good of his poore churches here, directe us in this arighte, and dispose it to a good issue. I am sorie we put you to so much trouble about this gentleman, espetialy at this time of great imploymente, but I know not how to avoyed it. I must againe intreate you, to let me know what charge & troble any of your people have been at aboute him, y' it may be recompenced. So with the true affection of a frind, desiring all happines to your selfe & yours, and to all my worthy friends with you (whom I love in ye Lord), I comende you to his grace & good providence, & rest

Your most assured friend,

JOHN WINTHROP.

Boston, May 5. 1631.

By occation wherof I will take a litle libertie to declare what fell out by this mans means & malice, complying with others. And though I doubt not but it will be more fully done by my honourd friends, whom it did more directly concerne, and have more perticuler knowledg of ye matter, yet I will here give a hinte of ye same, and Gods providence in preventing ye hurte that might have come by ye same. The intelligence I had by a letter from my much hon^d and beloved friend, Mr. John Winthrop, Govr of ye Massachusets.

S^r: Upon a petition exhibited by S^r. Christo: Gardner, S^r. Ferd: Gorges, Captaine Masson, &c., against you and us, the cause was heard before ye lords of ye Privie Counsell, and after reported to ye king, the sucsess wherof maks it evident to all, that ye Lord hath care of his people hear. The passages are admirable, and too long to write. I hartily wish an opportunitie to imparte them unto you, being mͣy sheets of paper. But ye conclusion was (against all mens expectation) an order for our incouragmente, and much blame and disgrace upon ye adversaries, wch calls for much thankfullnes from us all, which we purpose (ye Lord willing) to express in a day of thanks-giving to our mercifull God, (I doubt not but you will consider, if it be not fitt for you to joyne in it,) who, as he hath humbled us by his late correction, so he hath lifted us up, by an abundante rejoysing, in our deliverance out of so desperate a danger; so as that wch our enemies builte their hopes upon to ruine us by, He hath mercifully disposed to our great advantage, as I shall further aquainte you, when occasion shall serve.

The coppy of ye order follows.

At ye courte at Whit-hall ye 19. Jan: 1632.

Present

Sigillum Lord Privie Seale
Ea: of Dorsett
Lo: Vi: Falkland
Lo: Bp: of London
Lord Cottinton
M^r. Tre^r
M^r. Vic Chamb^r
M^r. Sec: Cooke
Maister Sec: Windebanck

Wheras his Matie hath latly been informed of great distraction and much disorder in y^t plantation in ye parts of America called New-England, which, if they be true, & suffered to rune on, would tende to ye great dishonour of this kingdome, and utter ruine of that plantation. For prevention wherof, and for ye orderly settling of goverment, according to ye intention of those patents which have been granted by his Matie and from his late royall father king James, it hath pleased his Matie that ye lords & others of his most honourable Privie Counsell, should take ye same into consideration. Their lordships in ye first place thought fitt to make a comitie of this bord, to take examination of ye matters informed; which comitties having called diverse of ye principall adventurers in y^t plantation, and heard those that are complanants against them, most of the things informed being deneyed, and resting to be proved by parties that must be called from y^t place, which required a long expence of time; and at presente their lordships finding the adventurers were upon dispatch of men, victles, and marchandice for y^t place, all which would be at a stand, if ye adventurers should have discouragmente, or take suspition that the state hear had no good opinion of y^t plantation; their lordships, not laying the faulte or fancies (if any be) of some perticuler men upon the generall govermente, or principall adventurers, (which in due time is further to be inquired into,) have thought fitt in ye meane time to declare, that the appearences were so faire, and hopes so greate, y^t the countrie would prove both beneficiall to this kingdom, and profitable to the perticuler adventurers, as y^t the adventurers had cause to goe on cherfully with their undertakings, and rest assured, if things were carried as was pretended when ye patents were granted, and accordingly as by the patentes it is appointed, his Majestie would not only maintaine the liberties & privileges heretofore granted, but supply any thing further that might tend to the good govermente, prosperitie, and comforte of his people ther of that place, &c.

WILLIAM TRUMBALL.

Anno Dom: 1632.

M^r. Allerton, returning for England, litle regarded his bound of a 1000^{li}. to performe covenants; for wheras he was bound by ye same to bring ye ship to [190] London, and to pay 30^{li}. per month for her hire, he did neither of boath, for he carried her to Bristoll againe, from whence he intended to sett her out againe, and so did ye 3. time, into these parts (as after will appeare); and though she had been 10. months upon ye former viage, at 30^{li}. p^r month, yet he never payed peney for hire. It should seeme he knew well enough how to deale with M^r. Sherley. And M^r. Sherley, though he would needs tye her & her accounte upon ye generall, yet he would dispose of her as him selfe pleased; for though M^r. Winslow had in their names protested against yᵉ receiving her on yᵗ accounte, or if ever they should hope to preveile in shuch a thing, yet never to suffer Mʳ. Allerton to have any more to doe in her, yet he yᵉ last year let her wholy unto him, and injoyned them to send all their supplye in her to their prejudice, as is before noted. And now, though he broke his bonds, kepte no covenante, paid no hire, nor was ever like to keep covenants, yet now he goes and sells him all, both ship, & all her accounts, from first to last (and in effecte he might as well have given him yᵉ same); and not only this, but he doth as good as provide a sanctuary for him, for he gives him one years time to prepare his accounte, and then to give up yᵉ same to them here; and then another year for him to make paymente of what should be due upon yᵗ accounte. And in yᵉ mean time writs ernestly to them not to interupte or hinder him from his bussines, or stay him aboute clearing accounts, &c.; so as he in yᵉ mean time gathers up all monies due for fraighte, and any other debtes belonging either to her, or yᵉ Frindship's accounts, as his owne perticuler; and after, sells ship, & ordnans, fish, & what he had raised, in Spaine, according to yᵉ first designe, in effecte; and who had, or what became of yᵉ money, he best knows. In yᵉ mean time their hands were bound, and could doe nothing but looke on, till he had made all away into other mens hands (save a few catle & a litle land & some small maters he had here at Plimoth), and so in yᵉ end removed, as he had allready his person, so all his from hence. This will better appere by Mʳ. Sherley's leter.

Sʳ: These few lines are further to give you to understand, that seeing you & we, that never differed yet but aboute yᵉ White-Angell, which somewhat troubleth us, as I perceive it doth you. And now Mʳ. Allerton beeing here, we have had some confferance with him about her, and find him very willing to give you & us all contente yᵗ possiblie he can, though he burthen him selfe. He is contente to take yᵉ White-Angell wholy on him selfe, notwithstanding he mett with pirates nere yᵉ coast of Ierland, which tooke away his best sayles & other provissions from her; so as verily if we should now sell her, she would yeeld but a small price, besids her ordnance. And to set her forth againe with fresh money we would not, she being now at Bristoll. Wherfore we thought it best, both for you & us, Mʳ. Allerton being willing to take her, to accepte of his bond of tow thousand pounds, to give [191] you a true & perfecte accounte, and take yᵉ whole charge of yᵉ Whit-Angell wholy to him selfe, from yᵉ first to yᵉ last. The accounte he is to make and perfecte within 12. months from yᵉ date of this letter, and then to pay you at 6. and 6. months after, what soever shall be due unto you and us upon the foote of yᵗ accounte. And verily, notwithstanding all yᵉ disasters he hath had, I am perswaded he hath enough to pay all men here and ther. Only they must have patience till he can gather in what is due to him ther. I doe not write this slightly, but upon some ground of what I have seen (and perhaps you know not of) under yᵉ hands & seals of some, &c. I rest

Your assured friend,

JAMES SHERLEY.

Des: 6. 1632.

But heres not a word of yᵉ breach of former bonds & covenants, or paimente of yᵉ ships hire; this is passt by as if no such thing had been; besids what bonds or obligments so ever they had of him, ther never came any into yᵉ hands or sight of yᵉ partners here. And for this yᵗ Mʳ. Sherley seems to intimate (as a secrete) of his abilitie, under yᵉ hands & seals of some, it was but a trick, having gathered up an accounte of what was owing form such base fellows as he had made traders for him, and other debts; and then got Mʳ. Mahue, & some others, to affirme under their hand & seale, that they had seen shuch accounts yᵗ were due to him.

Mr. Hatherley came over againe this year, but upon his owne occasions, and begane to make preparation to plant & dwell in yᵉ countrie. He with his former dealings had wound in what money he had in yᵉ patnership into his owne hands, and so gave off all partnership (excepte in name), as was found in yᵉ issue of things;

neither did he medle, or take any care aboute yᵉ same; only he was troubled about his ingagmente aboute yᵉ Friendship, as will after appeare. And now partly aboute yᵗ accounte, in some reconings betweene Mʳ. Allerton and him, and some debts yᵗ Mʳ. Allerton otherwise owed him upon dealing between them in perticuler, he drue up an accounte of above 2000ⁱⁱ., and would faine have ingaged yᵉ partners here with it, because Mʳ. Allerton had been their agent. But they tould him they had been fool'd longe enough with such things, and shewed him yᵗ it no way belonged to them; but tould him he must looke to make good his ingagment for yᵉ Freindship, which caused some trouble betweene Mʳ. Allerton and him.

Mʳ. William Peirce did yᵉ like, Mʳ. Allerton being wound into his debte also upon particuler dealings; as if they had been bound to make good all mens debts. But they easily shooke off these things. But Mʳ. Allerton herby rane into much trouble & vexation, as well as he had troubled others, for Mʳ. Denison sued him for yᵉ money he had disbursed for yᵉ 6. part of yᵉ Whit-Angell, & recovered yᵉ same with damages.

Though yᵉ partners were thus plūged into great ingagments, & oppresed with unjust debts, yet yᵉ Lord prospered their trading, that they made yearly large returnes, and had soone wound them selves out of all, if yet they had otherwise been well delt with all; as will more appear here after. [192] Also yᵉ people of yᵉ plantation begane to grow in their owtward estats, by reason[DG] of yᵉ flowing of many people into yᵉ cuntrie, espetially into yᵉ Bay of yᵉ Massachusets; by which means corne & catle rose to a great prise, by wᶜʰ many were much inriched, and comodities grue plentifull; and yet in other regards this benefite turned to their hurte, and this accession of strength to their weaknes. For now as their stocks increased, and yᵉ increse vendible, ther was no longer any holding them togeather, but now they must of necessitie goe to their great lots; they could not other wise keep their katle; and having oxen growne, they must have land for plowing & tillage. And no man now thought he could live, except he had catle and a great deale of ground to keep them; all striving to increase their stocks. By which means they were scatered all over yᵉ bay, quickly, and yᵉ towne, in which they lived

compactly till now, was left very thine, and in a short time allmost
desolate. And if this had been all, it had been less, thoug to much;
but yᵉ church must also be devided, and those yᵗ had lived so long
togeather in Christian & comfortable fellowship must now part and
suffer many divissions. First, those that lived on their lots on yᵉ
other side of the bay (called Duxberie) they could not long bring
their wives & children to yᵉ publick worship & church meetings
here, but with such burthen, as, growing to some competente
number, they sued to be dismissed and become a body of them
selves; and so they were dismiste (about this time), though very
unwillingly. But to touch this sadd matter, and handle things
together that fell out afterward. To prevent any further scatering
from this place, and weakning of yᵉ same, it was thought best to
give out some good farms to spetiall persons, yᵗ would promise to
live at Plimoth, and lickly to be helpfull to yᵉ church or
comonewelth, and so tye yᵉ lands to Plimoth as farmes for the
same; and ther they might keepe their catle & tillage by some
servants, and retaine their dwellings here. And so some spetiall
lands were granted at a place generall, called Greens Harbor, wher
no allotments had been in yᵉ former divission, a plase very weell
meadowed, and fitt to keep & rear catle, good store. But alass! this
remedy proved worse then yᵉ disease; for wᵗʰin a few years those
that had thus gott footing ther rente them selves away, partly by
force, and partly wearing yᵉ rest with importunitie and pleas of
necessitie, so as they must either suffer them to goe, or live in
continuall opposition and contention. And others still, as yᵉʸ
conceived them selves straitened, or to want accomodation, break
away under one pretence or other, thinking their owne conceived
necessitie, and the example of others, a warrente sufficente for
them. And this, I fear, will be yᵉ ruine of New-England, at least of
yᵉ churches of God ther, & will provock yᵉ Lords displeasure
against them.

[193] This year, Mʳ. William Perce came into yᵉ cuntry, &
brought goods and passengers, in a ship caled yᵉ Lyon, which
belonged cheefly to Mʳ. Sherley, and yᵉ rest of yᵉ London partners,
but these hear had nothing to doe with her. In this ship (besides

beaver which they had sent home before) they sent upwards of 800ᴸⁱ. in her, and some otter skines; and also yᵉ coppies of Mʳ. Allertons accounts, desiring that they would also peruse & examene them, and rectifie shuch things as they should find amise in them; and rather because they were better acquaynted with yᵉ goods bought ther, and yᵉ disbursments made, then they could bee here; yea, a great part were done by them selves, though Mʳ. Allerton brougt in yᵉ accounte, and sundry things seemed to them obscure and had need of clearing. Also they sente a booke of exceptions against his accounts, in such things as they could manifest, and doubted not but they might adde more therunto. And also shewed them how much Mʳ. Allerton was debtor to yᵉ accounte; and desired, seeing they had now put yᵉ ship White-Angell, and all, wholy into his power, and tyed their hands here, that they could not call him to accounte for any thinge, till yᵉ time was expired which they had given him, and by that time other men would get their debts of him, (as sume had done already by suing him,) and he would make all away here quickly out of their reach; and therfore prayed them to looke to things, and gett paymente of him ther, as it was all yᵉ reason they should, seeing they keept all yᵉ bonds & covenants they made with him in their owne hands; and here they could doe nothing by yᵉ course they had taken, nor had any thing to show if they should goe aboute it. But it pleased God, this ship, being first to goe to Verginia before she wente home, was cast away on yᵗ coast, not farr from Virginia, and their beaver was all lost (which was yᵉ first loss they sustained in that kind); but Mʳ. Peirce & yᵉ men saved their lives, and also their leters, and gott into Virginia, and so safly home. Yᵉ accounts were now sent from hence againe to them. And thus much of yᵉ passages of this year.

A part of Mʳ. Peirce his leter[DH] from Virginia.

It was dated in Des: 25. 1632. and came to their hand yᵉ 7. of Aprill, before they heard any thing from England.

Dear freinds, &c. Yᵉ bruit of this fatall stroke that yᵉ Lord hath brought both on me and you all will come to your ears before this cometh to your hands, (it is like,) and therfore I shall not need to inlarg in perticulers, &c. My whole estate (for ye most parte) is taken away; and so yours, in a great measure, by this and your former losses [he means by ye French & M^r. Allerton]. It is time to looke aboute us, before ye wrath of ye Lord breake forth to utter destruction. The good Lord give us all grace to search our harts and trie our ways, and turne unto ye Lord, and humble our selves under his mightie hand, and seeke atonemente, &c. Dear freinds, you may know y^t all your beaver, and ye books of your accounts, are swallowed up in ye sea; your letters remaine with me, and shall be delivered, if God bring me home. But what should I more say? Have we lost our outward estates? yet a hapy loss if our soules may gaine; ther is yet more in ye Lord Jehova than ever we had yet in ye world. Oh that our foolish harts could yet be wained from ye things here below, which are vanity and vexation of spirite; and yet we fooles catch after shadows, y^t flye away, & are gone in a momente, &c. Thus with my continuall remembrance of you in my poore desires to ye throne of grace, beseeching God to renew his love & favoure towards you all, in & through ye Lord Jesus Christ, both in spirituall & temporall good things, as may be most to the glory & praise of his name, and your everlasting good. So I rest,

Your afflicted brother in Christ,

WILLIAM PEIRCE.

Virginia, Des: 25. 1632.

Anno Dom: 1633.

This year M^r. Ed: Winslow was chosen Governor.

By the first returne this year, they had leters from M^r. Sherley of M^r. Allertons further ill success, and ye loss by M^r. Peirce, with many sadd complaints; but litle hope of any thinge to be gott of M^r. Allerton, or how their accounts might be either eased, or any way rectified by them ther; but now saw plainly y^t the burthen of all would be cast on their backs. The spetiall passages of his letters I shall here inserte, as shall be pertinente to these things; for though I

am weary of this tedious & uncomfortable subjecte, yet for yᵉ
clearing of yᵉ truth I am compelled to be more larg in yᵉ opening of
these matters, upon wᶜʰ [194] so much trouble hath insued, and so
many hard censures have passed on both sids. I would not be
partiall to either, but deliver yᵉ truth in all, and, as nere as I can, in
their owne words and passages, and so leave it to the impartiall
judgment of any that shall come to read, or veiw these things. His
leters are as folow, dated June 24. 1633.

Loving friends, my last[D1] was sente in yᵉ Mary & John, by Mʳ.
William Collier, &c. I then certified you of yᵉ great, &
uncomfortable, and unseasonable loss you & we had, in yᵉ loss of
Mʳ. Peirce his ship, yᵉ Lyon; but yᵉ Lords holy name be blessed,
who gives & taks as it pleaseth him; his will be done, Amen. I then
related unto you yᵗ fearfull accidente, or rather judgmente, yᵉ Lord
pleased to lay on London Bridge, by fire, and therin gave you a
touch of my great loss; the Lord, I hope, will give me patience to
bear it, and faith to trust in him, & not in these slipery and
uncertaine things of this world.

I hope Mʳ. Allerton is nere upon sayle with you by this; but he
had many disasters here before he could gett away; yet yᵉ last was a
heavie one; his ship, going out of yᵉ harbor at Bristoll, by stormie
weather was so farr driven on yᵉ shore, as it cost him above 100ˡⁱ.
before shee could be gott off againe. Verily his case was so
lamentable as I could not but afford him some help therin (and so
did some were strangers to him); besids, your goods were in her,
and if he had not been supported, he must have broke off his viage,
and so loss could not have been avoyded on all sides. When he first
bought her, I thinke he had made a saving match, if he had then
sunck her, and never set her forth. I hope he sees yᵉ Lords hand
against him, and will leave of these viages. I thinke we did well in
parting with her; she would have been but a clogge to yᵉ accounte
from time to time, and now though we shall not gett much by way
of satisfaction, yet we shall lose no more. And now, as before I
have writte, I pray you finish all yᵉ accounts and reconings with

him there; for here he hath nothing, but many debtes that he stands ingaged to many men for. Besids, here is not a man y' will spend a day, or scarce an hower, aboute ye accounts but my selfe, and y' bussines will require more time and help then I can afford. I shall not need to say any more; I hope you will doe y' which shall be best & just, to which adde mercie, and consider his intente, though he failed in many perticulers, which now cannot be helped, &c.

To morrow, or next day at furthest, we are to pay 300^{li}. and M^r. Beachamp is out of ye towne, yet ye bussines I must doe. Oh the greefe & trouble y' man, M^r. Allerton, hath brought upon you and us! I cannot forgett it, and to thinke on it draws many a sigh from my harte, and teares from my eyes. And now ye Lord hath visited me with an other great loss, yet I can undergoe it with more patience. But this I have follishly pulled upon my selfe, &c. [And in another, he hath this passage:] By M^r. Allertons faire propositions and large [195] promises, I have over rune my selfe; verily, at this time greefe hinders me to write, and tears will not suffer me to see; wherfore, as you love those that ever loved you, and y' plantation, thinke upon us. Oh what shall I say of that man, who hath abused your trust and wronged our loves! but now to complaine is too late, nither can I complaine of your backwardnes, for I am perswaded it lys as heavie on your harts, as it doth on our purses or credites. And had ye Lord sent M^r. Peirce safe home, we had eased both you and us of some of those debts; the Lord I hope will give us patience to bear these crosses; and that great God, whose care & providence is every where, and spetially over all those that desire truly to fear and serve him, direct, guid, prosper, & blesse you so, as y' you may be able (as I perswade my selfe you are willing) to discharge & take off this great & heavie burthen which now lyes upon me for your saks; and I hope in ye ende for ye good of you, and many thousands more; for had not you & we joyned & continued togeather, New-England might yet have been scarce knowne, I am perswaded, not so replenished & inhabited with honest English people, as it now is. The Lord increase & blesse them, &c. So, with my continuall praiers for you all, I rest

Your assured loving friend,

JAMES SHERLEY.

June 24. 1633.

By this it apperes when M^r. Sherly sould him ye ship & all her accounts, it was more for M^r. Allertons advantage then theirs; and if they could get any there, well & good, for they were like to have nothing here. And what course was held to hinder them there, hath allready beene manifested. And though M^r. Sherley became more sinsible of his owne condition, by these losses, and therby more sadly & plainly to complaine of M^r. Allerton, yet no course was taken to help them here, but all left unto them selves; not so much as to examene & rectifie ye accounts, by which (it is like) some hundereds of pounds might have been taken off. But very probable it is, the more they saw was taken off, ye less might come unto them selves. But I leave these maters, & come to other things.

M^r. Roger Williams (a man godly & zealous, having many precious parts, but very unsettled in judgmente) came over first to ye Massachusets, but upon some discontente left y^t place, and came hither, (wher he was friēdly entertained, according to their poore abilitie,) and exercised his gifts amongst them, & after some time was admitted a member of ye church; and his teaching well approoved, for ye benefite wherof I still blese God, and am thankfull to him, even for his sharpest admonitions & reproufs, so farr as they agreed with truth. He this year begane to fall into some strang oppiīons, and from opinion to practise; which caused some controversie betweene ye church & him, and in ye end some discontente on his parte, by occasion wherof he left them some thing abruptly. Yet after wards sued for his dismission to ye church of Salem, which was granted, with some caution to them concerning him, and what care they ought to have of him. But he soone fell into more things ther, both to their and ye governments troble and [196] disturbance. I shall not need to name perticulers, they are too well knowen now to all, though for a time ye church here wente under some hard censure by his occasion, from some that afterwards smarted them selves. But he is to be pitied, and prayed for, and so I shall leave yᵉ matter, and desire yᵉ Lord to shew him his errors, and reduse him into yᵉ way of truth, and give him a setled judgment and constancie in yᵉ same; for I hope he belongs to yᵉ Lord, and yᵗ he will shew him mercie.

Having had formerly converse and famliarity with yᵉ Dutch, (as is before remembred,) they, seeing them seated here in a barren quarter, tould them of a river called by them yᵉ Fresh River, but now is known by yᵉ name of Conightecute-River, which they often comended unto them for a fine place both for plantation and trade, and wished them to make use of it. But their hands being full otherwise, they let it pass. But afterwards ther coming a company of banishte Indeans into these parts, that were drivene out from thence by the potencie of yᵉ Pequents, which usurped upon them, and drive them from thence, they often sollisited them to goe thither, and they should have much trad, espetially if they would keep a house ther. And having now good store of comodities, and allso need to looke out wher they could advantage them selves to help them out of their great ingagments, they now begane to send that way to discover yᵉ same, and trade with yᵉ natives. They found it to be a fine place, but had no great store of trade; but yᵉ Indeans excused yᵉ same in regard of yᵉ season, and the fear yᵉ Indans were in of their enemise. So they tried diverce times, not with out profite, but saw yᵉ most certainty would be by keeping a house ther, to receive yᵉ trad when it came down out of yᵉ inland. These Indeans, not seeing them very forward to build ther, solisited them of yᵉ Massachusets in like sorte (for their end was to be restored to their countrie againe); but they in yᵉ Bay being but latly come, were not fitte for yᵉ same; but some of their cheefe made a motion to joyne wᵗʰ the partners here, to trad joyntly with them in yᵗ river, the which they were willing to imbrace, and so they should have builte, and put in equall stock togeather. A time of meeting was appointed at yᵉ Massachusets, and some of yᵉ cheefe here was appointed to treat with them, and went accordingly; but they cast many fears of deanger & loss and the like, which was perceived to be the maine obstacles, though they alledged they were not provided of trading goods. But those hear offered at presente to put in sufficiente for both, provided they would become ingaged for yᵉ halfe, and prepare against yᵉ nexte year. They conffessed more could not be offered, but thanked them, and tould them they had no mind to it. They then answered, they hoped it would be no offence unto [197] them, if them sellves wente on without them, if they saw it meete. They said ther was no reason they should; and thus this treaty broake of, and those here tooke conveniente time to made a begining ther; and were yᵉ first English that both discovered that place, and built in yᵉ same, though they were litle better then thrust out of it afterward as may appeare.

But yᵉ Dutch begane now to repente, and hearing of their purpose & preparation, indēoured to prevente them, and gott in a litle before them, and made a slight forte, and planted 2. peeces of ordnance, thretening to stopp their passage. But they having made a smale frame of a house ready, and haveing a great new-barke, they stowed their frame in her hold, & bords to cover & finishe it, having nayles & all other provisions fitting for their use. This they did yᵉ rather that they might have a presente defence against yᵉ Indeans, who weare much offended that they brought home & restored yᵉ right Sachem of yᵉ place (called Natawanute); so as they were to incounter with a duble danger in this attempte, both yᵉ Dutch and yᵉ Indeans. When they came up yᵉ river, the Dutch demanded what they intended, and whither they would goe; they answered, up yᵉ river to trade (now their order was to goe and seat above them). They bid them strike, & stay, or els they would shoote them; & stood by ther ordnance ready fitted. They answered they had comission from yᵉ Govʳ of Plimoth to goe up yᵉ river to such a place, and if they did shoote, they must obey their order and proceede; they would not molest them, but would goe one. So they passed along, and though the Dutch threatened them hard, yet they shoot not. Coming to their place, they clapt up their house quickly, and landed their provissions, and left yᵉ companie appoynted, and sent the barke home; and afterwards palisadoed their house aboute, and fortified them selves better. The Dutch sent word home to yᵉ Monhatas what was done: and in proces of time, they sent a band of aboute 70. men, in warrlike maner, with collours displayed, to assaulte them; but seeing them strengtened, & that it would cost blood, they came to parley, and returned in peace. And this was their enterance ther, who deserved to have held it, and not by freinds to have been thrust out, as in a sorte they were, as will after appere. They did y⁰ Dutch no wrong, for they took not a foote of any land they bought, but went to y⁰ place above them, and bought that tracte of land which belonged to these Indeans which they carried with them, and their friends, with whom y⁰ Dutch had nothing to doe. But of these matters more in another place.

It pleased y⁰ Lord to visite them this year with an infectious fevoure, of which many fell very sicke, and upward of 20. persons dyed, men and women, besids children, and sundry of them of their anciente friends which had lived in Holand; as Thomas Blossome, Richard Masterson, with sundry [198] others, and in y⁰ end (after he had much helped others) Samuell Fuller, who was their surgeon & phisition, and had been a great help and comforte unto them; as in his facultie, so otherwise, being a deacon of y⁰ church, a man godly, and forward to doe good, being much missed after his death; and he and y⁰ rest of their brethren much lamented by them, and caused much sadnes & mourning amongst them; which caused them to humble them selves, & seeke y⁰ Lord; and towards winter it pleased the Lord y⁰ sicknes ceased. This disease allso swept away many of y⁰ Indeans from all y⁰ places near adjoyning; and y⁰ spring before, espetially all y⁰ month of May, ther was such a quantitie of a great sorte of flies, like (for bignes) to wasps, or bumble-bees, which came out of holes in y⁰ ground, and replenished all y⁰ woods, and eate y⁰ green-things, and made such a constante yelling noyes, as made all y⁰ woods ring of them, and ready to deafe y⁰ hearers. They have not by y⁰ English been heard or seen before or since. But y⁰ Indeans tould them yᵗ sicknes would follow, and so it did in June, July, August, and y⁰ cheefe heat of somer.

It pleased y⁰ Lord to inable them this year to send home a great quantity of beaver, besids paing all their charges, & debts at home, which good returne did much incourage their freinds in England. They sent in beaver 3366ˡⁱ. waight, and much of it coat beaver, which yeeled 20ˢ. pʳ pound, & some of it above; and of otterskines[DJ] 346. sould also at a good prise. And thus much of yᵉ affairs of this year.

Anno Dom: 1634.

This year Mʳ. Thomas Prence was chosen Govʳ.

Mʳ. Sherleys letters were very breefe in answer of theirs this year. I will forbear to coppy any part therof, only name a head or 2. therm. First, he desirs they will take nothing ill in what he formerly write, professing his good affection towards them as before, &c. 2ˡʸ. For Mʳ. Allertons accounts, he is perswaded they must suffer, and yᵗ in no small sumes; and that they have cause enough to complaine, but it was now too late. And that he had failed them ther, those here, and him selfe in his owne aimes. And that now, having thus left them here, he feared God had or would leave him, and it would not be strang, but a wonder if he fell not into worse things, &c. 3ˡʸ. He blesseth God and is thankfull to them for yᵉ good returne made this year. This is yᵉ effecte of his letters, other things being of more private nature.

I am now to enter upon one of yᵉ sadest things that befell them since they came; but before I begine, it will be needfull to premise such parte of their patente as gives them right and priviledge at Kenebeck; as followeth:

[199] The said Counsell hath further given, granted, barganed, sold, infeoffed, alloted, assigned, & sett over, and by these presents doe clearly and absolutly give, grante, bargane, sell, alliene, enffeofe, allote, assigne, and confirme unto yᵉ said William Bradford, his heires, associates, and assignes, All that tracte of land or part of New-England in America afforesaid, which lyeth within or betweene, and extendeth it selfe from yᵉ utmost limits of Cobiseconte, which adjoyneth to yᵉ river of Kenebeck, towards the westerne ocean, and a place called yᵉ falls of Nequamkick in America, aforsaid; and yᵉ space of 15. English myles on each side of yᵉ said river, commonly called Kenebeck River, and all yᵉ said river called Kenebeck that lyeth within the said limits & bounds, eastward, westward, northward, & southward, last above

mentioned; and all lands, grounds, soyles, rivers, waters, fishing, &c. And by vertue of yᵉ authority to us derived by his said late Maᵗⁱˢ Lrēs patents, to take, apprehend, seise, and make prise of all such persons, their ships and goods, as shall attempte to inhabite or trade with yᵉ savage people of that countrie within yᵉ severall precincts and limits of his & their severall plantations, &c.

Now it so fell out, that one Hocking, belonging to yᵉ plantation of Pascataway, wente with a barke and comodities to trade in that river, and would needs press into their limites; and not only so, but would needs goe up yᵉ river above their house, (towards yᵉ falls of yᵉ river,) and intercept the trade that should come to them. He that was cheefe of yᵉ place forbad them, and prayed him that he would not offer them that injurie, nor goe aboute to infring their liberties, which had cost them so dear. But he answered he would goe up and trade ther in dispite of them, and lye ther as longe as he pleased. The other tould him he must then be forced to remove him from thence, or make seasure of him if he could. He bid him doe his worste, and so wente up, and anchored ther. The other tooke a boat & some men & went up to him, when he saw his time, and againe entreated him to departe by what perswasion he could. But all in vaine: he could gett nothing of him but ill words. So he considred that now was yᵉ season for trade to come downe, and if he should suffer him to lye, & take it from them, all ther former charge would be lost, and they had better throw up all. So, consulting with his men, (who were willing thertoe,) he resolved to put him from his anchores, and let him drive downe yᵉ river with yᵉ streame; but comanded yᵉ men yᵗ none should shoote a shote upon any occasion, except he comanded them. He spoake to him againe, but all in vaine; then he sente a cuple in a canow to cutt his cable, the which one of them performes; but Hocking taks up a pece which he had layed ready, and as yᵉ barke shered by yᵉ canow, he shote [200] him close under her side, in yᵉ head, (as I take it,) so he fell downe dead instantly. One of his fellows (that loved him well) could not hold, but with a muskett shot Hocking, who fell downe dead and never speake word. This was yᵉ truth of yᵉ thing. The rest of yᵉ men carried home the vessell and yᵉ sad tidings of these things. Now yᵉ Lord Saye & yᵉ Lord Brooks, with some other great persons, had a hand in this plantation; they write home to them, as much as they could to exasperate them in yᵉ matter, leaveing out all yᵉ circomstances, as if he had been kild without any offenc of his parte, conceling yᵗ he had kild another first, and yᵉ just occasion that he had given in offering such wrong; at wᶜʰ their Lordsᵖˢ were much offended, till they were truly informed of yᵉ mater.

The bruite of this was quickly carried all aboute, (and yᵗ in yᵉ worst maner,) and came into yᵉ Bay to their neighbours their. Their owne barke coming home, and bringing a true relation of yᵉ matter, sundry were sadly affected with yᵉ thing, as they had cause. It was not long before they had occasion to send their vessell into yᵉ Bay of yᵉ Massachusetts; but they were so prepossest with this matter, and affected with yᵉ same, as they comited Mʳ. Alden to prison, who was in yᵉ bark, and had been at Kenebeck, but was no actore in yᵉ bussines, but wente to carie them supply. They dismist yᵉ barke aboute her bussines, but kept him for some time. This was thought strang here, and they sente Capten Standish to give them true information, (togeather with their letters,) and yᵉ best satisfaction they could, and to procure Mʳ. Alden's release. I shall recite a letter or 2. which will show the passages of these things, as folloeth.

Good Sʳ:

I have received your lrēˢ by Captaine Standish, & am unfainedly glad of Gods mercie towards you in yᵉ recovery of your health, or some way thertoo. For yᵉ bussines you write of, I thought meete to answer a word or 2. to your selfe, leaving the answer of your Govᵒʳ lre to our courte, to whom yᵉ same, together with my selfe is directed. I conceive (till I hear new matter to yᵉ contrary) that your patente may warrente your resistance of any English from trading at Kenebeck, and yᵗ blood of Hocking, and yᵉ partie he slue, will be required at his hands. Yet doe I with your selfe & others sorrow for their deaths. I thinke likewise yᵗ your generall lrēs will satisfie our courte, and make them cease from any further inter medling in yᵉ mater. I have upon yᵉ same lre sett Mʳ. Alden at liberty, and his sureties, and yet, least I should seeme to neglecte y͏ᵉ opinion of our court & y͏ᵉ frequente speeches of others with us, I have bound Captaine Standish to appeare y͏ᵉ 3. of June at our nexte courte, to make affidavid for y͏ᵉ coppie of y͏ᵉ patente, and to manifest the circumstances of Hockins provocations; both which will tend to y͏ᵉ clearing of your inocencie. If any unkindnes hath ben taken from what we have done, let it be further & better considred of, I pray you; and I hope y͏ᵉ more you thinke of it, the lesse blame you will impute to us. At least you ought to be just in differencing them, whose opinions concurr [201] with your owne, from others who were opposites; and yet I may truly say, I have spoken w͏ᵗʰ no man in y͏ᵉ bussines who taxed you most, but they are such as have many wayes heretofore declared ther good affections towards your plantation. I further referr my selfe to y͏ᵉ reporte of Captaine Standish & M͏ʳ. Allden; leaving you for this presente to Gods blessing, wishing unto you perfecte recovery of health, and y͏ᵉ long continuance of it. I desire to be lovingly remembred to M͏ʳ. Prence, your Governor, M͏ʳ. Winslow, M͏ʳ. Brewster, whom I would see if I knew how. The Lord keepe you all. Amen.

Your very loving friend in our Lord Jesus,

THO: DUDLEY.

New-towne, y͏ᵉ 22. of May, 1631.

Another of his about these things as followeth.

S͏ʳ: I am right sorrie for y͏ᵉ news that Captaine Standish & other of your neigbours and my beloved freinds will bring now to Plimoth, wherin I suffer with you, by reason of my opinion, which differeth from others, who are godly & wise, amongst us here, the reverence of whose judgments causeth me to suspecte myne owne ignorance; yet must I remaine in it untill I be convinced therof. I thought not to have shewed your letter written to me, but to have done my best to have reconciled differences in y͏ᵉ best season & maner I could; but Captaine Standish requiring an answer therof publickly in y͏ᵉ courte,

I was forced to produce it, and that made yᵉ breach soe wide as he can tell you. I propounded to yᵉ courte, to answer Mʳ. Prences lre, your Govʳ, but our courte said it required no answer, it selfe being an answer to a former lre of ours. I pray you certifie Mʳ. Prence so much, and others whom it concereth, that no neglecte or ill maners be imputed to me theraboute. The late lres I received from England wrought in me divere fears[DK] of some trials which are shortly like to fall upon us; and this unhappie contention betweene you and us, and between you & Pascattaway, will hasten them, if God with an extraordinarie hand doe not help us. To reconcile this for yᵉ presente will be very difficulte, but time cooleth distempers, and a comone danger to us boath approaching, will necessitate our uniting againe. I pray you therfore, Sʳ. set your wisdom & patience a worke, and exhorte others to yᵉ same, that things may not proceede from bad to worse, so making our contentions like yᵉ barrs of a pallace, but that a way of peace may be kepte open, wherat yᵉ God of peace may have enterance in his owne time. If you suffer wrong, it shall be your honor to bear it patiently; but I goe to farr in needles putting you in mind of these things. God hath done great things for you, and I desire his blessings may be multiplied upon you more & more. I will commite no more to writing, but comending my selfe to your prayers, doe rest,

Your very loving friend in our Lord Jesus,

THO: DUDLEY.

June 4. 1634.

By these things it appars what troubls rise herupon, and how hard they were to be reconciled; for though they hear were hartily sorrie for what was fallen out, yet they conceived they were unjustly injuried, and provoked to what was done; and that their neigbours (haveing no jurisdiction over them) did more then was mete, thus to imprison one of theirs, and bind them to [202] their courte. But yet being assured of their Christian love, and perswaded what was done was out of godly zeale, that religion might not suffer, nor sinne any way covered or borne with, espetially ye guilte of blood, of which all should be very consciencious in any whom soever, they did indeavore to appease & satisfie them ye best they could; first, by informing them ye truth in all circomstances aboute ye matter; 2^ly, in being willing to referr ye case to any indifferante and equall hearing and judgmente of the thing hear, and to answere it els wher when they should be duly called therunto; and further they craved M^r. Winthrops, & other of ye reve^d magistrats ther, their advice & direction herein. This did mollifie their minds, and bring things to a good & comfortable issue in ye end.

For they had this advice given them by M^r. Winthrop, & others concurring with him, that from their courte, they should write to the neigboure plantations, & espetially that of ye lords, at Pascataway, and theirs of ye Massachusets, to appointe some to give them meeting at some fitt place, to consulte & determine in this matter, so as ye parties meeting might have full power to order & bind, &c. And that nothing be done to ye infringing or prejudice of ye liberties of any place. And for ye clearing of conscience, ye law of God is, y^t ye preist lips must be consulted with, and therfore it was desired that ye ministers of every plantation might be presente to give their advice in pointe of conscience. Though this course seemed dangerous to some, yet they were so well assured of ye justice of their cause, and ye equitie of their freinds, as they put them selves upon it, & appointed a time, of which they gave notice to ye severall places a month before hand; viz. Massachusets, Salem, & Pascataway, or any other y^t they would give notice too, and disired them to produce any evidence they could in ye case. The place for meeting was at Boston. But when ye day & time came, none apered, but some of ye magistrats and ministers of ye Massachusets, and their owne. Seeing none of Passcataway or other places came, (haveing been thus desired, & conveniente time given them for y^t end,) M^r. Winthrop & ye rest said they could doe no more then they had done thus to requeste them, ye blame must rest on them. So they fell into a fair debating of things them selves; and after all things had been fully opened & discussed, and ye opinione of each one demanded, both magistrats, and ministers, though they all could have wished these things had never been, yet they could not but lay y⁰ blame & guilt on Hockins owne head; and withall gave them such grave & godly exhortations and advice, as they thought meete, both for y⁰ presente & future; which they allso imbraced with love & thankfullnes, promising to indeavor to follow y⁰ same. And thus was this matter ended, and ther love and concord renewed; and also Mʳ. Winthrop & Mʳ. Dudley write in their behalfes to y⁰ Lord Ssay & other gentl-men that were interesed in yͭ plantation, very effectually, wᵗʰ which, togeather with their owne leters, and Mʳ. Winslows furder declaration of things unto them, they rested well satisfied.

[203] Mʳ. Winslow was sente by them this year into England, partly to informe and satisfie y⁰ Lord Say & others, in y⁰ former matter, as also to make answer and their just defence for y⁰ same, if any thing should by any be prosecuted against them at Counsell-table, or els wher; but this matter tooke end, without any further trouble, as is before noted. And partly to signifie unto y⁰ partners in England, that the terme of their trade with y⁰ company here was out, and therfore he was sente to finishe y⁰ accounts with them, and to bring them notice how much debtore they should remaine on yͭ accounte, and that they might know what further course would be best to hold. But y⁰ issue of these things will appear in y⁰ next years passages. They now sente over by him a great returne, which was very acceptable unto them; which was in beaver 3738ˡⁱ. waight, (a great part of it, being coat-beaver, sould at 20ˢ. pʳ pound,) and 234. otter skines;[ᴰᴸ] which alltogeather rise to a great sume of money.

This year (in y⁰ foreparte of y⁰ same) they sente forth a barke to trad at y⁰ Dutch-Plantation; and they mette ther with on Captaine Stone, that had lived in Christophers, one of y⁰ West-Ende Ilands, and now had been some time in Virginia, and came from thence into these parts. He kept company with y⁰ Dutch Goveʳ, and, I know not in what drunken fitt, he gott leave of y⁰ Govʳ to ceaise on their barke, when they were ready to come away, and had done their markett, haveing y⁰ valew of 500ˡⁱ. worth of goods abord her; having no occasion at all, or any collour of ground for such a thing,

but having made yᵉ Govʳ drunck, so as he could scarce speake a
right word; and when he urged him hear aboute, he answered him,
Als 't u beleeft.[DM] So he gat abord, (the cheefe of their men &
marchant being ashore,) and with some of his owne men, made yᵉ
rest of theirs waigh anchor, sett sayle, & carry her away towards
Virginia. But diverse of yᵉ Dutch sea-men, which had bene often at
Plimoth, and kindly entertayned ther, said one to another, Shall we
suffer our freinds to be thus abused, and have their goods carried
away, before our faces, whilst our Govʳ is drunke? They vowed
they would never suffer it; and so gott a vessell or 2. and pursued
him, & brought him in againe, and delivered them their barke &
goods againe.

After wards Stone came into yᵉ Massachusets, and they sent &
commensed suite against him for this facte; but by mediation of
freinds it was taken up, and yᵉ suite lett fall. And in yᵉ company of
some other gentle-men Stone came afterwards to Plimoth, and had
freindly & civill entertainmente amongst them, with yᵉ rest; but
revenge boyled within his brest, (though concelled,) for some
conceived he had a purpose (at one time) to have staped the Govʳ,
and put his hand to his dagger for that end, but by Gods providence
and yᵉ vigilance of some was prevented. He afterward returned to
Virginia, in a pinass, with one Captaine Norton & some others;
and, I know not for what occasion, they would needs goe up
Coonigtecutt River; and how they carried themselves I know not,
but yᵉ Indeans knoct him in yᵉ head, as he lay in his cabine, and had
thrown yᵉ covering over his face (whether out of fear or desperation
is uncertaine); this was his end. They likewise killed all yᵉ rest, but
Captaine Norton defended him selfe a long time against them all in
yᵉ cooke-roome, till by accidente the gunpowder tooke fire, which
(for readynes) he had sett in an open thing before him, which did so
burne, & scald him, & blind his eyes, as he could make no longer
resistance, but was slaine also by them, though they much
comended his vallour. And having killed yᵉ men, they made a pray
of what they had, and chafered away some of their things to yᵉ
Dutch that lived their. But it was not longe before a quarell fell

betweene the Dutch & them, and they would have cutt of their bark; but they slue ye cheef sachem wth ye shott of a murderer.[DN]

I am now to relate some strang and remarkable passages. Ther was a company of people lived in ye country, up above in ye river of Conigtecut, a great way from their trading house ther, and were enimise to those Indeans which lived aboute them, and of whom they stood in some fear (bing a stout people). About a thousand of them had inclosed them selves in a forte, which they had strongly palissadoed about. 3. or 4. Dutch men went up in ye begining of winter to live with them, to gett their trade, and prevente them for bringing it to ye English, or to fall into amitie with them; but at spring to bring all downe to their place. But their enterprise failed, for it pleased God to visite these Indeans with a great sicknes, and such a mortalitie that of a 1000. above 900. and a halfe of them dyed, and many of them did rott above ground for want of buriall, and ye Dutch men allmost starved before they could gett away, for ise and snow. But about Feb: they got with much difficultie to their trading house; whom they kindly releeved, being allmost spente with hunger and could. Being thus refreshed by them diverce days, they got to their owne place, and ye Dutch were very thankfull for this kindnes.

This spring, also, those Indeans that lived aboute their trading house there fell sick of ye small poxe, and dyed most miserably; for a sorer disease cannot befall them; they fear it more then ye plague; for usualy they that have this disease have them in abundance, and for wante of bedding & lining and other helps, they fall into a lamentable condition, as they lye on their hard matts, ye poxe breaking and mattering, and runing one into another, their skin cleaving (by reason therof) to the matts they lye on; when they turne them, a whole side will flea of at once, [204] (as it were,) and they will be all of a gore blood, most fearfull to behold; and then being very sore, what with could and other distempers, they dye like rotten sheep. The condition of this people was so lamentable, and they fell downe so generally of this diseas, as they were (in ye end) not able to help on another; no, not to make a fire, nor to fetch a litle water to drinke, nor any to burie ye dead; but would strivie as long as they could, and when they could procure no other means to make fire, they would burne yᵉ woden trayes & dishes they ate their meate in, and their very bowes & arrowes; & some would crawle out on all foure to gett a litle water, and some times dye by yᵉ way, & not be able to gett in againe. But those of yᵉ English house, (though at first they were afraid of yᵉ infection,) yet seeing their woefull and sadd condition, and hearing their pitifull cries and lamentations, they had compastion of them, and dayly fetched them wood & water, and made them fires, gott them victualls whilst they lived, and buried them when they dyed. For very few of them escaped, notwithstanding they did what they could for them, to yᵉ haszard of them selvs. The cheefe Sachem him selfe now dyed, & allmost all his freinds & kinred. But by yᵉ marvelous goodnes & providens of God not one of yᵉ English was so much as sicke, or in yᵉ least measure tainted with this disease, though they dayly did these offices for them for many weeks togeather. And this mercie which they shewed them was kindly taken, and thankfully acknowledged of all yᵉ Indeans that knew or heard of yᵉ same; and their mˢ here did much comend & reward them for yᵉ same.

Anno Dom: 1635.

Mʳ. Winslow was very wellcome to them in England, and yᵉ more in regard of yᵉ large returne he brought with him, which came all safe to their hands, and was well sould. And he was borne in hand, (at least he so apprehended,) that all accounts should be cleared before his returne, and all former differences ther aboute well setled. And so he writ over to them hear, that he hoped to cleare yᵉ accounts, and bring them over with him; and yᵗ the accounte of yᵉ White Angele would be taken of, and all things fairly ended. But it came to pass [205] that, being occasioned to answer some complaints made against the countrie at Counsell bord, more cheefly concerning their neigbours in yᵉ Bay then them selves hear, the which he did to good effecte, and further prosecuting such things as might tend to yᵉ good of yᵉ whole, as well them selves as others, aboute yᵉ wrongs and incroachments that the French & other strangers both had and were like further to doe unto them, if not prevented, he prefered this petition following to their Hon^rs that were deputed Comissioners for ye Plantations.

To ye right honorable ye Lords Comissioners for ye Plantations in America.

The humble petition of Edw: Winslow, on ye behalfe of ye plantations in New-England,

Humbly sheweth unto your Lordships, y^t wheras your petitioners have planted them selves in New England under his Ma^tis most gratious protection; now so it is, right Hon^bl, that ye French & Dutch doe indeaouer to devide ye land betweene them; for which purpose ye French have, on ye east side, entered and seased upon one of our houses, and carried away the goods, slew 2. of ye men in another place, and tooke ye rest prisoners with their goods. And ye Dutch, on ye west, have also made entrie upon Conigtecute River, within ye limits of his Maj^ts [-l]rs patent, where they have raised a forte, and threaten to expell your petitioners thence, who are also planted upon ye same river, maintaining possession for his Matie to their great charge, & hazard both of lives & goods.

In tender consideration hereof your petitioners humbly pray that your Lo^pps will either procure their peace wth those foraine states, or else to give spetiall warrante unto your petitioners and ye English Collonies, to right and defend them selves against all foraigne enimies. And your petitioners shall pray, &c.

This petition found good acceptation with most of them, and Mr. Winslow was heard sundry times by them, and appointed further to attend for an answer from their Lo^pps, espetially, having upon conferance with them laid downe a way how this might be doone without any either charge or trouble to ye state; only by furnishing some of ye cheefe of ye cuntry hear with authoritie, who would undertake it at their owne charge, and in such a way as should be without any publick disturbance. But this crossed both Sr Ferdinandos Gorges' & Cap: Masons designe, and ye arch-bishop of Counterberies by them; for Sr Ferd: Gorges (by ye arch-pps favore) was to have been sent over generall Govr into ye countrie, and to have had means from ye state for y^t end, and was now upon dispatch and conclude of ye bussines. And ye arch-bishops purposs & intente was, by his means, & some he should send with him, (to be furnished with Episcopall power,) [206] to disturbe ye peace of ye churches here, and to overthrow their proceedings and further growth, which was ye thing he aimed at. But it so fell out (by Gods providence) that though he in ye end crost this petition from taking any further effecte in this kind, yet by this as a cheefe means the plotte and whole bussines of his & Sr Ferdinandos fell to ye ground, and came to nothing. When M^r. Winslow should have had his suit granted, (as indeed upon ye pointe it was,) and should have been confirmed, the arch-bishop put a stop upon it, and M^r. Winslow, thinking to gett it freed, went to ye bord againe; but ye bishop, Sr Ferd: and Captine Masson, had, as it seemes, procured Morton (of whom mention is made before, & his base carriage) to complaine; to whose complaints M^r. Winslow made answer to ye good satisfaction of ye borde, who checked Morton and rebuked him sharply, & allso blamed Sr Fer^d Gorges, & Masson, for countenancing him. But ye bish: had a further end & use of his presence, for he now begane to question M^r. Winslow of many things; as of teaching in ye church publickly, of which Morton accused him, and gave evidence that he had seen and heard him doe it; to which M^r. Winslow answered, that some time (wanting a minster) he did exercise his gifte to help ye edification of his breethren, when they wanted better means, wch was not often. Then aboute mariage, the which he also confessed, that, haveing been called to place of magistracie, he had sometimes maried some. And further tould their lord^{ps} y^t mariage was a civille thinge, & he found no wher in ye word of God y^t it was tyed to ministrie. Again, they were necessitated so to doe, having for a long time togeather at first no minister; besids, it was no new-thing, for he had been so maried him selfe in Holand, by ye magistrats in their Statt-house. But in ye end (to be short), for these things, ye bishop, by vemente importunity, gott ye bord at last to consente to his comittemente; so he was comited to ye Fleete, and lay ther 17. weeks, or ther aboute, before he could gett to be released. And this was ye end of this petition, and this bussines; only yᵉ others designe was also frustrated hereby, with other things concurring, which was no smalle blessing to yᵉ people here.

But yᵉ charge fell heavie on them hear, not only in Mʳ. Winslows expences, (which could not be smale,) but by yᵉ hinderance of their bussines both ther and hear, by his personall imploymente. For though this was as much or more for others then for them hear, and by them cheefly he was put on this bussines, (for the plantation kēwe nothing of it till they heard of his imprisonmente,) yet yᵉ whole charge lay on them.

Now for their owne bussines; whatsoever Mʳ. Sherleys mind was before, (or Mʳ. Winslow apprehension of yᵉ same,) he now declared him selfe plainly, that he would neither take of yᵉ White-Angell from yᵉ accounte, nor [207] give any further accounte, till he had received more into his hands; only a pretty good supply of goods were sent over, but of yᵉ most, no note of their prises, or so orderly an invoyce as formerly; which Mʳ. Winslow said he could not help, because of his restrainte. Only now Mʳ. Sherley & Mʳ. Beachamp & Mʳ. Andrews sent over a letter of atturney under their hands & seals, to recovere what they could of Mʳ. Allerton for yᵉ Angells accounte; but sent them neither yᵉ bonds, nor covenants, or such other evidence or accounts, as they had aboute these matters. I shall here inserte a few passages out of Mʳ. Sherleys letters aboute these things.

Your leter of yᵉ 22. of July, 1634, by your trustie and our loving friend Mʳ. Winslow, I have received, and your larg parcell of beaver and otter skines. Blessed be our God, both he and it came safly to us, and we have sould it in tow parcells; yᵉ skin at 14ˢ. li. & some at 16.; yᵉ coate at 20ˢ. yᵉ pound. The accounts I have not sent you them this year, I will referr you to Mʳ. Winslow to tell you yᵉ reason of it; yet be assured yᵗ none of you shall suffer by yᵉ not having of them, if God spare me life. And wheras you say yᵉ 6. years are expired yᵗ yᵉ peopl put yᵉ trad into your & our hands for, for yᵉ discharge of yᵗ great debte wᶜʰ Mʳ. Allerton needlesly &

unadvisedly ran you & us into; yet it was promised it should continue till our disbursments & ingagements were satisfied. You conceive it is done; we feele & know other wise, &c. I doubt not but we shall lovingly agree, notwithstanding all y^t hath been writen, on boath sids, aboute ye Whit-Angell. We have now sent you a letter of atturney, therby giving you power in our names (and to shadow it ye more we say for our uses) to obtaine what may be of M^r. Allerton towards ye satisfing of that great charge of ye White Angell. And sure he hath bound him selfe, (though at present I cannot find it,) but he hath often affirmed, with great protestations, y^t neither you nor we should lose a peny by him, and I hope you shall find enough to discharg it, so as we shall have no more contesting aboute it. Yet, notwithstanding his unnaturall & unkind dealing with you, in ye midest of justice remember mercie, and doe not all you may doe, &c. Set us out of debte, and then let us recone & reason togeither, &c. M^r. Winslow hath undergone an unkind imprisonment, but I am perswaded it will turne much to all your good. I leave him to relate perticuleres, &c.

Your loving freind,

JAMES SHERLEY.

London, Sep: 7. 1635.

This year they sustained an other great loss from ye French. Monsier de Aulnay coming into ye harbore of Penobscote, and having before gott some of ye cheefe y^t belonged to ye house abord his vessell, by sutlty coming upon them in their shalop, he gott them to pilote him in; and after getting ye rest into his power, he tooke possession of ye house in ye name of ye king of France; and partly by threatening, & other wise, made Mr. Willett (their agente ther) to approve of ye sale of ye goods their unto him, of which he sett ye price him selfe [208] in effecte, and made an inventory therof, (yett leaving out sundry things,) but made no paymente for them; but tould them in convenient time he would doe it if they came for it. For ye house & fortification, &c. he would not alow, nor accounte any thing, saing that they which build on another mans ground doe forfite ye same. So thus turning them out of all, (with a great deale of complemente, and many fine words,) he let them have their shalop and some victualls to bring them home. Coming home and relating all the passages, they here were much troubled at it, & haveing had this house robbed by ye French once before, and lost then above 500^{li}. (as is before remembred), and now to loose house & all, did much move them. So as they resolved to consulte with their freinds in ye Bay, and if y^{ey} approved of it, (ther being now many ships ther,) they intended to hire a ship of force, and seeke to beat out ye Frenche, and recover it againe. Ther course was well approved on, if them selves could bear ye charge; so they hired a fair ship of above 300. tune, well fitted with ordnance, and agreed with ye m^r. (one Girling) to this effect: that he and his company should deliver them ye house, (after they had driven out, or surprised ye French,) and give them peacable possession therof, and of all such trading comodities as should ther be found; and give ye French fair quarter & usage, if they would yeeld. In consideration wherof he was to have 700^{li}. of beaver, to be delivered him ther, when he had done ye thing; but if he did not accomplish it, he was to loose his labour, and have nothing. With him they also sent their owne bark, and about 20. men, with Captaine Standish, to aide him (if neede weer), and to order things, if the house was regained; and then to pay him ye beaver, which they keept abord their owne barke. So they with their bark piloted him thither, and brought him safe into ye harbor. But he was so rash & heady as he would take no advice, nor would suffer Captaine Standish to have time to summone them, (who had comission & order so to doe,) neither would doe it him selfe; the which, it was like, if it had been done, & they come to affaire parley, seeing their force, they would have yeelded. Neither would he have patience to bring his ship wher she might doe execution, but begane to shoot at distance like a madd man, and did them no hurte at all; the which when those of ye plantation saw, they were much greeved, and went to him & tould him he would doe no good if he did not lay his ship beter to pass (for she might lye within pistoll shott of ye house). At last, when he saw his owne folly, he was perswaded, and layed her well, and bestowed a few shott to good purposs. But now, when he was in a way to doe some good, his powder was goone; for though he had ...[DO] peece of ordnance, it did now [209] appeare he had but a barrell of powder, and a peece; so he could doe no good, but was faine to draw of againe; by which means yᵉ enterprise was made frustrate, and yᵉ French incouraged; for all yᵉ while that he shot so unadvisedly, they lay close under a worke of earth, & let him consume him selfe. He advised with yᵉ Captaine how he might be supplyed with powder, for he had not to carie him home; so he tould him he would goe to yᵉ next plantation, and doe his indeour to procure him some, and so did; but understanding, by intelligence, that he intended to ceiase on yᵉ barke, & surprise yᵉ beaver, he sent him the powder, and brought yᵉ barke & beaver home. But Girling never assualted yᵉ place more, (seeing him selfe disapoyented,) but went his way; and this was yᵉ end of this bussines.

Upon yᵉ ill success of this bussines, the Govʳ and Assistants here by their leters certified their freinds in yᵉ Bay, how by this ship they had been abused and disapoynted, and yᵗ the French partly had, and were now likly to fortifie them selves more strongly, and likly to become ill neigbours to yᵉ English. Upon this they thus writ to them as folloeth:—

Worthy Sʳˢ: Upon yᵉ reading of your leters, & consideration of yᵉ waightines of yᵉ cause therin mentioned, the courte hath joyntly expressed their willingnes to assist you with men & munition, for yᵉ accomplishing of your desires upon yᵉ French. But because here are none of yours yᵗ have authority to conclude of any thing herein, nothing can be done by us for yᵉ presente. We desire, therfore, that you would with all conveniente speed send some man of trust, furnished with instructions from your selves, to make such agreemente with us about this bussines as may be usefull for you, and equall for us. So in hast we comite you to God, and remaine

Your assured loving freinds,

JOHN HAYNES, GOV^R.
RI: BELLINGHAM, DEP.
JO: WINTHROP.
THO: DUDLEY.
JO: HUMFRAY.
W^M: CODDINGTON.
W^M: PINCHON.
ATHERTON HOUGHE.
INCREAS NOWELL.
RIC: DUMER.
SIMON BRADSTRETE.

New-towne, Octo^r 9. 1635.

Upon the receite of ye above mentioned, they presently deputed 2. of theirs to treate with them, giving them full power to conclude, according to the instructions they gave them, being to this purposs: that if they would afford such assistance as, togeather with their owne, was like to effecte the thing, and allso bear a considerable parte of ye charge, they would goe on; if not, [210] they (having lost so much allready) should not be able, but must desiste, and waite further opportunitie as God should give, to help them selves. But this came to nothing, for when it came to ye issue, they would be at no charge, but sente them this letter, and referd them more at large to their owne messengers.

S^r: Having, upon ye consideration of your letter, with ye message you sente, had some serious consultations aboute ye great importance of your bussines with ye French, we gave our answer to those whom you deputed to conferr wth us aboute ye viage to Penobscote. We shewed our willingnes to help, but withall we declared our presente condition, & in what state we were, for our abilitie to help; which we for our parts shall be willing to improve, to procure you sufficiente supply of men & munition. But for matter of moneys we have no authority at all to promise, and if we should, we should rather disapoynte you, then incourage you by y^r

help, which we are not able to performe. We likewise thought it fitt to take yᵉ help of other Esterne plantations; but those things we leave to your owne wisdomes. And for other things we refer you to your owne comitties, who are able to relate all yᵉ passages more at large. We salute you, & wish you all good success in yᵉ Lord.

Your faithfull & loving friend,

RI: BELLINGHAM, Dep:

In yᵉ name of the rest of the Comities.

Boston, Octobʳ 16. 1635.

This thing did not only thus breake of, but some of their merchants shortly after sent to trad with them, and furnished them both with provissions, & poweder & shott; and so have continued to doe till this day, as they have seen opportunitie for their profite. So as in truth yᵉ English them selves have been the cheefest supporters of these French; for besids these, the plantation at Pemaquid (which lyes near unto them) doth not only supply them with what yᵉʸ wante, but gives them continuall intelligence of all things that passes among yᵉ English, (espetially some of them,) so as it is no marvell though they still grow, & incroach more & more upon yᵉ English, and fill yᵉ Indeans with gunes & munishtion, to yᵉ great deanger of yᵉ English, who lye open & unfortified, living upon husbandrie; and yᵉ other closed up in their forts, well fortified, and live upon trade, in good securitie. If these things be not looked too, and remeady provided in time, it may easily be conjectured what they may come toe; but I leave them.

This year, yᵉ 14. or 15. of August (being Saturday) was such a mighty storme of wind & raine, as none living in these parts, either English or Indeans, ever saw. Being like (for yᵉ time it continued) to those Hauricanes and Tuffons that writers make mention of in yᵉ Indeas. It began in yᵉ morning, a litle before day, and grue not by degrees, but came with violence in yᵉ begining, to yᵉ great amasmente of many. It blew downe sundry [211] houses, &

uncovered others; diverce vessells were lost at sea, and many more in extreme danger. It caused ye sea to swell (to ye southward of this place) above 20. foote, right up & downe, and made many of the Indeans to clime into trees for their saftie; it tooke of ye borded roofe of a house which belonged to the plantation at Manamet, and floted it to another place, the posts still standing in ye ground; and if it had continued long without ye shifting of ye wind, it is like it would have drouned some parte of ye cuntrie. It blew downe many hundered thowsands of trees, turning up the stronger by the roots, and breaking the hiegher pine trees of in the midle, and ye tall yonge oaks & walnut trees of good biggnes were wound like a withe, very strang & fearfull to behould. It begane in ye southeast, and parted toward ye south & east, and vered sundry ways; but ye greatest force of it here was from ye former quarters. It continued not (in ye extremitie) above 5. or 6. houers, but ye violence begane to abate. The signes and marks of it will remaine this 100. years in these parts wher it was sorest. The moone suffered a great eclips the 2. night after it.

Some of their neighbours in ye Bay, hereing of ye fame of Conightecute River, had a hankering mind after it, (as was before noted,) and now understanding that ye Indeans were swepte away with ye late great mortalitie, the fear of whom was an obstacle unto them before, which being now taken away, they begane now to prosecute it with great egernes. The greatest differances fell betweene those of Dorchester plantation and them hear; for they set their minde on that place, which they had not only purchased of ye Indeans, but wher they had builte; intending only (if they could not remove them) that they should have but a smale moyety left to ye house, as to a single family; whose doings and proceedings were conceived to be very injurious, to attempte not only to intrude them selves into ye rights & possessions of others, but in effect to thrust them out of all. Many were ye leters & passages that went betweene them hear aboute, which would be to long here to relate.

I shall here first inserte a few lines that was write by their own agente from thence.

Sʳ: &c. Yᵉ Masschuset men are coming almost dayly, some by water, & some by land, who are not yet determined wher to setle, though some have a great mind to yᵉ place we are upon, and which was last bought. Many of them look at that which this river will not afford, excepte it be at this place which we have, namly, to be a great towne, and have comodious dwellings for many togeather. So as what they will doe I cannot yet resolve you; for this place ther is none of them say any thing to me, but what I hear from their servants (by whom I perceive their minds). I shall doe what I can to withstand them. I hope they will hear reason; as that we were here first, and entred with much difficulty and danger, [212] both in regard of yᵉ Dutch & Indeans, and bought yᵉ land, (to your great charge, allready disbursed,) and have since held here a chargable possession, and kept yᵉ Dutch from further incroaching, which would els long before this day have possessed all, and kept out all others, &c. I hope these & such like arguments will stoppe them. It was your will we should use their persons & messengers kindly, & so we have done, and doe dayly, to your great charge; for yᵉ first company had well nie starved had it not been for this house, for want of victuals; I being forced to supply 12. men for 9. days togeather; and those which came last, I entertained the best we could, helping both them (& yᵉ other) with canows, & guids. They gott me to goe with them to yᵉ Dutch, to see if I could procure some of them to have quiet setling nere them; but they did peremtorily withstand them. But this later company did not once speak therof, &c. Also I gave their goods house roome according to their ernest request, and Mʳ. Pinchons letter in their behalfe (which I thought good to send you, here inclosed). And what trouble & charge I shall be further at I know not; for they are coming dayly, and I expecte these back againe from below, whither they are gone to veiw yᵉ countrie. All which trouble & charg we under goe for their occasion, may give us just cause (in yᵉ judgmente of all wise & understanding men) to hold and keep that we are setled upon. Thus with my duty remembred, &c. I rest

Yours to be comanded

JOHNNATHĀ BREWSTER.

Matianuck, July 6. 1635.

Amongst yᵉ many agitations that pased betweene them, I shal note a few out of their last letters, & for yᵉ present omitte yᵉ rest, except upon other occasion I may have fitter opportunity. After their thorrow veiw of yᵉ place, they began to pitch them selves upon their land & near their house; which occasioned much expostulation betweene them. Some of which are such as follow.

Brethren, having latly sent 2. of our body unto you, to agitate & bring to an issue some maters in difference betweene us, about some lands at Conightecutt, unto which you lay challeng; upon which God by his providence cast us, and as we conceive in a faire way of providence tendered it to us, as a meete place to receive our body, now upon removall.

We shall not need to answer all yᵉ passages of your larg letter, &c. But wheras you say God in his providence cast you, &c., we tould you before, and (upon this occasion) must now tell you still, that our mind is other wise, and yᵗ you cast rather a partiall, if not a covetous eye, upon that wᶜʰ is your neigbours, and not yours; and in so doing, your way could not be faire unto it. Looke yᵗ you abuse not Gods providence in such allegations.

Theirs.

Now allbeite we at first judged yᵉ place so free yᵗ we might with Gods good leave take & use it, without just offence to any man, it being the Lords [213] wast, and for yᵉ presente altogeather voyd of inhabitants, that indeede minded yᵉ imploymente therof, to yᵉ right ends for which land was created, Gen: 1. 28. and for future intentions of any, & uncertaine possibilities of this or that to be done by any, we judging them (in such a case as ours espetialy) not meete to be equalled with presente actions (such as ours was) much less worthy to be prefered before them; and therfore did we make some weake beginings in that good worke, in yᵉ place afforesaid.

Ans: Their answer was to this effecte. That if it was ye Lords wast, it was them selves that found it so, & not they; and have since bought it of ye right oweners, and maintained a chargable possession upon it al this while, as them selves could not but know. And because of present ingagments and other hinderances which lay at presente upon them, must it therfore be lawfull for them to goe and take it from them? It was well known that they are upon a barren place, wher they were by necessitie cast; and neither they nor theirs could longe continue upon ye same; and why should they (because they were more ready, & more able at presente) goe and deprive them of that which they had wth charg & hazard provided, & intended to remove to, as soone as they could & were able?

They had another passage in their letter; they had rather have to doe with the lords in England, to whom (as they heard it reported) some of them should say that they had rather give up their right to them, (if they must part with it,) then to ye church of Dorchester, &c. And that they should be less fearfull to offend ye lords, then they were them.

Answer: Their answer was, that what soever they had heard, (more then was true,) yet ye case was not so with them that they had need to give away their rights & adventurs, either to ye lords, or them; yet, if they might measure their fear of offence by their practise, they had rather (in that poynte) they should deal with ye lords, who were beter able to bear it, or help them selves, then they were.

But least I should be teadious, I will forbear other things, and come to the conclusion that was made in ye endd. To make any forcible resistance was farr from their thoughts, (they had enough of y^t about Kenebeck,) and to live in continuall contention with their freinds & brethren would be uncomfortable, and too heavie a burden to bear. Therfore for peace sake (though they conceived they suffered much in this thing) they thought it better to let them have it upon as good termes as they could gett; and so they fell to treaty. The first thing y^t (because they had made so many & long disputs aboute it) they would have them to grante was, y[t] they had right too it, or ells they would never treat aboute it. The[DP] which being acknowledged, & yeelded unto by them, this was y[e] conclusion they came unto in y[e] end after much adoe: that they should retaine their house, and have the 16. parte of all they had bought of y[e] Indeans; and y[e] other should have all y[e] rest of y[e] land; leaveing such a moyety to those [214] of New-towne, as they reserved for them. This 16. part was to be taken in too places; one towards y[e] house, the other towards New-townes proporrtion. Also they were to pay according to proportion, what had been disbursed to y[e] Indeans for y[e] purchass. Thus was y[e] controversie ended, but the unkindnes not so soone forgotten. They of New-towne delt more fairly, desireing only what they could conveniently spare, from a competancie reserved for a plantation, for them selves; which made them the more carfull to procure a moyety for them, in this agreement & distribution.

Amongst y[e] other bussinesses that M[r]. Winslow had to doe in England, he had order from y[e] church to provid & bring over some able & fitt man for to be their minister. And accordingly he had procured a godly and a worthy[DQ] man, one M[r]. Glover; but it pleased God when he was prepared for the viage, he fell sick of a feaver and dyed. Afterwards, when he was ready to come away, he became acquainted with M[r]. Norton, who was willing to come over, but would not ingage him selfe to this place, otherwise then he should see occasion when he came hear; and if he liked better else wher, to repay y[e] charge laid out for him, (which came to aboute 70[li].) and to be at his liberty. He stayed aboute a year with them, after he came over, and was well liked of them, & much desired by them; but he was invited to Ipswich, wher were many rich & able men, and sundry of his aquaintance; so he wente to them, & is their minister. Aboute half of y[e] charg was repayed, y[e] rest he had for y[e] pains he tooke amongst them.

Anno Dom: 1636.

M[r]. ED: WINSLOW was chosen Gov[r] this year.

In ye former year, because they perceived by M^r. Winslows later letters that no accounts would be sente, they resolved to keep ye beaver, and send no more, till they had them, or came to some further agreemente. At least they would forbear till M^r. Winslow came over, that by more full conferance with him they might better understand what was meete to be done. But when he came, though he brought no accounts, yet he perswaded them to send ye beaver, & was confident upon ye receite of y^t beaver, & his letters, they should have accounts ye nexte year; and though they thought his grounds but weake, that gave him this hope, & made him so confidente, yet by his importunitie they yeelded, & sente ye same, ther being a ship at ye latter end of year, by whom they sente 1150^li. waight of beaver, and 200. otter skins, besids sundrie small furrs, as 55. minks, 2. black foxe skins, &c. And this year, in the spring, came in a Dutch man, who thought to have traded at ye Dutch-forte; [215] but they would not suffer him. He, having good store of trading goods, came to this place, & tendred them to sell; of whom they bought a good quantitie, they being very good & fitte for their turne, as Dutch roll, ketles, &c., which goods amounted to ye valew of 500^li., for ye paymente of which they passed bills to M^r. Sherley in England, having before sente ye forementioned parcell of beaver. And now this year (by another ship) sente an other good round parcell that might come to his hands, & be sould before any of these bills should be due. The quantity of beaver now sent was 1809^li. waight, and of otters 10. skins, and shortly after (ye same year) was sent by another ship (Mr. Langrume maister), in beaver 0719^li. waight, and of otter skins 199. concerning which M^r. Sherley thus writs.

Your leters I have received, with 8. hoggsheads of beaver by Ed: Wilkinson, master of ye Falcon. Blessed be God for ye safe coming of it. I have also seen & acceped 3. bills of exchainge, &c. But I must now acquainte you how the Lords heavie hand is upon this kingdom in many places, but cheefly in this cittie, with his judgmente of ye plague. The last weeks bill was 1200. & odd, I fear this will be more; and it is much feared it will be a winter sicknes. By reason wherof it is incredible ye number of people y^t are gone into yᵉ cuntry & left yᵉ citie. I am perswaded many more then went out yᵉ last sicknes; so as here is no trading, carriers from most places put downe; nor no receiving of any money, though long due. Mʳ. Hall ows us more then would pay these bills, but he, his wife, and all, are in yᵉ cuntrie, 60. miles from London. I write to him, he came up, but could not pay us. I am perswaded if I should offer to sell yᵉ beaver at 8s. pʳ pound, it would not yeeld money; but when yᵉ Lord shall please to cease his hand, I hope we shall have better & quicker markets; so it shall lye by. Before I accepted yᵉ bills, I acquainted Mʳ. Beachamp & Mʳ. Andrews with them, & how ther could be no money made nor received; and that it would be a great discredite to you, which never yet had any turned back, and a shame to us, haveing 1800ˡⁱ. of beaver lying by us, and more oweing then yᵉ bills come too, &c. But all was nothing; neither of them both will put too their finger to help. I offered to supply my 3. parte, but they gave me their answer they neither would nor could, &c. How ever, your bils shall be satisfied to yᵉ parties good contente; but I would not have thought they would have left either you or me at this time, &c. You will and may expect I should write more, & answer your leters, but I am not a day in yᵉ weeke at home at towne, but carry my books & all to Clapham; for here is yᵉ miserablest time yᵗ I thinke hath been known in many ages. I have know 3. great sickneses, but none like this. And that which should be a means to pacifie yᵉ Lord, & help us, that is taken away, preaching put downe in many places, not a sermone in Westminster on yᵉ saboth, nor in many townes aboute us; yᵉ Lord in mercie looke uppon us. In the begining of yᵉ year was a great [216] drought, & no raine for many weeks togeather, so as all was burnte up, haye, at 5ˡⁱ. a load; and now all raine, so as much sommer come & later haye is spoyled. Thus yᵉ Lord sends judgmente after judgmente, and yet we cannot see, nor humble our selves; and therfore may justly fear heavier judgments, unless we speedyly repente, & returne unto him, which yᵉ Lord give us grace to doe, if it be his blessed will. Thus desiring you to remember us in your prayers, I ever rest

Your loving friend,

JAMES SHERLEY.

Sep: 14. 1636.

This was all the answer they had from M. Sherley, by which M. Winslow saw his hops failed him. So they now resoloved to send no more beaver in y way which they had done, till they came to some issue or other aboute these things. But now came over letters from M. Andrews & M. Beachamp full of complaints, that they marveled y nothing was sent over, by which any of their moneys should be payed in; for it did appear by y accounte sente in An 1631. that they were each of them out, aboute a leven hundred pounds a peece, and all this while had not received one penie towards y same. But now M. Sherley sought to draw more money from them, and was offended because they deneyed him; and blamed them hear very much that all was sent to M. Sherley, & nothing to them. They marvelled much at this, for they conceived that much of their moneis had been paid in, & y yearly each of them had received a proportionable quantity out of y larg returnes sent home. For they had sente home since y accounte was received in An 1631. (in which all & more then all their debts, w y years supply, was charged upon them) these sumes following.

Novbr 8.	Ano 1631.	By M. Peirce	0400li.	waight of beaver, & otters	20.
July 13.	Ano 1632.	By M. Griffin	1348li.	beaver, & otters	147.
	Ano 1633.	By M. Graves	3366li.	bever, & otters	346.
	Ano 1634.	By M. Andrews	3738li.	beaver, & otters	234.

	An⁰ 1635.	By Mʳ. Babb	1150ˡⁱ.	beaver, & otters	200.
June 24.	An⁰ 1636.	By Mʳ. Wilkinson	1809ˡⁱ.	beaver, & otters	010.
	Ibidem.	By Mʳ. Langrume	0719ˡⁱ.	beaver, & otters	199.
			———		———
			[DR]12150ˡⁱ.		1156.

All these sumes were safly rceived & well sould, as appears by leters. The coat beaver usualy at 20ˢ. pʳ pound, and some at 24ˢ.; the skin at 15. & sometimes 16. I doe not remember any under 14. It may be yᵉ last year might be something lower, so also ther were some small furrs that are not recconed in this accounte, & some black beaver at higer rates, to make up yᵉ defects. [217] It was conceived that yᵉ former parcells of beaver came to litle less then 10000ˡⁱ. sterling, and yᵉ otter skins would pay all yᵉ charge, & they wᵗʰ other furrs make up besids if any thing wanted of yᵉ former sume. When yᵉ former accounte was passed, all their debts (those of White-Angelle & Frendship included) came but to 4770ˡⁱ. And they could not estimate that all yᵉ supplies since sent them, & bills payed for them, could come to above 2000ˡⁱ. so as they conceived their debts had been payed, with advantage or intrest. But it may be objected, how comes it that they could not as well exactly sett downe their receits, as their returnes, but thus estimate it. I answer, 2. things were yᵉ cause of it; the first & principall was, that yᵉ new accountante, which they in England would needs presse upon them, did wholy faile them, & could never give them any accounte; but trusting to his memorie, & lose papers, let things rune into such confusion, that neither he, nor any with him, could bring things to rights. But being often called upon to perfecte his accounts, he desired to have such a time, and such a time of leasure, and he would doe it. In yᵉ intrime he fell into a great sicknes, and in conclusion it fell out he could make no accounte at all. His books were after a litle good begining left altogeather unperfect; and his papers, some were lost, & others so confused, as he knew not what to make of them him selfe, when they came to be searched & examined. This was not unknowne to Mʳ. Sherley; and they came to smarte for it to purposs, (though it was not their faulte,) both thus in England, and also here; for they conceived they lost some hundreds of pounds for goods trusted out in yᵉ place, which were lost for want of clear accounts to call them in. Another reason of this mischeefe was, that after Mʳ. Winslow was sente into England to demand accounts, and to excepte against yᵉ Whit-Angell, they never had any price sent with their goods, nor any certaine invoyce of them; but all things stood in confusion, and they were faine to guesse at yᵉ prises of them.

They write back to Mʳ. Andrews & Mʳ. Beachamp, and tould them they marveled they should write they had sent nothing home since yᵉ last accounts; for they had sente a great deale; and it might rather be marveled how they could be able to send so much, besids defraying all charg at home, and what they had lost by the French, and so much cast away at sea, when Mʳ. Peirce lost his ship on yᵉ coast of Virginia. What they had sente was to them all, and to them selves as well as Mʳ. Sherley, and if they did not looke after it, it was their owne falts; they must referr them to Mʳ. Sherley, who had received [218] it, to demand it of him. They allso write to Mʳ. Sherley to yᵉ same purposs, and what the others complaints were.

This year 2. shallops going to Coonigtecutt with goods from yᵉ Massachusetts of such as removed theither to plante, were in an easterly storme cast away in coming into this harbore in yᵉ night; the boats men were lost, and the goods were driven all alonge the shore, and strowed up & downe at high-water marke. But yᵉ Govʳ caused them to be gathered up, and drawn togeather, and appointed some to take an inventory of them, and others to wash & drie such things as had neede therof; by which means most of y⁰ goods were saved, and restored to y⁰ owners. Afterwards anotheir boate of theirs (going thither likwise) was cast away near unto Manoanscusett, and such goods as came a shore were preserved for them. Such crosses they mette with in their beginings; which some imputed as a correction from God for their intrution (to y⁰ wrong of others) into yᵗ place. But I dare not be bould with Gods judgments in this kind.

In y⁰ year 1634, the Pequents (a stoute and warlike people), who had made warrs with sundry of their neigbours, and puft up with many victories, grue now at varience with y⁰ Narigansets, a great people bordering upon them. These Narigansets held correspondance and termes of freindship with y⁰ English of y⁰ Massachusetts. Now y⁰ Pequents, being conscious of y⁰ guilte of Captain-Stones death, whom they knew to be an-English man, as also those yᵗ were with him, and being fallen out with y⁰ Dutch, least they should have over many enemies at once, sought to make freindship with y⁰ English of y⁰ Massachusetts; and for yᵗ end sent both messengers & gifts unto them, as appears by some letters sent from y⁰ Govʳ hither.

Dear & worthy Sʳ: &c. To let you know somwhat of our affairs, you may understand that y⁰ Pequents have sent some of theirs to us, to desire our freindship, and offered much wampam & beaver, &c. The first messengers were dismissed without answer; with y⁰ next we had diverce dayes conferance, and taking y⁰ advice of some of our ministers, and seeking the Lord in it, we concluded a peace & freindship with them, upon these conditions: that they should deliver up to us those men who were guilty of Stones death, &c. And if we desired to plant in Conightecute, they should give up their right to us, and so we would send to trade with them as our freinds (which was y⁰ cheefe thing we aimed at, being now in warr with y⁰ Dutch and y⁰ rest of their neigbours). To this they readily agreed; and that we should meadiate a peace betweene them and the Narigansetts; for which end they were contente we should give the Narigansets parte of yᵗ presente, they would bestow on us (for they stood [219][DS] so much on their honour, as they would not be seen to give any thing of them selves). As for Captein Stone, they tould us ther were but 2. left of those who had any hand in his death; and that they killed him in a just quarell, for (say they) he surprised 2. of our men, and bound them, to make them by force to shew him yᵉ way up yᵉ river;[DT] and he with 2. other coming on shore, 9. Indeans watched him, and when they were a sleepe in yᵉ night, they kiled them, to deliver their owne men; and some of them going afterwards to yᵉ pinass, it was suddainly blowne up. We are now preparing to send a pinass unto them, &c.

In an other of his, dated yᵉ 12. of yᵉ first month, he hath this.

Our pinass is latly returned from yᵉ Pequents; they put of but litle comoditie, and found them a very false people, so as they mean to have no more to doe with them. I have diverce other things to write unto you, &c.

Yours ever assured,

Jo: WINTHROP.

Boston, 12. of yᵉ 1. month, 1634.

After these things, and, as I take, this year, John Oldom, (of whom much is spoken before,) being now an inhabitant of yᵉ Massachusetts, went wᵗʰ a small vessell, & slenderly mand, a trading into these south parts, and upon a quarell betweene him & yᵉ Indeans was cutt of by them (as hath been before noted) at an iland called by yᵉ Indeans Munisses, but since by yᵉ English Block Iland. This, with yᵉ former about the death of Stone, and the baffoyling of yᵉ Pequents with yᵉ English of yᵉ Massachusetts, moved them to set out some to take revenge, and require satisfaction for these wrongs; but it was done so superfitially, and without their acquainting of those of Conightecute & other neighbours with yᵉ same, as they did litle good. But their neigbours had more hurt done, for some of yᵉ murderers of Oldome fled to yᵉ Pequents, and though the English went to yᵉ Pequents, and had some parley with them, yet they did but delude them, & yᵉ English returned without doing any thing to purpose, being frustrate of their oppertunitie by yᵉ others deceite. After yᵉ English were returned, the Pequents tooke their time and oppertunitie to cut of some of yᵉ English as they passed in boats, and went on fouling, and assaulted them yᵉ next spring at their habytations, as will appear in its place. I doe but touch these things, because I make no question they wall be more fully & distinctly handled by them selves, who had more exacte knowledg of them, and whom they did more properly concerne.

This year Mʳ. Smith layed downe his place of ministrie, partly by his owne willingnes, as thinking it too heavie a burthen, and partly at the desire, and by yᵉ perswasion, of others; and the church sought out for [220]ᴰᵁ some other, having often been disappointed in their hops and desires heretofore. And it pleased the Lord to send them an able and a godly man,ᴰⱽ and of a meeke and humble spirite, sound in yᵉ truth, and every way unreproveable in his life & conversation; whom, after some time of triall, they chose for their teacher, the fruits of whose labours they injoyed many years with much comforte, in peace, & good agreemente.

Anno Dom: 1637.

In yᵉ fore parte of this year, the Pequents fell openly upon yᵉ English at Conightecute, in yᵉ lower parts of yᵉ river, and slew sundry of them, (as they were at work in yᵉ feilds,) both men & women, to yᵉ great terrour of yᵉ rest; and wente away in great prid & triumph, with many high threats. They allso assalted a fort at yᵉ rivers mouth, though strong and well defended; and though they did not their prevaile, yet it struk them with much fear & astonishmente to see their bould attempts in the face of danger; which made them in all places to stand upon their gard, and to prepare for resistance, and ernestly to solissite their freinds and confederats in yᵉ Bay of Massachusets to send them speedy aide, for they looked for more forcible assaults. Mʳ. Vane, being then Govʳ, write from their Generall Courte to them hear, to joyne with them in this warr; to which they were cordially willing, but tooke opportunitie to write to them aboute some former things, as well as presente, considerable hereaboute. The which will best appear in yᵉ Govʳ answer which he returned to yᵉ same, which I shall here inserte.

Sʳ: The Lord having so disposed, as that your letters to our late Govʳ is fallen to my lott to make answer unto, I could have wished I might have been at more freedome of time & thoughts also, that I might have done it more to your & my owne satisfaction. But what shall be wanting now may be supplyed hereafter. For yᵉ matters which from your selfe & counsell were propounded & objected to us, we thought not fitte to make them so publicke as yᵉ cognizance of our Generall Courte. But as they have been considered by those of our counsell, this answer we thinke fitt to returne unto you. (1.) Wereas you signifie your willingnes to joyne with us in this warr against yᵉ Pequents, though you cannot ingage your selves without yᵉ consente of your Generall Courte, we acknowledg your good affection towards us, (which we never had cause to doubt of,) and are willing to attend your full resolution, when it may most seasonably be ripened. (2ˡʸ.) Wheras you make this warr to be our peopls, and not [221] to conceirne your selves, otherwise then by consequence, we do in parte consente to you therin; yet we suppose, that, in case of perill, you will not stand upon such terms, as we hope we should not doe towards you; and withall we conceive that you looke at yᵉ Pequents, and all other Indeans, as a comone enimie, who, though he may take occasion of yᵉ begining of his rage, from some one parte of yᵉ English, yet if he prevaile, will surly pursue his advantage, to yᵉ rooting out of yᵉ whole nation. Therfore when we desired your help, we did it not without respecte to your owne saftie, as ours. (3ˡʸ.) Wheras you desire we should be ingaged to aide you, upon all like occasions; we are perswaded you doe not doubte of it; yet as we now deale with you as a free people, and at libertie, so as we cannot draw you into this warr with us, otherwise then as reason may guid & provock you; so we desire we may be at yᵉ like freedome, when any occasion may call for help from us. And wheras it is objected to us, that we refused to aide you against yᵉ French; we conceive yᵉ case was not alicke; yet we cannot wholy excuse our failing in that matter. (4ˡʸ.) Weras you objecte that we began yᵉ warr without your privitie, & managed it contrary to your advise; the truth is, that our first intentions being only against Block Iland, and yᵉ interprice seeming of small difficultie, we did not so much as consider of taking advice, or looking out for aide abroad. And when we had resolved upon yᵉ Pequents, we sent presently, or not long after, to you aboute it; but yᵉ answer received, it was not seasonable for us to chaing our counsells, excepte we had seen and waighed your grounds, which might have out wayed our owne.

(5ˡʸ.) For our peoples trading at Kenebeck, we assure you (to our knowledge) it hath not been by any allowance from us; and what we have provided in this and like cases, at our last Courte, Mʳ. E. W. can certifie you.

And (6ˡʸ); wheras you objecte to us yᵗ we should hold trade & correspondancie with yᵉ French, your enemise; we answer, you are misinformed, for, besids some letters which hath passed betweene our late Govʳ and them, to which we were privie, we have neither sente nor incouraged ours to trade with them; only one vessell or tow, for yᵉ better conveāce of our letters, had licens from our Govʳ to sayle thither.[DW]

Diverce other things have been privatly objected to us, by our worthy freind, wherunto he received some answer; but most of them concerning yᵉ apprehention of perticuler discurteseis, or injueries from some perticuler persons amongst us. It concernes us not to give any other answer to them then this; that, if yᵉ offenders shall be brought forth in a right way, we shall be ready to doe justice as yᵉ case shall require. In the meane time, we desire you to rest assured, that such things are without our privity, and not a litle greeveous to us.

Now for yᵉ joyning with us in this warr, which indeed concerns us no other wise then it may your selves, viz.: the releeving of our freinds & Christian [222] breethren, who are now first in yᵉ danger; though you may thinke us able to make it good without you, (as, if yᵉ Lord please to be with us, we may,) yet 3. things we offer to your consideration, which (we conceive) may have some waight with you. (First) y¹ if we should sinck under this burden, your opportunitie of seasonable help would be lost in 3. respects. 1. You cannot recover us, or secure your selves ther, with 3. times yᵉ charge & hazard which now yᵉ may. 2ˡʸ. The sorrowes which we should lye under (if through your neglect) would much abate of yᵉ acceptablenes of your help afterwards. 3ˡʸ. Those of yours who are now full of courage and forwardnes, would be much damped, and so less able to undergoe so great a burden. The (2.) thing is this, that it concernes us much to hasten this warr to an end before yᵉ end of this somer, otherwise yᵉ newes of it will discourage both your & our freinds from coming to us next year; with what further hazard & losse it may expose us unto, your selves may judge.

The (3.) thing is this, that if yᵉ Lord shall please to blesse our endeaours, so as we end yᵉ warr, or put it in a hopefull way without you, it may breed such ill thoughts in our people towards yours, as will be hard to entertaine such opinione of your good will towards us, as were fitt to be nurished among such neigbours & brethren as we are. And what ill consequences may follow, on both sids, wise men may fear, & would rather prevente then hope to redress. So with my harty salutations to you selfe, and all your counsell, and other our good freinds with you, I rest

Yours most assured in yᵉ Lord,

JO: WINTHROP.

Boston, yᵉ 20. of yᵉ 3. month, 1637.

In yᵉ mean time, the Pequents, espetially in yᵉ winter before, sought to make peace with yᵉ Narigansets, and used very pernicious arguments to move them therunto: as that yᵉ English were stranegers and begane to overspred their countrie, and would deprive them therof in time, if they were suffered to grow & increse; and if yᵉ Narigansets did assist yᵉ English to subdue them, they did but make way for their owne overthrow, for if they were rooted out, the English would soone take occasion to subjugate them; and if they would harken to them, they should not neede to fear yᵉ strength of yᵉ English; for they would not come to open battle with them, but fire their houses, kill their katle, and lye in ambush for them as they went abroad upon their occasions; and all this they might easily doe without any or litle danger to them selves. The which course being held, they well saw the English could not long subsiste, but they would either be starved with hunger, or be forced to forsake the countrie; with many yᵉ like things; insomuch that yᵉ Narigansets were once wavering, and were halfe minded to have made peace with them, and joyed against yᵉ English. But againe when they considered, how much wrong they had received from the Pequents, and what an oppertunitie they now had by yᵉ help of yᵉ English to right them selves, revenge was so sweete unto them, as it prevailed above all yᵉ rest; so as they resolved to joyne with yᵉ English against them, & did. [223] The Court here agreed forwith to send 50. men at their owne charg; and wᵗʰ as much speed as posiblie they could, gott them armed, and had made them ready under sufficiente leaders, and provided a barke to carrie them provisions & tend upon them for all occasions; but when they were ready to march (with a supply from yᵉ Bay) they had word to stay, for yᵉ enimy was as good as vanquished, and their would be no neede.

I shall not take upon me exactly to describe their proceedings in these things, because I expecte it will be fully done by them selves, who best know the carrage & circumstances of things; I shall therfore but touch them in generall. From Connightecute (who were most sencible of yᵉ hurt sustained, & yᵉ present danger), they sett out a partie of men, and an other partie mett them from yᵉ Bay, at yᵉ Narigansets, who were to joyne with them. Yᵉ Narigansets were ernest to be gone before yᵉ English were well rested and refreshte, espetially some of them which came last. It should seeme their desire was to come upon yᵉ enemie sudenly, & undiscovered. Ther was a barke of this place, newly put in ther, which was come from Conightecutte, who did incourage them to lay hold of yᵉ Indeans forwardnes, and to shew as great forwardnes as they, for it would incorage them, and expedition might prove to their great advantage. So they went on, and so ordered their march, as the Indeans brought them to a forte of y⁰ enimies (in which most of their cheefe men were) before day. They approached y⁰ same with great silence, and surrounded it both with English & Indeans, that they might not breake out; and so assualted them with great courage, shooting amongst them, and entered y⁰ forte with all speed; and those yᵗ first entered found sharp resistance from the enimie, who both shott at & grapled with them; others rane into their howses, & brought out fire, and sett them on fire, which soone tooke in their matts, &, standing close togeather, with y⁰ wind, all was quickly on a flame, and therby more were burnte to death then was otherwise slain; it burnte their bowstrings, and made them unservisable. Those yᵗ scaped y⁰ fire were slaine with y⁰ sword; some hewed to peeces, others rune throw with their rapiers, so as they were quickly dispatchte, and very few escaped. It was conceived they thus destroyed about 400. at this time. It was a fearfull sight to see them thus frying in y⁰ fyer, and y⁰ streams of blood quenching y⁰ same, and horrible was y⁰ stinck & sente ther of; but y⁰ victory seemed a sweete sacrifice, and they gave the prays therof to God, who had wrought so wonderfuly for them, thus to inclose their enimise in their hands, and give them so speedy a victory over so proud & insulting an enimie. The Narigansett Indeans, all this while, stood round aboute, but aloofe from all danger, and left y⁰ whole [224] execution to y⁰ English, exept it were y⁰ stoping of any yᵗ broke away, insulting over their enimies in this their ruine & miserie, when they saw them dancing in y⁰ flames, calling them by a word in their owne language, signifing, O brave Pequents! which they used familierly among them selves in their own prayes, in songs of triumph after their victories. After this servis was thus happily accomplished, they marcht to the water side, wher they mett with some of their vesells, by which they had refreishing with victualls & other necessaries. But in their march y⁰ rest of y⁰ Pequents drew into a body, and acoasted them, thinking to have some advantage against them by[DX] reason of a neck of land; but when they saw the English prepare for them, they kept a loofe, so as they neither did hurt, nor could receive any. After their refreishing & repair to geather for further counsell & directions, they resolved to pursue their victory, and follow yᵉ warr against yᵉ rest, but yᵉ Narigansett Indeans most of them forsooke them, and such of them as they had with them for guids, or otherwise, they found them very could and backward in yᵉ bussines, ether out of envie, or yᵗ they saw yᵉ English would make more profite of yᵉ victorie then they were willing they should, or els deprive them of such advantage as them selves desired by having them become tributaries unto them, or yᵉ like.

For yᵉ rest of this bussines, I shall only relate yᵉ same as it is in a leter which came from Mʳ. Winthrop to yᵉ Govʳ hear, as followeth.

Worthy Sʳ: I received your loving letter, and am much provocked to express my affections towards you, but straitnes of time forbids me; for my desire is to acquainte you with yᵉ Lords greate mercies towards us, in our prevailing against his & our enimies; that you may rejoyce and praise his name with us. About 80. of our men, haveing costed along towards yᵉ Dutch plantation, (some times by water, but most by land,) mett hear & ther with some Pequents, whom they slew or tooke prisoners. 2. sachems they tooke, & beheaded; and not hearing of Sassacous, (the cheefe sachem,) they gave a prisoner his life, to goe and find him out. He wente and brought them word where he was, but Sassacouse, suspecting him to be a spie, after he was gone, fled away with some 20. more to yᵉ Mowakes, so our men missed of him. Yet, devideing them selves, and ranging up & downe, as yᵉ providence of God guided them (for yᵉ Indeans were all gone, save 3. or 4. and they knew not whither to guid them, or els would not), upon yᵉ 13. of this month, they light upon a great company of them, viz. 80. strong men, & 200. women & children, in a small Indean towne, fast by a hideous swamp, which they all slipped into before our men could gett to them. Our captains were not then come togeither, but ther was Mʳ. Ludlow and Captaine Masson, with some 10. [225] of their men, & Captaine Patrick with some 20. or more of his, who, shooting at yᵉ Indeans, Captaine Trask with 50. more came soone in at yᵉ noyse.

Then they gave order to surround yᵉ swampe, it being aboute a mile aboute; but Levetenante Davenporte & some 12. more, not hearing that comand, fell into yᵉ swampe among yᵉ Indeans. The swampe was so thicke with shrub-woode, & so boggie with all, that some of them stuck fast, and received many shott. Levetenant Davenport was dangerously wounded aboute his armehole, and another shott in yᵉ head, so as, fainting, they were in great danger to have been taken by yᵉ Indeans. But Sargante Rigges, & Jeffery, and 2. or 3. more, rescued them, and slew diverse of yᵉ Indeans with their swords. After they were drawne out, the Indeans desired parley, & were offered (by Thomas Stanton, our interpretour) that, if they would come out, and yeeld them selves, they should have their lives, all that had not their hands in yᵉ English blood. Wherupon yᵉ sachem of yᵉ place came forth, and an old man or 2. & their wives and children, and after that some other women & children, and so they spake 2. howers, till it was night. Then Thomas Stanton was sente into them againe, to call them forth; but they said they would selle their lives their, and so shott at him so thicke as, if he had not cried out, and been presently rescued, they had slaine him. Then our men cutt of a place of yᵉ swampe with their swords, and cooped the Indeans into so narrow a compass, as they could easier kill them throw yᵉ thickets. So they continued all yᵉ night, standing aboute 12. foote one from an other, and yᵉ Indeans, coming close up to our men, shot their arrows so thicke, as they pierced their hatte brimes, & their sleeves, & stockins, & other parts of their cloaths, yet so miraculously did the Lord preserve them as not one of them was wounded, save those 3. who rashly went into yᵉ swampe. When it was nere day, it grue very darke, so as those of them which were left dropt away betweene our men, though they stood but 12. or 14. foote assunder; but were presenly discovered, & some killed in yᵉ pursute. Upon searching of yᵉ swampe, yᵉ next morning, they found 9. slaine, & some they pulled up, whom yᵉ Indeans had buried in yᵉ mire, so as they doe thinke that, of all this company, not 20. did escape, for they after found some who dyed in their flight of their wounds received. The prisoners were devided, some to those of yᵉ river, and the rest to us. Of these we send yᵉ male children to Bermuda,[DY] by Mʳ. William Peirce, & yᵉ women & maid children are disposed aboute in the townes. Ther have been now slaine & taken, in all, aboute 700. The rest are dispersed, and the Indeans in all quarters so terrified as all their friends are affraid to receive them. 2. of yᵉ sachems of Long Iland came to Mʳ. Stoughton and tendered them selves to be tributaries under our protection. And 2. of yᵉ Neepnett sachems have been with me to seeke our frendship. Amonge the prisoners we have yᵉ wife & children of Mononotto, a womon of a very modest countenance and behaviour. It was by her mediation that the[DZ] 2. English [226] maids were spared from death, and were kindly used by her; so that I have taken charge of her. One of her first requests was, that the English would not abuse her body, and that her children might not be taken from her. Those which were wounded were fetched of soone by John Galopp, who came with his shalop in a happie houre, to bring them victuals, and to carrie their wounded men to yᵉ pinass, wher our cheefe surgeon was, wᵗʰ Mʳ. Willson, being aboute 8. leagues off. Our people are all in health, (yᵉ Lord be praised,) and allthough they had marched in their armes all yᵉ day, and had been in fight all yᵉ night, yet they professed they found them selves so fresh as they could willingly have gone to such another bussines.

This is yᵉ substance of that which I received, though I am forced to omite many considerable circomstances. So, being in much straitnes of time, (the ships being to departe within this 4. days, and in them the Lord Lee and Mʳ. Vane,) I hear breake of, and with harty saluts to, &c., I rest

Yours assured,

JO: WINTHROP.

The 28. of yᵉ 5. month, 1637.

The captains reporte we have slaine 13. sachems; but Sassacouse & Monotto are yet living.

That I may make an end of this matter: this Sassacouse (yᵉ Pequents cheefe sachem) being fled to yᵉ Mowhakes, they cutt of his head, with some other of yᵉ cheefe of them, whether to satisfie yᵉ English, or rather yᵉ Narigansets, (who, as I have since heard, hired them to doe it,) or for their owne advantage, I well know not; but thus this warr tooke end. The rest of yᵉ Pequents were wholy driven from their place, and some of them submitted them selves to yᵉ Narigansets, & lived under them; others of them betooke them selves to yᵉ Monhiggs, under Uncass, their sachem, wᵗʰ the approbation of yᵉ English of Conightecutt, under whose protection Uncass lived, and he and his men had been faithful to them in this warr, & done them very good service. But this did so vexe the Narrigansetts, that they had not yᵉ whole sweay over them, as they have never ceased plotting and contriving how to bring them under, and because they cannot attaine their ends, because of yᵉ English who have protected them, they have sought to raise a generall conspiracie against yᵉ English, as will appear in an other place.

They had now letters againe out of England from Mʳ. Andrews & Mʳ. Beachamp, that Mʳ. Sherley neither had nor would pay them any money, or give them any accounte, and so with much discontent desired them hear to send them some, much blaming them still, that they had sent all to Mʳ. Sherley, & none to them selves. Now, though they might have justly referred them to their former answer, and insisted ther upon, & some wise men counselled them so to doe, yet because they beleeved that [227] they were realy out round sumes of money, (espetialy Mʳ. Andrews,) and they had some in their hands, they resolved to send them what bever they had.[EA] Mʳ. Sherleys letters were to this purpose: that, as they had left him in yᵉ paiment of yᵉ former bills, so he had tould them he would leave them in this, and beleeve it, they should find it true. And he was as good as his word, for they could never gett peney from him, nor bring him to any accounte, though Mr. Beachamp sued him in yᵉ Chancerie. But they all of them turned their complaints against them here, wher ther was least cause, and who had suffered most unjustly; first from Mʳ. Allerton & them, in being charged with so much of yᵗ which they never had, nor drunke for; and now in paying all, & more then all (as they conceived), and yet still thus more demanded, and that with many heavie charges. They now discharged M^r. Sherley from his agencie, and forbad him to buy or send over any more goods for them, and prest him to come to some end about these things.

Anno Dom: 1638.

This year M^r. Thomas Prence was chosen Govr.

Amongst other enormities that fell out amongst them, this year 3. men were (after due triall) executed for robery & murder which they had committed; their names were these, Arthur Peach, Thomas Jackson, and Richard Stinnings; ther was a 4., Daniel Crose, who was also guilty, but he escaped away, and could not be found. This Arthur Peach was ye cheefe of them, and ye ring leader of all ye rest. He was a lustie and a desperate yonge man, and had been one of ye souldiers in ye Pequente warr, and had done as good servise as ye most ther, and one of ye forwardest in any attempte. And being now out of means, and loath to worke, and falling to idle courses & company, he intended to goe to ye Dutch plantation; and had alured these 3., being other mens servants and apprentices, to goe with him. But another cause ther was allso of his secret going away in this maner; he was not only rune into debte, but he had gott a maid with child, (which was not known till after his death,) a mans servante in ye towne, and fear of punishmente made him gett away. The other 3. complotting with him, ranne away from their maisters in the night, and could not be heard of, for they went not ye ordinarie way, but shaped such a course as they thought to avoyd ye pursute of any [228]. But falling into ye way that lyeth betweene ye Bay of Massachusetts and the Narrigansets, and being disposed to rest them selves, struck fire, and took tobaco, a litle out of ye way, by ye way side. At length ther came a Narigansett Indean by, who had been in ye Bay a trading, and had both cloth & beads aboute him. (They had meett him ye day before, & he was now returning.) Peach called him to drinke tobaco with them, and he came & sate downe with them. Peach tould ye other he would kill him, and take what he had from him. But they were some thing afraid; but he said, Hang him, rogue, he had killed many of them. So they let him alone to doe as he would; and when he saw his time, he tooke a rapier and rane him through the body once or twise, and tooke from him 5. fathume of wampam, and 3. coats of cloath, and wente their way, leaving him for dead. But he scrabled away, when they were gone, and made shift to gett home, (but dyed within a few days after,) by which means they were discovered; and by subtilty the Indeans tooke them. For they desiring a canow to sett them over a water, (not thinking their facte had been known,) by ye sachems command they were carried to Aquidnett Iland, & ther accused of ye murder, and were examend & comitted upon it by ye English ther. The Indeans sent for M^r. Williams, & made a greeveous complainte; his freinds and kinred were ready to rise in armes, and provock the rest therunto, some conceiving they should now find ye Pequents words trew: that ye English would fall upon them. But M^r. Williams pacified them, & tould them, they should see justice done upon ye offenders; & wente to ye man, & tooke M^r. James, a phisition, with him. The man tould him who did it, & in what maner it was done; but the phisition found his wounds mortall, and that he could not live, (as he after testified upon othe, before the jurie in oppen courte,) and so he dyed shortly after, as both Mr. Williams, M^r. James, & some Indeans testified in courte. The Govr in the Bay were aquented with it, but refferrd it hither, because it was done in this jurisdiction;[FB] but pressed by all means y^t justice might be done in it; or els ye countrie must rise & see justice done, otherwise it would raise a warr. Yet some of ye rude & ignorante sorte murmured that any English should be put to death for ye Indeans. So at last they of ye iland brought them hither, and being often examened, and ye evidence prodused, they all in the end freely confessed in effect all y^t the Indean accused them of, & that they had done it, in ye maner afforesaid; and so, upon ye forementioned evidence, were cast by ye jurie, & condemned, & executed for the same. And some of ye Narigansett Indeans, & of ye parties freinds, were presente when it was done, which gave them & all ye countrie good satisfaction. But it was a matter of much sadnes to them hear, and was ye 2.

execution which they had since they came; being both for wilfull murder, as hath bene before related. Thus much of this mater.

[229] They received this year more letters from England full of reneued complaints, on yᵉ one side, that they could gett no money nor accounte from Mʳ. Sherley; & he againe, yᵗ he was pressed therto, saying he was to accounte with those hear, and not with them, &c. So, as was before resolved, if nothing came of their last letters, they would now send them what they could, as supposing, when some good parte was payed them, that Mʳ. Sherley & they would more easily agree aboute yᵉ remainder.

So they sent to Mʳ. Andrews and Mʳ. Beachamp, by Mʳ. Joseph Yonge, in yᵉ Mary & Anne, 1325ˡⁱ. waight of beaver, devided betweene them. Mʳ. Beachamp returned an accounte of his moyety, that he made 400ˡⁱ. starling of it, fraight and all charges paid. But Mʳ. Andrews, though he had yᵉ more and beter parte, yet he made not so much of his, through his owne indiscretion; and yet turned yᵉ loss[EC] upon them hear, but without cause.

They sent them more by bills & other paimente, which was received & acknowledged by them, in money[ED] & yᵉ like; which was for katle sould of Mʳ. Allertons, and yᵉ price of a bark sold, which belonged to yᵉ stock, and made over to them in money, 434ˡⁱ. sterling. The whole sume was 1234ˡⁱ. sterling, save what Mʳ. Andrews lost in yᵉ beaver, which was otherwise made good. But yet this did not stay their clamors, as will apeare here after more at large.

It pleased God, in these times, so to blesse yᵉ cuntry with such access & confluance of people into it, as it was therby much inriched, and catle of all kinds stood at a high rate for diverce years together. Kine were sould at 20ˡⁱ. and some at 25ˡⁱ. a peece, yea, some times at 28ˡⁱ. A cow-calfe usually at 10ˡⁱ. A milch goate at 3ˡⁱ. & some at 4ˡⁱ. And femall kids at 30ˢ. and often at 40ˢ. a peece. By which means yᵉ anciente planters which had any stock begane to grow in their estats. Corne also wente at a round rate, viz. 6ˢ. a bushell. So as other trading begane to be neglected; and the old partners (having now forbidden Mʳ. Sherley to send them any more goods) broke of their trade at Kenebeck, and, as things stood, would follow it no longer. But some of them, (with other they joyned with,) being loath it should be lost by discontinuance, agreed with yͤ company for it, and gave them aboute yͤ 6. parte of their gaines for it; [230][EE] with yͤ first fruits of which they builte a house for a prison; and the trade ther hath been since continued, to yͤ great benefite of yͤ place; for some well fore-sawe that these high prises of corne and catle would not long continue, and that then yͤ comodities ther raised would be much missed.

This year, aboute yͤ 1. or 2. of June, was a great & fearfull earthquake; it was in this place heard before it was felte. It came with a rumbling noyse, or low murmure, like unto remoate thunder; it came from yͤ norward, & pased southward. As yͤ noyse aproched nerer, they earth begane to shake, and came at length with that violence as caused platters, dishes, & such like things as stoode upon shelves, to clatter & fall downe; yea, persons were afraid of yͤ houses them selves. It so fell oute yᵗ at yͤ same time diverse of yͤ cheefe of this towne were mett together at one house, conferring with some of their freinds that were upon their removall from yͤ place, (as if yͤ Lord would herby shew yͤ signes of his displeasure, in their shaking a peeces & removalls one from an other.) How ever it was very terrible for yͤ time, and as yͤ men were set talking in yͤ house, some women & others were without yͤ dores, and yͤ earth shooke with yᵗ violence as they could not stand without catching hould of yͤ posts & pails yᵗ stood next them; but yͤ violence lasted not long. And about halfe an hower, or less, came an other noyse & shaking, but nether so loud nor strong as yͤ former, but quickly passed over; and so it ceased. It was not only on yͤ sea coast, but yͤ Indeans felt it within land; and some ships that were upon yͤ coast were shaken by it. So powerfull is yͤ mighty hand of yͤ Lord, as to make both the earth & sea to shake, and the mountaines to tremble before him, when he pleases; and who can stay his hand? It was observed that yͤ somers, for divers years togeather after this earthquake, were not so hotte & seasonable for yͤ ripning of corne & other fruits as formerly; but more could & moyst, & subjecte to erly & untimly frosts, by which, many times, much Indean corne came not to maturitie; but whether this was any cause, I leave it to naturallists to judge.

Anno Dom: 1639. & Anno Dom: 1640.

These 2. years I joyne togeather, because in them fell not out many things more then y⁰ ordinary passages of their comone affaires, which are not needfull to be touched. [231] Those of this plantation having at sundrie times granted lands for severall townships, and amongst y⁰ rest to y⁰ inhabitants of Sityate, some wherof issewed from them selves, and allso a large tracte of land was given to their 4. London partners in y⁰ place, viz. Mʳ. Sherley, Mʳ. Beacham, Mʳ. Andrews, & Mʳ. Hatherley. At Mʳ. Hatherley's request and choys it was by him taken for him selfe and them in yᵗ place; for the other 3. had invested him with power & trust to chose for them. And this tracte of land extended to their utmoste limets that way, and bordered on their neigbours of y⁰ Massachusets, who had some years after seated a towne (called Hingam) on their lands next to these parts. So as now ther grue great differance betweene these 2. townships, about their bounds, and some meadow grownds that lay betweene them. They of Hingam presumed to alotte parte of them to their people, and measure & stack them out. The other pulled up their stacks, & threw them. So it grew to a controversie betweene the 2. goverments, & many letters and passages were betweene them aboute it; and it hunge some 2. years in suspense. The Courte of Massachusets, appointed some to range their line according to y⁰ bounds of their patente, and (as they wente to worke) they made it to take in all Sityate, and I know not how much more. Againe, on y⁰ other hand, according to y⁰ line of the patente of this place, it would take in Hingame and much more within their bounds.

In y⁰ end boath Courts agreed to chose 2. comissioners of each side, and to give them full & absolute power to agree and setle y⁰ bounds betwene them; and what they should doe in y⁰ case should stand irrevocably. One meeting they had at Hingam, but could not conclude; for their comissioners stoode stiffly on a clawes in their graunte, That from Charles-river, or any branch or parte therof, they were to extend their limits, and 3. myles further to ye southward; or from ye most southward parte of ye Massachusets Bay, and 3. mile further. But they chose to stand on ye former termes, for they had found a smale river, or brooke rather, that a great way with in land trended southward, and issued into some part of y^t river taken to be Charles-river, and from ye most southerly part of this, & 3. mile more southward of ye same, they would rune a line east to ye sea, aboute 20. mile; which will (say they) take in a part of Plimoth itselfe. Now it is to be knowne y^t though this patente & plantation were much the ancienter, yet this inlargemente of the same (in which Sityate stood) was granted after theirs, and so theirs were first to take place, before this inlargmente. Now their answer was, first, that, however according to their owne plan, they could noway come upon any part of their ancieante grante. [232] Secondly. They could never prove y^t to be a parte of Charles-river, for they knew not which was Charles-river, but as ye people of this place, which came first, imposed such a name upon y^t river, upon which, since, Charles-towne is builte (supposing y^t was it, which Captaine Smith in his mapp so named). Now they y^t first named it have best reason to know it, and to explaine which is it. But they only tooke it to be Charles river, as fare as it was by them navigated, and y^t was as farr as a boate could goe. But y^t every runlett or small brooke, y^t should, farr within land, come into it, or mixe their stremes with it, and were by ye natives called by other & differente names from it, should now by them be made Charles-river, or parts of it, they saw no reason for it. And gave instance in Humber, in Old England, which had ye Trente, Ouse, and many others of lesser note fell into it, and yet were not counted parts of it; and many smaler rivers & broks fell into ye Trente, & Ouse, and no parts of them, but had nams aparte, and divisions & nominations of them selves. Againe, it was pleaded that they had no east line in their patente, but were to begine at ye sea, and goe west by a line, &c. At this meeting no conclution was made, but things discussed & well prepared for an issue. The next year ye same comissioners had their power continued or renewed, and mett at Sityate, and concluded ye mater, as followeth.

The agreemente of ye bounds betwixte Plimoth and Massachusetts.

Wheras ther were tow comissiones granted by ye 2. jurisdictions, ye one of Massachsets Govermente, granted unto John Endecott, gent: and Israell Stoughton, gent: the other of New-Plimoth Govermente, to William Bradford, Govr, and Edward Winslow, gent: and both these for ye setting out, setling, & determining of ye bounds & limitts of ye lands betweene ye said jurisdictions, wherby not only this presente age, but ye posteritie to come may live peaceably & quietly in y^t behalfe. And for as much as ye said comissioners on both sids have full power so to doe, as appeareth by ye records of both jurisdictions; we therfore, ye said comissioners above named, doe hearby with one consente & agreemente conclude, detirmine, and by these presents declare, that all ye marshes at Conahasett y^t lye of ye one side of ye river next to Hingam, shall belong to ye jurisdition of Massachusetts Plantation; and all ye marshes y^t lye on ye other side of ye river next to Sityate, shall be long to ye jurisdiction of New-Plimoth; excepting 60. acers of marsh at ye mouth of ye river, on Sityate side next to the sea, which we doe herby agree, conclude, & detirmine shall belong to ye jurisdition of Massachusetts. And further, we doe hearby agree, determine, and conclude, y^t the bounds of ye limites betweene both ye said jurisditions are as followeth, viz. from ye mouth of ye brook y^t runeth into Chonahasett marches (which we call by ye name of Bound-brooke) with a stright & directe line to ye midle of a great ponde, y^t lyeth on ye right hand of ye uper path, or commone way, y^t leadeth betweene Waimoth and Plimoth, close to ye path as [233] we goe alonge, which was formerly named (and still we desire may be caled) Accord pond, lying aboute five or 6. myles from Weimoth southerley; and from thence with a straight line to ye souther-most part of Charles-river,[EF] & 3. miles southerly, inward into ye countrie, according as is expresed in ye patente granted by his Matie to ye Company of ye Massachusetts Plantation. Provided allways and never ye less concluded & determined by mutuall agreemente betweene yᵉ said comissioners, yᵗ if it fall out yᵗ the said line from Accord-pond to yᵉ sothermost parte of Charles-river, & 3. myles southerly as is before expresed, straiten or hinder any parte of any plantation begune by yᵉ Goveⁿ of New-Plimoth, or hereafter to be begune within 10. years after yᵉ date of these psⁿˢ, that then, notwithstanding yᵉ said line, it shall be lawfull for yᵉ said Govⁿ of New-Plimoth to assume on yᵉ northerly side of yᵉ said line, wher it shall so intrench as afforesaid, so much land as will make up yᵉ quantity of eight miles square, to belong to every shuch plantation begune, or to [be] begune as afforesaid; which we agree, determine, & conclude to appertaine & belong to yᵉ said Govⁿ of New-Plimoth. And wheras yᵉ said line, from yᵉ said brooke which runeth into Choahassett saltmarshes, called by us Bound-brooke, and yᵉ pond called Accord-pond, lyeth nere yᵉ lands belonging to yᵉ tounships of Sityate & Hingam, we doe therfore hereby determine & conclude, that if any devissions allready made and recorded, by either yᵉ said townships, doe crose the said line, that then it shall stand, & be of force according to yᵉ former intents and purposes of the said townes granting them (the marshes formerly agreed on exepted). And yᵗ no towne in either jurisdiction shall hereafter exceede, but containe them selves within yᵉ said lines expressed. In witnes wherof we, the comissioners of both jurisdictions, doe by these presents indented set our hands & scales yᵉ ninth day of yᵉ 4. month in 16. year of our soveraine lord, king Charles; and in yᵉ year of our Lord, 1640.

WILLIAM BRADFORD, GOVᴿ.
ED: WINSLOW.
JO: ENDECOTT.
ISRAELL STOUGHTON.

Wheras yᵉ patente was taken in yᵉ name of William Bradford, (as in trust,) and rane in these termes: To him, his heires, and associats & assignes; and now yᵉ noumber of free-men being much increased, and diverce tounships established and setled in severall quarters of yᵉ govermente, as Plimoth, Duxberie, Sityate, Tanton,

Sandwich, Yarmouth, Barnstable, Marchfeeld, and not longe after, Seacunke (called afterward, at ye desire of ye inhabitants, Rehoboth) and Nawsett, it was by ye Courte desired that William Bradford should make a surrender of the same into their hands. The which he willingly did, in this maner following.

Wheras William Bradford, and diverce others ye first instruments of God in the begining of this great work of plantation, togeather with such as ye allordering hand of God in his providence soone added unto them, have been at very great charges to procure ye lands, priviledges, & freedoms from all intanglments, as may appeare by diverse & sundrie deeds, inlargments of grants, purchases, and payments of debts, &c., by reason wherof ye title to ye day of these presents [234] remaineth in ye said William Bradford, his heires, associats, and assignes: now, for ye better setling of ye estate of the said lands (contained in ye grant or pattente), the said William Bradford, and those first instruments termed & called in sondry orders upon publick recorde, Y^e Purchasers, or Old comers; witnes 2. in spetiall, the one bearing date ye 3. of March, 1639. the other in Des: the 1. An^o 1640. wherunto these presents have spetiall relation & agreemente, and wherby they are distinguished from other ye freemen & inhabitants of ye said corporation. Be it knowne unto all men, therfore, by these presents, that the said William Bradford, for him selfe, his heires, together with ye said purchasers, doe only reserve unto them selves, their heires, and assignes those 3. tractes of land mentioned in ye said resolution, order, and agreemente, bearing date ye first of Des: 1640. viz. first, from ye bounds of Yarmouth, 3. miles to ye eastward of Naemschatet, and from sea to sea, crose the neck of land. The 2. of a place called Acoughcouss, which lyeth in ye botome of ye bay adjoyning to ye west-side of Pointe Perill, and 2. myles to ye westerne side of ye said river, to an other place called Acushente river, which entereth at ye westerne end of Nacata, and 2. miles to ye eastward therof, and to extend 8. myles up into ye countrie. The 3. place, from Sowansett river to Patucket river, (with Cawsumsett neck,) which is ye cheefe habitation of ye Indeans, & reserved for them to dwell upon, extending into ye land 8. myles through ye whole breadth therof. Togeather with such other small parcells of lands as they or any of them are personally possessed of or intressed in, by vertue of any former titles or grante whatsoever. And ye said William Bradford doth, by ye free & full consente, approbation, and agreemente of ye said old-planters, or purchasers, together with ye liking, approbation, and acceptation of ye other parte of ye said corporation, surrender into ye hands of ye whole courte, consisting of ye free-men of this corporation of New-Plimoth, all y^t other right & title, power, authority, priviledges, immunities, & freedomes granted in ye said letters patents by ye said right Honb^{le} Counsell for New-England; reserveing his & their personall right of freemen, together wth the said old planters afforesaid, excepte ye said lands before excepted, declaring the freemen of this corporation, togeather with all such as shal be legally admitted into ye same, his associats. And ye said William Bradford, for him, his heiers, & assignes, doe hereby further promise and grant to doe & performe whatsoever further thing or things, acte or actes, which in him lyeth, which shall be needfull and expediente for ye better confirming and establishing the said premises, as by counsel lerned in ye lawes shall be reasonably advised and devised, when he shall be ther unto required. In witness wherof, the said William Bradford hath in publick courte surrendered the said letters patents actually into ye hands & power of ye said courte, binding him selfe, his heires, executors, administrators, and assignes to deliver up whatsoever spetialties are in his hands that doe or may concerne the same.

[235] In these 2. years they had sundry letters out of England to send one over to end the buissines and accounte with M^r. Sherley; who now professed he could not make up his accounts without ye help of some from hence, espetialy M^r. Winslows. They had serious thoughts of it, and ye most parte of ye partners hear thought it best to send; but they had formerly written such bitter and threatening letters as M^r. Winslow was neither willing to goe, nor y^t any other of ye partners should; for he was perswaded, if any of them wente, they should be arested, and an action of such a sume layed upon them as they should not procure baele, but must lye in

prison, and then they would bring them to what they liste; or other wise they might be brought into trouble by ye arch-bishops means, as ye times then stood. But, notwithstanding, they weer much inclined to send, & Captaine Standish was willing to goe, but they resolved, seeing they could not all agree in this thing, and that it was waighty, and ye consequence might prove dangerous, to take M^r. Winthrops advise in ye thing, and ye rather, because M^r. Andrews had by many letters acquaynted him with ye differences betweene them, and appoynted him for his assigne to receive his parte of ye debte. (And though they deneyed to pay him any as a debte, till ye controversie was ended, yet they had deposited 110^li. in money in his hands for M^r. Andrews, to pay to him in parte as soone as he would come to any agreement with ye rest.) But M^r. Winthrop was of M^r. Winslows minde, and disswaded them from sending; so they broak of their resolution from sending, and returned this answer: that the times were dangerous as things stood with them, for they knew how M^r. Winslow had suffered formerley, and for a small matter was clapte up in ye Fleete, & it was long before he could gett out, to both his & their great loss and damage; and times were not better, but worse, in y^t respecte. Yet, that their equall & honest minds might appeare to all men, they made them this tender: to refferr ye case to some gentle-men and marchants in ye Bay of ye Massachusetts, such as they should chuse, and were well knowne unto them selves, (as they perceived their wer many of their aquaintance and freinds ther, better knowne to them then ye partners hear,) and let them be informed in ye case by both sids, and have all ye evidence y^t could be prodused, in writing, or other wise; and they would be bound to stand to their determination, and make good their award, though it should cost them all they had in ye world. But this did not please them, but they were offended at it, without any great reasone for ought I know, (seeing nether side could give in clear accountes, ye partners here could not, by reason they (to their smarte) were failed by ye accountante they sent them, and M^r. Sherley pretened he could not allso,) save as they conceived it a disparagmente to yeeld to their inferiours in respecte of ye place and other concurring circomstances. So this came to nothing; and afterward M[r]. Sherley write, y[t] if M[r]. Winslow would mett him in France, y[e] Low-Countries, or Scotland, let y[e] place be knowne, and he [236] come to him ther. But in regard of y[e] troubles that now begane to arise in our owne nation, and other reasons, this did not come to any effecte. That which made them so desirous to bring things to an end was partly to stope y[e] clamours and aspertions raised & cast upon them hereaboute; though they conceived them selves to sustaine the greatest wrong, and had most cause of complainte; and partly because they feared y[e] fall of catle, in which most parte of their estats lay. And this was not a vaine feare; for they fell indeede before they came to a conclusion, and that so souddanly, as a cowe that but a month before was worth 20[li]., and would so have passed in any paymente, fell now to 5[li]. and would yeeld no more; and a goate that wente at 3[li]. or 50[s]. would now yeeld but 8. or 10[s]. at most. All men feared a fall of catle, but it was thought it would be by degrees; and not to be from y[e] highest pitch at once to y[e] lowest, as it did, which was greatly to y[e] damage of many, and y[e] undoing of some. An other reason was, they many of them grew aged, (and indeed a rare thing it was that so many partners should all live together so many years as these did,) and saw many changes were like to befall; so as they were loath to leave these intanglments upon their children and posteritie, who might be driven to remove places, as they had done; yea, them selves might doe it yet before they dyed. But this bussines must yet rest; y[e] next year gave it more ripnes, though it rendred them less able to pay, for y[e] reasons afforesaid.

Anno Dom: 1641.

M[r]. Sherley being weary of this controversie, and desirous of an end, (as well as them selves,) write to M[r]. John Atwode and M[r]. William Collier, 2. of y[e] inhabitants of this place, and of his speatiall aquaintance, and desired them to be a means to bring this bussines to an end, by advising & counselling the partners hear, by some way to bring it to a composition, by mutuall agreemente. And he write to them selves allso to yᵗ end, as by his letter may apear; so much therof as concernse yᵉ same I shall hear relate.

Sʳ. My love remembered, &c. I have writte so much concerning yᵉ ending of accounts betweexte us, as I profess I know not what more to write, &c. If you desire an end, as you seeme to doe, ther is (as I conceive) but 2. waise; that is, to parfecte all accounts, from yᵉ first to yᵉ last, &c. Now if we find this difficulte, and tedious, haveing not been so stricte & carefull as we should and oughte to have done, as for my owne parte I doe confess I have been somewhat to remisse, and doe verily thinke so are you, &c. I fear you can never make a perfecte accounte of all your pety viages, out, & home too & againe, &c.[EG] So then yᵉ second way must be, by biding, or [237] compounding; and this way, first or last, we must fall upon, &c. If we must warr at law for it, doe not you expecte from me, nether will I from you, but to cleave yᵉ heare, and then I dare say yᵉ lawyers will be most gainers, &c. Thus let us set to yᵉ worke, one way or other, and end, that I may not allways suffer in my name & estate. And you are not free; nay, yᵉ gospell suffers by your delaying, and causeth yᵉ professors of it to be hardly spoken of, that you, being many, & now able, should combine & joyne togeather to oppress & burden me, &c. Fear not to make a faire & reasonable offer; beleeve me, I will never take any advantage to plead it against you, or to wrong you; or else let Mʳ. Winslow come over, and let him have such full power & authority as we may ende by compounding; or else, yᵉ accounts so well and fully made up, as we may end by reconing. Now, blesed be God, yᵉ times be much changed here, I hope to see many of you returne to you native countrie againe, and have such freedome & libertie as yᵉ word of God prescribs. Our bishops were never so near a downfall as now; God hath miraculously confounded them, and turned all their popish & Machavillian plots & projects on their owne heads, &c. Thus you see what is fitt to be done concerning our perticulere greevances. I pray you take it seriously into consideration; let each give way a litle that we may meete, &c. Be you and all yours kindly saluted, &c. So I ever rest,

Your loving friend,

JAMES SHERLEY.

Clapham, May 18, 1641.

Being thus by this leter, and allso by M^r. Atwodes & M^r. Colliers mediation urged to bring things to an end, (and ye continuall clamors from ye rest,) and by none more urged then by their own desires, they tooke this course (because many scandals had been raised upon them). They apoynted these 2. men before mentioned to meet on a certaine day, and called some other freinds on both sids, and M^r. Free-man, brother in law to M^r. Beachamp, and having drawne up a collection of all ye remains of ye stock, in what soever it was, as housing, boats, bark, and all implements belonging to ye same, as they were used in ye time of ye trad, were they better or worce, with ye remaines of all comodities, as beads, knives, hatchetts, cloth, or any thing els, as well ye refuse as ye more vendible, with all debts, as well those y^t were desperate as others more hopefull; and having spent diverce days to bring this to pass, having ye helpe of all bookes and papers, which either any of them selves had, or Josias Winslow, who was their accountante; and they found ye sume in all to arise (as ye things were valued) to aboute 1400^{li}. And they all of them tooke a voluntary but a sollem oath, in ye presence one of an other, and of all their frends, ye persons abovesaid y^t were now presente, that this was all that any of them knew of, or could remember; and Josias Winslow did ye like for his parte. But ye truth is they wrongd them selves much in ye valuation, for they reconed some catle as they were taken of M^r. Allerton, as for instance a cowe in ye hands of one cost 25^{li}. and so she was valued in this accounte; but when she came to be past away in parte of paymente, after ye agreemente, she would be accepted but a 4^{li}. 15^s. [238] Also being tender of their oaths, they brought in all they know owing to ye stock; but they had not made ye like diligente search what ye stocke might owe to any, so as many scattering debts fell upon afterwards more then now they know of.

Upon this they drew certaine articles of agreemente betweene M^r. Atwode, on M^r. Sherleys behalfe, and them selves. The effecte is as folloeth.

Articles of agreemente made and concluded upon ye 15. day of October, 1641. &c.

Imp: Wheras ther was a partnership for diverce years agreed upon betweene James Sherley, John Beacham, and Richard Andrews, of London, marchants, and William Bradford, Edward Winslow, Thomas Prence, Myles Standish, William Brewster, John Aldon, & John Howland, wth Isaack Allerton, in a trade of beaver skines & other furrs arising in New-England; the terme of which said partnership being expired, and diverse sumes of money in goods adventured into New-England by ye said James Sherley, John Beachamp, & Richard Andrews, and many large returnes made from New-England by ye said William Bradford, Ed: Winslow, &c.; and differance arising aboute ye charge of 2. ships, the one called ye White Angele, of Bristow, and ye other ye Frindship, of Barnstable, and a viage intended in her, &c.; which said ships & their viages, ye said William Bradford, Ed: W. &c. conceive doe not at all appertaine to their accounts of partnership; and weras ye accounts of ye said partnership are found to be confused, and cannot orderley appeare (through ye defaulte of Josias Winslow, ye booke keeper); and weras ye said W. B. &c. have received all their goods for ye said trade from the foresaid James Sherley, and have made most of their returnes to him, by consente of ye said John Beachamp & Richard Andrews; and wheras also ye said James Sherley hath given power & authoritie to M^r. John Atwode, with ye advice & consente of William Collier, of Duxborow, for and on his behalfe, to put such an absolute end to ye said partnership, with all and every accounts, reconings, dues, claimes, demands, whatsoever, to ye said James Sherley, John Beacham, & Richard Andrews, from ye said W. B. &c. for and concerning ye said beaver trade, & also ye charge ye said 2. ships, and their viages made or pretended, whether just or unjuste, from ye worlds begining to this presente, as also for ye paimente of a purchas of 1800ˡⁱ. made by Isaack Allerton, for and on yᵉ behalfe of yᵉ said W. B., Ed: W., &c., and of yᵉ joynt stock, shares, lands, and adventurs, what soever in New-England aforesaid, as apeareth by a deede bearing date yᵉ 6. Novᵇʳ. 1627; and also for and from such sume and sumes of money or goods as are received by William Bradford, Tho: Prence, & Myles Standish, for yᵉ recovery of dues, by accounts betwexte them, yᵉ said James Sherly, John Beachamp, & Richard Andrews, and Isaack Allerton, for yᵉ ship caled yᵉ White Angell. Now yᵉ said John Attwode, with advice & counsell of yᵉ said William Collier, having had much comunication & spente diverse days in agitation of all yᵉ said differances & accounts with yᵉ said W. B., E. W., &c.; and yᵉ said W. B., E. W., &c. have also, with yᵉ said book-keeper spente much time in collecting & gathering togeither yᵉ remainder of yᵉ stock of partnership for yᵉ said trade, and what soever hath beene received, or is due by yᵉ said attorneyship before expresed, and all, and all manner of goods, debts, and dues therunto belonging, as well those debts that are weake and doubtfull [239] and desperate, as those yᵗ are more secure, which in all doe amounte to yᵉ sume of 1400ˡⁱ. or ther aboute; and for more full satisfaction of yᵉ said James Sherley, John Beachamp, & Richard Andrews, the said W. B. and all yᵉ rest of yᵉ abovesaid partners, togeither with Josias Winslow yᵉ booke keeper, have taken a voluntarie oath, yᵗ within yᵉ said sume of 1400ˡⁱ. or theraboute, is contained whatsoever they knew, to yᵉ utmost of their rememberance.

In consideration of all which matters & things before expressed, and to yᵉ end yᵗ a full, absolute, and finall end may be now made, and all suits in law may be avoyded, and love & peace continued, it is therfore agreed and concluded betweene yᵉ said John Attwode, with yᵉ advice & consent of yᵉ said William Colier, for & on yᵉ behalfe of yᵉ said James Sherley, to and with yᵉ said W. B., &c. in maner and forme following: viz. that yᵉ said John Attwode shall procure a sufficiente release and discharge, under yᵉ hands & seals of yᵉ said James Sherley, John Beachamp, & Richard Andrews, to be delivered fayer & unconcealed unto yᵉ said William Bradford, &c., at or before yᵉ last day of August, next insuing yᵉ date hereof, whereby yᵉ said William Bradford &c., their heires, executors, & administrators, & every of them shall be fully and absolutly aquited & discharged of all actions, suits, reconings, accounts, claimes, and demands whatsoever concerning yᵉ generall stock of beaver trade, paymente of yᵉ said 1800ˡⁱ. for yᵉ purchass, and all demands, reckonings, and accounts, just or unjuste, concerning the tow ships Whit-Angell and Frendship aforesaid, togeather with whatsoever hath been received by yᵉ said William Bradford, of yᵉ goods or estate of Isaack Allerton, for satisfaction of yᵉ accounts of yᵉ said ship called yᵉ Whit Angele, by vertue of a lre of attourney to him, Thomas Prence, & Myles Standish, directed from yᵉ said James Sherley, John Beachamp, & Richard Andrews, for yᵗ purpose as afforesaid.

It is also agreed & concluded upon betweene the said parties to these presents, that the said W. B., E. W., &c. shall now be bound in 2400ˡⁱ. for paymente of 1200ˡⁱ. in full satisfaction of all demands as afforesaid; to be payed in maner & forme following; that is to say, 400ˡⁱ. within 2. months next after yᵉ receite of the aforesaid releases and discharges, one hundred and ten pounds wherof is allready in yᵉ hands of John Winthrop senior of Boston, Esquire, by the means of Mʳ. Richard Andrews afforesaid, and 80ˡⁱ. waight of beaver now deposited into yᵉ hands of yᵉ said John Attwode, to be both in part of paimente of yᵉ said 400ˡⁱ. and yᵉ other 800ˡⁱ. to be payed by 200ˡⁱ. pʳ anume, to such assignes as shall be appointed, inhabiting either in Plimoth or Massachusetts Bay, in such goods & comodities, and at such rates, as the countrie shall afford at yᵉ time of delivery & paymente; and in yᵉ mean time yᵉ said bond of 2400ˡⁱ. to be deposited into yᵉ hands of yᵉ said John Attwode. And it is agreed upon by & betweene yᵉ said parties to these presents, that if yᵉ said John Attwode shall not or cannot procure such said releases & discharges as afforesaid from yᵉ said James Sherley, John Bachamp, & Richard Andrews, at or before yᵉ last day of August next insuing yᵉ date hear of, yᵗ then yᵉ said John Attwode shall, at yᵉ said day precisely, redeliver, or cause to [240] be delivered unto ye said W. B., E. W., &c. their said bond of 2400ˡⁱ. and yᵉ said 80ˡⁱ. waight of beaver, or yᵉ due valew therof, without any fraud or further delay; and for performance of all & singuler y⁶ covenants and agreements hearin contained and expressed, which on y⁶ one parte and behalfe of y⁶ said James Sherley are to be observed & performed, shall become bound in y⁶ sume of 2400ˡⁱ. to them, y⁶ said William Bradford, Edward Winslow, Thomas Prence, Myles Standish, William Brewster, John Allden, and John Howland. And it is lastly agreed upon betweene y⁶ said parties, that these presents shall be left in trust, to be kepte for boath parties, in y⁶ hands of Mr. John Reanour, teacher of Plimoth. In witnes wherof, all y⁶ said parties have hereunto severally sett their hands, y⁶ day and year first above writen.

JOHN ATWODE, WILLIAM BRADFORD, EDWARD WINSLOW, &c. In y⁶ presence of

> EDMOND FREEMAN,
> WILLIAM THOMAS,
> WILLIAM PADY,
> NATHANIELL SOUTHER.

The nexte year this long and tedious bussines came to some issue, as will then appeare, though not to a finall ende with all y⁶ parties; but this much for y⁶ presente.

I had forgoten to inserte in its place how y⁶ church here had invited and sent for Mʳ. Charles Chansey,[EH] a reverend, godly, and very larned man, intending upon triall to chose him pastor of y⁶ church hear, for y⁶ more comfortable performance of y⁶ ministrie with Mr. John Reinor, the teacher of the same. But ther fell out some differance aboute baptising, he holding it ought only to be by diping, and putting y⁶ whole body under water, and that sprinkling was unlawfull. The church yeelded that immersion, or diping, was lawfull, but in this could countrie not so conveniente. But they could not nor durst not yeeld to him in this, that sprinkling (which all y⁶ churches of Christ doe for y⁶ most parte use at this day) was unlawfull, & an humane invention, as y⁶ same was prest; but they were willing to yeeld to him as far as y⁶ʸ could, & to y⁶ utmost; and were contented to suffer him to practise as he was perswaded; and when he came to minister that ordnance, he might so doe it to any y' did desire it in y' way, provided he could peacably suffer Mr. Reinor, and such as desired to have theirs otherwise baptised by him, by sprinkling or powering on of water upon them; so as ther might be no disturbance in ye church hereaboute. But he said he could not yeeld herunto. Upon which the church procured some other ministers to dispute ye pointe with him publikly; as Mr. Ralfe Partrich, of Duxberie, who did it sundrie times, very ablie and sufficently, as allso some other ministers within this govermente. But he was not satisfied; so ye church sent to many other churches to crave their help and advise in [241] this mater, and, with his will & consente, sent them his arguments writen under his owne hand. They sente them to ye church at Boston in ye Bay of Massachusets, to be comunicated with other churches ther. Also they sent ye same to the churches of Conightecutt and New-Haven, with sundrie others; and received very able & suffcent answers, as they conceived, from them and their larned ministers, who all concluded against him. But him selfe was not satisfied therwth. Their answers are too large hear to relate. They conceived ye church had done what was meete in ye thing, so M^r. Chansey, having been ye most parte of 3. years here, removed him selfe to Sityate, wher he now remaines a minister to ye church ther. Also about these times, now y' catle & other things begane greatly to fall from their former rates, and persons begane to fall into more straits, and many being allready gone from them, (as is noted before,) both to Duxberie, Marshfeeld, and other places, & those of ye cheefe sorte, as M^r. Winslow, Captaine Standish, Mr. Allden, and many other, & stille some dropping away daly, and some at this time, and many more unsetled, it did greatly weaken ye place, and by reason of ye straitnes and barrennes of ye place, it sett ye thoughts of many upon removeall; as will appere more hereafter.

Anno Dom: 1642.

Marvilous it may be to see and consider how some kind of wickednes did grow & breake forth here, in a land wher the same was so much witnesed against, and so narrowly looked unto, & severly punished when it was knowne; as in no place more, or so much, that I have known or heard of; insomuch as they have been somewhat censured, even by moderate and good men, for their severitie in punishments. And yet all this could not suppress ye breaking out of sundrie notorious sins, (as this year, besids other, gives us too many sad presidents and instances,) espetially drunkennes and unclainnes; not only incontinencie betweene persons unmaried, for which many both men & women have been punished sharply enough, but some maried persons allso. But that which is worse, even sodomie and bugerie, (things fearfull to name,) have broak forth in this land, oftener then once. I say it may justly be marveled at, and cause us to fear & tremble at the consideration of our corrupte natures, which are so hardly bridled, subdued, & mortified; nay, cannot by any other means but ye powerfull worke & grace of Gods spirite. But (besids this) one reason may be, that ye Divell may carrie a greater spite against the churches of Christ and ye gospell hear, by how much ye more they indeaour to preserve holynes and puritie amongst them, and strictly punisheth the contrary when it ariseth either in church or comone wealth; that he might cast a [242] blemishe & staine upon them in ye eyes of [y^e] world, who use to be rash in judgmente. I would rather thinke thus, then that Satane hath more power in these heathen lands, as som have thought, then in more Christian nations, espetially over Gods servants in them.

2. An other reason may be, that it may be in this case as it is with waters when their streames are stopped or damed up, when they gett passage they flow with more violence, and make more noys and disturbance, then when they are suffered to rune quietly in their owne chanels. So wikednes being here more stopped by strict laws, and ye same more nerly looked unto, so as it cannot rune in a comone road of liberty as it would, and is inclined, it searches every wher, and at last breaks out wher it getts vente.

3. A third reason may be, hear (as I am verily perswaded) is not more evills in this kind, nor nothing nere so many by proportion, as in other places; but they are here more discoverd and seen, and

made publick by due serch, inquisition, and due punishment; for yᵉ churches looke narrowly to their members, and yᵉ magistrats over all, more strictly then in other places. Besids, here the people are but few in comparison of other places, which are full & populous, and lye hid, as it were, in a wood or thickett, and many horrible evills by yᵗ means are never seen nor knowne; wheras hear, they are, as it were, brought into yᵉ light, and set in yᵉ plaine feeld, or rather on a hill, made conspicuous to yᵉ veiw of all.

But to proceede; yᵉʳ came a letter from yᵉ Govʳ in yᵉ Bay to them here, touching matters of yᵉ forementioned nature, which because it may be usefull I shall hear relate it, and yᵉ passages ther aboute.

Sʳ: Having an opportunitie to signifie yᵉ desires of our Generall Court in toow things of spetiall importance, I willingly take this occasion to imparte them to you, yᵗ you may imparte them to yᵉ rest of your magistrats, and also to your Elders, for counsell; and give us your advise in them. The first is concerning heinous offences in point of uncleannes; yᵉ perticuler cases, with yᵉ circomstances, and yᵉ questions ther upon, you have hear inclosed. The 2. thing is concerning yᵉ Ilanders at Aquidnett; yᵗ seeing the cheefest of them are gone from us, in offences, either to churches, or comone welth, or both; others are dependants on them, and yᵉ best sorte are such as close with them in all their rejections of us. Neither is it only in a faction yᵗ they are devided from us, but in very deed they rend them selves from all yᵉ true churches of Christ, and, many of them, from all yᵉ powers of majestracie. We have had some experience hereof by some of their underworkers, or emissaries, who have latly come amongst us, and have made publick defiance against magistracie, ministrie, churches, & church covenants, &c. as antichristian; secretly also sowing yᵉ seeds of Familisme, and Anabaptistrie, to yᵉ infection of some, and danger of others; so that we are not willing to joyne with them in any league or confederacie at all, but rather that you would consider & advise with us how we may avoyd them, and keep ours from being infected by them. Another thing I should mention to you, for yᵉ maintenance of yᵉ trad of beaver; if ther be not a company to order it in every jurisdition among yᵉ English, which companies should agree in generall of their way in trade, I supose that ye trade will be overthrowne, and the Indeans will abuse us. For this cause we have latly put it into order amongst us, hoping of incouragmente from you (as we have had) y^t we may continue ye same. Thus not further to trouble you, I rest, with my loving remembrance to your selfe, &c.

Your loving friend,

RI: BELLINGHAM.

Boston, 28. (1.) 1642.

The note inclosed follows on ye other side.[E1]

[244] Worthy & beloved S^r:

Your letter (with ye questions inclosed) I have comunicated with our Assistants, and we have refered ye answer of them to such Rev^{ēd} Elders as are amongst us, some of whose answers thertoo we have here sent you inclosed, under their owne hands; from ye rest we have not yet received any. Our farr distance hath bene ye reason of this long delay, as also y^t they could not conferr their counsells togeather.

For our selves, (you know our breedings & abillities,) we rather desire light from your selves, & others, whom God hath better inabled, then to presume to give our judgments in cases so difficulte and of so high a nature. Yet under correction, and submission to better judgments, we propose this one thing to your prudent considerations. As it seems to us, in ye case even of willfull murder, that though a man did smite or wound an other, with a full pourpose or desire to kill him, (wch is murder in a high degree, before God,) yet if he did not dye, the magistrate was not to take away ye others life.[E1] So by proportion in other grosse & foule sines, though high attempts & nere approaches to ye same be made, and such as in the sight & account of God may be as ill as ye accomplishmente of ye foulest acts of y^t sine, yet we doute whether it may be safe for ye magistrate to proceed to death; we thinke, upon ye former grounds, rather he may not. As, for instance, in y^e

case of adultrie, (if it be admitted y' it is to be punished wth death, which to some of us is not cleare,) if ye body be not actually defiled, then death is not to be inflicted. So in sodomie, & beastialitie, if ther be not penetration. Yet we confess foulnes of circomstances, and frequencie in ye same, doth make us remaine in ye darke, and desire further light from you, or any, as God shall give.

As for ye 2. thing, concerning ye Ilanders? we have no conversing with them, nor desire to have, furder then necessitie or humanity may require.

And as for trade? we have as farr as we could ever therin held an orderly course, & have been sory to see ye spoyle therof by others, and fear it will hardly be recovered. But in these, or any other things which may concerne ye comone good, we shall be willing to advise & concure with you in what we may. Thus wth my love remembered to your selfe, and ye rest of our worthy friends, your Assistants, I take leave, & rest,

Your loving friend,

W. B.

Plim: 17. 3. month, 1642.

Now follows ye ministers answers. And first Mr. Reynors.

Qest: What sodmiticall acts are to be punished with death, & what very facte (ipso facto) is worthy of death, or, if ye fact it selfe be not capitall, what circomstances concurring may make it capitall?

Ans: In ye judiciall law (ye moralitie wherof concerneth us) it is manyfest y' carnall knowledg of man, or lying wth man, as with woman, cum penetratione corporis, was sodomie, to be punished with death; what els can be understood by Levit: 18. 22. & 20. 13. & Gen: 19. 5? 2^ly. It seems allso y' this foule sine might be capitall, though ther was not penitratio corporis, but only contactus & fricatio usq ad effusionem seminis, for these reasons: [245] 1. Because it was sin to be punished with death, Levit. 20. 13. in ye man who was lyen withall, as well as in him y' lyeth with him; now his sin is not mitigated wher ther is not penitration, nor augmented wher it is; wheras its charged upon y' women, y' they were guilty of this unnaturall sine, as well as men, Rom. 1. 26. 27. Y' same thing doth furder apeare, 2. because of y' proportion betwexte this sin & beastialitie, wherin if a woman did stand before, or aproach to, a beast, for y' end, to lye downe therto, (whether penetration was or not,) it was capitall, Levit: 18. 23. & 20. 16. 3'y. Because something els might be equivalent to penetration wher it had not been, viz. y' fore mentioned acts with frequencie and long continuance with a high hand, utterly extinguishing all light of nature; besids, full intention and bould attempting of y' foulest acts may seeme to have been capitall here, as well as coming presumptuously to slay with guile was capitall. Exod: 21. 14.

Yet it is not so manyfest y' y' same acts were to be punished with death in some other sines of uncleannes, w' yet by y' law of God were capitall crimes; besids other reasons, (1.) because sodomie, & also beastialitie, is more against y' light of nature then some other capitall crimes of unclainnes, which reason is to be attended unto, as y' which most of all made this sin capitall; (2.) because it might be comited with more secrecie & less suspition, & therfore needed y' more to be restrained & suppresed by y' law; (3'y) because ther was not y' like reason & degree of sining against family & posteritie in this sin as in some other capitall sines of uncleannes.

2. Quest: How farr a magistrate may extracte a confession from a delinquente, to acuse him selfe of a capitall crime, seeing Nemo tenetur prodere seipsum.

Ans: A majestrate cannot without sin neglecte diligente inquision into y' cause brought before him. Job 29. 16. Pro: 24. 11. 12. & 25. 2. (2'y.) If it be manifest y' a capitall crime is committed, & y' comone reporte, or probabilitie, suspition, or some complainte, (or y' like,) be of this or y' person, a magistrate ought to require, and by all due means to procure from y' person (so farr allready bewrayed) a naked confession of y' fact, as apears by y' which is morall & of perpetuall equitie, both in y' case of uncertaine murder, Deut: 21. 1.

9. and slander, Deut: 22. 13. 21; for though nemo tenetur prodere seipsum, yet by that wch may be known to ye magistrat by ye forenamed means, he is bound thus to doe, or els he may betray his countrie & people to ye heavie displeasure of God, Levit: 18. 24. 25. Jos: 22. 18. Psa: 106. 30; such as are inocente to ye sinfull, base, cruell lusts of ye profane, & such as are delinquents, and others with them, into ye hands of ye stronger temptations, & more bouldness, & hardnes of harte, to comite more & worse villany, besids all ye guilt & hurt he will bring upon him selfe. (3^{ly}.) To inflicte some punishmente meerly for this reason, to extracte a conffession of a capitall crime, is contrary to ye nature of vindictive justice, which always hath respecte to a know crime comitited by ye person punished; and it will therfore, for any thing which can before be knowne, be ye provocking and forcing of wrath, compared to ye wringing of ye nose, Pro: 30. 33. which is as well forbiden ye fathers of ye countrie as of ye family, Ephe. 6. 4. as produsing many sad & dangerous effects. That an oath (ex officio) for such a purpose is no due means, hath been abundantly proved by ye godly learned, & is well known.

Q. 3. In what cases of capitall crimes one witnes with other circomstances shall be sufficiente to convince? or is ther no conviction without 2. witneses?

Ans: In taking away ye life of man, one witnes alone will not suffice, ther must be tow, or y^t which is instar; ye texts are manifest, Numb: 35. 30. Deut: 17. 6. & 19. 15. 2^{ly}. Ther may be conviction by one witnes, & some thing y^t hath ye force of another, as ye evidencie of ye fact done by such an one, & not an other; unforced confession when ther was no fear or danger of suffering for ye fact, hand writings acknowledged & confessed.

JOHN REYNOR.

[246] *M^r. Partrich his writing, in ans: to ye questions.*

What is y^t sodomiticall acte which is to be punished with death?

Though I conceive probable y^t a voluntary effusion of seed per modum concubitus of man with man, as of a man with woman, though in concubitu ther be not penetratio corporis, is y^t sin which is forbiden, Levit: 18. 22. & adjudged to be punished with death, Levit: 20. 13. because, though ther be not penetratio corporis, yet ther may be similitudo concubitus muliebris, which is y^t the law specifieth; yet I dar not be con-[EK] (1.) because, Gen: 19. 5. ye intended acte of ye Sodomits (who were ye first noted maisters of this unnaturall act of more then brutish filthines) is expressed by carnall copulation of man with woman: Bring them out unto us, y^t we may know them; (2^{ly}.) because it is observed among ye nations wher this unnaturall unclainnes is comited, it is wth penetration of ye body; (3^{ly}.) because, in ye judiciall proceedings of ye judges in England, ye indict: so rune (as I have been informed).

Q. How farr may a magistrat extracte a confession of a capitall crime from a suspected and an accused person?

Ans. I conceive y^t a magistrate is bound, by carfull examenation of circomstances & waighing of probabilities, to sifte ye accused, and by force of argumente to draw him to an acknowledgment of ye truth; but he may not extracte a confession of a capitall crime from a suspected person by any violent means, whether it be by an oath imposed, or by any punishmente inflicted or threatened to be inflicted, for so he may draw forth an acknowledgmente of a crime from a fearfull inocente; if guilty, he shall be compelled to be his owne accuser, when no other can, which is against ye rule of justice.

Q. In what cases of capitall crimes one witnes with other circomstances shall be sufficente to convicte; or is ther no conviction without two witnesses?

Ans: I conceive y^t, in ye case of capitall crimes, ther can be no safe proceedings unto judgmente without too witnesses, as Numb: 35. 30. Deut: 19. 15. excepte ther can some evidence be prodused as aveilable & firme to prove ye facte as a witnes is, then one witnes may suffice; for therin ye end and equitie of ye law is attained. But to proceede unto sentence of death upon presumptions, wher probably ther may subesse falsum, though ther be y͏ᵉ testimony of one wittnes, I supose it cannot be a safe way; better for such a one to be held in safe custodie for further triall, I conceive.

RALPH PARTRICH.

The Answer of M͏ʳ. Charles Chancy.

An contactus et fricatio usq ad seminis effusiōnem sine penetratione corporis sit sodomia morte plectenda?

Q. The question is what sodomiticall acts are to be punished w͏ᵗʰ death, & what very facte committed, (ipso facto,) is worthy of death, or if y͏ᵉ facte it selfe be not capitall, what circomstances concuring may make it capitall. The same question may be asked of rape, inceste, beastialitie, unnaturall sins, presumtuous sins. These be y͏ᵉ words of y͏ᵉ first question.

Ans: The answer unto this I will lay downe (as God shall directe by his word & spirite) in these following conclusions: (1.) That y͏ᵉ judicials of Moyses, that are appendances to y͏ᵉ morall law, & grounded on y͏ᵉ law of nature, or y͏ᵉ decalogue, are imutable, and ppetuall, w͏ᶜʰ all orthodox devines acknowledge; see y͏ᵉ authors following. Luther, Tom. 1. Whitenberge: fol. 435. & fol. 7. Melanethon, in loc: com loco de conjugio. Calvin, 1. 4. Institu. c. 4. sect. 15. Junious de politia Moysis, thes. 29. & 30. Hen: Bulin: Decad. 3. sermo. 8. Wolf: Muscu. loc: com: in 6. precepti explicaci: Bucer de regno Christi, 1. 2. c. 17. Theo: Beza, vol: 1. de hereti: puniendis, fol. 154. Zanch: in 3. præcept: Ursin: Pt. 4. explicat. contra John. Piscat: in Aphorismi Loc. de lege dei aphorism. 17. And more might be added. I forbear, for brevities sake, to set downe their very words; this being y͏ᵉ constante & generall oppinion of y͏ᵉ best devines, I will rest in this as undoubtedly true, though much more might be said to confirme it.

2. That all y͏ᵉ sines mentioned in y͏ᵉ question were punished with death by y͏ᵉ judiciall law of Moyses, as adultry, Levit: 20. 10. Deut: 22. 22. Esech: 16. 38. Jhon. 8. 5. which is to be understood not only of double adultrie, when as both parties are maried, (as some

conceive,) but whosoever (besids her husband) lyes with a married woman, whether yᵉ man be maried or not, as in yᵉ place, Deut: 22. 22. or whosoever, being a maried man, lyeth with another woman (besids his wife), as P. Martire saith, loc: com: which in diverce respects maks yᵉ sine worse on yᵉ maried mans parte; for yᵉ Lord in this law hath respect as well to publick honesty, (the sin being so prejudicall to yᵉ church & state,) as yᵉ private wrongs (saith Junious). So incest is to be punished with death, Levit: 20. 11. 22. Beastiality likwise, Lev: 20. 15. Exod: 22. 19. Raps in like maner, Deut: 22. 25. Sodomie in like sort, Levit: 18. 22. & 20. 13. And all presumptuous sins, Numb: 15. 30. 31.

3. That yᵉ punishmente of these foule sines wᵗʰ death is grounded on yᵉ law of nature, & is agreeable to the morall law. (1.) Because yᵉ reasons anexed shew them to be perpetuall. Deut. 22. 22. So shalt thou put away evill. Incest, beastiality, are caled confusion, & wickednes. (2.) Infamie to yᵉ whole humane nature, Levit: 22. 12. Levit: 18. 23. Raps are as murder, Deut: 22. 25. Sodomie is an abomination, Levit: 22. 22. [247] No holier & juster laws can be devised by any man or angele then have been by yᵉ Judg of all yᵉ world, the wisdome of yᵉ Father, by whom kings doe raigne, &c. (3.) Because, before yᵉ giving of yᵉ Law, this punishmente was anciently practised, Gen: 26. 11. 38. 29. 39. 20. & even by the heathen, by yᵉ very light of nature, as P. Martire shews. (4ˡʸ.) Because yᵉ land is defiled by such sins, and spews out yᵉ inhabitants, Levit: 18. 24, 25. & that in regard of those nations yᵗ were not acquainted wᵗʰ the law of Moyses. 5. All yᵉ devins above specified consent in this, that yᵉ unclean acts punishable with death by yᵉ law of God are not only yᵉ grose acts of uncleannes by way of carnall copulation, but all yᵉ evidente attempts therof, which may appeare by those severall words yᵗ are used by yᵉ spirite of God, expressing yᵉ sins to be punished with death; as yᵉ discovering of nakednes, Levit: 18. 20. which is retegere pudenda, as parts pʳ euphemismum (saith Junius), or detegere ad cubandum (saith Willett), to uncover yᵉ shamefull parts of yᵉ body (saith Ainsworth), which, though it reaches to yᵉ grose acts, yet it is plaine it doth comprehend ye other foregoing immodest attempts, as contactum,

fricationem, &c.; likwise ye phrase of lying with, so often used, doth not only signifie carnall copulation, but other obscene acts, pᶜceding yᵉ same, is implyed in Pauls word [Greek: arsenokoitai], 1. Cor: 6. 9. & men lying with men, 1. Tim: 1. 9. men defiling them selves wᵗʰ mankind, men burning with lust towards men, Rom: 1. 26. & Levit: 18.[EL] 22. sodom & sin going after strange flesh, Jud: v. 7. 8. and lying with mankind as with a woman, Levit: 18. 22. Abulentis says yᵗ it signifies omnes modos quibus masculus masculo abutatur, changing yᵉ naturall use into yᵗ which is against nature, Rom: 1. 26. arrogare sibi cubare, as Junius well translats Levit: 20. 15. to give consente to lye withall, so approaching to a beast, & lying downe therto, Levit: 20. 16. ob solum conatú[EM] (saith Willett) or for going about to doe it. Add to this a notable speech of Zepperus de legibus (who hath enough to end controversies of this nature). L. 1. he saith: In crimine adulterii voluntas (understanding manifeste) sine effectu subsecuto de jure attenditur; and he proves it out of good laws, in these words: Solicitatores[EN] alienum nuptiām itemq matrimonīum interpellatores, etsi effectu sceleris potiri non possunt, propter voluntatem tamen perniciosæ libidinis extra ordinem puniuntur; nam generale est quidem affectū sine effectu [non] puniri, sed contrarium observatur in atrocioribus & horum similibus.

5. In concluding punishments from yᵉ judiciall law of Moyses yᵗ is perpetuall, we must often pᶜceed by analogicall proportion & interpretation, as a paribus similibus, minore ad majus, &c.; for ther will still fall out some cases, in every comone-wealth, which are not in so many words extante in holy write, yet yᵉ substance of yᵉ matter in every kind (I conceive under correction) may be drawne and concluded out of yᵉ scripture by good consequence of an equevalent nature; as, for example, ther is no express law against destroying conception in yᵉ wombe by potions, yet by anologie with Exod: 21. 22, 23. we may reason yᵗ life is to be given for life. Againe, yᵉ question, An contactus & fricatio, &c., and methinks yᵗ place Gen: 38. 9. in yᵉ punishmente of Onans sin, may give some cleare light to it; it was (saith Pareus) beluina crudelitas quam Deus pari loco cum parricidio habuit, nam semen corrumpere, quid fuit

aliud quam hominem ex semine generandum occidere? Propterea juste a Deo occisus est. Observe his words. And againe, Discamus quantopere Deus abominetur omnem seminis genitalis abusum, illicitā effusionem, & corruptionē, &c., very pertinente to this case. That allso is considerable, Deut: 25. 11, 12. God comanded yᵗ, if any wife drue nigh to deliver her husband out of yᵉ hand of him yᵗ smiteth him, &c., her hand should be cutt off. Yet such a woman in yᵗ case might say much for her selfe, yᵗ what she did was in trouble & perplexitie of her minde, & in her husbands defence; yet her hand must be cutt of for such impuritie (and this is morall, as I conceive). Then we may reason from yᵉ less to yᵉ greater, what greevous sin in yᵉ sight of God it is, by yᵉ instigation of burning lusts, set on fire of hell, to proceede to contactum & fricationem ad emissionem seminis, &c., & yᵗ contra naturam, or to attempte yᵉ grosse acts of unnaturall filthines. Againe, if yᵗ unnaturall lusts of men with men, or woman with woman, or either with beasts, be to be punished with death, then a pari naturall lusts of men towards children under age are so to be punished.

6. Circumstantiæ variant vis e actiunes, (saith yᵉ lawiers,) & circomstances in these cases cannot possibly be all reckēd up; but God hath given laws for those causes & cases that are of greatest momente, by which others are to be judged of, as in yᵉ differance betwixte chanc medley, & willfull murder; so in yᵉ sins of uncleannes, it is one thing to doe an acte of uncleannes by sudden temptation, & another to lye in waite for it, yea, to make a comune practise of it; this mightily augments & multiplies yᵉ sin. Againe, some sines of this nature are simple, others compound, as yᵗ is simple adultrie, or inceste, or simple sodomie; but when ther is a mixture of diverce kinds of lust, as when adultery & sodomie & pᵈditio seminis goe togeather in yᵉ same acte of uncleannes, this is capitall, double, & trible. Againe, when adultrie or sodomie is comited by pfessors or church members, I fear it coms too near yᵉ sine of yᵉ preists daughters, forbidden, & comanded to be punished, Levit: 21. 9. besids yᵉ presumption of yᵉ sines of such. Againe, when uncleannes is comited with those whose chastity they are

bound to p'serve, this coms very nere the incestious copulation, I feare; but I must hasten to yͤ other questions.

[248] 2. Question yͤ second, upon yͤ pointe of examination, how farr a magistrate may extracte a confession from a delinquente to accuse him selfe in a capitall crime, seeing Nemo tenetur prodere seipsum.

Ans: The words of yͤ question may be understood of extracting a confession from a delinquente either by oath or bodily tormente. If it be mente of extracting by requiring an oath, (ex officio, as some call it,) & that in capitall crimes, I fear it is not safe, nor warented by Gods word, to extracte a confession from a delinquente by an oath in matters of life and death. (1.) Because yͤ practise in yͤ Scripturs is other wise, as in yͤ case of Achan, Jos: 7. 19. Give, I pray yͤ, glorie to yͤ Lord God of Israll, and make a confession to him, & tell me how thou hast done. He did not compell him to sweare. So when as Johnathans life was indangered, 1. Sam. 14. 43. Saule said unto Johnathan, Tell me what thou hast done; he did not require an oath. And notable is yͭ, Jer: 38. 14. Jeremiah was charged by Zedechias, who said, I will aske the a thing, hide it not from me; & Jeremiah said, If I declare it unto yͤ, wilt thou not surely put me to death? impling yͭ, in case of death, he would have refused to answer him. (2.) Reason shews it, & experience; Job: 2. 4. Skin for skin, &c. It is to be feared yͭ those words (whatsoever a man hath) will comprehend also yͤ conscience of an oath, and yͤ fear of God, and all care of religion; therfore for laying a snare before yͤ guiltie, I think it ought not to be donn. But now, if yͤ question be mente of inflicting bodyly torments to extracte a confession from a mallefactor, I conceive yͭ in maters of higest consequence, such as doe conceirne yͤ saftie or ruine of stats or countries, magistrats may proceede so farr to bodily torments, as racks, hote-irons, &c., to extracte a conffession, espetially wher presumptions are strounge; but otherwise by no means. God sometims hids a sinner till his wickednes is filled up.

Question 3. In what cases of capitall crimes, one witnes with other circumstances shall be sufficente to convicte, or is ther no conviction without 2. witnesses?

Deut: 19. 25. God hath given an express rule yᵗ in no case one witness shall arise in judgmente, espetially not in capitall cases. God would not put our lives into yᵉ power of any one toungue. Besids, by yᵉ examination of more wittneses agreeing or disagreeing, any falshood ordenarilly may be discovered; but this is to be understood of one witnes of another; but if a man witnes against him selfe, his owne testimony is sufficente, as in yᵉ case of yᵉ Amalakite, 2. Sam: 1. 16. Againe, when ther are sure & certaine signes & evidences by circumstances, ther needs no witnes in this case, as in yᵉ bussines of Adoniah desiring Abishage yᵉ Shunamite to wife, that therby he might make way for him selfe unto yᵉ kingdome, 1. King: 2. 23, 24. Againe, probably by many concurring circumstances, if probability may have yᵉ strength of a witnes, somthing may be this way gathered, me thinks, from Sallomons judging betweexte yᵉ true mother, and yᵉ harlote, 1. King. 3. 25. Lastly, I see no cause why in waighty matters, in defecte of witneses & other proofes, we may not have recourse to a lott, as in yᵉ case of Achan, Josu: 7. 16. which is a clearer way in such doubtfull cases (it being solemnely & religiously performed) then any other that I know, if it be made yᵉ last refuge. But all this under correction.

The Lord in mercie directe & prosper yᵉ desires of his servants that desire to walk before him in truth & righteousnes in the administration of justice, and give them wisdome and largnes of harte.

CHARLES CHANNCY.

Besids yᵉ occation before mentioned in these writings concerning the abuse of those 2. children, they had aboute yᵉ same time a case of buggerie fell out amongst them, which occasioned these questions, to which these answers have been made.

And after y⁰ time of y⁰ writĩg of these things befell a very sadd accidente of the like foule nature in this governmente, this very year, which I shall now relate. Ther was a youth whose name was Thomas Granger; he was servant to an honest man of Duxbery, being aboute 16. or 17. years of age. (His father & mother lived at the same time at Sityate.) He was this year detected of buggery (and indicted for y⁰ same) with a mare, a cowe, tow goats, five sheep, 2. calves, and a turkey. Horrible [249] it is to mention, but y⁰ truth of y⁰ historie requires it. He was first discovered by one y¹ accidentally saw his lewd practise towards the mare. (I forbear perticulers.) Being upon it examined and comitted, in y⁰ end he not only confest y⁰ fact with that beast at that time, but sundrie times before, and at severall times with all y⁰ rest of y⁰ forenamed in his indictmente; and this his free-confession was not only in private to y⁰ magistrats, (though at first he strived to deney it,) but to sundrie, both ministers & others, and afterwards, upon his indictmente, to y⁰ whole court & jury; and confirmed it at his execution. And wheras some of y⁰ sheep could not so well be knowne by his description of them, others with them were brought before him, and he declared which were they, and which were not. And accordingly he was cast by y⁰ jury, and condemned, and after executed about y⁰ 8. of Sept, 1642. A very sade spectakle it was; for first the mare, and then y⁰ cowe, and y⁰ rest of y⁰ lesser catle, were kild before his face, according to y⁰ law, Levit: 20. 15. and then he him selfe was executed. The catle were all cast into a great & large pitte that was digged of purposs for them, and no use made of any part of them.

Upon y⁰ examenation of this person, and also of a former that had made some sodomiticall attempts upon another, it being demanded of them how they came first to y⁰ knowledge and practice of such wickednes, the one confessed he had long used it in old England; and this youth last spoaken of said he was taught it by an other that had heard of such things from some in England when he was ther, and they kept catle togeather. By which it appears how one wicked person may infecte many; and what care all ought to have what servants they bring into their families.

But it may be demanded how came it to pass that so many wicked persons and profane people should so quickly come over into this land, & mixe them selves amongst them? seeing it was religious men yᵗ begane yᵉ work, and they came for religions sake. I confess this may be marveilled at, at least in time to come, when the reasons therof should not be knowne; and yᵉ more because here was so many hardships and wants mett withall. I shall therfore indeavor to give some answer hereunto. And first, according to yᵗ in yᵉ gospell, it is ever to be remembred that wher yᵉ Lord begins to sow good seed, ther yᵉ envious man will endeavore to sow tares. 2. Men being to come over into a wildernes, in which much labour & servise was to be done aboute building & planting, &c., such as wanted help in yᵗ respecte, when they could not have such as yᵉʸ would, were glad to take such as they could; and so, many untoward servants, sundry of them proved, that were thus brought over, both men & women kind: who, when their times were expired, became families of them selves, which gave increase hereunto. 3. An other and a maine reason hearof was, that men, finding so many godly disposed persons willing to come into these parts, some begane to make a trade of it, to transeport passengers & their goods, and hired ships for that end; and then, to make up their fraight and advance their profite, cared not who yᵉ persons were, so they had money to pay them. And by this means the cuntrie became pestered with many unworthy persons, who, being come over, crept into one place or other. 4. Againe, the Lords blesing usually following his people, as well in outward as spirituall things, (though afflictions be mixed withall,) doe make many to adhear to yᵉ people of God, as many followed Christ, for yᵉ loaves sake, John 6. 26. and a mixed multitud came into yᵉ willdernes with yᵉ people of God out of Eagipte of old, Exod. 12. 38; so allso ther were sente by their freinds some under hope yᵗ they would be made better; others that they might be eased of such burthens, and they kept from shame at home yᵗ would necessarily follow their dissolute courses. And thus, by one means or other, in 20. years time, it is a question whether yᵉ greater part be not growne yᵉ worser.

[250] I am now come to yᵉ conclusion of that long & tedious bussines betweene yᵉ partners hear, & them in England, the which I shall manifest by their owne letters as followeth, in such parts of them as are pertinente to yᵉ same.

Mʳ. Sherleys to Mʳ. Attwood.

Mʳ. Attwood, my approved loving friend: Your letter of yᵉ 18. of October last I have received, wherin I find you have taken a great deall of paines and care aboute yᵗ troublesome bussines betwixte our Plimoth partners & freinds, & us hear, and have deeply ingaged your selfe, for which complements & words are no reall satisfaction, &c. For yᵉ agreemente you have made with Mʳ. Bradford, Mʳ. Winslow, & yᵉ rest of yᵉ partners ther, considering how honestly and justly I am perswaded they have brought in an accounte of yᵉ remaining stock, for my owne parte I am well satisfied, and so I thinke is Mʳ. Andrewes, and I supose will be Mʳ. Beachampe, if most of it might acrew to him, to whom yᵉ least is due, &c. And now for peace sake, and to conclud as we began, lovingly and freindly, and to pass by all failings of all, the conclude is accepted of; I say this agreemente yᵗ you have made is condesended unto, and Mʳ. Andrews hath sent his release to Mʳ. Winthrop, with such directions as he conceives fitt; and I have made bould to trouble you with mine, and we have both sealed in yᵉ presence of Mʳ. Weld, and Mʳ. Peeters, and some others, and I have also sente you an other, for the partners ther, to seale to me; for you must not deliver mine to them, excepte they seale & deliver one to me; this is fitt and equall, &c.

Yours to comand in what I may or can,

JAMES SHERLEY.

June 14. 1642.

His to yᵉ partners as followeth.

Loving freinds,

M^r. Bradford, M^r. Winslow, M^r. Prence, Captaine Standish, M^r. Brewster, M^r. Alden, & M^r. Howland, give me leave to joyne you all in one letter, concerning ye finall end & conclude of y^t tedious & troublsome bussines, & I thinke I may truly say uncomfurtable & unprofitable to all, &c. It hath pleased God now to put us upon a way to sease all suits, and disquieting of our spirites, and to conclude with peace and love, as we began. I am contented to yeeld & make good what M^r. Attwood and you have agreed upon; and for y^t end have sente to my loving friend, M^r. Attwood, an absolute and generall release unto you all, and if ther wante any thing to make it more full, write it your selves, & it shall be done, provided y^t all you, either joyntly or severally, seale ye like discharge to me. And for y^t end I have drawne one joyntly, and sent it to M^r. Attwood, with y^t I have sealed to you. Mr. Andrews hath sealed an aquitance also, & sent it to M^r. Winthrop, whith such directions as he conceived fitt, and, as I hear, hath given his debte, which he maks 544^{li}. unto ye gentlemen of ye Bay. Indeed, M^r. Welld, M^r. Peters, & M^r. Hibbens have taken a great deale of paines with M^r. Andrews, M^r. Beachamp, & my selfe, to bring us to agree, and to y^t end we have had many meetings and spent much time aboute it. But as they are very religious & honest gentle-men, yet they had an end y^t they drove at & laboured to accomplish (I meane not any private end, but for ye generall good of their patente). It had been very well you had sent one over. M^r. Andrew wished you might have one 3. parte of ye 1200^{li}. & the Bay 2. thirds; but then we 3. must have agreed togeather, which were a hard mater now. But M^r. Weld, M^r. Peters, & M^r. Hibbens, & I, have agreed, they giving you bond (so to compose with M^r. Beachamp, as) to procure his generall release, & free you from all trouble & charge y^t he may put you too; which indeed is nothing, for I am perswaded M^r. Weld will in time gaine him to give them all that is dew to [251] him, which in some sorte is granted allready; for though his demands be great, yet M^r. Andrewes hath taken some paines in it, and makes it appear to be less then I thinke he will consente to give them for so good an use; so you neede not fear, that for taking bond ther to save you harmles, you be safe and well. Now our accord is, y' you must pay to y⁰ gentle-men of y⁰ Bay 900ˡⁱ.; they are to bear all chargs yᵗ may any way arise concerning y⁰ free & absolute clearing of you from us three. And you to have y⁰ other 300ˡⁱ. &c.

Upon y⁰ receiving of my release from you, I will send you your bonds for y⁰ purchass money. I would have sent them now, but I would have Mʳ. Beachamp release as well as I, because you are bound to him in them. Now I know if a man be bound to 12. men, if one release, it is as if all released, and my discharge doth cutt them of; wherfore doubte you not but you shall have them, & your commission, or any thing els that is fitt. Now you know ther is tow years of y⁰ purchass money, that I would not owne, for I have formerley certified you yᵗ would but pay 7. years; but now you are discharged of all, &c.

Your loving and kind friend in what I may or can,

JAMES SHERLEY.

June 14. 1642.

The coppy of his release is as followeth.

Wheras diverce questions, differences, & demands have arisen & depended betweene William Bradford, Edward Winslow, Thomas Prence, Mylest Standish, William Brewster, John Allden, and John Howland, gent: now or latly inhabitants or resident at New-Plimoth, in New-England, on y⁰ one party, and James Sherley of London, marchante, and others, in th' other parte, for & concerning a stocke & partable trade of beaver & other comodities, and fraighting of ships, as y⁰ White Angell, Frindship, or others, and y⁰ goods of Isaack Allerton which were seazed upon by vertue of a leter of atturney made by y⁰ said James Sherley and John Beachamp and Richard Andrews, or any other maters concerning y⁰ said trade, either hear in Old-England or ther in New-England or elsewher, all which differences are since by mediation of freinds composed, compremissed, and all y⁰ said parties agreed. Now know all men by these presents, that I, the said James Sherley, in performance of y⁰ said compremise & agreemente, have remised, released, and quite claimed, & doe by these presents remīse, release, and for me, myne heires, executors, & Administrators, and for every of us, for ever quite claime unto y⁰ said William Bradford, Edward Winslow, Thomas Prence, Myles Standish, William Brewster, John Allden, & John Howland, and every of them, their & every of their heires, executors, and administrators, all and all maner of actions, suits, debts, accounts, rekonings, comissions, bonds, bills, specialties, judgments, executions, claimes, challinges, differences, and demands whatsoever, with or against y⁰ said William Bradford, Edward Winslow, Thomas Prence, Myles Standish, William Brewster, John Allden, and John Howland, or any of them, ever I had, now have, or in time to come can, shall, or may have, for any mater, cause, or thing whatsoever from y⁰ begining of y⁰ world untill y⁰ day of y⁰ date of these presents. In witnes wherof I have hereunto put my hand & seale, given the second day of June, 1642, and in y⁰ eighteenth year of y⁰ raigne of our soveraigne lord, king Charles, &c.

JAMES SHERLEY.

Sealed and delivered
in y⁰ presence of

> THOMAS WELD,
> HUGH PETERS,
> WILLIAM HIBBINS.
> ARTHUR TIRREY, Scr.
> THO: STURGS, his servante.

Mʳ. Andrews his discharg was to y⁰ same effecte; he was by agreemēte to have 500ˡⁱ. of y⁰ money, the which he gave to them in y⁰ Bay, who brought his discharge and demanded y⁰ money. And they tooke in his release and paid y⁰ money according to agreemēte, viz. one third of the 500ˡⁱ. they paid downe in hand, and y⁰ rest in 4. equall payments, to be paid yearly, for which they gave their bonds. And wheras 44ˡⁱ. was more demanded, they conceived they could take it of with M^r. Andrews, and therfore it was not in the bonde. [252] But M^r. Beachamp would not parte with any of his, but demanded 400^{li}. of ye partners here, & sent a release to a friend, to deliver it to them upon ye receite of ye money. But his relese was not perfecte, for he had left out some of ye partners names, with some other defects; and besids, the other gave them to understand he had not near so much due. So no end was made with him till 4. years after; of which in it plase. And in y^t regard, that them selves did not agree, I shall inserte some part of M^r. Andrews letter, by which he conceives ye partners here were wronged, as followeth. This leter of his was write to M^r. Edmond Freeman, brother in law to M^r. Beachamp.

M^r. Freeman,

My love remembred unto you, &c. I then certified ye partners how I found M^r. Beachamp & M^r. Sherley, in their perticuler demands, which was according to mens principles, of getting what they could; allthough ye one will not shew any accounte, and ye other a very unfaire and unjust one; and both of them discouraged me from sending ye partners my accounte, M^r. Beachamp espetially. Their reason, I have cause to conceive, was, y^t allthough I doe not, nor ever intended to, wrong ye partners or ye bussines, yet, if I gave no accounte, I might be esteemed as guiltie as they, in some degree at least; and they might seeme to be ye more free from taxation in not delivering their accounts, who have both of them charged ye accounte with much intrest they have payed forth, and one of them would likwise for much intrest he hath not paid forth, as appeareth by his accounte, &c. And seeing ye partners have now made it appear y^t ther is 1200^{li}. remaining due between us all, and that it may appear by my accounte I have not charged ye bussines with any intrest, but doe forgive it unto ye partners, above 200^{li}. if M^r. Sherley & M^r. Beachamp, who have betweene them wronged ye bussines so many 100^{li}. both in principall & intrest likwise, and have therin wronged me as well and as much as any of ye partners; yet if they will not make & deliver faire & true accounts of ye same, nor be contente to take what by computation is more then can be justly due to either, that is, to M^r. Beachamp 150^{li}. as by M^r.

Allertons accounte, and M^r. Sherleys accounte, on oath in chancerie; and though ther might be nothing due to M^r. Sherley, yet he requirs 100^{li}. &c. I conceive, seing ye partners have delivered on their oaths ye sume remaining in their hands, that they may justly detaine ye 650^{li}. which may remaine in their hands, after I am satisfied, untill M^r. Sherley & M^r. Beachamp will be more fair & just in their ending, &c. And as I intend, if ye partners fayrly end with me, in satisfing in parte and ingaging them selves for ye rest of my said 544^{li}. to returne back for ye poore my parte of ye land at Sityate, so likwise I intend to relinquish my right & intrest in their dear patente, on which much of our money was laid forth, and also my right & intrest in their cheap purchass, the which may have cost me first & last 350^{li}.^[EO] But I doubte whether other men have not charged or taken on accounte what they have disbursed in ye like case, which I have not charged, neither did I conceive any other durst so doe, untill I saw ye accounte of the one and heard ye words of ye other; the which gives me just cause to suspecte both their accounts to be unfaire; for it seemeth they consulted one with another aboute some perticulers therin. Therfore I conceive ye partners ought ye rather to require just accounts from each of them before they parte with any money to either of them. For marchants understand how to give an acounte; if they mean fairley, they will not deney to give an accounte, for they keep memorialls to helpe them to give exacte acounts in all perticulers, and memoriall cannot forget his charge, if ye man will remember. I desire not to wrong M^r. Beachamp or M^r. Sherley, nor may be silente in such apparente probabilities of their wronging ye partners, and me likwise, either in deneying to deliver or shew any accounte, or in delivering one very unjuste in some perticulers, and very suspitious in many more; either of which, being from understanding marchants, cannot be from weaknes or simplisitie, and therfore ye more unfaire. So comending you & yours, and all ye Lord's people, unto ye gratious protection and blessing of ye Lord, and rest your loving friend,

RICHARD ANDREWES.

Aprill 7. 1643.

This leter was write yᵉ year after yᵉ agreement, as doth appear; and what his judgmente was herein, yᵉ contents doth manifest, and so I leave it to yᵉ equall judgmente of any to consider, as they see cause.

Only I shall adde what Mʳ. Sherley furder write in a leter of his, about yᵉ same time, and so leave this bussines. His is as followeth on yᵉ other side.[EP]

[253] Loving freinds, Mʳ. Bradford, Mʳ. Winslow, Cap: Standish, Mʳ. Prence, and yᵉ rest of yᵉ partners wᵗʰ you; I shall write this generall leter to you all, hoping it will be a good conclude of a generall, but a costly & tedious bussines I thinke to all, I am sure to me, &c.

I received from Mʳ. Winslow a letter of yᵉ 28. of Sept: last, and so much as concernes yᵉ generall bussines I shall answer in this, not knowing whether I shall have opportunitie to write perticuler letters, &c. I expected more letters from you all, as some perticuler writs,[EQ] but it seemeth no fitt opportunity was offered. And now, though yᵉ bussines for yᵉ maine may stand, yet some perticulers is alltered; I say my former agreemente with Mʳ. Weld & Mʳ. Peters, before they[ER] could conclude or gett any grante of Mʳ. Andrews, they sought to have my release; and ther upon they sealed me a bond for a 110ˡⁱ. So I sente my acquittance, for they said without mine ther would be no end made (& ther was good reason for it). Now they hoped, if yᵉʸ ended with me, to gaine Mʳ. Andrews parte, as they did holy, to a pound, (at which I should wonder, but yᵗ I observe some passages,) and they also hoped to have gotten Mʳ. Beachamps part, & I did thinke he would have given it them. But if he did well understand him selfe, & that acounte, he would give it; for his demands make a great sound.[ES] But it seemeth he would not parte with it, supposing it too great a sume, and yᵗ he might easily gaine it from you. Once he would have given them 40ˡⁱ. but now they say he will not doe that, or rather I suppose they will not take it; for if they doe, & have Mʳ. Andrewses, then they must pay me their bond of 110ˡⁱ. 3 months hence. Now it will fall out farr better for you, y^t they deal not with Mr. Beachamp, and also for me, if you be as kind to me as I have been & will be to you; and y^t thus, if you pay M^r. Andrews, or ye Bay men, by his order, 544^{li}. which is his full demande; but if looked into, perhaps might be less. The man is honest, & in my conscience would not wittingly doe wronge, yett he may forgett as well as other men; and M^r. Winslow may call to minde wherin he forgetts; (but some times it is good to buy peace.) The gentlemen of ye Bay may abate 100^{li}. and so both sids have more right & justice then if they exacte all, &c. Now if you send me a 150^{li}. then say M^r. Andrews full sume, & this, it is nere 700^{li}. M^r. Beachamp he demands 400^{li}. and we all know that, if a man demands money, he must shew wherfore, and make proofe of his debte; which I know he can never make good proafe of one hunderd pound dew unto him as principall money; so till he can, you have good reason to keep ye 500^{li}. &c. This I proteste I write not in malice against M^r. Beachamp, for it is a reall truth. You may partly see it by M^r. Andrews making up his accounte, and I think you are all perswaded I can say more then M^r. Andrews concerning that accounte. I wish I could make up my owne as plaine & easily, but because of former discontents, I will be sparing till I be called; & you may injoye ye 500^{li}. quietly till he begine; for let him take his course hear or ther, it shall be all one, I will doe him no wronge; and if he have not on peney more, he is less loser then either M^r. Andrews or I. This I conceive to be just & honest; ye having or not having of his release matters not; let him make such proafe of his debte as you cannot disprove, and according to your first agreemente you will pay it, &c.

Your truly affectioned friend,

JAMES SHERLEY.

London, Aprill 27. 1643.

Anno Dom: 1643.

I am to begine this year whith that which was a mater of great saddnes and moūring unto them all. Aboute yᵉ 18. of Aprill dyed their Reveᵈ Elder, and my dear & loving friend, Mʳ. William Brewster; a man that had done and suffered much for yᵉ Lord Jesus and yᵉ gospells sake, and had bore his parte in well and woe with this poore persecuted church above 36. years [254] in England, Holand, and in this wildernes, and done yᵉ Lord & them faithfull service in his place & calling. And notwithstanding yᵉ many troubls and sorrows he passed throw, the Lord upheld him to a great age. He was nere fourskore years of age (if not all out) when he dyed. He had this blesing added by yᵉ Lord to all yᵉ rest, to dye in his bed, in peace, amongst yᵉ mids of his freinds, who mourned & wepte over him, and ministered what help & comforte they could unto him, and he againe recomforted them whilst he could. His sicknes was not long, and till yᵉ last day therof he did not wholy keepe his bed. His speech continued till somewhat more then halfe a day, & then failed him; and aboute 9. or 10. a clock that evīng he dyed, without any pangs at all. A few howers before, he drew his breath shorte, and some few minuts before his last, he drew his breath long, as a man falen into a sound slepe, without any pangs or gaspings, and so sweetly departed this life unto a better.

I would now demand of any, what he was yᵉ worse for any former sufferings? What doe I say, worse? Nay, sure he was yᵉ better, and they now added to his honour. *It is a manifest token* (saith yᵉ Apostle, 2. Thes: 1. 5, 6, 7.) *of yᵉ righeous judgmente of God that you may be counted worthy of yᵉ kingdome of God, for which ye allso suffer; seing it is a righteous thing with God to recompence tribulation to them yᵗ trouble you: and to you who are troubled, rest with us, when yᵉ Lord Jesus shall be revealed from heaven, with his mighty angels.* 1. Pet. 4. 14. *If you be reproached for yᵉ name of Christ, hapy are ye, for yᵉ spirite of glory and of God resteth upon you.* What though he wanted yᵉ riches and pleasurs of yᵉ world in this life, and pompous monuments at his funurall? yet yᵉ memoriall of yᵉ just shall be blessed, when yᵉ name of yᵉ wicked shall rott (with their marble monuments). Pro: 10. 7.

I should say something of his life, if to say a litle were not worse then to be silent. But I cannot wholy forbear, though hapily more may be done hereafter. After he had attained some learning, viz. yᵉ knowledg of yᵉ Latine tongue, & some insight in yᵉ Greeke, and spent some small time at Cambridge, and then being first seasoned with yᵉ seeds of grace and vertue, he went to yᵉ Courte, and served that religious and godly gentlman, Mʳ. Davison, diverce years, when he was Secretary of State; who found him so discreete and faithfull as he trusted him above all other that were aboute him, and only imployed him in all matters of greatest trust and secrecie. He esteemed him rather as a sonne then a servante, and for his wisdom & godlines (in private) he would converse with him more like a freind & familier then a maister. He attended his mʳ. when he was sente in ambassage by the Queene into yᵉ Low-Countries, in yᵉ Earle of Leicesters time, as for other waighty affaires of state, so to receive possession of the cautionary townes, and in token & signe therof the keyes of Flushing being delivered to him, in her maᵗⁱˢ name, he kepte them some time, and comitted them to this his servante, who kept them under his pilow, on which he slepte yᵉ first night. And, at his returne, yᵉ States honoured him with a gould chaine, and his maister comitted it to him, and comanded him to wear it when they arrived in England, as they ridd thorrow the country, till they came to yᵉ Courte. He afterwards remained with him till his troubles, that he was put from his place aboute yᵉ death of yᵉ Queene of Scots; and some good time after, doeing him manie faithfull offices of servise in yᵉ time of his troubles. Afterwards he wente and lived in yᵉ country, in good esteeme amongst his freinds and yᵉ gentle-men of those parts, espetially the godly & religious. He did much good in yᵉ countrie wher he lived, in promoting and furthering religion, not only by his practiss & example, and provocking and incouraging of others, but by procuring of good preachers to yᵉ places theraboute, and, drawing on of others to assiste & help forward in such a worke; he him selfe most comonly deepest in yᵉ charge, & some times above his abillitie. And in this state he continued many years, doeing yᵉ best good he could, and walking according to yᵉ light he saw, till yᵉ Lord reveiled further unto him. And in yᵉ end, by yᵉ tirrany of yᵉ bishops against godly preachers & people, in silenceing the one & persecuting yᵉ other, he and many more of those times begane to looke further into things, and to see into yᵉ unlawfullnes of their callings, and yᵉ burthen of many anti-christian corruptions, which both he and they endeavored to cast of; as yᵉʸ allso did, as in yᵉ begining of this treatis is to be seene. [255] After they were joyned togither in comunion, he was a spetiall stay & help unto them. They ordinarily mett at his house on yᵉ Lords day, (which was a manor of yᵉ bishops,) and with great love he entertained them when they came, making provission for them to his great charge. He was yᵉ cheefe of those that were taken at Boston, and suffered yᵉ greatest loss; and of yᵉ seven that were kept longst in prison, and after bound over to yᵉ assises. Affter he came into Holland he suffered much hardship, after he had spente yᵉ most of his means, haveing a great charge, and many children; and, in regard of his former breeding & course of life, not so fitt for many imployments as others were, espetially such as were toylesume & laborious. But yet he ever bore his condition with much cherfullnes and contentation. Towards yᵉ later parte of those 12. years spente in Holland, his outward condition was mended, and he lived well & plentifully; for he fell into a way (by reason he had yᵉ Latine tongue) to teach many students, who had a disire to lerne yᵉ English tongue, to teach them English; and by his method they quickly attained it with great facilitie; for he drew rules to lerne it by, after yᵉ Latine maner; and many gentlemen, both Danes & Germans, resorted to him, as they had time from other studies, some of them being great mens sones. He also had means to set up printing, (by yᵉ help of some freinds,) and so had imploymente inoughg, and by reason of many books which would not be alowed to be printed in England, they might have had more then they could doe. But now removeing into this countrie, all these things were laid aside againe, and a new course of living must be framed unto; in which he was no way unwilling to take his parte, and to bear his burthen with yᵉ rest, living many times without bread, or corne, many months together, having many times nothing but fish, and often wanting that also; and drunke nothing but water for many years togeather, yea, till within 5. or 6. years of his death. And yet he lived (by y⁰ blessing of God) in health till very old age. And besids yᵗ, he would labour with his hands in y⁰ feilds as long as he was able; yet when the church had no other minister, he taught twise every Saboth, and yᵗ both powerfully and profitably, to y⁰ great contentment of y⁰ hearers, and their comfortable edification; yea, many were brought to God by his ministrie. He did more in this behalfe in a year, then many that have their hundreds a year doe in all their lives. For his personall abilities, he was qualified above many; he was wise and discreete and well spoken, having a grave & deliberate utterance, of a very cherfull spirite, very sociable & pleasante amongst his freinds, of an humble and modest mind, of a peaceable disposition, under vallewing him self & his owne abilities, and some time over valewing others; inoffencive and inocente in his life & conversation, wᶜʰ gained him y⁰ love of those without, as well as those within; yet he would tell them plainely of their faults & evills, both publickly & privatly, but in such a maner as usually was well taken from him. He was tender harted, and compassionate of such as were in miserie, but espetialy of such as had been of good estate and ranke, and were fallen unto want & poverty, either for goodnes & religions sake, or by y⁰ injury & oppression of others; he would say, of all men these deserved to be pitied most. And none did more offend & displease him then such as would hautily and proudly carry & lift up themselves, being rise from nothing, and haveing litle els in them to comend them but a few fine cloaths, or a litle riches more then others. In teaching, he was very moving & stirring of affections, also very plaine & distincte in what he taught; by which means he became y⁰ more profitable to y⁰ hearers. He had a singuler good gift in prayer, both publick & private, in ripping up y⁰ hart & conscience before God, in the humble confession of sinne, and begging y⁰ mercies of God in Christ for y⁰ pardon of y⁰ same. He always thought it were better for ministers to pray oftener, and devide their prears, then be longe & tedious in the same (excepte upon sollemne & spetiall occations, as in days of humiliation & y⁰ like). His reason was, that y⁰ harte & spirits of all, espetialy yᵉ weake, could hardly continue & stand bente (as it were) so long towards God, as they ought to doe in yᵗ duty, without flagging and falling of. For yᵉ govermente of yᵉ church, (which was most [256] proper to his office,) he was carfull to preserve good order in yᵉ same, and to preserve puritie, both in yᵉ doctrine & comunion of yᵉ same; and to supress any errour or contention that might begine to rise up amongst them; and accordingly God gave good success to his indeavors herein all his days, and he saw yᵉ fruite of his labours in that behalfe. But I must breake of, having only thus touched a few, as it were, heads of things.

I cannot but here take occasion, not only to mention, but greatly to admire yᵉ marvelous providence of God, that notwithstanding yᵉ many changes and hardships that these people wente throwgh, and yᵉ many enemies they had and difficulties they mette with all, that so many of them should live to very olde age! It was not only this reveᵈ mans condition, (for one swallow maks no summer, as they say,) but many more of them did yᵉ like, some dying aboute and before this time, and many still living, who attained to 60. years of age, and to 65. diverse to 70. and above, and some nere 80. as he did. It must needs be more then ordinarie, and above naturall reason, that so it should be; for it is found in experience, that chaing of aeir, famine, or unholsome foode, much drinking of water, sorrows & troubls, &c., all of them are enimies to health, causes of many diseaces, consumers of naturall vigoure and yᵉ bodys of men, and shortners of life. And yet of all these things they had a large parte, and suffered deeply in yᵉ same. They wente from England to Holand, wher they found both worse air and dyet then that they came from; from thence (induring a long imprisonmente, as it were, in yᵉ ships at sea) into New-England; and how it hath been with them hear hath allready beene showne; and what crosses, troubls, fears, wants, and sorrowes they had been lyable unto, is easie to conjecture; so as in some sorte they may say with yᵉ Apostle, 2. Cor: 11. 26, 27. they were *in journeyings often, in perils of waters, in perills of robers, in perills of their owne nation, in perils among yᵉ heathen, in perills in yᵉ willdernes, in perills in yᵉ sea, in perills among false breethern; in wearines & painfullnes, in watching often, in hunger and thirst, in fasting often, in could and nakednes.* What was it then that upheld them? It was Gods vissitation that preserved their spirits. Job 10. 12. *Thou hast given me life and grace, and thy vissitation hath preserved my spirite.* He that upheld yᵉ Apostle upheld them. *They were persecuted, but not forsaken, cast downe, but perished not.* 2. Cor: 4. 9. *As unknowen, and yet knowen; as dying, and behold we live; as chastened, and yett not kiled.* 2. Cor: 6. 9. God, it seems, would have all men to behold and observe such mercies and works of his providence as these are towards his people, that they in like cases might be incouraged to depend upon God in their trials, & also blese his name when they see his goodnes towards others. Man lives not by bread only, Deut: 8. 3. It is not by good & dainty fare, by peace, & rest, and harts ease, in injoying yᵉ contentments and good things of this world only, that preserves health and prolongs life. God in such examples would have yᵉ world see & behold that he can doe it without them; and if yᵉ world will shut ther eyes, and take no notice therof, yet he would have his people to see and consider it. Daniell could be better liking with pulse then others were with yᵉ kings dainties. Jaacob, though he wente from one nation to another people, and passed thorow famine, fears, & many afflictions, yet he lived till old age, and dyed sweetly, & rested in yᵉ Lord, as infinite others of Gods servants have done, and still shall doe, (through Gods goodnes,) notwithstanding all yᵉ malice of their enemies; *when yᵉ branch of yᵉ wicked shall be cut of before his day*, Job. 15. 32. *and the bloody and deceitfull men shall not live out halfe their days.* Psa: 55. 23.

By reason of yᵉ plottings of the Narigansets, (ever since yᵉ Pequents warr,) the Indeans were drawne into a generall conspiracie against yᵉ English in all parts, as was in part discovered yᵉ yeare before; and now made more plaine and evidente by many discoveries and free-conffessions of sundrie Indeans (upon severall occasions) from diverse places, concuring in one; with such other concuring circomstances as gave them suffissently to understand the trueth therof, and to thinke of means, how to prevente yᵉ same, and secure them selves. Which made them enter into this more nere union & confederation following.

[257] Articles of Confederation betweene yᵉ Plantations under yᵉ Govermente of Massachusets, yᵉ Plantations under yᵉ Govermente of New-Plimoth, yᵉ Plantations under yᵉ Govermente of Conightecute, and yᵉ Govermente of New-Haven, with yᵉ Plantations in combination therwith.

Wheras we all came into these parts of America with one and yᵉ same end and aime, namly; to advance the kingdome of our Lord Jesus Christ, & to injoye yᵉ liberties of yᵉ Gospell in puritie with peace; and wheras in our setling (by a wise providence of God) we are further disperced upon yᵉ sea coasts and rivers then was at first intended, so yᵗ we cannot, according to our desires, with convenience comunicate in one govermente & jurisdiction; and wheras we live encompassed with people of severall nations and strang languages, which hereafter may prove injurious to us and our posteritie; and for as much as yᵉ natives have formerly committed sundrie insolencies and outrages upon severall plantations of yᵉ English, and have of late combined them selves against us; and seeing, by reason of those distractions in England (which they have heard of) and by which they know we are hindered from yᵗ humble way of seeking advice or reaping those comfurtable fruits of protection which at other times we might well expecte; we therfore doe conceive it our bounden duty, without delay, to enter into a presente consociation amongst our selves, for mutuall help & strength in all our future concernments. That as in nation and religion, so in other respects, we be & continue one, according to yᵉ tenor and true meaning of the insuing articles. (1) Wherfore it is fully agreed and concluded by & betweene yᵉ parties or jurisdictions above named, and they joyntly & severally doe by these presents agree & conclude, that they all be and henceforth be called by yᵉ name of The United Colonies of New-England.

2. The said United Collonies, for them selves & their posterities, doe joyntly & severally hereby enter into a firme & perpetuall

league of frendship & amitie, for offence and defence, mutuall advice and succore upon all just occasions, both for preserving & propagating yᵉ truth of yᵉ Gospell, and for their owne mutuall saftie and wellfare.

3. It is further agreed that the plantations which at presente are or hereafter shall be setled with[in] yᵉ limites of yᵉ Massachusets shall be for ever under yᵉ Massachusets, and shall have peculier jurisdiction amonge them selves in all cases, as an intire body. And yᵗ Plimoth, Conightecutt, and New-Haven shall each of them have like peculier jurisdition and govermente within their limites and in refference to yᵉ plantations which allready are setled, or shall hereafter be erected, or shall setle within their limites, respectively; provided yᵗ no other jurisdition shall hereafter be taken in, as a distincte head or member of this confederation, nor shall any other plantation or jurisdiction in presente being, and not allready in combination or under yᵉ jurisdiction of any of these confederats, be received by any of them; nor shall any tow of yᵉ confederats joyne in one jurisdiction, without consente of yᵉ rest, which consete to be interpreted as is expresed in yᵉ sixte article ensewing.

4. It is by these conffederats agreed, yᵗ the charge of all just warrs, whether offencive or defencive, upon what parte or member of this confederation soever they fall, shall, both in men, provissions, and all other disbursments, be borne by all yᵉ parts of this confederation, in differente proportions, according to their differente abillities, in maner following: namely, yᵗ the comissioners for each jurisdiction, from time to time, as ther shall be occasion, bring a true accounte and number of all their males in every plantation, or any way belonging too or under their severall jurisdictions, of what qualitie or condition soever they be, from 16. years old to 60, being inhabitants ther; and yᵗ according to yᵉ differente numbers which from time to time shall be found in each jurisdiction upon a true & just accounte, the service of men and all charges of yᵉ warr be borne by yᵉ pole; each jurisdiction or plantation being left to their owne just course & custome of rating them selves and people according to their differente estates, with due respects to their qualities and exemptions amongst them selves,

though the confederats take no notice of any such priviledg. And yᵗ according to their differente charge of each jurisdiction & plantation, the whole advantage of yᵉ warr, (if it please God to blesse their indeaours,) whether it be in lands, goods, or persons, shall be proportionably devided amonge yᵉ said confederats.

5. It is further agreed, that if these jurisdictions, or any plantation under or in combynacion with them, be invaded by any enemie whomsoever, upon notice & requeste of any 3. [258] magistrats of yᵗ jurisdiction so invaded, yᵉ rest of yᵉ confederats, without any further meeting or expostulation, shall forthwith send ayde to yᵉ confederate in danger, but in differente proportion; namely, yᵉ Massachusets an hundred men sufficently armed & provided for such a service and journey, and each of yᵉ rest forty five so armed & provided, or any lesser number, if less be required according to this proportion. But if such confederate in danger may be supplyed by their nexte confederates, not exeeding yᵉ number hereby agreed, they may crave help ther, and seeke no further for yᵉ presente; yᵉ charge to be borne as in this article is exprest, and at yᵉ returne to be victuled & suplyed with powder & shote for their jurney (if ther be need) by yᵗ jurisdiction which imployed or sent for them. But none of yᵉ jurisdictions to exceede these numbers till, by a meeting of yᵉ comissioners for this confederation, a greater aide appear nessessarie. And this proportion to continue till upon knowlege of greater numbers in each jurisdiction, which shall be brought to yᵉ nexte meeting, some other proportion be ordered. But in such case of sending men for presente aide, whether before or after such order or alteration, it is agreed yᵗ at yᵉ meeting of yᵉ comissioners for this confederation, the cause of such warr or invasion be duly considered; and if it appeare yᵗ the falte lay in yᵉ parties so invaded, yᵗ then that jurisdiction or plantation make just satisfaction both to yᵉ invaders whom they have injured, and beare all yᵉ charges of yᵉ warr them selves, without requiring any allowance from yᵉ rest of yᵉ confederats towards yᵉ same. And further, yᵗ if any jurisdiction see any danger of any invasion approaching, and ther be time for a meeting, that in such a case 3. magistrats of yᵗ jurisdiction may sumone a meeting, at such conveniente place as them selves shall

thinke meete, to consider & provid against ye threatened danger, provided when they are mett, they may remove to what place they please; only, whilst any of these foure confederats have but 3 magistrats in their jurisdiction, their requeste, or summons, from any 2. of them shall be accounted of equall force with ye 3. mentioned in both the clauses of this article, till ther be an increase of majestrats ther.

6. It is also agreed y^t, for ye managing & concluding of all affairs propper, & concerning the whole confederation, tow comissioners shall be chosen by & out of each of these 4. jurisdictions; namly, 2. for ye Massachusets, 2. for Plimoth, 2. for Conightecutt, and 2. for New-Haven, being all in church fellowship with us, which shall bring full power from their severall Generall Courts respectively to hear, examene, waigh, and detirmine all affairs of warr, or peace, leagues, aids, charges, and numbers of men for warr, divissions of spoyles, & whatsoever is gotten by conquest; receiving of more confederats, or plantations into combination with any of ye confederates, and all things of like nature, which are ye proper concomitants or consequences of such a confederation, for amitie, offence, & defence; not inter-medling with ye govermente of any of ye jurisdictions, which by ye 3. article is preserved entirely to them selves. But if these 8. comissioners when they meete shall not all agree, yet it concluded that any 6. of the 8. agreeing shall have power to setle & determine ye bussines in question. But if 6. doe not agree, that then such propositions, with their reasons, so farr as they have been debated, be sente, and referred to ye 4. Generall Courts, viz. ye Massachusets, Plimoth, Conightecutt, and New-haven; and if at all ye said Generall Courts ye bussines so referred be concluded, then to be prosecuted by ye confederats, and all their members. It was further agreed that these 8. comissioners shall meete once every year, besids extraordinarie meetings, (according to the fifte article,) to consider, treate, & conclude of all affaires belonging to this confederation, which meeting shall ever be the first Thursday in September. And y^t the next meeting after the date of these presents, which shall be accounted ye second meeting, shall be at Boston in ye Massachusets, the 3. at Hartford, the 4. at New-

Haven, the 5. at Plimoth, and so in course successively, if in ye meane time some midle place be not found out and agreed on, which may be comodious for all ye jurisdictions.

7. It is further agreed, y^t at each meeting of these 8. comissioners, whether ordinarie, or extraordinary, they all 6. of them agreeing as before, may chuse a presidente out of them selves, whose office & work shall be to take care and directe for order, and a comly carrying on of all proceedings in ye present meeting; but he shall be invested with no such power or respecte, as by which he shall hinder ye propounding or progrese of any bussines, or any way cast ye scailes otherwise then in ye precedente article is agreed.

[259] 8. It is also agreed, y^t the comissioners for this confederation hereafter at their meetings, whether ordinary or extraordinarie, as they may have comission or opportunitie, doe indeaover to frame and establish agreements & orders in generall cases of a civill nature, wherin all ye plantations are interested, for ye preserving of peace amongst them selves, and preventing as much as may be all occasions of warr or difference with others; as aboute ye free & speedy passage of justice, in every jurisdiction, to all ye confederats equally as to their owne; not receiving those y^t remove from one plantation to another without due certificate; how all ye jurisdictions may carry towards ye Indeans, that they neither growe insolente, nor be injured without due satisfaction, least warr breake in upon the confederats through such miscarriages. It is also agreed, y^t if any servante rune away from his maister into another of these confederated jurisdictions, that in such case, upon ye certificate of one magistrate in the jurisdiction out of which ye said servante fledd, or upon other due proofe, the said servante shall be delivered, either to his maister, or any other y^t pursues & brings such certificate or proofe. And y^t upon ye escape of any prisoner whatsoever, or fugitive for any criminall cause, whether breaking prison, or getting from ye officer, or otherwise escaping, upon the certificate of 2. magistrats of ye jurisdiction out of which ye escape is made, that he was a prisoner, or such an offender at ye time of ye escape, they magistrats, or sume of them of the jurisdiction wher for ye presente the said prisoner or fugitive abideth, shall forthwith

grante such a warrante as ye case will beare, for ye apprehending of any such person, & the delivering of him into ye hands of ye officer, or other person who pursues him. And if ther be help required, for ye safe returning of any such offender, then it shall be granted to him y^t craves ye same, he paying the charges therof.

9. And for y^t the justest warrs may be of dangerous consequence, espetially to ye smaler plantations in these United Collonies, it is agreed y^t neither ye Massachusets, Plimoth, Conightecutt, nor New-Haven, nor any member of any of them, shall at any time hear after begine, undertake, or ingage them selves, or this confederation, or any parte therof, in any warr whatsoever, (sudden[ET] exegents, with ye necessary consequents therof excepted, which are also to be moderated as much as ye case will permitte,) without ye consente and agreemente of ye forementioned 8. comissioners, or at the least 6. of them, as in ye sixt article is provided. And y^t no charge be required of any of they confederats, in case of a defensive warr, till ye said comissioners have mett, and approved ye justice of ye warr, and have agreed upon ye sume of money to be levied, which sume is then to be paid by the severall confederats in proportion according to ye fourth article.

10. That in extraordinary occasions, when meetings are summoned by three magistrates of any jurisdiction, or 2. as in ye 5. article, if any of ye comissioners come not, due warning being given or sente, it is agreed y^t 4. of the comissioners shall have power to directe a warr which cannot be delayed, and to send for due proportions of men out of each jurisdiction, as well as 6. might doe if all mett; but not less then 6. shall determine the justice of ye warr, or alow ye demands or bills of charges, or cause any levies to be made for ye same.

11. It is further agreed, y^t if any of ye confederats shall hereafter breake any of these presente articles, or be any other ways injurious to any one of ye other jurisdictions, such breach of agreemente or injurie shall be duly considered and ordered by ye comissioners for ye other jurisdiction; that both peace and this presente confederation may be intirly preserved without violation.

12. Lastly, this perpetuall confederation, and yᵉ severall articles therof being read, and seriously considered, both by yᵉ Generall Courte for yᵉ Massachusets, and by yᵉ comissioners for Plimoth, Conigtecute, & New-Haven, were fully alowed & confirmed by 3. of yᵉ forenamed confederats, namly, yᵉ Massachusets, Conightecutt, and New-Haven; only yᵉ comissioners for Plimoth haveing no comission to conclude, desired respite till they might advise with their Generall Courte; wher upon it was agreed and concluded by yᵉ said Courte of yᵉ Massachusets, and the comissioners for yᵉ other tow confederats, that, if Plimoth consente, then the whole treaty as it stands in these present articls is, and shall continue, firme & stable without alteration. But if Plimoth come not in, yet yᵉ other three confederats doe by these presents [260] confeirme yᵉ whole confederation, and the articles therof; only in September nexte, when yᵉ second meeting of yᵉ comissioners is to be at Boston, new consideration may be taken of yᵉ 6. article, which concerns number of comissioners for meeting & concluding the affaires of this confederation, to yᵉ satisfaction of yᵉ Courte of yᵉ Massachusets, and yᵉ comissioners for yᵉ other 2. confederats, but yᵉ rest to stand unquestioned. In yᵉ testimonie wherof, yᵉ Generall Courte of yᵉ Massachusets, by ther Secretary, and yᵉ comissioners for Conightecutt and New-Haven, have subscribed these presente articles this 19. of yᵉ third month, comonly called May, Anno Dom: 1643.

At a meeting of yᵉ comissioners for yᵉ confederation held at Boston yᵉ 7. of Sept: it appearing that the Generall Courte of New-Plimoth, and yᵉ severall towneshipes therof, have read & considered & approved these articles of confederation, as appeareth by comission from their Generall Courte bearing date yᵉ 29. of August, 1643. to Mʳ. Edward Winslow and Mʳ. William Collier, to ratifie and confirme yᵉ same on their behalfes. We, therfore, yᵉ Comissioners for yᵉ Massachusets, Conightecutt, & New Haven, doe also, for our severall goverments, subscribe unto them.

JOHN WINTHROP, Govʳ. of yᵉ Massachusest.
THO: DUDLEY.
GEO: FENWICK.

THOMAS GREGSON.
THEOPH: EATON.
EDWA: HOPKINS.
THOMAS GREGSON.

These were yᵉ articles of agreemente in yᵉ union and confederation which they now first entered into; and in this their first meeting, held at Boston yᵉ day & year abovesaid, amongst other things they had this matter of great consequence to considere on: the Narigansets, after yᵉ subduing of yᵉ Pequents, thought to have ruled over all yᵉ Indeans aboute them; but yᵉ English, espetially those of Conightecutt holding correspondencie & frenship with Uncass, sachem of yᵉ Monhigg Indeans which lived nere them, (as yᵉ Massachusets had done with yᵉ Narigansets,) and he had been faithful to them in yᵉ Pequente warr, they were ingaged to supporte him in his just liberties, and were contented yᵗ such of yᵉ surviving Pequents as had submited to him should remaine with him and quietly under his protection. This did much increase his power and augmente his greatnes, which yᵉ Narigansets could not indure to see. But Myantinomo, their cheefe sachem, (an ambitious & politick man,) sought privatly and by trearchery (according to yᵉ Indean maner) to make him away, by hiring some to kill him. Sometime they assayed to poyson him; that not takeing, then in yᵉ night time to knock him on yᵉ head in his house, or secretly to shoot him, and such like attempts. But none of these taking effecte, he made open warr upon him (though it was against yᵉ covenants both betweene yᵉ English & them, as also betweene them selves, and a plaine breach of yᵉ same). He came suddanly upon him with 900. or 1000. men (never denouncing any warr before). Yᵉ others power at yᵗ presente was not above halfe so many; but it pleased God to give Uncass yᵉ victory, and he slew many of his men, and wounded many more; but yᵉ cheefe of all was, he tooke Miantinomo prisoner. And seeing he was a greate man, and yᵉ Narigansets a potente people & would seeke revenge, he would doe nothing in yᵉ case without yᵉ advise of yᵉ English; so he (by yᵉ help & direction of those of Conightecutt) kept him prisoner till this meeting of yᵉ comissioners. The comissioners weighed yᵉ cause and passages, as they were clearly represented & sufficently evidenced betwixte Uncass and Myantinomo; and the things being duly considered, the comissioners apparently saw yⁱ Uncass could not be safe whilst Miantynomo lived, but, either by secrete trechery or open force, his life would still be in danger. Wherfore they thought he might justly put such a false & bloud-thirstie enimie to death; but in his owne jurisdiction, not in yᵉ English plantations. And they advised, in yᵉ maner of his death all mercy and moderation should be showed, contrary to yᵉ practise of yᵉ Indeans, who exercise torturs and cruelty. And, [261] Uncass having hitherto shewed him selfe a freind to yᵉ English, and in this craving their advise, if the Narigansett Indeans or others shall unjustly assaulte Uncass for this execution, upon notice and request, yᵉ English promise to assiste and protecte him as farr as they may agaīste such violence.

This was yᵉ issue of this bussines. The reasons and passages hereof are more at large to be seene in yᵉ acts & records of this meeting of yᵉ comissioners. And Uncass follewd this advise, and accordingly executed him, in a very faire maner, acording as they advised, with due respecte to his honour & greatnes. But what followed on yᵉ Narigansets parte will appear hear after.

Anno Dom: 1644.

Mᴿ. EDWARD WINSLOW was chosen Govʳ this year.

Many having left this place (as is before noted) by reason of the straightnes & barrennes of yᵉ same, and their finding of better accommodations elsewher, more sutable to their ends & minds; and sundrie others still upon every occasion desiring their dismissions, the church begane seriously to thinke whether it were not better joyntly to remove to some other place, then to be thus weakened, and as it were insensibly dissolved. Many meetings and much consultation was held hearaboute, and diverse were mens minds and opinions. Some were still for staying togeather in this place, aledging men might hear live, if they would be contente with their condition; and yᵗ it was not for wante or necessitie so much yᵗ they removed, as for yᵉ enriching of them selves. Others were resolute upon removall, and so signified yᵗ hear yᵉʸ could not stay; but if yᵉ church did not remove, they must; insomuch as many were swayed, rather then ther should be a dissolution, to condescend to a removall, if a fitt place could be found, that might more conveniently and comfortablie receive yᵉ whole, with such accession of others as might come to them, for their better strength & subsistence; and some such like cautions and limitations. So as, with yᵉ afforesaide provissos, yᵉ greater parte consented to a removall to a place called Nawsett, which had been superficially veiwed and yᵉ good will of yᵉ purchassers (to whom it belonged) obtained, with some addition thertoo from yᵉ Courte. But now they begane to see their errour, that they had given away already the best & most comodious places to others, and now wanted them selves; for this place was about 50. myles from hence, and at an outside of yᵉ countrie, remote from all society; also, that it would prove so straite, as it would not be competente to receive yᵉ whole body, much less be capable of any addition or increase; so as (at least in a shorte time) they should be worse ther then they are now hear. The which, with sundery other like considerations and inconveniences, made them chaing their resolutions; but such as were before resolved upon removall tooke advantage of this agreemente, & wente on notwithstanding, neither could yᵉ rest hinder them, they haveing made some begining. And thus was this poore church left, like an anciente mother, growne olde, and forsaken of her children, (though not in their affections,) yett in regarde of their bodily presence and personall helpfullness. Her anciente members being most of them worne away by death; and these of later time being like children translated into other families, and she like a widow left only to trust in God. Thus she that had made many rich became her selfe poore.

[262] Some things handled, and pacified by yᵉ comissioner this year.

Wheras, by a wise providence of God, tow of yᵉ jurisdictions in yᵉ westerne parts, viz. Conightecutt & New-haven, have beene latly exercised by sundrie insolencies & outrages from yᵉ Indeans; as, first, an Englishman, runing from his mʳ out of yᵉ Massachusets, was murdered in yᵉ woods, in or nere yᵉ limites of Conightecute jurisdiction; and aboute 6. weeks after, upon discovery by an Indean, yᵉ Indean sagamore in these parts promised to deliver the murderer to yᵉ English, bound; and having accordingly brought him within yᵉ sight of Uncaway, by their joynte consente, as it is informed, he was ther unbound, and left to shifte for him selfe; wherupon 10. Englishmen forthwith coming to yᵉ place, being sente by Mʳ. Ludlow, at yᵉ Indeans desire, to receive yᵉ murderer, who seeing him escaped, layed hold of 8. of yᵉ Indeans ther presente, amongst whom ther was a sagamore or 2. and kept them in hold 2. days, till 4. sagamors ingaged themselves within one month to deliver yᵉ prisoner. And about a weeke after this agreemente, an Indean came presumtuously and with guile, in yᵉ day time, and murtherously assalted an English woman in her house at Stamford, and by 3. wounds, supposed mortall, left her for dead, after he had robbed yᵉ house. By which passages yᵉ English were provoked, & called to a due consideration of their owne saftie; and yᵉ Indeans generally in those parts arose in an hostile maner, refused to come to yᵉ English to carry on treaties of peace, departed from their wigwames, left their corne unweeded, and shewed them selves tumultuously about some of yᵉ English plantations, & shott of peeces within hearing of yᵉ towne; and some Indeans came to yᵉ English & tould them yᵉ Indeans would fall upon them. So yᵗ most of yᵉ English thought it unsafe to travell in those parts by land, and some of yᵉ plantations were put upon strong watchs and ward, night & day, & could not attend their private occasions, and yet distrusted their owne strength for their defence. Wherupon Hartford & New-Haven were sent unto for aide, and saw cause both to send into yᵉ weaker parts of their owne jurisdiction thus in danger, and New-Haven, for conveniencie of situation, sente aide to Uncaway, though belonging to Conightecutt. Of all which passages they presently acquainted yᵉ comissioners in yᵉ Bay, & had yᵉ allowance & approbation from yᵉ Generall Courte ther, with directions neither to hasten warr nor to bear such insolencies too longe. Which courses, though chargable to them selves, yet through Gods blessing they hope fruite is, & will be, sweete and wholsome to all yᵉ collonies; the murderers are since delivered to justice, the publick peace preserved for yᵉ presente, & probabillitie it may be better secured for yᵉ future.

Thus this mischeefe was prevented, and yᵉ fear of a warr hereby diverted. But now an other broyle was begune by yᵉ Narigansets; though they unjustly had made warr upon Uncass, (as is before declared,) and had, yᵉ winter before this, ernestly presed yᵉ Goveʳ of yᵉ Massachusets that they might still make warr upon them to revenge the death of their sagamore, wᶜʰ, being taken prisoner, was by them put to death, (as before was noted,) pretending that they had first received and accepted his ransome, and then put him to death. But yᵉ Goveʳ refused their presents, and tould them yᵗ it was them selves had done yᵉ wronge, & broaken yᵉ conditions of peace; and he nor yᵉ English neither could nor would allow them to make any further warr upon him, but if they did, must assiste him, & oppose them; but if it did appeare, upon good proofe, that he had received a ransome for his life, before he put him to death, when yᵉ comissioners mett, they should have a fair hearing, and they would cause Uncass to returne yᵉ same. But notwithstanding, at yᵉ spring of yᵉ year they gathered a great power, and fell upon Uncass, and slue sundrie of his men, and wounded more, and also had some loss them selves. Uncass cald for aide from yᵉ English; they tould him what yᵉ Narigansets objected, he deney the same; they tould him it must come to triall, and if he was inocente, if yᵉ Narigansets would not desiste, they would aide & assiste him. So at this meeting they [263] sent both to Uncass & yᵉ Narrigansets, and required their sagamors to come or send to yᵉ comissioners now mete at Hartford, and they should have a faire & inpartiall hearing in all their greevances, and would endeavor yᵗ all wrongs should be rectified wher they should be found; and they promised that they should safly come and returne without any danger or molestation; and sundry yᵉ like things, as appears more at large in yᵉ messengers instructions. Upon wᶜʰ the Narigansets sent one sagamore and some other deputies, with full power to doe in yᵉ case as should be meete.

Uncass came in person, accompanyed with some cheefe aboute him. After the agitation of yᵉ bussines, yᵉ issue was this. The comissioners declared to the Narigansett deputies as followeth.

1. That they did not find any proofe of any ransome agreed on.

2. It appeared not yᵗ any wampam had been paied as a ransome, or any parte of a ransome, for Myantinomos life.

3. That if they had in any measure proved their charge against Uncass, the comissioners would have required him to have made answerable satisfaction.

4. That if hereafter they can make satisfing profe, yᵉ English will consider yᵉ same, & proceed accordingly.

5. The comissioners did require yᵗ neither them selves nor yᵉ Nyanticks make any warr or injurious assaulte upon Unquass or any of his company untill they make profe of yᵉ ransume charged, and yᵗ due satisfaction be deneyed, unless he first assaulte them.

6. That if they assaulte Uncass, the English are engaged to assist him.

Hearupon yᵉ Narigansette sachim, advising with yᵉ other deputies, ingaged him selfe in the behalfe of yᵉ Narigansets & Nyanticks that no hostile acts should be comitted upon Uncass, or any of his, untill after yᵉ next planting of corne; and yᵗ after that, before they begine any warr, they will give 30. days warning to yᵉ Goveʳ of the Massachusets or Conightecutt. The comissioners approving of this offer, and taking their ingagmente under their hands, required Uncass, as he expected yᵉ continuance of yᵉ favour of the English, to observe the same termes of peace with yᵉ Narigansets and theirs.

These foregoing conclusions were subscribed by yᵉ comissioners, for yᵉ severall jurisdictions, yᵉ 19. of Sept: 1644.

EDWA: HOPKINS, Presidente.
SIMON BRADSTREETE.
WILLᴹ. HATHORNE.
EDW: WINSLOW.
JOHN BROWNE.

GEOR: FENWICK.
THEOPH: EATON.
THO: GREGSON.

The forenamed Narigansets deputies did further promise, that if, contrary to this agreemente, any of yᵉ Nyantick Pequents should make any assaulte upon Uncass, or any of his, they would deliver them up to yᵉ English, to be punished according to their demerits; and that they would not use any means to procure the Mowacks to come against Uncass during this truce.

These were their names subscribed with their marks.

WEETOWISH.
PAMPIAMETT.
CHINÑOUGH.
PUMMUNISH.

[264] *Anno Dom: 1645.*

The comissioners this year were caled to meete to-gither at Boston, before their ordinarie time; partly in regard of some differances falen betweene yᵉ French and yᵉ govermente of the Massachusets, about their aiding of Munseire Latore against Munsseire de Aulney, and partly aboute yᵉ Indeans, who had broaken yᵉ former agreements aboute the peace concluded yᵉ last year. This meeting was held at Boston, yᵉ 28. of July.

Besids some underhand assualts made on both sids, the Narigansets gathered a great power, and fell upon Uncass, and slew many of his men, and wounded more, by reason yᵗ they farr exseeded him in number, and had gott store of peeces, with which they did him most hurte. And as they did this withoute yᵉ knowledg and consente of yᵉ English, (contrary to former agreemente,) so they were resolved to prosecute yᵉ same, notwithstanding any thing yᵉ English said or should doe against them. So, being incouraged by ther late victorie, and promise of assistance from yᵉ Mowaks, (being a strong, warlike, and desperate people,) they had allready devoured Uncass & his, in their hops; and surly they had done it in deed, if the English had not timly sett in for his aide. For those of Conightecute sent him 40. men, who were a garison to him, till yᵉ comissioners could meete and take further order.

Being thus mett, they forthwith sente 3. messengers, viz. Sargent John Davis, Benedicte Arnold, and Francis Smith, with full & ample instructions, both to yᵉ Narigansets and Uncass; to require them yᵗ they should either come in person or send sufficiente men fully instructed to deale in yᵉ bussines; and if they refused or delayed, to let them know (according to former agreements) yᵗ the English are engaged to assiste against these hostile invasions, and yᵗ they have sente their men to defend Uncass, and to know of yᵉ Narigansets whether they will stand to yᵉ former peace, or they will assaulte yᵉ English also, that they may provid accordingly.

But yᵉ messengers returned, not only with a sleighting, but a threatening answer from the Narigansets (as will more appear hereafter). Also they brought a letter from Mʳ. Roger Williams, wherin he assures them that yᵉ warr would presenly breake forth, & yᵉ whole country would be all of a flame. And yᵗ the sachems of yᵉ Narigansets had concluded a newtrality with yᵉ English of Providence and those of Aquidnett Iland. Wherupon yᵉ comissioners, considering yᵉ great danger & provocations offered, and yᵉ necessitie we should be put unto of making warr with yᵉ Narigansetts, and being also carfull, in a matter of so great waight & generall concernmente, to see yᵉ way cleared, and to give satisfaction to all yᵉ colonies, did thinke fitte to advise with such of yᵉ magistrats & elders of yᵉ Massachusets as were then at hand, and also with some of yᵉ cheefe millitary comanders ther; who being assembled, it was then agreed,——

First, yᵗ our ingagmente bound us to aide & defend Uncass. 2. That this ayde could not be intended only to defend him & his forte, or habitation, but (according to yᵉ comone acceptation of such covenants, or ingagments, considered with yᵉ grounds or occasion therof) so to ayde him as he might be preserved in his liberty and estate. 3ˡʸ. That this ayde [265] must be speedy, least he might be swalowed up in ye mean time, and so come to late. 4^{ly}. The justice of this warr being cleared to our selves and ye rest then presente, it was thought meete y^t the case should be stated, and ye reasons & grounds of ye warr declared and published. 5^{ly}. That a day of humilliation should be apoynted, which was ye 5. day of ye weeke following. 6^{ly}. It was then allso agreed by ye comissioners that ye whole number of men to be raised in all ye colonies should be 300. Wherof from ye Massachusets a 190. Plimoth, 40. Conightecute, 40. New-Haven, 30. And considering y^t Uncass was in present danger, 40. men of this number were forthwith sente from ye Massachusets for his sucoure; and it was but neede, for ye other 40. from Conightecutt had order to stay but a month, & their time being out, they returned; and ye Narigansets, hearing therof, tooke the advantage, and came suddanly upon him, and gave him another blow, to his further loss, and were ready to doe ye like againe; but these 40. men being arrived, they returned, and did nothing.

The declaration which they sett forth I shall not transcribe, it being very larg, and put forth in printe, to which I referr those y^t would see ye same, in which all passages are layed open from ye first. I shall only note their prowd carriage, and answers to ye 3. messengers sent from ye comissioners. They received them with scorne & contempte, and tould them they resolved to have no peace without Uncass his head; also they gave them this further answer: that it mattered not who begane ye warr, they were resolved to follow it, and that ye English should withdraw their garison from Uncass, or they would procure ye Mowakes against them; and withall gave them this threatening answer: that they would lay ye English catle on heaps, as high as their houses, and y^t no English-man should sturr out of his dore to pisse, but he should be kild. And wheras they required guids to pass throw their countrie, to deliver their message to Uncass from ye comissioners, they deneyed them, but at length (in way of scorne) offered them an old Pequente woman. Besids allso they conceived them selves in danger, for whilst ye interpretour was speakeing with them about ye answer he should returne, 3. men came & stood behind him with ther hatchets, according to their murderous maner; but one of his fellows gave him notice of it, so they broak of & came away; with sundry such like affrontes, which made those Indeans they carryed with them to rune away for fear, and leave them to goe home as they could.

Thus whilst yᵉ comissioners in care of yᵉ publick peace sought to quench yᵉ fire kindled amongst yᵉ Indeans, these children of strife breath out threatenings, provocations, and warr against yᵉ English them selves. So that, unless they should dishonour & provoak God, by violating a just ingagmente, and expose yᵉ colonies to contempte & danger from yᵉ barbarians, they cannot but exerciese force, when no other means will prevaile to reduse yᵉ Narigansets & their confederats to a more just & sober temper.

So as here upon they went on to hasten yᵉ preparations, according to yᵉ former agreemente, and sent to Plimoth to send forth their 40. men with all speed, to lye at Seacunke, least any deanger should befalle it, before yᵉ rest were ready, it lying next yᵉ enemie, and ther to stay till yᵉ Massachusetts should joyne with them. Allso Conigtecute & Newhaven forces were to joyne togeather, and march with all speed, and yᵉ Indean confederats of those parts with them. All which was done accordingly; and the souldiers of this place were at Seacunk, the place of their rendevouze, 8. or 10. days before yᵉ rest were ready; they were well armed all with snaphance peeces, and wente under yᵉ camand of Captain [266] Standish. Those from other places were led likwise by able comanders,[EU] as Captaine Mason for Conigtecute, &c.; and Majore Gibons was made generall over yᵉ whole, with such comissions & instructions as was meete.

Upon yᵉ suden dispatch of these souldiears, (the present necessitie requiring it,) the deputies of yᵉ Massachusetts Courte (being now assembled imediatly after yᵉ setting forth of their 40. men) made a question whether it was legally done, without their comission. It was answered, that howsoever it did properly belong to yᵉ authority of yᵉ severall jurisdictions (after yᵉ warr was agreed upon by yᵉ comissioners, & the number of men) to provid yᵉ men & means to carry on yᵉ warr; yet in this presente case, the proceeding of ye comissioners and ye comission given was as sufficiente as if it had been done by ye Generall Courte.

First, it was a case of such presente & urgente necessitie, as could not stay ye calling of ye Courte or Counsell. 2^{ly}. In ye Articles of Confederation, power is given to ye comissioners to consult, order, & determine all affaires of warr, &c. And ye word *determine* comprehends all acts of authority belonging therunto.

3^{ly}. The comissioners are ye judges of ye necessitie of the expedition.

4^{ly}. The Generall Courte have made their owne comissioners their sole counsell for these affires.

5^{ly}. These counsels could not have had their due effecte excepte they had power to proceede in this case, as they have done; which were to make ye comissioners power, and ye maine end of ye confederation, to be frustrate, and that mearly for observing a ceremony.

6^{ly}. The comissioners haveing sole power to manage ye warr for number of men, for time, place, &c., they only know their owne counsells, & *determinations*, and therfore none can grante comission to acte according to these but them selves.

All things being thus in readines, and some of ye souldiers gone forth, and the rest ready to march, the comissioners thought it meete before any hostile acte was performed, to cause a presente to be returned, which had been sente to ye Gove^r of the Massachusetts from ye Narigansett sachems, but not by him received, but layed up to be accepted or refused as they should carry them selves, and observe ye covenants. Therfore they violating the same, & standing out thus to a warr, it was againe returned, by 2. messengers & an interpretour. And further to let know that their men already sent to Uncass (& other wher sent forth) have hitherto had express order only to stand upon his & their owne defence, and not to attempte any invasion of ye Narigansetts country; and yet if they may have due reperation for what is past, and good securitie for ye future, it shall appear they are as desirous of peace, and shall be as tender of ye Narigansets blood as ever. If therefore Pessecuss, Innemo, writh other sachemes, will (without further delay) come along with you to Boston, the comissioners doe promise & assure them, they shall have free liberty to come, and retourne without molestation or any just greevance from ye English. But deputies will not now serve, nor may the preparations in hand be now stayed, or ye directions given recalled, till ye forementioned sagamors come, and some further order be taken. But if they will have nothing but warr, the English are providing, and will proceede accordingly.

Pessecouss, Mixano, & Witowash, 3. principall sachems of ye Narigansett Indeans, and Awasequen, deputie for ye Nyanticks, with a large traine of men, within a few days after came to Boston.

And to omitte all other circomstances and debats y^t past betweene them and the comissioners, they came to this conclusion following.

[267] 1. It was agreed betwixte ye comissioners of ye United Collonies, and ye forementioned sagamores, & Niantick deputie, that ye said Narigansets & Niantick sagamores should pay or cause to be payed at Boston, to ye Massachusets comissioners, ye full sume of 2000. fathome of good white wampame, or a third parte of black wampampeage, in 4. payments; namely, 500. fathome within 20. days, 500. fathome within 4. months, 500. fathome at or before next planting time, and 500. fathome. within 2. years next after ye date of these presents; which 2000. fathome ye comissioners accepte for satisfaction of former charges expended.

2. The foresaid sagamors & deputie (on ye behalfe of ye Narigansett & Niantick Indeans) hereby promise & covenante that they upon demand and profe satisfie & restore unto Uncass, ye Mohigan sagamore, all such captives, whether men, or women, or children, and all such canowes, as they or any of their men have taken, or as many of their owne canowes in ye roome of them, full as good as they were, with full satisfaction for all such corne as they or any of theire men have spoyled or destroyed, of his or his mens, since last planting time; and ye English comissioners hereby promise y^t Uncass shall doe ye like.

3. Wheras ther are sundry differences & greevances betwixte Narigansett & Niantick Indeans, and Uncass & his men, (which in Uncass his absence cannot now be detirmined,) it is hearby agreed yᵗ Nariganset & Niantick sagamores either come them selves, or send their deputies to yᶜ next meeting of yᶜ comissioners for yᶜ collonies, either at New-Haven in Sepᵗ 1646. or sooner (upon conveniente warning, if yᶜ said comissioners doe meete sooner), fully instructed to declare & make due proofe of their injuries, and to submite to yᶜ judgmente of yᶜ comissioners, in giving or receiving satisfaction; and yᶜ said comissioners (not doubting but Uncass will either come him selfe, or send his deputies, in like maner furnished) promising to give a full hearing to both parties with equall justice, without any partiall respects, according to their allegations and profs.

4. The said Narigansett & Niantick sagamors & deputies doe nearby promise & covenante to keep and maintaine a firme & perpetuall peace, both with all yᶜ English United Colonies & their successors, and with Uncass, yᶜ Monhegen sachem, & his men; with Ossamequine, Pumham, Sokanoke, Cutshamakin, Shoanan, Passaconaway, and all other Indean sagamors, and their companies, who are in freindship with or subjecte to any of yᶜ English; hearby ingaging them selves, that they will not at any time hearafter disturbe yᶜ peace of yᶜ cuntry, by any assaults, hostile attempts, invasions, or other injuries, to any of yᶜ Unnited Collonies, or their successors; or to yᶜ afforesaid Indeans; either in their persons, buildings, catle, or goods, directly or indirectly; nor will they confederate with any other against them; & if they know of any Indeans or others yᵗ conspire or intend hurt against yᶜ said English, or any Indeans subjecte to or in freindship with them, they will without delay acquainte & give notice therof to yᶜ English comissioners, or some of them.

Or if any questions or differences shall at any time hereafter arise or grow betwext them & Uncass, or any Endeans before mentioned they will, according to former ingagments (which they hearby confirme & ratifie) first acquainte yᶜ English, and crave their judgments & advice therin; and will not attempte or begine any warr, or hostille invasion, till they have liberty and alowance from yᶜ comissioners of yᶜ United Collonies so to doe.

5. The said Narigansets & Niantick sagamores & deputies doe hearby promise yᵗ they will forthwᵗʰ deliver & restore all such Indean fugitives, or captives which have at any time fled from any of yᶜ English, and are now living or abiding amongst them, or give due satisfaction for them to yᶜ comissioners for yᶜ Massachusets; and further, that they will (without more delays) pay, or cause to be payed, a yearly tribute, a month before harvest, every year after this, at Boston, to yᶜ English Colonies, for all such Pequents as live amongst them, according to yᶜ former treaty & agreemente, made at Hartford, 1638. namly, one fathome of white wampam for every Pequente man, & halfe a fathume for each Pequente youth, and one hand length for each mal-child. And if Weequashcooke refuse to pay this tribute for any Pequents with him, the Narigansetts sagamores promise to assiste yᶜ English against him. And they further covenante yᵗ they will resigne & yeeld up the whole Pequente cuntrie, and every parte of it, to yᶜ English collonies, as due to them by conquest.

6. The said Narigansett & Niantick sagamores & deputie doe hereby promise & covenante yᵗ within 14. days they will bring & deliver to yᶜ Massachusetts comissioners on the behalf of yᶜ collonies, [268] foure of their children, viz. Pessecous his eldest son, the sone Tassaquanawite, brother to Pessecouss, Awashawe his sone, and Ewangsos sone, a Niantick, to be kepte (as hostages & pledges) by yᶜ English, till both yᶜ forementioned 2000. fathome of wampam be payed at yᶜ times appoynted, and yᶜ differences betweexte themselves & Uncass be heard & ordered, and till these artickles be under writen at Boston, by Jenemo & Wipetock. And further they hereby promise & covenante, yᵗ if at any time hearafter any of yᶜ said children shall make escape, or be conveyed away from yᶜ English, before yᶜ premisses be fully accomplished, they will either bring back & deliver to yᶜ Massachusett comissioners yᶜ same children, or, if they be not to be founde, such & so many other children, to be chosen by yᶜ comissioners for yᶜ United Collonies, or their assignes, and yᵗ within 20. days after demand,

and in yᵉ mean time, untill yᵉ said 4. children be delivered as hostages, yᵉ Narigansett & Niantick sagamors & deputy doe, freely & of their owne accorde, leave with yᵉ Massachusett comissioners, as pledges for presente securitie, 4. Indeans, namely, Witowash, Pumanise, Jawashoe, Waughwamino, who allso freely consente, and offer them selves to stay as pledges, till yᵉ said children be brought & delivered as abovesaid.

7. The comissioners for yᵉ United Collonies doe hereby promise & agree that, at yᵉ charge of yᵉ United Collonies, yᵉ 4. Indeans now left as pledges shall be provided for, and yᵗ the 4. children to be brought & delivered as hostages shall be kepte & maintained at yᵉ same charge; that they will require Uncass & his men, with all other Indean sagamors before named, to forbear all acts of hostilitie againste yᵉ Narigansetts and Niantick Indeans for yᵉ future. And further, all yᵉ promises being duly observed & kept by yᵉ Narigansett & Niantick Indians and their company, they will at yᵉ end of 2. years restore yᵉ said children delivered as hostiages, and retaine a firme peace with yᵉ Narigansets & Nianticke Indeans and their successours.

8. It is fully agreed by & betwixte yᵉ said parties, yᵗ if any hostile attempte be made while this treaty is in hand, or before notice of this agreemente (to stay further preparations & directions) can be given, such attempts & yᵉ consequencts therof shall on neither parte be accounted a violation of this treaty, nor a breach of yᵉ peace hear made & concluded.

9. The Narigansets & Niantick sagamors & deputie hereby agree & covenante to & with yᵉ comissioners of yᵉ United Collonies, yᵗ henceforth they will neither give, grante, sell, or in any maner alienate, any parte of their countrie, nor any parcell of land therin, either to any of yᵉ English or others, without consente or allowance of yᵉ comissioners.

10. Lastly, they promise that, if any Pequente or other be found & discovered amongst them who hath in time of peace murdered any of yᵉ English, he or they shall be delivered to just punishmente.

    In witness wherof yᵉ parties above named have interchaingablie subscribed these presents, the day & year above writen.

JOHN WINTHROP, President.

HERBERT PELHAM.

THO: PRENCE.

JOHN BROWNE.

GEO: FENWICK.

EDWA: HOPKINS.

THEOPH: EATON.

STEVEN GOODYEARE.

PESSECOUSS his mark

MEEKESANO his mark

WITOWASH his mark

AUMSEQUEN his mark the Niantick deputy.

ABDAS his mark

PUMMASH his mark

CUTCHAMAKIN his mark

This treaty and agreemente betwixte the comissioners of y͇ United Collonies and y͇ sagamores and deputy of Narrigansets and Niantick Indeans was made and concluded, Benedicte Arnold being interpretour upon his oath; Sergante Callicate & an Indean, his man, being presente, and Josias & Cutshamakin, tow Indeans aquainted with y͇ English language, assisting therin; who opened & cleared the whole treaty, & every article, to y͇ sagamores and deputie there presente.

And thus was y͇ warr at this time stayed and prevented.

[269] *Anno Dom: 1646.*

About y͇ midle of May, this year, came in 3. ships into this harbor, in warrlike order; they were found to be men of warr. The captains name was Crumwell, who had taken sundrie prizes from y͇ Spaniards in y͇ West Indies. He had a comission from y͇ Earle of Warwick. He had abord his vessels aboute 80. lustie men, (but very unruly,) who, after they came ashore, did so distemper them selves with drinke as they became like madd-men; and though some of them were punished & imprisoned, yet could they hardly be restrained; yet in yᵉ ende they became more moderate & orderly. They continued here aboute a month or 6. weeks, and then went to yᵉ Massachusets; in which time they spente and scattered a great deale of money among yᵉ people, and yet more sine (I fear) then money, notwithstanding all yᵉ care & watchfullnes that was used towards them, to prevente what might be.

In which time one sadd accidente fell out. A desperate fellow of yᵉ company fell a quarling with some of his company. His captine comanded him to be quiet & surcease his quarelling; but he would not, but reviled his captaine with base language, & in yᵉ end halfe drew his rapier, & intended to rune at his captien; but he closed with him, and wrasted his rapier from him, and gave him a boxe on yᵉ earr; but he would not give over, but still assaulted his captaine. Wherupon he tooke yᵉ same rapier as it was in yᵉ scaberd, and gave him a blow with yᵉ hilts; but it light on his head, & yᵉ smal end of yᵉ bar of yᵉ rapier hilts peirct his scull, & he dyed a few days after. But yᵉ captaine was cleared by a counsell of warr. This fellow was so desperate a quareller as yᵉ captaine was faine many times to chaine him under hatches from hurting his fellows, as yᵉ company did testifie; and this was his end.

This Captaine Thomas Cromuell sett forth another vioage to the Westindeas, from the Bay of the Massachusets, well maned & victuled; and was out 3. years, and tooke sundry prises, and returned rich unto the Massachusets, and ther dyed the same somere, having gott a fall from his horse, in which fall he fell on his rapeir hilts, and so brused his body as he shortly after dyed therof, with some other distempers, which brought him into a feavor. Some observed that ther might be somthing of the hand of God herein; that as the forenamed man dyed of yᵉ blow he gave him with yᵉ rapeir hilts, so his owne death was occationed by a like means.

This year M^r. Edward Winslow went into England, upon this occation: some discontented persons under ye govermente of the Massachusets sought to trouble their peace, and disturbe, if not innovate, their govermente, by laying many [270] scandals upon them; and intended to prosecute against them in England, by petitioning & complaining to the Parlemente. Allso Samuell Gorton & his company made complaints against them; so as they made choyse of M^r. Winslow to be their agente, to make their defence, and gave him comission & instructions for that end; in which he so carried him selfe as did well answer their ends, and cleared them from any blame or dishonour, to the shame of their adversaries. But by reason of the great alterations in the State, he was detained longer then was expected; and afterwards fell into other imployments their, so as he hath now bene absente this 4. years, which hath been much to the weakning of this govermente, without whose consente he tooke these imployments upon him.

Anno 1647. And Anno 1648.

APPENDIX.

APPENDIX.

No. I.

[Passengers of the Mayflower.]

The names of those which came over first, in yᵉ year 1620. and were by the blessing of God the first beginers and (in a sort) the foundation of all the Plantations and Colonies in New-England; and their families.

Mʳ. John Carver; Kathrine, his wife; Desire Minter; & 2. man-servants, John Howland, Roger Wilder; William Latham, a boy; & a maid servant, & a child yᵗ was put to him, called Jasper More.

| 8. |

Mʳ. William Brewster; Mary, his wife; with 2. sons, whose names were Love & Wrasling; and a boy was put to him called Richard More; and another of his brothers. The rest of his children were left behind, & came over afterwards.

| 6. |

Mʳ. Edward Winslow; Elizabeth, his wife; & 2. men servants, caled Georg Sowle and Elias Story; also a litle girle was put to him, caled Ellen, the sister of Richard More.

| 5. |

William Bradford, and Dorothy, his wife; having but one child, a sone, left behind, who came afterward.

| 2. |

Mʳ. Isaack Allerton, and Mary, his wife; with 3. children, Bartholmew, Remember, & Mary; and a servant boy, John Hooke.

| 6. |

| 2. |

M^r. Samuell Fuller, and a servant, caled William Butten. His wife was behind, & a child, which came afterwards.

John Crakston, and his sone, John Crakston.

Captin Myles Standish, and Rose, his wife.

2
2.

M^r. Christopher Martin, and his wife, and 2. servants, Salamon Prower and John Langemore.

4.

M^r. William Mullines, and his wife, and 2. children, Joseph & Priscila; and a servant, Robart Carter.

5.

M^r. William White, and Susana, his wife, and one sone, caled Resolved, and one borne a ship-bord, caled Peregriene; & 2. servants, named William Holbeck & Edward Thomson.

6.

M^r. Steven Hopkins, & Elizabeth, his wife, and 2. children, caled Giles, and Constanta, a doughter, both by a former wife; and 2. more by this wife, caled Damaris & Oceanus; the last was borne at sea; and 2. servants, called Edward Doty and Edward Litster.

8.

M^r. Richard Warren; but his wife and children were lefte behind, and came afterwards.

1.

John Billinton, and Elen, his wife; and 2. sones, John & Francis.

4.

Edward Tillie, and Ann, his wife; and 2. children that were their cossens, Henery Samson and Humillity Coper.

4.

John Tillie, and his wife; and Eelizabeth, their doughter.

Francis Cooke, and his sone John. But his wife & other children came afterwards.

3
2.

Thomas Rogers, and Joseph, his sone. His other children came afterwards.

2.

Thomas Tinker, and his wife, and a sone.

John Rigdale, and Alice, his wife.

3 [EV]
2.

3.

James Chilton, and his wife, and Mary, their dougter. They had an other doughter, yᵗ was maried, came afterward.

Edward Fuller, and his wife, and Samuell, their sonne.

John Turner, and 2. sones. He had a doughter came some years after to Salem, wher she is now living.

Francis Eaton, and Sarah, his wife, and Samuell, their sone, a yong child.

Moyses Fletcher, John Goodman, Thomas Williams, Digerie Preist, Edmond Margeson, Peter Browne, Richard Britterige, Richard Clarke, Richard Gardenar, Gilbart Winslow.

John Alden was hired for a cooper, at South-Hampton, wher the ship victuled; and being a hopfull yong man, was much desired, but left to his owne liking to go or stay when he came here; but he stayed, and maryed here.

John Allerton and Thomas Enlish were both hired, the later to goe mʳ of a shalop here, and yᵉ other was reputed as one of yᵉ company, but was to go back (being a seaman) for the help of others behind. But they both dyed here, before the shipe returned.

There were allso other 2. seamen hired to stay a year here in the country, William Trevore, and one Ely. But when their time was out, they both returned.

3	
3.	
3.	
10.	
1.	
2.	
2.	

These, bening aboute a hundred sowls, came over in this first ship; and began this worke, which God of his goodnes hath hithertoo blesed; let his holy name have yᵉ praise.

And seeing it hath pleased him to give me to see 30. years compleated since these beginings; and that the great works of his providence are to be observed, I have thought it not unworthy my paines to take a veiw of the decreasings & increasings of these persons, and such changs as hath pased over them & theirs, in this thirty years. It may be of some use to such as come after; but, however, I shall rest in my owne benefite.

I will therfore take them in order as they lye.

M^r. Carver and his wife dyed the first year; he in ye spring, she in ye somer; also, his man Roger and ye litle boy Jasper dyed before either of them, of ye commone infection. Desire Minter returned to her freinds, & proved not very well, and dyed in England. His servant boy Latham, after more then 20. years stay in the country, went into England, and from thence to the Bahamy Ilands in ye West Indies, and ther, with some others, was starved for want of food. His maid servant maried, & dyed a year or tow after, here in this   place.

His servant, John Howland, maried the doughter of John Tillie, Elizabeth, and they are both now living, and have 10. children, now all living; and their eldest daughter hath 4. children. And ther 2. daughter, 1. all living; and other of their children mariagable. So 15. are come of them.

15.

M^r. Brewster lived to very old age; about 80. years he was when he dyed, having lived some 23. or 24. years here in ye countrie; & though his wife dyed long before, yet she dyed aged. His sone Wrastle dyed a yonge man unmaried; his sone Love lived till this year 1650. and dyed, & left 4. children, now living. His doughters which came over after him are dead, but have left sundry children alive; his eldst sone is still liveing, and hath 9. or 10 children; one maried, who hath a child or 2.

4.
2.

Richard More his brother dyed the first winter; but he is maried, and hath 4. or 5. children, all living.

4.

2.

Mr. Ed: Winslow his wife dyed the first winter; and he maried with the widow of Mr. White, and hath 2. children living by her marigable, besids sundry that are dead.

One of his servants dyed, as also the litle girle, soone after the ships arivall. But his man, Georg Sowle, is still living, and hath 8. childrē.

| 8. |

William Bradford his wife dyed soone after their arivall; and he maried againe; and hath 4. children, 3. wherof are maried.

| 4. |

Mr. Allerton his wife dyed with the first, and his servant, John Hooke. His sone Bartle is maried in England, but I know not how many children he hath. His doughter Remember is maried at Salem, & hath 3. or 4. children living. And his doughter Mary is maried here, & hath 4. children. Him selfe maried againe with ye doughter of Mr. Brewster, & hath one sone living by her, but she is long since dead. And he is maried againe, and hath left this place long agoe. So I account his increase to be 8. besids his sons in England.

| 8. |

Mr. Fuller his servant dyed at sea; and after his wife came over, he had tow children by her, which are living and growne up to years; but he dyed some 15. years agoe.

| 2. |

John Crakston dyed in the first mortality; and about some 5. or 6. years after, his sone dyed; having lost him selfe in ye wodes, his feet became frosen, which put him into a feavor, of which he dyed.

[EW] Captain Standish his wife dyed in the first sicknes, and he maried againe, and hath 4. sones liveing, and some *are dead.*

| 4. |

Mr. Martin, he & all his, dyed in the first infection not long after the arivall.

Mr. Molines, and his wife, his sone, and his servant, dyed the first winter. Only his dougter Priscila survied, and maried with John Alden, who are both living, and have 11. children. And their eldest daughter is maried, & hath five children.

| 15. |

Mr. White and his 2. servants dyed soone after ther landing. His wife maried with M^r. Winslow (as is before noted). His 2. sons are maried, and Resolved hath 5. children, Perigrine tow, all living. So their increase are 7.

| 7. |

M^r. Hopkins and his wife are now both dead, but they lived above 20. years in this place, and had one sone and 4. doughters borne here. Ther sone became a seaman, & dyed at Barbadoes; one daughter dyed here, and 2. are maried; one of them hath 2. children; & one is yet to mary. So their increase which still survive are 5. But his sone Giles is maried, and hath 4. children.

| 5. |
| 4. |

His doughter Constanta is also maried, and hath 12. children, all of them living, and one of them maried.

| 12. |

M^r. Richard Warren lived some 4. or 5. years, and had his wife come over to him, by whom he had 2. sons before dyed; and one of them is maryed, and hath 2. children. So his increase is 4. But he had 5. doughters more came over with his wife, who are all maried, & living, & have many children.

| 4. |

John Billinton, after he had bene here 10. yers, was executed for killing a man; and his eldest sone dyed before him; but his 2. sone is alive, and maried, & hath 8. children.

| 8. |

Edward Tillie and his wife both dyed soon after their arivall; and the girle Humility, their cousen, was sent for into England, and dyed ther. But the youth Henery Samson is still liveing, and is maried, & hath 7. children.

| 7. |

John Tillie and his wife both dyed a litle after they came ashore; and their daughter Elizabeth maried with John Howland, and hath issue as is before noted.

Francis Cooke is still living, a very olde man, and hath seene his childrens children have children; after his wife came over, (with other of his children,) he hath 3. still living by her, all maried, and have 5. children; so their encrease is 8. And his sone John, which came over with him, is maried, and hath 4, chilldren living.

| 8. |
| 4. |

| 6. |

Thomas Rogers dyed in the first sicknes, but his sone Joseph is still living, and is maried, and hath 6. children. The rest of Thomas Rogers [children] came over, & are maried, & have many children.

Thomas Tinker and his wife and sone all dyed in the first sicknes.

And so did John Rigdale and his wife.

James Chilton and his wife also dyed in the first infection. But their daughter Mary is still living, and hath 9. children; and one daughter is maried, & hath a child; so their increase is 10.

10.

Edward Fuller and his wife dyed soon after they came ashore; but their sone Samuell is living, & maried, and hath 4. children or more.

4.

John Turner and his 2. sones all dyed in the first sikness. But he hath a daugter still living at Salem, well maried, and approved of.

Francis Eaton his first wife dyed in the generall sicknes; and he maried againe, & his 2. wife dyed, & he maried the 3. and had by her 3. children. One of them is maried, & hath a child; the other are living, but one of them is an ideote. He dyed about 16. years 1. agoe. His sone Samuell, who came over a sucking child, is allso maried, & hath a child.

4.
1.

Moyses Fletcher, Thomas Williams, Digerie Preist, John Goodman, Edmond Margeson, Richard Britteridge, Richard Clarke. All these dyed sone after their arivall, in the generall sicknes that befell. But Digerie Preist had his wife & children sent hither afterwards, she being Mr. Allertons sister. But the rest left no posteritie here.

Richard Gardinar became a seaman, and died in England, or at sea.

Gilbert Winslow, after diverse years aboad here, returned into England, and dyed ther.

6.

Peter Browne maried twise. By his first wife he had 2. children, who are living, & both of them maried, and the one of them hath 2. children; by his second wife he had 2. more. He dyed about 16. years since.

Thomas English and John Allerton dyed in the generall siknes.

John Alden maried with Priscila, M^r. Mollines his doughter, and had issue by her as is before related.

Edward Doty & Edward Litster, the servants of M^r. Hopkins. Litster, after he was at liberty, went to Virginia, & ther dyed. But Edward Doty by a second wife hath 7. children, and both he and they are living.

Of these 100. persons which came first over in this first ship together, the greater halfe dyed in the generall mortality; and most of them in 2. or three monthes time. And for those which survied, though some were ancient & past procreation, & others left ye place and cuntrie, yet of those few remaining are sprunge up above 160. persons, in this 30. years, and are now living in this presente year, 1650. besids many of their children which are dead, and come not within this account.

And of the old stock (of one & other) ther are yet living this present year, 1650. nere 30. persons. Let the Lord have ye praise, who is the High Preserver of men.

[EX] Twelfe persons liveing of the old stock this present yeare, 1679.

Two persons liveing that came over in the first shipe 1620, this present yeare, 1690. Resolved White and Mary Chusman,[EY] the daughter of M^r. Allerton.

And John Cooke, the son of Frances Cooke, that came in the first ship, is still liveing this present yeare, 1694; & Mary Cushman is still living, this present year, 1698.

No. II.

[Commission for Regulating Plantations.]

Charles by yᵉ grace of God king of England, Scotland, France, and Ireland, Defender of yᵉ Faith, &c.[EZ]

To the most Reveᵈ father in Christ, our wellbeloved & faithfull counsellour, William, by devine providence Archbishop of Counterbery, of all England Primate & Metropolitan; Thomas Lord Coventry, Keeper of our Great Seale of England; the most Reverente father in Christ our wellbeloved and most faithful Counselour, Richard, by devine providence Archbishop of Yorke, Primate & Metropolitan; our wellbeloved and most faithfull coussens & Counselours, Richard, Earle of Portland, our High Treasurer of England; Henery, Earle of Manchester, Keeper of our Privie Seale; Thomas, Earle of Arundalle & Surry, Earle Marshall of England; Edward, Earle of Dorsett, Chamberline of our most dear consorte, the Queene; and our beloved & faithfull Counselours, Francis Lord Cottington, Counseler, and Undertreasurour of our Eschequour; Sʳ: Thomas Edmonds, knight, Treasourer of our houshould; Sʳ: Henery Vane, Knight, controuler of yᵉ same houshould; Sʳ: John Cooke, Knight, one of our Privie Secretaries; and Francis Windebanck, Knight, another of our Privie Secretaries,

Wheras very many of our subjects, & of our late fathers of beloved memory, our sovereigne lord James, late king of England, by means of licence royall, not only with desire of inlarging yᵉ teritories of our empire, but cheefly out of a pious & religious affection, & desire of propagating yᵉ gospell of our Lord Jesus Christ, with great industrie & expences have caused to be planted large Collonies of yᵉ English nation, in diverse parts of yᵉ world altogether unmannred, and voyd of inhabitants, or occupied of the barbarous people that have no knowledg of divine worship. We being willing to provid a remedy for yᵉ tranquillity & quietnes of those people, and being very confidente of your faith & wisdom, justice & providente circomspection, have constituted you yᵉ aforesaid Archbishop of Counterburie, Lord Keeper of yᵉ Great Seale of England, yᵉ Archbishop of Yorke, &c. and any 5. or more, of you, our Comissioners; and to you, and any 5. or more of you, we doe give and comite power for yᵉ govermente & saftie of yᵉ said collonies, drawen, or which, out of yᵉ English nation into those parts hereafter, shall be drawne, to make lawes, constitutions, & ordinances, pertaining ether to yᵉ publick state of these collonies, or yᵉ private profite of them; and concerning yᵉ lands, goods, debts, & succession in those parts, and how they shall demaine them selves, towards foraigne princes, and their people, or how they shall bear them selves towards us, and our subjects, as well in any foraine parts whatsoever, or on yᵉ seas in those parts, or in their returne sayling home; or which may pertaine to yᵉ clergie govermente, or to yᵉ cure of soules, among yᵉ people ther living, and exercising trad in those parts; by designing out congruente porcions arising in tithes, oblations, & other things ther, according to your sound discretions, in politicall & civill causes; and by haveing yᵉ advise of 2. or 3. bishops, for yᵉ setling, making, & ordering of yᵉ bussines, for yᵉ designeing of necessary ecclesiasticall, and clargie porcions, which you shall cause to be called, and taken to you. And to make provission against yᵉ violation of those laws, constitutions, and ordinances, by imposing penealties & mulets, imprisonmente if ther be cause, and yᵗ yᵉ quality of yᵉ offence doe require it, by deprivation of member, or life, to be inflicted. With power allso (our assente being had) to remove, & displace yᵉ governours or rulers of those collonies, for causes which to you shall seeme lawfull, and others in their stead to constitute; and require an accounte of their rule & govermente, and whom you shall finde culpable, either by deprivation from their place, or by imposition of a mulete upon yᵉ goods of them in those parts to be levied, or banishmente from those provinces in wᶜʰ they have been goveʳ or otherwise to cashier according to yᵉ quantity of yᵉ offence. And to constitute judges, & magistrats politicall & civill, for civill causes and under yᵉ power and forme, which to you 5. or more of you shall seeme expediente. And judges & magistrats & dignities, to causes Ecclesiasticall, and under yᵉ power & forme which to you 5. or more of you, with the bishops vicegerents (provided by yᵉ Archbishop of Counterbure for yᵉ time being), shall seeme expediente; and to ordaine courts, pretoriane and tribunall, as well ecclesiasticall, as civill, of judgmentes; to detirmine of yᵉ formes and maner of procceedings in yᵉ same; and of appealing from them in matters & causes as well criminall, as civill, personall, reale, and mixte, and to their seats of justice, what may be equall & well ordered, and what crimes, faults, or exessess, of contracts or injuries ought to belonge to yᵉ Ecclesiasticall courte, and what to yᵉ civill courte, and seate of justice.

Provided never yᵉ less, yᵗ the laws, ordinances, & constitutions of this kinde, shall not be put in execution, before our assent be had therunto in writing under our signet, signed at least, and this assente being had, and yᵉ same publikly proclaimed in yᵉ provinces in which they are to be executed, we will & comand yᵗ those lawes, ordinances, and constitutions more fully to obtaine strength and be observed[FA] shall be inviolably of all men whom they shall concerne.

Notwithstanding it shall be for you, or any 5. or more of you, (as is afforsaid,) allthough those lawes, constitutions, and ordinances shalbe proclaimed with our royall assente, to chainge, revocke, & abrogate them, and other new ones, in forme afforsaid, from time to time frame and make as afforesaid; and to new evills arissing, or new dangers, to apply new remedyes as is fitting, so often as to you it shall seeme expediente. Furthermore you shall understand that we have constituted you, and every 5. or more of you, the afforesaid Archbishop of Counterburie, Thomas Lord Coventrie, Keeper of yᵉ Great Seale of England, Richard, Bishop of Yorke, Richard, Earle of Portland, Henery, Earle of Manchester, Thomas, Earle of Arundale & Surry, Edward, Earell of Dorsett, Francis Lord Cottinton, Sʳ Thomas Edmonds,[FB] knighte, Sʳ Henry Vane, knight, Sʳ Francis Windebanke, knight, our comissioners to hear, & determine, according to your sound discretions, all maner of complaints either against those collonies, or their rulers, or govenours, at ye instance of ye parties greeved, or at their accusation brought concerning injuries from hence, or from thence, betweene them, & their members to be moved, and to call ye parties before you; and to the parties or to their procurators, from hence, or from thence being heard ye full complemente of justice to be exhibted. Giving unto you, or any 5. or more of you power, y^t if you shall find any of ye collonies afforesaid, or any of ye cheefe rulers upon ye jurisdictions of others by unjust possession, or usurpation, or one against another making greevance, or in rebelion against us, or withdrawing from our alegance, or our comandments, not obeying, consultation first with us in y^t case had, to cause those colonies, or ye rulers of them, for ye causes afforesaid, or for other just causes, either to returne to England, or to comand them to other places designed, even as according to your sounde discretions it shall seeme to stand with equitie, & justice, or necessitie. Moreover, we doe give unto you, & any 5. or more of you, power & spetiall comand over all ye charters, leters patents, and rescripts royall, of ye regions, provinces, ilands, or lands in foraigne parts, granted for raising colonies, to cause them to be brought before you, & ye same being received, if any thing surrepticiously or unduly have been obtained, or y^t by the same priviledges, liberties, & prerogatives hurtfull to us, or to our crowne, or to foraigne princes, have been prejudicially suffered, or granted; the same being better made knowne unto you 5. or more of you, to comand them according to ye laws and customs of England to be revoked, and to doe such other things, which to ye profite & safgard of ye afforesaid collonies, and of our subjects residente in ye same, shall be necessary. And therfore we doe comand you that aboute ye premisses at days & times, which for these things you shall make provission, that you be diligente in attendance, as it becometh you; giving in precepte also, & firmly injoyning, we doe give comand to all and singuler cheefe rulers of provinces into which ye colonies afforesaid have been drawne, or shall be drawne, & concerning ye colonies themselves, & concerning others, y^t have been interest therein, y^t they give atendance upon you, and be observante and obediente unto your warrants in those affaires, as often as, and even as in our name they shall be required, at their perill. In testimoney wherof, we have caused these our letters to be made pattente. Wittnes our selfe at Westminster the 28. day of Aprill, in yͤ tenth year of our Raigne.

By write from yͤ privie seale,

WILLIES.

Anno Dom: 1634.

FOOTNOTES:

[A] The Hon. Charles Francis Adams.

[B] Lib. 2 Chap. 22.

[C] In the text, parentheses are used frequently, apparently in place of commas. For this reason, many are omitted in the reprint.

[D] Acts & Mon: pag. 1587. editi: 2.

[E] Ens: lib: 6. Chap. 42.

[F] Pag. 421.

[G] A note of the author at this place, written subsequent to this portion of the narrative, on the reverse pages of his History.

[H] All these and subsequent passages are quoted from the Geneva version of the Bible.

[I] Em: meter: lib: 25. col. 119.

[J] The reformed churches shapen much neerer yͤ primitive patterne *then England*, for they cashered yͤ Bishops wth al their courts, cannons, and ceremoneis, at the first; and left them amongst yͤ popish tr.... to ch wch they pertained. (The last word in the note is uncertain in the MS.)

[K] Goulden booke, &c.

[L] Sr Robert Nanton.

[M] NOTE.—O sacred bond, whilst inviollably preserved! how sweete and precious were the fruits that flowed from ye same, but when this fidelity decayed, then their ruine approached. O that these anciente members had not dyed, or been dissipated, (if it had been the will of God) or els that this holy care and constante faithfullnes had still lived, and remained with those that survived, and were in times afterwards added unto them. But (alass) that subtill serpente hath slylie wound in himselfe under faire pretences of necessitie and ye like, to untwiste these sacred bonds and tyes, and as it were insensibly by degrees to dissolve, or in a great measure to weaken, ye same. I have been happy, in my first times, to see, and with much comforte to injoye, the blessed fruits of this sweete communion, but it is now a parte of my miserie in old age, to find and feele ye decay and wante therof (in a great measure), and with greefe and sorrow of hart to lamente & bewaile ye same. And for others warning and admonnition, and my owne humiliation, doe I hear note ye same.

[The above reflections of the author were penned at a later period, on the reverse pages of his History, at this place.]

[N] Bishops.

[O] M^r. Tho: Weston, &c.

[P] *Yowthers* in the manuscript, an illegibly written word, doubtless intended for "ye others."

[Q] This word is enclosed in brackets in the manuscript.

[R] In Governor Bradford's Collection of Letters, these subscribers are thus wrote out at length: SAMUEL FULLER, WILLIAM BRADFORD, ISAAC ALLERTON, ED. WINSLOW.—*Prince.*

[S] June 11. O. S. is Lord's day, and therefore 't is likely the date of this letter should be June 10, the same with the date of the letter following.—*Prince.*

[T] He was a minister.

[U] Of some 60 tune.

[V] Heb. 11.

[W] This was about 22. of July.

[X] It was well for them y^t this was not accepted.

[Y] This letter is omitted in Governor Bradford's *Collection of Letters.*—*Prince.*

[Z] In Governor Bradford's *Collection of Letters*, this is Edward Southworth.—*Prince.*

[AA] He was governour in ye biger ship, & M^r. Cushman assistante.

[AB] I thinke he was deceived in these things.

[AC] This was found true afterward.

[AD] In the manuscript it is "strive dayly," but a pen has been drawn through the latter word.

[AE] For Governor Bradford's list of passengers in the Mayflower, see Appendix, No. I.

[AF] Because y^{ey} tooke much of y^t fishe ther.

[AG] Epist: 53.

[AH] Act. 28.

[AI] Deu: 26. 5, 7.

[AJ] 107 Psa: v. 1, 2, 4, 5, 8.

[AK] Which was this author him selfe.

[AL] Page 17.

[AM] *Thing* in the manuscript

[AN] She came ye 9. to ye Cap.

[AO] Nay, they were faine to spare ye shipe some to carry her home.

[AP] *Yeeled* in the manuscript.

[AQ] *Adventures* in the manuscript.

[AR] I know not wch way.

[AS] *Adventures* in the manuscript.

[AT] See how his promisss is fulfild.

[AU] *But yᵉ [he] left not his own men a bite of bread.*

[AV] The number is repeated in the Ms.

[AW] Mr. Hunter writes, "Here is an error in Bradford's pagination. He passes from 79 to 90. No part of the manuscript is here lost." 79 is repeated in the paging.

[AX] W^{th} in the manuscript.

[AY] *They* in the MS.

[AZ] I may not here omite how, notwithstand all their great paines & industrie, and yᵉ great hops of a large cropp, the Lord seemed to blast, & take away the same, and to threaten further & more sore famine unto them, by a great drought which continued from yᵉ 3. weeke in May, till about yᵉ midle of July, without any raine, and with great heat (for yᵉ most parte), insomuch as yᵉ corne begane to wither away, though it was set with fishe, the moysture wherof helped it much. Yet at length it begane to languish sore, and some of yᵉ drier grounds were partched like withered hay, part wherof was never recovered. Upon which they sett a parte a solemne day of humilliation, to seek yᵉ Lord by humble & fervente prayer, in this great distrese. And he was pleased to give them a gracious & speedy answer, both to their owne, & the Indeans admiration, that lived amongest them. For all yᵉ morning, and greatest part of the day, it was clear weather & very hotte, and not a cloud or any signe of raine to be seen, yet toward evening it begane to overcast, and shortly after to raine, with shuch sweete and gentle showers, as gave them cause of rejoyceing, & blesing God. It came, without either wind, or thunder, or any violence, and by degreese in yᵗ abundance, as that yᵉ earth was thorowly wete and soked therwith. Which did so apparently revive & quicken yᵉ decayed corne & other fruits, as was wonderfull to see, and made yᵉ Indeans astonished to behold; and afterwards the Lord sent them shuch seasonable showers, with enterchange of faire warme weather, as, through his blessing, caused a fruitfull & liberall harvest, to their no small comforte and rejoycing. For which mercie (in time conveniente) they also sett aparte a day of thanksgiveing. This being overslipt in its place, I thought meet here to inserte ye same.

[The above is written on the reverse of page 103 of the original, and should properly be inserted here. This passage, "being overslipt in its place," the author at first wrote it, or the most of it, under the preceding year; but, discovering his error before completing it, drew his pen across it, and wrote beneath, "This is to be here rased out, and is to be placed on page 103, wher it is inserted."]

[BA] *On.*

[BB] I. R.

[BC] This proved rather, a propheti, then advice.

[BD] *Contend* in the manuscript.

[BE] In MS. also 145.

[BF] In MS. also 146.

[BG] He dyed afterwards at Bristoll, in ye time of the warrs, of ye sicknes in y^t place.

[BH] With her flages, & streamers, pendents, & wastcloaths, &c.

[BI] *And* is repeated in the MS.

[BJ] *Adventures* in the manuscript.

[BK] He means Mr. Robinson.

[BL] But this lasted not long, they had now provided Lyford & others to send over.

[BM] It is worthy to be observed, how ye Lord doth chaing times & things; for what is now more plentifull then wine? and that of ye best, coming from Malago, ye Cannaries, and other places, sundry ships lading in a year. So as ther is now more cause to complaine of ye excess and ye abuse of wine (through mens corruption) even to drunkennes, then of any defecte or wante of the same. Witnes this year 1646. The good Lord lay not ye sins & unthankfullnes of men to their charge in this perticuler.

[BN] This was John Oldome & his like.

[BO] M^r. Westons men.

[BP] *Notabe* in MS.

[BQ] Plin: lib: 18. chap. 2.

[BR] Of wh^{ch} were many witneses.

[BS] Jer. 41. 6.

[BT] 121 is repeated in the paging of the original.

[BU] *Inurious* in MS.

[BV] *Receive* in the manuscript.

[BW] This was Lyford himselfe.

[BX] *Is it not* in the MS.

[BY] *Bet-* in MS.

[BZ] If I mistake not, it was not much less. [30^{li} in the manuscript.]

[CA] First written as in the text, then altered to *standerss*.

[CB] Note.

[CC] Here occurs another error in the paging of the original; 142 is omitted.

[CD] Below are the names of the adventurers subscribed to this paper, taken from Bradford's Letter-Book, 1 Mass. Hist. Coll., III. 48; being forty-two in number. The names of six of these persons are found subsequently among the members of the Massachusetts Company, viz. John White, John Pocock, Thomas Goffe, Samuel Sharpe, John Revell, and Thomas Andrews. Mr. Haven, who edited the Records of the Massachusetts Company, is of opinion that the first person on the list is the celebrated clergyman of Dorchester, the reputed author of the Planter's Plea. Emnu. Alltham is probably the same person named in the Council Records, under date January 21. 1622-3: "Emanuel Altum to command the Pinnace built for Mr.

Peirce's Plantation." Smith speaks of "Captaine *Altom*" as commanding this vessell, but Morton says the name of the master of the Little James was Mr. Bridges, who it appears was drowned at Damariscove, in March, 1624. See Coll. of the Amer. Antiq. Soc., III. 26, 62, Preface; Felt's MS. Memoranda from the Council Records; Smith's Generall Historie, p. 239; Morton's Memorial, p. 48.

John White,
John Pocock,
Robert Kean,
Edward Bass,
William Hobson,
William Penington,
William Quarles,
Daniel Poynton,
Richard Andrews,
Newman Rookes,
Henry Browning,
Richard Wright,
John Ling,
Thomas Goffe,
Samuel Sharpe,
Robert Holland,
James Sherley,
Thomas Mott,
Thomas Fletcher,
Timothy Hatherly,
Thomas Brewer,
John Thorned,
Myles Knowles,
William Collier,
John Revell,
Peter Gudburn,
Emnu. Alltham,
John Beauchamp,

Thomas Hudson,
Thomas Andrews,
Thomas Ward,
Fria. Newbald,
Thomas Heath,
Joseph Tilden,
William Perrin,
Eliza Knight,
Thomas Coventry,
Robert Allden,
Lawrence Anthony,
John Knight,
Matthew Thornhill,
Thomas Millsop.

[CE] The orthography of some of these words differs from the modern way of spelling them; and we have no means of ascertaining the accuracy of Bradford's copy from the original letter. This passage may be rendered thus:—

"Noble, worshipful, wise, and prudent Lords, the Governor and Councillors residing in New Plymouth, our very dear friends:—The Director and Council of New Netherland wish to your Lordships, worshipful, wise, and prudent, happiness in Christ Jesus our Lord, with prosperity and health, in soul and body."

[CF] Nov. 6. 1627. Page 238. [Reference is here made to the page of the original manuscript.]

[CG] 155 omitted in original MS.—COM.

[CH] Another leter of his, that should have bene placed before:—

We cannot but take notice how ye Lord hath been pleased to crosse our proseedings, and caused many disasters to befale us therin. I conceive ye only reason to be, we, or many of us, aimed at other ends then Gods glorie; but now I hope y^t cause is taken away; the bargen being fully concluded, as farr as our powers will reach, and confirmed under our hands & seals, to M^r. Allerton & ye rest of his &

your copartners. But for my owne parte, I confess as I was loath to hinder ye full confirming of it, being ye first propounder ther of at our meeting; so on ye other side, I was as unwilling to set my hand to ye sale, being ye receiver of most part of ye adventurs, and a second causer of much of ye ingagments; and one more threatened, being most envied & aimed at (if they could find any stepe to ground their malice on) then any other whosoever. I profess I know no just cause they ever had, or have, so to doe; neither shall it ever be proved y^t I have wronged them or any of ye adventurers, wittingly or willingly, one peny in ye disbursing of so many pounds in those 2. years trouble. No, ye sole cause why they maligne me (as I & others conceived) was y^t I would not side with them against you, & the going over of ye Leyden people. But as I then card not, so now I litle fear what they can doe; yet charge & trouble I know they may cause me to be at. And for these reasons, I would gladly have perswaded the other 4. to have sealed to this bargaine, and left me out, but they would not; so rather then it should faile, M^r. Alerton having taken so much pains, I have sealed with ye rest; with this proviso & promise of his, y^t if any trouble arise hear, you are to bear halfe ye charge. Wherfore now I doubt not but you will give your generallitie good contente, and setle peace amongst your selves, and peace with the natives; and then no doubt but ye God of Peace will blese your going out & your returning, and cause all y^t you sett your hands unto to prosper; the which I shall ever pray ye Lord to grante if it be his blessed will. Asuredly unless ye Lord be mercifull unto us & ye whole land in generall, our estate & condition is farr worse then yours. Wherfore if ye Lord should send persecution or trouble hear, (which is much to be feared,) and so should put into our minds to flye for refuge, I know no place safer then to come to you, (for all Europ is at varience one with another, but cheefly wth us,) not doubting but to find such frendly entertainmente as shall be honest & conscionable, notwithstanding what hath latly passed. For I profess in ye word of an honest man, had it not been to procure your peace & quiet from some turbulent spirites hear, I would not have sealed to this last deed; though you would have given me all my adventure and debte ready downe. Thus desiring ye Lord to blesse & prosper you, I cease ever resting,

Your faithfull & loving friend,
to my power,
JAMES SHERLEY.

Des: 27.

[The above letter was written on the reverse of page 154 of the original manuscript.]

[CI] Peag.

[CJ] 1629, May 25, the first letter concerning the former company of Leyden people.—*Prince.*

[CK] 1629-30, March 8th, the second letter concerning the latter company of Leyden people.—*Prince.*

[CL] This word is here substituted for *recovering* in the manuscript, on the authority of Bradford's Letter-Book.

[CM] This paragraph is written on the reverse of the page immediately preceding, in the original manuscript.

[CN] *Fractions* in the manuscript.

[CO] Thomas Willett.

[CP] 177 is omitted in MS.

[CQ] Oporto, called by the Dutch *Port a port.*

[CR] Hubbard, on page 101, notices the execution of Billington as taking place "about September" of this year. "The murtherer expected that, either for want of power to execute for capital offences, or for want of people to increase the plantation, he should have his life spared; but justice otherwise determined, and rewarded him, the first murtherer of his neighbour there, with the deserved punishment of death, for a warning to others." The first offence committed in the colony was by Billington, in 1621, who, for contempt of the Captain's lawful command, with opprobious speeches, was adjudged to have his neck and heels tied together. Prince, I. 103, from Bradford's pocket-book.

[CS] This paragraph was written on the reverse of page 180 of the original manuscript, near this place.

[CT] Wth in manuscript.

[CU] This was about ye selling ye ship in Spaine.

[CV] They were too short in resting on M^r. Hatherleys honest word, for his order to discharg them from ye Friendship's accounte, when he and M^r. Allerton made ye bargane with them, and they delivered them the rest of the goods; and therby gave them oppertunitie also to receive all the fraight of boath viages, without seeing an order (to have such power) under their hands in writing, which they never doubted of, seeing he affirmed he had power; and they both knew his honestie, and y^t he was spetially imployed for their agente at this time. And he was as shorte in resting on a verball order from them; which was now denyed, when it came to a perticuler of loss; but he still affirmed the same. But they were both now taught how to deale in ye world, espetially with marchants, in such cases. But in ye end this light upon these here also, for M^r. Allerton had gott all into his owne hand, and M^r. Hatherley was not able to pay it, except they would have uterlie undon him, as ye sequell will manifest.

[CW] This comission is abused; he never had any for shuch end, as they well knew, nether had they any to pay this money, nor would have paid a peny, if they had not pleased for some other respecte.

[CX] o in MS.

[CY] The last two words not found in the MS. but obviously intended.

[CZ] About ye Whit-Angell they all mette at a certaine taverne in London, wher they had a diner prepared, and had a conference with a factore aboute selling of her in Spaine, or at Port a porte, as hath been before mentioned; as M^r. Hatherley manifested, & M^r. Allerton could not deney.

[DA] Mr. Winslow deposed, ye same time, before ye Govr afore said, &c. that when he came into England, and the partners inquired of ye success of ye Whit Angell, which should have been laden wth bass and so sent for Port. of Porting-gall, and their ship & goods to be sould; having informed them that they were like to faile in their lading of bass, that then M^r. James Sherley used these termes: Feck, we must make one accounte of all; and ther upon presed him, as agente for ye partners in Neu-England, to accepte ye said ship Whit-Angell, and her accounte, into ye joynte partner-ship; which he refused, for many reasons; and after received instructions from New-Engl: to refuse her if she should be offered, which instructions he shewed them; and wheras he was often pressed to accept her, he ever refused her, &c.

[DB] So as a while before, wheras their great care was how to pay the purchase, and those other few debts which were upon them, now it was with them as it was some times with Saule's father, who left careing for ye Asses, and sorrowed for his sonn. 1. Sam. 10. 2. So that which before they looked at as a heavie burthen, they now esteeme but a small thing and a light mater, in comparison of what was now upon them. And thus ye Lord oftentimes deals with his people to teach them, and humble them, that he may doe them good in ye later end.

[DC] This word is obscure in MS.

[DD] The above paragraph was written on the reverse of page 188 of the original manuscript.

[DE] The following account of Sir Christopher Gardiner, with the documents accompanying it, extending to page 357, does not appear in the text of the original manuscript,—having been perhaps inadvertently omitted,—but was written on the reverse of pages 189-191.

[DF] That is, in the original manuscript.

[DG] *Rea*-in the manuscript.

[DH] This letter was written on the reverse of folio 192 of the original manuscript, and may be properly inserted here.

[DI] March 22.

[DJ] The skin was sold at 14^s. and 15. ye pound.

[DK] Ther was cause enough of these feares, which arise by ye underworking of some enemies to ye churches here, by which this Comission following was procured from his Matie. (See this paper in appendix, No. 11.)

[DL] And ye skin at 14^s.

[DM] That is, "If you please."

[DN] The two paragraphs above were written on the reverse of folios 202 and 203 of the original manuscript, under this year.

[DO] Blank in the original.

[DP] *They* in MS.

[DQ] Before this word in the margin appears a capital *N*.

[DR] Not correctly cast; it should be 12530^{li}.

[DS] 119 in MS.

[DT] Ther is little trust to be given to their relations in these things.

[DU] 120 in MS.

[DV] Mr John Reinor.

[DW] But by this means they did furnish them, & have still continued to doe.

[DX] *Be* in manuscript.

[DY] But y^{ey} were carried to ye West-Indeas.

[DZ] *They* in the manuscript.

[EA] But staid it till ye next year.

[EB] And yet afterwards they laid claime to those parts in the controversie about Seacunk.

[EC] Being about 40^{li}.

[ED] And devided betweene them.

[EE] 130 in MS.

[EF] Which is Charles River may still be questioned.

[EG] This was but to pretend advantage, for it could not be done, neither did it need.

[EH] M^r. Chancey came to them in ye year 1638. and staid till ye later part of this year 1641.

[EI] A leaf is here wanting in the original manuscript, it having been cut out.

[EJ] Exod: 21. 22. Deu: 19. 11. Num: 35. 16. 18.

[EK] "Confident"?

[EL] *8* in MS.

[EM] *Contic* in MS.

[EN] Solicitations in MS.

[EO] This he means of ye first adventures, all which were lost, as hath before been shown; and what he here writs is probable at least.

[EP] Being the conclusion, as will be seen, of page 252 of the original.

[EQ] Perhaps *write* for *wrote*.

[ER] *The* in the manuscript.

[ES] This was a misterie to them, for they heard nothing hereof from any side ye last year, till now ye conclution was past, and bonds given.

[ET] Substituted for *sundry* on the authority of the original MS. Records.

[EU] *Comander* in the MS.

[EV] Written 2 in MS.

[EW] Who dyed 3. of Octob. 1655.

[EX] The following memoranda are in a later hand.

[EY] Obviously intended for Cushman.

[EZ] See page 381. This document was written on the reverse of folio 201 et seq. of the original manuscript, and for the sake of convenience is transferred to this place.

[FA] A superfluous *and* comes after "observed" in the manuscript.

[FB] *Edwards* in the manuscript.

Printed in Dunstable, United Kingdom

68365103R00255